C000180716

FOURTEENTH CENTURY ENGLAND

V

The essays collected here present the fruits of the most recent research on aspects of the politics and culture of fourteenth-century England. Among the topics considered are the size and structure of magnates' households and retinues, Edward II's relationship with Piers Gaveston, court venues and the image presented by royal justice, the pattern of clergy ordinations, and the Despensers' patronage of Tewkesbury Abbey. Three essays deal with aspects of Richard II's reign, two reassessing the so-called 'tyranny', and a third looking at the inter-relation of English and Irish politics. The final essays look at general but related themes, the administration of royal justice and the role of morality in the exercise of public office.

NIGEL SAUL is Professor of Medieval History at Royal Holloway, University of London.

Fourteenth Century England

ISSN 1471–3020

The series aims to provide a forum for the most recent research into the political, social, economic, ecclesiastical and cultural history of the fourteenth century in England. Contributions are currently invited for the next volume, which will appear in 2010; draft submissions should be sent by June 2009 to Professor Chris Given-Wilson at the following address:

Department of Medieval History
University of St Andrews
St Andrews
Fife
Scotland
KY16 9AL

Email: cjg2@st-andrews.ac.uk

FOURTEENTH CENTURY ENGLAND

V

Edited by Nigel Saul

THE BOYDELL PRESS

First published 2008
The Boydell Press, Woodbridge

ISBN 978–1–84383–387–1

The Boydell Press is an imprint of Boydell & Brewer Ltd
PO Box 9, Woodbridge, Suffolk IP12 3DF, UK
and of Boydell & Brewer Inc.
Mt Hope Avenue, Rochester, NY 14620, USA
website: www.boydellandbrewer.com

A catalogue record for this book is available
from the British Library

This publication is printed on acid-free paper

Printed in Great Britain by
Antony Rowe Ltd, Chippenham, Wiltshire

CONTENTS

ILLUSTRATIONS

CONTRIBUTORS

Alison Marshall is a part-time tutor in the School of Historical Studies, University of Bristol

Elizabeth H. Will is an independent scholar

Jochen Burgtorf is Professor of Medieval History at California State University, Fullerton

David Robinson was the County Archivist of Surrey and is a member of the Canterbury and York Society

Martyn Lawrence is a publisher at Emerald Group Publishing Ltd

Peter Crooks is a Research Fellow at the Institute of Historical Research, London

G. B. Stow is Professor of History, La Salle University, Philadelphia

Terry Jones is an independent scholar and author of *Who Murdered Chaucer?* (London, 2003)

Anthony Musson is Professor of Legal History, University of Exeter

Christopher Fletcher is a Drapers' Research Fellow, Pembroke College, Cambridge

PREFACE

Fourteenth Century England, now in its fifth volume, publishes biennially a representative sample of recent and innovative work on the history of the fourteenth century, with particular emphasis on the politics and political culture of England. It is organised under the co-editorship of Chris Given-Wilson (University of St Andrews), Jeffrey Hamilton (Baylor University, Texas), Mark Ormrod (University of York) and Nigel Saul (Royal Holloway, University of London).

Fourteenth Century England does not publish the proceedings of a conference, although some of the contributions naturally originate in conference papers. In particular, a number of the articles published here were first aired at the International Congress on Medieval Studies, Western Michigan University, Kalamazoo, and at sessions organised by the Society for Fourteenth-Century Studies at the International Medieval Congress at the University of Leeds. The editors of *Fourteenth Century England*, some of whom organise sessions at these two conferences, are especially grateful to the Society of the White Hart for its continued support of international research on later medieval English history.

Rather than centring on a single theme, the contributions in the volume represent a cross-section of recent research in fourteenth-century studies and reflect the concerns and trends of current scholarship in the field. The book opens with two complementary studies of big magnate retinues. Alison Marshall offers a sharply focused study of the retinue of Thomas of Brotherton, Edward II's half brother, shedding new light on the following of a magnate not usually regarded as one of the best documented figures of his day. Elizabeth Will then looks at a hitherto neglected set of sources for John of Gaunt's household – the check rolls and journal of his household in the East Sussex Record Office, Lewes – showing how they shed light on the size and composition of the largest retinue of the age. Turning to political culture, Jochen Burgtorf re-examines the much debated relationship between Edward II and his favourite Piers Gaveston, arguing that there is no evidence of sexual intimacy between the two men and that what the magnates objected to was essentially the exclusiveness of the relationship and the degree of trust which Edward placed in his friend. David Robinson, turning to ecclesiastical history, reviews the evidence for clergy ordinations, finding a broad correlation between the level of ordinations and the level and distribution of wealth locally; the main exceptions, he finds, are to be found on the northern border, an area impoverished by warfare, and the south-east, where there were many alternative sources of employment. Martyn Lawrence, staying with ecclesiastical history, explores the Despensers' patronage of Tewkesbury Abbey (Gloucestershire), arguing for greater recognition of Hugh III's involvement in the great rebuilding programme and showing how religious and dynastic imperatives came together in the family's patronage of the abbey. In the first of three essays on aspects of Richard II's reign, Peter Crooks re-examines Irish politics in the 1380s, making sense of some tangled local disputes and demonstrating a closer interaction between Irish affairs and those of the court than is often supposed. In a couple of essays which neatly complement each other, George Stow and Terry Jones look at the last years of Richard II's reign, the period of so-called 'tyranny'. George Stow shows how a key source for the modern view of the king as a tyrant – the passage in the *Eulogium* chronicle describing his crown wearings – is almost certainly a Lancastrian interpolation, designed to blacken the king's reputation, while Terry Jones argues that Richard's exalted kingly style, elevating the crown above magnate factions, corresponds in large measure to the advice given in the 'mirrors for princes' manuals. Two essays taking a broader canvas complete the book. Anthony Musson, considering legal culture, shows how public justice was sometimes administered in private surroundings, and asks how this environment affected perceptions of justice, while Christopher Fletcher, looking at the fourteenth-century literature of complaint, suggests that it served the function of internal moral regulation, inculcating in office-holders the values by which were to discharge the responsibilities of their office.

Once again, the editors would like to thank the staff of Boydell and Brewer, especially Richard Barber and Caroline Palmer, for their support of *Fourteenth Century England* and their assistance in the production of this book.

Nigel Saul
January 2008

ABBREVIATIONS

BIHR	*Bulletin of the Institute of Historical Research*
BL	British Library, London
CCR	*Calendar of Close Rolls*
CFR	*Calendar of Fine Rolls*
CIPM	*Calendar of Inquisitions Post Mortem*
CPR	*Calendar of Patent Rolls*
EHR	*English Historical Review*
TNA: PRO	The National Archives (Public Record Office), Kew
TRHS	Transactions of the Royal Historical Society
VCH	*Victoria County History*

This book is produced with the assistance of
a grant from Isobel Thornley's Bequest to the University of London

AN EARLY FOURTEENTH-CENTURY AFFINITY: THE EARL OF NORFOLK AND HIS FOLLOWERS

Alison Marshall

In the last generation or so, the affinities of a number of later medieval magnates, among them the dukes of Lancaster and the earls of Pembroke and Warwick, have been studied in some detail and to great effect. These studies, however, relate to only a small proportion of the retinues which flourished in the fourteenth and fifteenth centuries.[1] Research has naturally tended to focus on the few magnates about whose retinues a considerable body of evidence survives, while opportunities to research other lords and their followers have usually been overlooked because of the supposed paucity of material. Yet even in cases where no indentures of retinue, livery rolls or household accounts have come down to us, it is still possible to discover a great deal about such matters as size, composition and inner workings. Charters, correspondence, estate accounts, bishops' registers and, of course, the ever important body of government records, can all be brought together to build up a picture. Only by studying more magnate affinities can generalizations be avoided, and arguments corroborated or dismissed. One retinue which it is possible to reconstruct in a fair degree of detail is that of Thomas of Brotherton, earl of Norfolk (d. 1338).

In its widest sense, the affinity consisted not only of the lord's knights and men-at-arms, but also of his household and estate officials and domestic servants. The size of a lord's affinity was an important factor in itself, not only because it provided a strong force in wartime, but because it served as a highly visible affirmation of his status, wealth and social standing in times of peace. The following attached to Norfolk's childhood household, which was created for him in 1301 by his father, Edward I, rivalled that of many contemporary noblemen in terms of size and magnificence.[2] In his adult life it was only natural for Norfolk, as the half-brother of Edward II and uncle of Edward III, to wish to demonstrate his wealth and status over and above his peers by means of his affinity. It is therefore little surprise to find that his following appears to have compared highly favourably with – and in most cases to have exceeded – those of his contemporaries in terms of size. Of course, because of the overall lack of generosity shown by Edward II towards his male siblings (which

1 J. R. S. Phillips, *Aymer de Valence Earl of Pembroke 1307–1324: Baronial Politics in the Reign of Edward II* (Oxford, 1972), 253–68; J. R. Maddicott, *Thomas of Lancaster, 1307–1322: A Study in the Reign of Edward II* (Oxford, 1970), 40–66; S. Walker, *The Lancastrian Affinity 1361–1399* (Oxford, 1990); N. B. Lewis, 'Indentures of Retinue with John of Gaunt, Duke of Lancaster, Enrolled in Chancery, 1367–1399', *Camden Miscellany*, xxii (Camden Society, 4th series, 1, 1964), 77–112; K. Fowler, *The King's Lieutenant: Henry of Grosmont* (London, 1969), 175–86; C. Carpenter, 'The Beauchamp Affinity: A Study of Bastard Feudalism at Work', *EHR*, 95 (1980), 514–32.

2 A. Marshall, 'The Childhood and Household of Edward II's Half-Brothers, Thomas of Brotherton and Edmund of Woodstock', in G. Dodd and A. Musson (eds.), *The Reign of Edward II: New Perspectives* (York, 2006), 192–6.

starkly contrasted with the lavish rewards granted to his favourites),[3] Norfolk's retinue would have been nowhere near as large as that of John of Gaunt towards the end of the century, which numbered around 170 indentured men, and which probably represents the largest magnate affinity of the later medieval period.[4] Nor could it have compared with the following of Thomas of Lancaster, which – according to Maddicott's estimate – numbered at its height around fifty-five indentured knights. This sizeable force was maintained by Lancaster's annual revenue from his vast estates of about £11,000.[5]

Nevertheless, with a yearly income of £4,500 or more, Norfolk could afford to maintain a following appropriate to his status as one of the premier magnates of the realm, and some idea of the comparative size of his military retinue can be gleaned from the government records.[6] The king's wardrobe book covering the period from 1 May 1322 to 19 October 1323, for instance, is of particular interest since it records the wages paid to magnates and their contingents for serving in the Scottish campaign during the summer of 1322. The document reveals that Norfolk was paid a total of £321 2s. 0d. for serving between 4 August and 10 September 1322 with a contingent of 123 men. His body of men comprised three bannerets who each received 4s. per day, twenty-nine knights who were paid 2s. a day, and ninety-one men-at-arms on a wage of 12d. per day.[7] By comparison, the earl of Pembroke's force was the second largest recorded in the document – he received £282 14s. in wages for himself and for ninety-five other men, who included two bannerets and nineteen knights. The earl of Kent served with two bannerets, eighteen knights and sixty-six men-at-arms, and was paid a total of £224 4s. 0d. in wages, whilst the earl of Arundel received £184 2s. 0d. for serving with a contingent of seventy-four men, two of whom were bannerets and sixteen of whom were knights.[8]

The lists of protections issued by Edward II in 1320 and 1322 paint a similar picture as to the comparative size of Norfolk's force. On 26 February 1320, the king granted protections to Norfolk and to thirty-eight of his followers, who were all shortly to accompany Edward II on his expedition to pay homage to Philip V of France.[9] Protections were also granted during February and March to the earl of Kent and twenty-six of his men, to Hugh Despenser the elder together with ten others, and to the earl of Richmond and the bishop of Hereford, who each took with them seven men.[10] Similarly, on 20 July 1322 Norfolk and thirty-seven members of his affinity were granted protections by the king in preparation for the Scottish campaign planned for that summer. By this time Despenser the elder, recently created earl of Winchester, had expanded his following better to reflect his new position, and received protections for forty-four other men. Pembroke was issued

3 Edward II's attitude towards his half-brothers is discussed in greater detail in A. Marshall, 'Thomas of Brotherton, Earl of Norfolk and Marshal of England: A Study in Early Fourteenth-Century Aristocracy' (unpublished Ph.D. thesis, University of Bristol, 2006), 47–50, 77–84, 95–7. See also P. Chaplais, *Piers Gaveston: Edward II's Adoptive Brother* (Oxford, 1994), 30–5.

4 Walker, *Lancastrian Affinity*, 18; Lewis, 'Indentures of Retinue', 77–8.

5 Maddicott, *Thomas of Lancaster*, 45.

6 For an estimate of Norfolk's annual revenue, see Marshall, 'Thomas of Brotherton', 170–7.

7 BL, MS Stowe 553, fol. 56v.

8 BL, MS Stowe 553, fol. 45r–v.

9 *CPR 1317–1321*, 427.

10 *CPR 1317–1321*, 419, 426–7, 435.

with protections for thirty-two others, while Richmond again had relatively few companions – thirteen of his men were named.[11]

The extent of Norfolk's household, consisting of his administrative officials and domestic servants, would no doubt have been as impressive as his military retinue, although its size and composition are more difficult to reconstruct given the lack of household records. Once again, however, contemporary government records prove their worth. In March 1337 Norfolk was summoned before the king's council to answer charges of oppression caused by his household's 'lack of discreet rule and good array'. As a result, an East Anglian landowner and royal servant, Sir Constantine Mortimer, was appointed to survey Norfolk's household and to make any necessary changes that he should see fit. It was recorded in the patent rolls that a letter to this effect was to be sent to Norfolk's steward, together with a list of individuals who were authorized to serve in his household . Only those men who were named in the list were to be allowed to continue in Norfolk's service.[12] Fortunately this list, entitled '*Le Meisnee le Counte*', has survived.[13] It begins with Norfolk's two stewards – Sir Ralph Bocking, steward of his estates, and Sir John Hales, steward of his household. It then names nine household clerks, of whom the most important were Peter Denton, the treasurer, Richard Burghstede, keeper of the great seal, and a parson named only as Nicholas, who acted as keeper of the privy seal. William de Radenhale was named as Norfolk's chaplain and almoner, whilst his second wife Mary was recorded as having her own chaplain, John Jermye, as well as a clerk to writer letters for her. The remaining three clerks were attached to the chapel or to the other household offices. After the clerks, six serjeants are listed. These were the men who had charge of the household departments such as the chamber, hall, pantry and buttery, and ten squires, of whom two were tailors by profession. There were seventeen valets, whose duties ranged from making candles and shoeing horses in the stables, to purveying supplies such as hay and other essential items. There were also four ladies in the entourage of Norfolk's wife, two laundresses and twelve pageboys.

In total, sixty-two individuals are listed as members of Norfolk's 'hospicium' in 1337. In reality, his entire household would have been significantly larger than this. Prestwich has pointed out that the 1337 list did not include Norfolk's huntsmen, carters, or other menial servants.[14] Furthermore, the list represents a scaled-down version of Norfolk's household in accordance with the demands of the king's council and Constantine Mortimer. The household provided by Edward I for Norfolk and his brother, Kent, between 1301 and 1312, consisted of up to seventy individuals paid for by an annual allowance of around £1,500, and it seems highly unlikely that Norfolk would have retained a smaller number of servants during his adult life despite enjoying an income which was significantly greater.[15] Precise estimates are impossible, but in reality it would seem likely that Norfolk's household was about twice the size of the 1337 list. When one adds Norfolk's estate officials to his domestic servants and military retinue – the attorneys, auditors, constables, bailiffs, reeves, haywards and parkers who are all evidenced by the sole surviving estate

11 *CPR 1321–1324*, 185–9.
12 *CPR 1334–1338*, 426, 434.
13 TNA:PRO, C49/7/4.
14 M. Prestwich, *Plantagenet England 1225–1360* (Oxford, 2005), 374.
15 Marshall, 'Childhood and Household', 195–6.

account for Norfolk's manor of Framlingham (Suffolk) in 1324–5, as well as other sources[16] – it is clear that the total number of his followers would have numbered in the hundreds.

Of course it was not only the size of a magnate's retinue that attested his power, prestige and influence. The composition of the affinity, the status of its members, the geographical areas from which they were drawn, and the various ties which bound them to their lord and to each other, were also important. Norfolk's highest ranking follower was undoubtedly Robert Umfraville, earl of Angus, whom he seems to have retained in 1320 (probably only for a short-term) to accompany him to France on the occasion of Edward II's homage to Philip V.[17] This was a prestigious event at which Norfolk would have been keen to display his status in front of his English and French royal relations, and the presence of the earl of Angus amongst his followers would certainly have had this effect. Whilst the king might retain his earls to serve him on campaigns in return for a fee, only the most wealthy and influential of this group could hope to imitate the king by retaining one of their peers. Lancaster was certainly wealthy enough to do this, and he also retained the earl of Angus in return for the sum of 100 marks. Lancaster additionally retained the earl of Warenne in 1309 (probably for the occasion of the Dunstable tournament), and he may also have counted David Strathbogie, earl of Atholl, amongst his followers.[18] It was by no means usual, however, for one earl to retain another in his service, and Norfolk was one of the very few earls apart from Lancaster to do so during the early fourteenth century, thereby demonstrating the superiority of his wealth and status.

Other prominent knights in Norfolk's service included Robert Ufford, Walter Mauny, Robert Morley, Richard Grey of Codnor and John Verdon. Of these individuals, the first two were particular favourites of Norfolk's nephew, Edward III. Sir Robert Ufford originated from an important family of land owners based at Ufford in Suffolk. He first appears in Norfolk's retinue in 1322, and thereafter was associated with Norfolk and his followers on a number of royal commissions.[19] He also became a trusted companion of Edward III since he was involved in the coup of 1330, in which year he was also appointed a banneret in the royal household and was granted the castle of Orford in Suffolk to hold for life.[20] Ufford received the ultimate royal reward when he was created earl of Suffolk by the king in 1337, but the fact that he witnessed Norfolk's deeds in 1333, 1336 and 1337 suggests that he remained in the earl's employ.[21]

Unlike Robert Ufford, who came from a family with a long tradition of royal service, Walter Mauny originated from Hainault and only arrived in England in 1327 as a page in Queen Philippa's household. However, he soon rose to prominence and served as a yeoman and esquire in the king's household before being knighted at the king's command in 1331, and then appointed keeper of Harlech Castle and

16 *Medieval Framlingham: Select Documents 1270–1524*, ed. J. Ridgard (Woodbridge, 1985), 51–85.

17 *CPR 1317–1321*, 427.

18 Maddicott, *Thomas of Lancaster*, 56.

19 *CPR 1321–1324*, 187; *CPR 1324–1327*, 311, 315–16; *CPR 1327–1330*, 214.

20 C. Shenton, 'Edward III and the Coup of 1330', in J. S. Bothwell (ed.), *The Age of Edward III* (York, 2001), 13–34; *Oxford Dictionary of National Biography in Association with the British Academy: From the Earliest Times to the Year 2000*, ed. H. C. G. Matthew and B. Harrison (60 vols., Oxford, 2004), lv, 856–8.

21 TNA:PRO, E328/108, m. 5; Suffolk Record Office, Ipswich, HD1538/202/1/127, HD1538/202/1/128.

sheriff of Merioneth in 1332.[22] On 1 April 1331 Norfolk granted 35 marks a year to Mauny from the sum that he received annually from his comital county, and later that year the earl (who had held the marshalship of England since 1316 with the power to appoint deputies) further granted him the position of the serjeanty of the marshalsea to hold for the term of his life.[23] Bothwell has interpreted Norfolk's patronage of Walter Mauny as evidence for the general acceptance by the established aristocracy (and in particular by members of the royal family) of Edward III's 'new men', and this is certainly a valid argument.[24] Not only did Norfolk patronize Walter Mauny, he also created a marriage alliance in 1333 with another of Edward III's favourites, William Montagu. Furthermore, he appointed one of the king's yeomen, Adam de Ashurst, to act as his clerk marshal within the royal household in 1335, and he retained one of Edward III's yeomen, Thomas Pabenham, to serve as his own yeoman-at-arms in 1337.[25] This may well denote an acceptance by Norfolk of members of Edward III's inner circle, but it should also be noted that Norfolk might also potentially benefit from his associations with such men. As Given-Wilson and Fryde have suggested, there seems to have been little affection between Norfolk and Edward III, and by retaining the king's favourites or creating alliances with them, he may have hoped to increase his own favour and influence at court.[26]

Of the other individuals mentioned above, Sir Richard Grey of Codnor (Derbyshire) also had a successful career as a royal servant, in addition to serving in Norfolk's retinue. Although he had briefly sided with the Marcher lords against the Despensers in 1321, he received a pardon and was subsequently appointed steward of Gascony in 1324. Between 14 December 1325 and 26 October 1330 he acted as constable of Nottingham Castle. In 1331 he received from Norfolk the significant grant of the manor of Segrave in Leicestershire to hold during the minority of the heir, John de Segrave, whose wardship belonged to the earl.[27] Sir Robert Morley was likewise an active soldier, who received numerous royal commissions during his lifetime (often in association with Norfolk), and who was regularly summoned to parliament between 1317 and 1357. According to the author of the *Annales Paulini*, he helped to organize a prestigious tournament at Stepney in 1331, at which he fought on the side of Norfolk and the king.[28] Sir John Verdon came from a family that had settled in Norfolk shortly after the Norman Conquest. Born in June 1299, he was a member of Norfolk's contingent on the Scottish campaign of 1322, witnessed

22 *Oxford Dictionary of National Biography* xxxvii, 445–8; J. S. Bothwell, *Edward III and the English Peerage: Royal Patronage, Social Mobility and Political Control in Fourteenth-Century England* (Woodbridge, 2004), 22.

23 *CPR 1330–1334*, 96, 179.

24 Bothwell, *Edward III*, 133, 136–7.

25 TNA:PRO, E328/108, m. 5; *CCR 1333–1337*, 85; *CPR 1334–1338*, 467; *CPR 1338–1340*, 55.

26 C. Given-Wilson, *The English Nobility in the Late Middle Ages: The Fourteenth-Century Political Community* (London, 1987), 34; N. Fryde, *The Tyranny and Fall of Edward II 1321–1326* (Cambridge, 1979), 224. The reasons for Norfolk's unpopularity with his nephew and his attempts to regain the king's favour are discussed in greater detail in Marshall, 'Thomas of Brotherton', 121–32.

27 *CPR 1330–1334*, 112; *Oxford Dictionary of National Biography* xxiii, 861; *The Complete Peerage of England, Scotland, Ireland, Great Britain and the United Kingdom*, ed. G. E. C., revised by Vicary Gibbs, H. A. Doubleday and Lord Howard de Walden, 13 vols. (London, 1910–57), i, 149–50.

28 'Annales Paulini', in *Chronicles of the Reigns of Edward I and Edward II*, ed. W. Stubbs (2 vols., London, 1882–3), i, 353–4; *CCR 1323–1327*, 168; *CPR 1321–1324*, 402; *CPR 1327–1330*, 213–14, 233–4; *CPR 1330–1334*, 292–3, 296–7; *Complete Peerage* ix, 211–14.

several of his charters during the 1330s, and was militarily active in both Scotland and France during the reigns of Edward II and Edward III.[29]

Robert Ufford, John Verdon and Robert Morley were all prominent East Anglian landholders; and men from Norfolk and Suffolk, or the bordering counties of Lincolnshire, Cambridgeshire, Bedfordshire and Essex, also dominate the lower ranks of Norfolk's affinity. Aside from the inquisitions post mortem, this can most clearly be seen from the number of men in Norfolk's service whose surnames originate from place-names in the region. Just a few examples can be cited; these include Sir Giles and Sir Roger de Trumpington of Trumpington (Cambridgeshire), Richard de Therston, William de Calthorp, Thomas de Hickling, Robert and William de Langham, Richard de Repps and Thomas de Shelton (Norfolk), Robert de Mildenhall and William de Clopton (Suffolk).[30] Of course there are exceptions (such as Sir Richard Grey of Codnor in Derbyshire and William de Newport), but in general men from more distant English counties and, more particularly, from Norfolk's Welsh and Irish lordships, form a minority.

Does this suggest that Norfolk deliberately pursued a policy of retaining the majority of his men from the East Anglian region? It is possible, but a more plausible explanation may be that Norfolk's estates were concentrated in this area. Out of the thirty-five manors which came into his possession along with the title to the earldom of Norfolk in 1312, twenty-six were located in Norfolk and Suffolk.[31] He was much the greatest and wealthiest landholder in the region, and it may have been primarily for this reason that men from the area flocked to his service. Saul has similarly found that knights and esquires in Gloucestershire tended to be local in their outlook, and were most likely to enter into the service of a lord near their base.[32] Furthermore, the dearth of men in Norfolk's service from his Welsh and Irish lordships may be attributable to the fact that he rarely seems to have visited Chepstow during his adult life, and never ventured overseas to Carlow.

Nevertheless, the idea that Norfolk, like Lancaster, realized the importance of a strong, localized power base should not be entirely dismissed.[33] The regions from which an influential and powerful magnate like him drew his retainers depended not only on the location of his estates, but also to a degree upon his political attitude. Thus Phillips has argued that the earl of Pembroke's retinue consisted of men from such a wide geographical spread not only because his estates were scattered, but also because he was so rarely in opposition to the crown that he had little need to create a strong system of local support.[34] Although Norfolk was rarely in open oppo-

29 *CPR 1321–1324*, 187; *CPR 1334*–1338, 236; *Complete Peerage*, xii.ii, 241.

30 These men all accompanied Norfolk on either the 1320 expedition to France or the 1322 Scottish campaign: *CPR 1317–1321*, 427; *CPR 1321–1324*, 187. The de Trumpingtons were a particularly wealthy family. They were responsible for rebuilding Trumpington parish church on the most lavish scale in the early fourteenth century. Sir Giles prepared a magnificent canopied tomb for himself in the north aisle, which was in the event appropriated for the use of his son Roger, who predeceased him. On this tomb is the famous brass, *c.* 1326, one of the oldest of a knight in England: see W. Lack, H. M. Stuchfield, P. Whittemore, *The Monumental Brasses of Cambridgeshire* (London, 1995), 236–7.

31 Marshall, 'Thomas of Brotherton', 177–8.

32 N. E. Saul, *Knights and Esquires: The Gloucestershire Gentry in the Fourteenth Century* (Oxford, 1981), 70–82.

33 For the geographical composition of Lancaster's affinity and its implications, see Maddicott, *Thomas of Lancaster*, 54–8, 65–6.

34 Phillips, *Aymer de Valence*, 258–9.

sition to the king, his fall from royal favour following the battle of Boroughbridge in 1322, and again after his role in the Lancastrian rebellion of 1328–9, may have persuaded him of the importance of building up a powerful regional following in and around his comital county.

Whether or not Norfolk's recruitment of men from East Anglia was a deliberate policy, it would certainly have been significant at the time of Isabella and Mortimer's invasion in September 1326. Fryde has been one of the few historians to recognize that 'the stand taken by the earl of Norfolk against his half-brother was no doubt decisive in giving Isabella an initial foothold on the east coast'.[35] During the first half of 1326 Edward II had appointed Norfolk as captain and surveyor of the array in the crucial areas of Norfolk, Suffolk and Essex, whilst two of his retainers, Robert Ufford and Thomas Latimer, were ordered to equip ships from ports in Suffolk in support of the royal fleet.[36] Neither force nor fleet materialized in support of the king, and instead Norfolk was the first to give his allegiance to the invaders after their unopposed landing at Orwell in Suffolk, inviting them to spend their first night on English soil at his nearby castle of Walton.[37] The fact that Isabella and Mortimer were able to land without losing a single man undoubtedly owed something to Norfolk's influence in the region, and by adding his own considerable and largely local force to the invading army (which numbered only 1,500 men), Norfolk swelled their numbers and strengthened their cause.[38]

Returning to the composition of Norfolk's affinity and the ties which held it together, it is notable that some of his retainers were also his tenants. Robert Ufford's manor of the same name, for example, was held of Norfolk by the service of one knight's fee, Robert Aspale held a messuage, pasture and woodland of the earldom of Norfolk for a moiety of a fourth of a knight's fee, and John Weyland held the manor of Charsfield in Suffolk from Norfolk for a fourth of a knight's fee.[39] Other names familiar from Norfolk's affinity appear in an undated roll of rents compiled by his bailiffs.[40] Maddicott and Phillips have also found that a number of Lancaster's and Pembroke's retainers were their tenants, and many of Gaunt's knights held land from him.[41] It is only to be expected in the retinues of extensive landholders such as Norfolk, Lancaster, Pembroke and Gaunt that some of their followers would also have been their tenants, and Maddicott has suggested that 'feudal loyalties were no longer sufficient to bind lord and man without the reinforcement of a fee'.[42] Nevertheless, the idea that land tenure might still in this period have an influence on the composition of a magnate's retinue should not be entirely dismissed. As McFarlane argued, traditional associations based on land tenure might still sway a man's choice of lord, and 'if their ancestors had been bound in feudal times by

35 Fryde, *Tyranny*, 5, 185–7.

36 *CPR 1324–1327*, 220, 268, 302, 311, 315–16; *Parliamentary Writs and Writs of Military Summons*, ed. F. Palgrave (2 vols., London, 1827–34), II.ii, 737, 748, 754.

37 *Adae Murimuth Continuatio Chronicarum*, ed. E. M. Thompson (London, 1889), 46–7; *Flores Historiarum*, ed. H. R. Luard (3 vols., London, 1890) iii, 233.

38 'Annales Paulini', 314; *Chronicle of Lanercost 1272–1346*, ed. H. Maxwell (Glasgow, 1913), 251; Marshall, 'Thomas of Brotherton', 85–9; Fryde, *Tyranny*, 186; R. M. Haines, *King Edward II: Edward of Caernarfon, his Life, his Reign and its Aftermath, 1284–1330* (Montreal, 2003), 174.

39 *CIPM*, vi, 44; *CIPM*, v, 196; *CIPM*, vii, 37–8.

40 BL, Egerton Charters 8761, mm. 1–2.

41 Maddicott, *Thomas of Lancaster*, 58; Phillips, *Aymer de Valence*, 256; K. B. McFarlane, 'Bastard Feudalism', *BIHR*, 20 (1945), 169.

42 Maddicott, *Thomas of Lancaster*, 58.

close ties to a particular family there was a natural presumption that … the tradition would survive'.[43]

Within Norfolk's affinity there were familial as well as tenurial ties of loyalty. Following Norfolk's marriage to his first wife, Alice Hales, a number of her relatives entered Norfolk's service.[44] The clearest evidence for this is provided by a charter between two of Norfolk's followers, Sir Robert Morley and Sir Walter Hales, whereby the former granted his manor of Carbrooke in Norfolk to the latter. This charter, dated 1 January 1326, was witnessed by Norfolk himself and by other members of his affinity. The witnesses included Roger and John Hales, and William and John Jermye (the family into which Alice Hales' sister, Joan, married).[45] Whether or not Norfolk similarly employed relatives of his second wife, Mary de Braose, is less clear, but the fact that he granted a valuable manor to one of her kinsmen, Peter de Braose, suggests that he did.[46] This retention by Norfolk of his wives' kinsmen should not necessarily be regarded as typical. A magnate could usually be expected to marry into a family whose wealth was such that they could provide for their own lesser members. Norfolk, however, made surprisingly lowly matches – his first wife Alice was the daughter of a Norfolk knight and coroner, and although his second wife Mary was of somewhat higher status, she was still hardly the spouse to be expected of a son of Edward I. Nevertheless, such strong family ties within Norfolk's service would certainly have served to strengthen his affinity, and long after Alice's death in around 1330 her kinsmen were still in his employ. The 1337 list of Norfolk's household members shows that Sir John Hales was acting as the steward of his household, Roger Hales was serving as one of his squires, and John Jermye was being employed as chaplain to Norfolk's second wife, Mary de Braose.[47]

The relationship between a lord and his followers was a reciprocal one, and the emoluments due to a retainer, such as his fee, livery and right to 'bouche of court', might be detailed in a formal contract, or indenture. Although none of Norfolk's original indentures of retinue have survived, it is clear from government records that he did make formal contracts with some of his followers. For instance, it was recorded in the patent rolls of 1332 that in return for serving as Norfolk's constable of Framlingham Castle, Geoffrey Quincy was to receive 5s. per week from the earl, as well as hay for two horses, half a bushel of oats for every knight serving under his authority, and yearly livery.[48] Similarly, in 1337 Edward III confirmed a grant from Norfolk to Thomas Pabenham of the hundred of Loose in Suffolk, which he was to hold for life by way of a fee in return for staying in Norfolk's 'comitiva' in the capacity of yeoman-at-arms.[49] The size of the fee that a retainer could expect varied greatly, depending on factors such as the wealth and generosity of the lord, the role and status of the follower and to an extent, no doubt, his success in winning

[43] McFarlane, 'Bastard Feudalism', 169.

[44] The precise date of Norfolk's marriage to Alice Hales has escaped record, but probably took place during the early 1320s since they had a son of marriageable age by 1328, and had certainly occurred by 1324–5 when she is mentioned in an account roll for Framlingham Castle: *Medieval Framlingham*, 67; Marshall, 'Thomas of Brotherton', 138–40.

[45] TNA:PRO, E327/3784.

[46] TNA:PRO, C49/7/4, m. 2.

[47] Ibid.

[48] *CPR 1330–1334*, 260.

[49] *CPR 1334–1338*, 467.

his lord's particular favour. One of the highest paid members of Norfolk's affinity was William de Newport, a clerk who received the considerable sum of £125 11s. 7d. in wages, paid directly from the profits of Framlingham manor while he was serving as the keeper of Norfolk's wardrobe in 1324–5.[50] One of Norfolk's chief parkers, John Fourneux, received the manor of Earsham in Norfolk for the duration of his life by way of his fee – a grant which was worth about £50 per annum.[51] Given that Lancaster retained the earl of Angus for only 100 marks (about £66), and that a knight might serve his lord in return for £20 or £30 a year during this period, these two examples represent very generous fees.[52] Another of Norfolk's parkers, Robert Wafre, received what was probably a much more typical fee for a man of his status, being paid a total of £6 15s. 8½d. in 1324–5.[53]

The means by which a retainer received his fee might also vary. No doubt many of Norfolk's followers, such as Geoffrey Quincy, received their wages directly from the earl's wardrobe or from a receivership. Others, however, were given either an annuity from a manor (or manors), or were enfeoffed in a property for a defined number of years or for the duration of their lives. For example, Norfolk made use of the wardship of John de Segrave by granting most of the latter's manors to his own retainers, to hold until the heir reached his majority.[54] Furthermore, the inquiry into Norfolk's household by Sir Constantine Mortimer in 1337 found that the earl had granted lands, farms and rents worth a total of £314 13s. 4d. per annum to fourteen of his family members and followers. It was clearly felt that this was beyond Norfolk's means, as Mortimer ordered all of these grants to be repealed and the lands and rents to be restored to Norfolk in aid of his sustenance.[55] This would presumably have caused a certain amount of discontent within Norfolk's affinity, but may have been a necessary measure, since there is some evidence to suggest that Norfolk became increasingly indebted to the crown at this time, and the task of maintaining such a large retinue (and paying generous fees) was no doubt a contributory factor.[56]

By making lifelong grants of manors to his followers, Norfolk did incur the risk that some of them might fail to fulfil their obligations to him, and yet would still have a legal claim to the lands. There is, though, only one surviving example of a land dispute between Norfolk and one of his retainers. In about 1334 Robert Morley and his wife Joan brought a plea of novel disseisin against Norfolk concerning the manor of Earsham (Norfolk), which they claimed he had granted to them for life. There is not enough extant evidence to ascertain why Norfolk then seized back this manor (subsequently granting it to his chief parker, John Forneux), but the dispute was in any case peaceably settled when Robert and Joan Morley accepted

50 *Medieval Framlingham*, 66.

51 TNA:PRO, C49/7/4, m. 2; *CPR 1338–1340*, 7.

52 Maddicott, *Thomas of Lancaster*, 56.

53 *Medieval Framlingham*, 62–3.

54 Richard Grey of Codnor, William Giffard and John Jermye – all prominent members of Norfolk's affinity – benefited from lands pertaining to the wardship, which Norfolk had been granted on 3 March 1327: *CPR 1327–1330*, 23; *A Catalogue of the Medieval Muniments at Berkeley Castle*, ed. B. Wells-Furby (2 vols., Bristol, 2004), ii, 713–14.

55 TNA:PRO, C49/7/4, m. 2.

56 Norfolk's indebtedness should not, however, be exaggerated, since it seems to have amounted to no more than a few hundred pounds at the time of his death in August 1338: *CCR 1337–1339*, 159, 243, 504, 537, 560; *CFR 1337–1347*, 91–2.

in compensation an area of 'great marsh' in Halvergate, Norfolk, and quitclaimed all of their rights to Earsham.[57]

There were numerous other ways in which a retainer might be rewarded for his services in addition to those outlined above. Favoured clerks, for instance, might reasonably expect to be rewarded with a benefice. Norfolk, like many other magnates, jealously guarded his right to make presentations to benefices in his gift for precisely this reason. In the 1330s Edward III found himself in the unenviable position of having to revoke presentations that he had made to a number of benefices, including those of Clopton (Suffolk) and Newnham (Gloucestershire), because Norfolk had successfully demonstrated that these advowsons belonged to him.[58] Both clerks and knights might desire Norfolk to find positions for other members of their families in his service, and examples of individuals who share a surname are common in his affinity. Just a few examples are Henry and Sir Maurice le Brun, Sir Giles and Sir Roger de Trumpington, John and Roger Courson, Robert and William de Langham, and Thomas and Nicholas Latimer.[59] Norfolk's followers might also expect him to further their prospects in the service of the crown: for not only could he use his influence (especially as a member of the royal family) to find them positions on royal commissions, as marshal of England he was also able to reward a number of his followers with offices in the king's marshalsea. His right to appoint a deputy marshal and a clerk within the royal household was particularly valuable given the proximity of these officials to the king's person; however, he could additionally appoint subordinates within the exchequer, the court of king's bench, the court of common pleas and the Fleet prison, and a number of Norfolk's followers profited from such appointments, including Walter Mauny and Geoffrey Quincy.[60]

An important aspect of a lord's obligations to his followers was to aid them in legal disputes and attempts to remedy injustices. An excellent example of his support is provided by the case of Norfolk's long-serving butler, Gassocus de Ruele. Prior to her death in 1318, Norfolk's mother Queen Margaret had granted lands in Kent and Suffolk to Ruele to hold to himself and his heirs, in return for services rendered to her and her sons. Following Margaret's death the lands seem to have officially passed to Queen Isabella, and the grant to Ruele was only renewed at Norfolk's insistence. Following the coup of 1330 Isabella's estates were confiscated, and the lands which Ruele claimed were granted by Edward III to John of Florence. It was only as a result of Norfolk's repeated petitioning of the king that the lands were restored to Ruele in 1331 for the duration of his life, and that in 1334 this grant was extended to include his heirs.[61]

The means by which Norfolk defended the rights of Gassocus de Ruele were entirely legal, but of course there were also less scrupulous means by which both lords and their retainers could profit – most notably through bribery, corruption and plunder. In 1328, for example, Norfolk found it necessary to request royal pardons for four of his followers who (by his own admission) he had sent during November

[57] *CPR 1338–1340*, 97.

[58] *CCR 1327–1330*, 321, 326; *CPR 1330–1334*, 274.

[59] These men all served Norfolk in either 1320 or 1322: *CPR 1317–1321*, 427; *CPR 1321–1324*, 187.

[60] For examples of the appointment of Norfolk's followers to offices within the marshalsea, see: *CCR 1327–1330*, 150; *CPR 1317–1321*, 189; *CPR 1330–1334*, 40, 179.

[61] TNA:PRO, SC8/143/7117; *CCR 1330–1334*, 184; *CPR 1334–1338*, 21.

1326 to pillage the lands of the Despensers,[62] and the fact that Norfolk was called to answer complaints of oppression against his household in 1337 suggests that he was allowing his officials to take provisions while paying little or nothing in return for them.[63] Norfolk's retainers sometimes acted as commissioners on cases of oyer and terminer in which he had an interest,[64] and in 1337 Isolda Inge (who was involved in a dispute of novel disseisin with Norfolk) complained that the original jury had been changed by force – presumably by Norfolk's men.[65] The extent of corruption within Norfolk's affinity should not, however, be exaggerated: complaints against his conduct are far from extensive, and there is no extant evidence to suggest that he regularly paid fees to the king's justices, sheriffs or other local officials. This is in contrast to both Thomas of Lancaster, who paid fees to the king's pleaders and gave liveries to his justices in 1318–19, and John of Gaunt, who retained at least twenty-four men who also acted as sheriffs.[66]

The bonds within Norfolk's affinity and the rewards open to his followers were incentive enough to ensure that many of these men served him loyally for lengthy periods. In fact, at least five of the men who served the earl during the 1320s and 1330s had previously been members of his childhood household between 1301 and 1312.[67] Many of Norfolk's other retainers can be shown to have served him for much of his adult life. Sir Robert Aspale, for instance, can be traced as a member of Norfolk's affinity for around a decade. In a letter written to the king in early 1322, Norfolk described Aspale as his 'trescher Bachelor', and by 1330 (after a period acting as his steward) he was serving as Norfolk's attorney.[68] Even longer serving were Sir Robert Ufford, Sir John Verdon and Sir William Giffard, who all accompanied Norfolk to Scotland in 1322 and who were still acting as witnesses to his various deeds during the later 1330s.[69] There is no evidence to suggest that long-serving retainers such as these were concurrently employed by other lords, which serves to corroborate Saul's suggestion that 'there does seem to be an absence for the first half of the fourteenth century at least of those shifting relationships that have led some writers to complain of the unstable nature of "bastard feudalism" '.[70] Of course individuals who were only retained by Norfolk for one or two campaigns

62 *CPR 1327–1330*, 268. See also Fryde, *Tyranny*, 187–9.

63 *CPR 1334–1338*, 426, 434. According to the chroniclers, Norfolk's brother Kent was unpopular because he similarly allowed his household to take liberties in the localities: *Adae Murimuth Continuatio Chronicarum*, ed. E. M. Thompson (London, 1889), 60; *Chronicon Galfridi Le Baker de Swynbroke*, ed. E. M. Thompson (Oxford, 1889), 44.

64 In August 1327, for example, three of his retainers were given a commission of oyer and terminer on complaint by Norfolk that one of his parks in Derbyshire had been broken into, his deer hunted and stolen: *CPR 1327–1330*, 206.

65 Norfolk later compensated Isolda with 100 marks: TNA:PRO, SC8/119/5904; *CCR 1337–1339*, 521.

66 Maddicott, *Thomas of Lancaster*, 63; Walker, *Lancastrian Affinity*, 241.

67 These five men were William de Newport, Ambrose de Newbury, William Bas, Peter Bordet and Richard de la More. At least two other men who served in the childhood household – John Golde and Roger Wellesford – continued in the service of Norfolk's brother, Edmund of Kent, long after 1312: *CPR 1317–1321*, 189, 419, 427, 435; *CPR 1321–1324*, 187; Marshall, 'Thomas of Brotherton', 164–5.

68 TNA:PRO, SC1/36/8; *CCR 1323–1327*, 168; *CPR 1321–1324*, 402; *CPR 1327–1330*, 508; *Medieval Framlingham*, 64, 70.

69 Suffolk Record Office, Ipswich, HD1538/202/1/127; HD1538/202/1/128; *CPR 1321–1324*, 187; *CPR 1334–1338*, 236.

70 Saul, *Knights and Esquires*, 94.

in order to swell the numbers of his force would have been far more likely to seek further employment elsewhere. It has already been noted that the earl of Angus served both Norfolk and Thomas of Lancaster on occasion, and similarly Richard de la Rivere, who followed Norfolk on the Scottish campaign of 1322, was also in the service of Pembroke in 1313, 1318 and 1322, and acted as Henry of Lancaster's steward of Kidwelly in Wales in 1308, 1319 and 1322.[71] Within the core of Norfolk's affinity, however, there does seem to have been a considerable degree of allegiance and stability.

In conclusion, a great deal of valuable information can be gleaned about a nobleman's retinue even when no indentures of retinue or household rolls and liveries have survived, and this in turn provides essential new evidence with which to examine later medieval magnate affinities as a whole. As befitted his status, Norfolk possessed a sizeable following at the heart of which was a body of long-term retainers, bound to him not only by the fee but also often by familial, tenurial and geographical ties. The extant evidence suggests that Norfolk was a generous lord, and this factor combined with the scale of his retinue occasionally led to financial difficulties towards the end of his life. Norfolk was fortunate, however, that in addition to the normal channels of patronage he could also use his influence with the crown as a member of the royal family to gain commissions for his followers, as well as appointing deputies within the marshalsea. Despite the negative connotations often associated with later medieval magnate retinues, there is no evidence that corruption was rife in Norfolk's affinity, and many of his followers appear to have served him loyally and exclusively for lengthy periods of time.

[71] Phillips, *Aymer de Valence*, 256–7.

JOHN OF GAUNT'S HOUSEHOLD: ATTENDANCE ROLLS IN THE GLYNDE ARCHIVE, MS 3469*

Elizabeth H. Will

John of Gaunt was one of the foremost figures of the late fourteenth century in both England's domestic affairs and European affairs more generally. At the root of his power lay the wealth of the Lancastrian estates and the income acquired by right of his wife Blanche. Gaunt was a highly controversial figure. In his own time his loyalties were considered to be deeply suspect and he provoked strong feelings, frequently of enmity. He was widely disliked by the Londoners in 1377 and the rebels in 1381, and among the chroniclers only Knighton, who wrote under his patronage, was openly sympathetic. Yet while he was unquestionably ambitious, it is likely that his concerns were to defend the royal prerogative and uphold royal authority, and his ambition was directed at the pursuit not of the throne of England, but a of foreign kingdom from where he could promote English interests, in accordance with Edward III's intentions for all his children.

Little material relates to Gaunt's household or domestic matters, although the first biography[1] was followed by the publication of two key records from the archives of the Duchy of Lancaster, *John of Gaunt's Register* for 1372–76 in 1911,[2] and that for 1379–83 in 1937.[3] These contain copies of documents made by the Lancastrian chancery, mostly those passing under the duke's privy seal, and cover the full range of the duke's concerns. Amongst much else there is information on his retainers, their wages, provision for his family, and the running of his household. Robert Somerville, editor of the second Register, went on to publish a history of the Duchy of Lancaster which contains a chapter on John of Gaunt's duchy administration, and a list of his estate and household officers.[4]

Shortly before the publication of Anthony Goodman's biography in 1992,[5] Simon Walker published a detailed study of the duke's affinity[6] which drew extensively on records of the Duchy and Palatinate of Lancaster as well as other sources, including a little-known document of a relatively rare type in the East Sussex Record Office: seventeen check-rolls and three membranes of a household journal from the records

* I would like to thank Nigel Saul for his encouragement and for commenting on the drafts of this article. I would also like to thank Christopher Whittick for his advice and help with GLY 3469.

1 S. Armitage-Smith, *John of Gaunt* (London, 1904).

2 S. Armitage-Smith (ed.), *John of Gaunt's Register* (2 vols., Camden Society, 3rd series, 20–1, 1911). Hereafter *Register I*.

3 E. C. Lodge and R. Somerville (eds.), *John of Gaunt's Register 1379–83* (2 vols., Camden Society, 3rd series, 56–7, 1937). Hereafter *Register II*.

4 R. Somerville, *History of the Duchy of Lancaster*, i (London, 1953), 90–110, 363–385. The list of central and estate officials has been added to and corrected by S. Walker, *The Lancastrian Affinity 1361–1399* (Oxford, 1990), 285–291.

5 A. Goodman, *John of Gaunt. The Exercise of Princely Power in Fourteenth-Century Europe* (London, 1992).

6 Walker, *The Lancastrian Affinity*.

of John of Gaunt, now GLY 3469 (1–20). These parchment rolls had been used as a backing of the Waleys Cartulary,[7] compiled, probably in London, to provide a copy of deeds to be handed over following the division of the estates of John Waleys of Sussex after his death in 1419. The cartulary consisted of two rolls measuring 22 and 24 feet, each made up of paper sheets measuring approximately 17½ inches x 11¾ inches (44.5 cm x 30 cm), pasted onto a parchment backing which was discovered when the cartulary was repaired. To preserve the paper and read the backing rolls, the two were separated at the Bodleian Library in 1955. The membranes were examined with the help of K. B. McFarlane, put into a suggested date order and numbered, with reference also to which roll they had been part of, A or B, and the order in which they had been when used as backing. A description of the membranes was given in Richard Dell's catalogue of the Glynde Place Archive published in 1964.[8] These rolls are the only known records of Gaunt's household[9] other than a fragment of a wardrobe account of 1383–4,[10] and Receiver General's and estate accounts which provide some incidental information.[11] Yet they have been little used since being catalogued by Dell.

The purpose here is to review the dates of the accounts given by Dell and in some cases to reconsider Dell's dates or to offer an alternative. All the membranes have now been dated, securely or with some certainty (although two only in part), and a new order is suggested (see Appendix, p. 24 below).

The organisation and administration of a household the size of Gaunt's was a major undertaking. As well as providing a secure and agreeable environment for the duke and his family, whether in residence or travelling, the household was the centre of the wider affinity employed by the duke to accompany him, in England and across Europe, in peace, war and diplomacy. Attendance rolls and household journals formed only a small part of the system controlling the administration of the vast Lancastrian estates. Nonetheless, these fragments when combined with other sources provide a limited but focused picture of the numbers and deployment of individual members of the household.

The membranes were originally filed at the head, cut away when re-used. All would have been of a standard size, but were severely trimmed down to fit their new purpose and now measure between 12 and 11 inches (30.5 to 28 cm) in width and 34 and 26 inches (87 to 66 cm) in length.[12] Apart from the severe cropping, the membranes are in good condition and quite legible, other than in some small areas of slight damage and a little fading. There is also a fair amount of presumably fifteenth-century glue still present on the faces to which the paper pages of the Waleys cartulary were pasted. Each check-roll seems originally to have had a heading, with the regnal year and possibly other information such as location, now

[7] East Sussex Record Office, MS GLY 1139. R. F. Dell (ed.), *Glynde Place Archives* (Lewes, 1964), 97.

[8] Dell, *Glynde Place Archives*, 260–2.

[9] C. M. Woolgar (ed.), *Household Accounts from Medieval England* (2 vols., Oxford, 1993), ii, 704.

[10] Cambridge, Peterhouse MS 42, fols. 1–2 1383–4. M. R. James (ed.), *Catalogue of the Manuscripts of Peterhouse, Cambridge* (Cambridge, 1899), 60–3, gives a transcription; see also M. Sharp, 'A Fragmentary Household Account of John of Gaunt', *BIHR*, 13 (1935/6), 154–160.

[11] Receiver General's Accounts, DL 28/3/1, 50 Edward III – 1 Richard II; DL 28/3/2, 15–16 Richard II; DL 28/3/5, 20–21 Richard II. All DL references are to Duchy of Lancaster documents in The National Archives (formerly Public Record Office) London.

[12] The exception is III/3 which is 19 inches (48.25 cm) wide and 12 inches (30.5 cm) long.

lost. The sole surviving vestige of a main heading is in IV/2, July 1381, where the words *Julij anno quarto* can be made out. Sub-headings at the top of recto and verso, of which two-thirds (twenty-three of thirty-four) survive if only in part, have initials or abbreviations for days of the week, and roman numerals for dates of the month.[13] Typically, each membrane records attendance at a particular place for one month. Names of members of the household are listed down the left-hand side, and against each name is an entry under each day: *venit* (abbreviated to *ven'* or *vet'*), *0* when present, *vacat* (*vat'* or *vac'*), or left blank when absent. Household horses and their fodder rations follow. The lists have the appearance of being fair copies and were perhaps compiled from a system of checking-in or tallies, and written up at the end of a month or when the household moved on.

In 1381 the average number of all household members on the check-rolls was 160, a figure which by the 1390s had increased to around 180 (see Table, p. 23 below). The number of knights and senior officials remained at about twenty; esquires increased over the same period from an average of twenty-three to thirty-seven;[14] valets remained at just under forty; the next rank, however, that of grooms, of whom there were some twenty in 1381, more than doubled to nearly fifty by the early 1390s, then fell to under forty in the middle of the decade. To arrive at the total number of staff, unnamed servants in the stables and kitchens would have to be included, as well as washerwomen employed by the two laundresses, and many pages too menial or too young to achieve the check-roll.[15] Unfortunately any estimate of the numbers of these anonymous servants would be mere guesswork.

The seventeen check-rolls divide into three groups, the first for January, April, June, July and September 1381.[16] Ten years then elapse before the second series, for November, December 1391, January, February, March, and September 1392[17] with a concurrent roll for periods which the duke spent in London in December, January (two) and February.[18] The final group, of five rolls, runs from November 1393 to March 1394.[19] In addition there are three membranes from a household journal for parts of July, August, and September 1383.[20]

In the summer of 1381 – the year of the Peasants' Revolt – members of the household must have felt particularly under threat, not least because of their allegiance to the duke. In membrane II/4, April 1381, the duke and his retinue returned to Leicester after a glittering banquet at The Savoy, held as part of the negotiations for Richard II's marriage to Anne of Bohemia, and possibly one of the last times

13 On membrane X/9 *December*, *Januarius*, and *Februarius*, and on XIV/15 *November*, appear in the sub-headings.

14 The *Nomina militum et scutiferorum* compiled in 1382 with revisions made up to mid-1385, printed in *Register II*, 6–9, contains names of 99 knights and 126 esquires of the *retinentia domini*, the inner core of the duke's following, who could be summoned for military service. The names of 17 knights and 29 esquires from this list appear in the check-rolls. See also Walker, *The Lancastrian Affinity*, 310–11.

15 James, in *Catalogue of the Manuscripts of Peterhouse*, 60–3, records several pages in various departments identified by first name only, paid annual *calciatura* and ad hoc amounts for specified periods or journeys.

16 I/1, II/4, III/3, IV/2, V/5.

17 VI/6, VII/11, VIII/7, IX/8, XI/10, and XII/17 (from which names have been cut away).

18 X/9.

19 XIII/12, XIV/15 (names cut away), XV/13, XVI/14, and XVII/16 (names cut away).

20 XVIII/18, XIX/19 and XX/20.

when the palace would be used for such an event.[21] One of the most intriguing rolls, III/3, for Tuesday 4 – Sunday 30 June 1381 is also unfortunately the most severely cut-down, and although sub-headings survive on the verso, only a small part, perhaps a quarter, of the original roll remains. The duke had passed through Leicester in the middle of May,[22] stopping at Knaresborough on his way to Scotland to hold a March Day,[23] and this roll may record the attendance of those who had accompanied him as far as Knaresborough, and remained there intending to await his return. Following the destruction of The Savoy on 13 June,[24] threats to Leicester Castle and damage to Hertford Castle, on 17 June the duke ordered the household to assemble at Pontefract.[25] The recto of what remains of III/3 begins with an orderly record from 4 to 30 June of the duchess's servants and horses, who remain throughout the period.[26] Then, from 20 June, below these routine entries, people appear to be recorded as they arrive, irrespective of rank: some pages, two of the duke's councillors, his confessor, the master cook, a valet, and some musicians. The membrane is then cut. In the next roll, IV/2 for July, following the duke's orders, the household is presumably at Pontefract. Constance with her own servants and some of the household valets, grooms and clerks is found already in residence there, when on 18 June the duke arrived from Edinburgh with a company of nearly fifty knights, esquires and valets.[27] In response to the duke's further instructions, money, plate, and emergency supplies were being sent urgently from various of the duke's estates to Pontefract,[28] presumably causing considerable disorder as they arrived: however the valets, usually paid *iiij d* a day, were receiving *vij d ob* daily, an esquire's rate, for the extra work. In September the duke was at York investigating with other justices the recent 'various treasons, insurrections and other evils' in Yorkshire.[29]

No attendance rolls are known from November 1381 to November 1391. When the next sequence begins at Hertford in November 1391, the household had changed considerably, though not beyond recognition. A period of disruption was initiated in July 1386, when the duke, taking his wife Constance and a large part of their household,[30] went to Spain and Portugal to make good after fourteen years their claim to the throne of Castile. In November 1389 they returned, the situation resolved by the marriages of the duke's daughters, Philippa to João I of Portugal,[31] and Katherine to Enrique of Castile.[32] Numerous names disappeared from the lists between 1381

21 Goodman, *John of Gaunt*, 78; N. E. Saul, *Richard II* (New Haven and London, 1997), 87.

22 *Register II*, 525, 554–5.

23 Entries in *Register II* are dated at Knaresborough from 26 May (1049) to 2 June (528–9, 542). The duke then continued to Scotland, the first warrant dated at Edinburgh is on 25 June (559).

24 L. C. Hector and B. F. Harvey (eds.), *The Westminster Chronicle, 1381–1394* (Oxford, 1982), 5.

25 *Register II*, 541.

26 This raises the question of where the story might fit of the duchess's night flight from Knaresborough to Pontefract (a distance of some 30 miles). The presence of the duchess's servants on the next roll is also constant. Armitage-Smith, *John of Gaunt*, 249; Goodman, *John of Gaunt*, 79; G. H. Martin (ed.), *Knighton's Chronicle, 1337–1396* (Oxford, 1995), 230.

27 Following his altercation with the earl of Northumberland, the duke briefly returned to Edinburgh (Goodman, *John of Gaunt*, 80–3).

28 *Register II*, 541, 549–551.

29 Goodman, *John of Gaunt*, 89.

30 Saul, *Richard II*, 149.

31 Philippa married João I of Portugal in February 1387, F. Lopes, *The English in Portugal 1367–87*, ed. D. W. Lomax and R. J. Oakley (Warminster, 1989), 229.

32 Katherine married Enrique, grandson of Enrique of Trastámara in September 1388, and became

and 1391, and many had died in Spain,[33] more perhaps from disease than combat.[34] But the duke recruited new retainers, and continued to do so throughout the period of the accounts, and up to his death.

The membranes of the next sequence run from November 1391 to March 1392. The duke spent Christmas and the New Year at Hertford with Constance, Henry of Derby, who had been crusading in Prussia during the summer,[35] and the four Beauforts. Roll X/9 simultaneously records some of the household in London for sessions of parliament in December and January and the king's council in February.[36] In the last roll of this series, XI/10,[37] for part of February and the whole of March 1392, the duke travelled via Dover and Calais to meet Charles VI at Amiens.[38] At the start he was accompanied by nearly 120 members of the household of whom, on 7 March, the date on or close to which the duke crossed to Calais,[39] about thirty, mostly household officials and the servants of the duchess, left the main retinue, presumably at Dover.

The last group, for October–November to February–March 1393–4, despite each membrane being cut away to some extent, shows the whole household again spending Christmas and New Year at Hertford.[40] There was jousting for which Henry of Derby, who had been travelling through Europe to the Holy Land,[41] bought a quantity of arms and armour for himself and his half-brother Thomas Beaufort.[42] Celebrating the season with the duke were Constance, Henry and Mary of Derby, 'Meistre Henry de Derby' (the future Henry V), then about six years old, Katherine Swynford, John Beaufort, Jane Beaufort (now Ferrers), and Thomas Beaufort, all in residence by 20 December.[43]

Throughout the records patterns of attendance show that the majority of the duke's servants, though based wherever the household was situated, frequently made journeys away. Leaving the household did not mean abandoning the duke's interests. On the contrary, as the Registers record, many of these journeys would have been made on the duke's business. The largest groups arrived and departed with the duke on formal or state business. When the duke went to London for sessions of parlia-

queen in 1390: Armitage-Smith, *John of Gaunt*, 333. P. E. Russell, *The English Intervention in Spain and Portugal in the Time of Edward III and Richard II* (Oxford, 1955), 508–10.

33 *Westminster Chronicle*, 191; Goodman, *John of Gaunt*, 125–6.

34 Philippa Chaucer died between 18 June and 7 November 1387 (M. M. Crow and C. C. Olson (eds.), *Chaucer Life-Records* (Oxford, 1966), 84. The large contingent accompanying the duke and duchess in 1386 included ladies attending Constance, of whom Philippa, a long-established *demoiselle* of the duchess (she is mentioned as such in the *Registers* from 1372 and appears in the check-rolls for 1381), should have been one. It seems possible that Philippa, too, may have been a victim of one of the epidemics that ravaged the duke's army. The duke himself fell sick.

35 L. Toulmin Smith (ed.), *Expeditions to Prussia and the Holy Land made by Henry Earl of Derby (afterwards King Henry IV) in the Years 1390–1 and 1392–3* (Camden Society, 52, 1894), ix.

36 Goodman, *John of Gaunt*, 149.

37 There are no horses on this roll.

38 Goodman, *John of Gaunt*, 150–1.

39 DL 28/3/2 m. 16 cites a warrant dated at Calais on 7 March.

40 Goodman, *John of Gaunt*, 153.

41 Toulmin Smith, *Expeditions to Prussia*, x.

42 Goodman, *John of Gaunt*, 153.

43 The knights' names are cut away but a horse of Thomas Swynford is present on the verso and it seems likely that he was also there. Henry Beaufort is listed but not present. Thomas, the son of Geoffrey and Philippa Chaucer, retained as *esquire familier* in 1389 and listed throughout the rolls for the 1390s, is also there.

ment in late 1391 and early 1392 (X/9) between seventy and ninety people went with him; when he went to Amiens in March 1392 (XI/10), he was accompanied by a retinue of more than ninety.[44] Constance and her *demoiselles* and servants travelled too, but not as frequently as the duke. The only members of the household to be in residence at all times were clerks of the secretariat who seem to have travelled only when the whole household moved to a new location.

In each roll all members of the household are grouped by rank, each group probably having some internal hierarchy which is not now apparent. Where the left-hand margin survives, a daily allowance is written: for knights *xij d*, esquires *vij d ob*, valets *iiij d*, grooms *ij d*, pages, *j d*. Information for valets, grooms, and pages is of course scarcer than for knights and esquires, but there is some in the Registers and estate records. Although members of the entourage are carefully segregated by rank, the rolls give little information about employment. The chancellor, treasurer and controller, 'Le Manservant', and 'Le Register' are listed by title, and the names of some of those working in household departments are suggestive of occupation. Information for others can be found principally in the Registers, where the addressees or those named are further described as duke's esquire, valet, groom or clerk of, for example, a household department, or one of an array of occupations: the duke's avener, almoner, armourer, barber, ewerer and naperer, valet of his jewels, minstrel, pavilioner, tailor, trumpeter, usher, are only some of those mentioned.

Nowhere in the attendance rolls are the duke or members of his family referred to directly, but the presence of these people can be inferred from the presence of their horses. For the duke himself, the horses of his chamber probably give the best indication that he is present. The duchess Constance and, in the earlier group, Philippa of Lancaster, have servants and horses identified as theirs, and it must be assumed they are in residence when their servants and horses are. Elizabeth of Lancaster, when countess of Pembroke living at the king's court,[45] appears when she visits Leicester in April 1381 and her horses are in the stable list.[46] In the household journal Constance is mentioned when she left Kenilworth, on 25 July 1383, to go to Tutbury *cum parte familie*.[47] Katherine of Lancaster, sent to live in the household of Lady de Mohun, a wealthy heiress and particular friend of the duke,[48] is also mentioned in 1383 when expenses for a visit to Kenilworth are noted.[49] Henry of Derby does not feature in the attendance rolls of 1381, but from 1391 his horses are included in the stable lists, as are those of his wife Mary and son Henry.

Stable lists follow those for the household. Although most left-hand margins are lost, a few details of fodder rations survive. Horses are also listed by groups or sections. The first, usually between twenty and thirty, are described by colour, sometimes by kind (destrier, palfrey, &c) and a name, either, occasionally, their own, but more often their owner's or, following common practice at the time, that of the

44 Only one roll for London, X/9, and one for travel to France, XI/10, have been identified and it is not possible to know how typical they are. XIII/12 and XVI/14 have a similar format to X/9 but are as yet only partly dated.

45 Armitage-Smith, *John of Gaunt*, 459.

46 II/4.

47 XIX/19. She appears to have gone to Tutbury to meet the duke, who arrived there from Scotland on 26 July (*Register II*, 900). See n. 62, below.

48 Armitage-Smith, *John of Gaunt*, 226–7; Goodman, *John of Gaunt*, 293.

49 XX/20.

previous owner, or place of origin.[50] The second section is for horses of the household departments; then horses for the family, the duchess Constance and her servants, Katherine Swynford and, from 1391, Henry of Derby, and the Beauforts. The horses of heralds, messengers, and musicians come next; then carters or carriage drivers and their horses in teams of up to seven; horses of personal servants, and last and infrequently, longer-term visitors. Some who received a daily allowance were also allocated a horse or horses; other servants were allocated horses but were named only in the stable list, and presumably had annual wages but no daily allowance.[51]

Two hundred and more horses[52] require a large number of attendants, but none are named in the attendance roll and, although someone must have undertaken this major role, no marshal of the stables has been identified. The marchalsea would have kept its own records and entries under *vadia* in the household journal, also in the Glynde material, included daily wages of stable, and possibly kitchen, staff.

A reordered list of the check-rolls is given in the Appendix. Where a date can be confirmed in some cases it is then possible to identify the location. *Register II* for 1379–83, contemporary with the 1381 rolls, is of considerable value. The dates of warrants make it possible to outline an itinerary for the duke, and there is much information about members as well as activities of the household. In contrast, the Receiver's Accounts for 1391–2 and 1394–5[53] provide a much sparser background for the two series of the 1390s.

Dell gave firm dates for seven of the seventeen check-rolls: I/1, III/3, IX/8, X/9, XI/10, XIV/15, and XVII/16. He offered two alternatives for V/5, VI/6, and XV/13, three alternatives for VIII/7 and XII/17; and suggested a range of possibilities within limits for VII/11, XIII/12, and XVI/14.

Dell dated II/4, to July 1381 and IV/2 to April 1381. However although II/4 has a sub-heading for thirty-one days, the last day, *Mercurii*, is crossed through and entries beneath are for a thirty-day month, i.e. April. IV/2 is the only membrane with part of a main heading to survive: *Julij anno quarto*. The dates are therefore correct, but the membranes should be transposed.

With no main headings, attempts at dating must rely on internal evidence, of which, fortunately, there is more than appears at first sight and even incomplete sub-headings can offer possibilities where there is a combination of day and date.

Dell dated Roll VII/11 to before March 1392.[54] It is for a thirty-one day month and contains an internal reference to December. Entries for names of those absent on this roll for *Veneris primo* to *Lune iiij* match those present for the same four days in X/9a, making the date of this roll December 1391. For VIII/7, Dell suggested three possible dates but there is a similar internal reference to January, and again

50 Horses with names of the Scottish nobility, Carrick, Douglas, Lindsay, Stewart, appear in IV/2 and V/5 after the duke's sojourn in Scotland.

51 They may have been paid a daily wage with stable servants, accounted for in the *vadia* of the household journal.

52 Most household knights and esquires were required to provide horses for themselves and their servants, and to arrange and pay for stabling, according to the terms of their indentures. The figure of 200 excludes these, but they may have been stabled with or close by horses of the household. Thomas of Lancaster stabled more than 400 horses at Pontefract in 1318–19. (C. M. Woolgar, *The Great Household in Late Medieval England* (New Haven and London, 1999), 191.)

53 DL 28/3/2, DL 28/3/5.

54 Jane Beaufort is referred to as Jane Ferrers after her marriage to Robert Ferrers in March 1392.

entries of those absent here match those present on X/9b and c for January 1392; likewise those absent in IX/8 match those present in X/9d. Names on roll XII/17 have been cut away but sub-headings remain and there are two entries which mention September (1392).

Where rolls appear to run consecutively possibilities can be confirmed, or not, by matching name by name entries for the last days of one against the first days of the next: thus VI/6 matches with VII/11, and VII/11 with VIII/7.

In some cases the corroboration is more circumstantial. Dell offered two alternatives for V/5, September or December 1381, both months when the first day is Sunday. At the start of December the duke was staying in the bishop of London's palace at Fulham[55] for a session of parliament which adjourned on 13 December;[56] he then went to meet Anne of Bohemia when she arrived at Dover towards the end of the month for her marriage to Richard II, and took her to Leeds Castle for Christmas.[57] No such pattern of movement is reflected in the account however. In September the duke was in York investigating with other justices the 'various treasons, insurrections and other evils' of the summer. This more settled pattern of attendances fits the account much better. September therefore seems the more likely month.

In the final group of check-rolls, entries in XV/13 extend over nearly six weeks and Dell suggested two possible alternatives, July and August 1392, or December and January 1393–4. Throughout July and August 1392 the duke was travelling continuously,[58] but this roll shows no such movement. Members of the household arrived throughout the first month until there was almost full attendance by the twentieth; they then remained until at least the third day of the second month. The pattern of movement in XV/13 must be for December and January 1393–1394.

XIII/12, which possibly includes 7–15 October and 7–16 November 1393, and XVI/14, which possibly includes 1–2 December 1393 and 4–8 January 1394,[59] are similar in format to X/9 for London in 1391–2 and may also be for periods when the duke and some of its members were away from the main household.

The last membrane to be dated with certainty is XVII/16, for 1 February to 24 March 1394 and, although without names, and with the location unidentified, there is a clear pattern of activity. The duke is known to have left England for France with his brother Thomas of Woodstock on 10 March to negotiate an extension to the truce of Leulingham.[60] On this roll a large group is found assembling on 10 March, most of whom left again on 17 March. Constance is thought to have died on 24 March,[61] but there is no activity around this date which might be related to the event, and the roll probably therefore records movements somewhere on the way to Calais.

The three membranes of the household journal come chronologically between the first and second groups of attendance rolls and are for 5–19 July, 20 July–1

55 After the destruction of The Savoy the duke stayed in Fulham, at La Neyte, the bishop of London's palace, in November and December 1381. Goodman, *John of Gaunt*, 90; *Register II*, 588, 610–13, 615 and passim.

56 *Register II*, 623–40 and passim, 704; Armitage-Smith, *John of Gaunt*, 256n.

57 Goodman, *John of Gaunt*, 91; *Westminster Chronicle*, 23.

58 DL 23/3/2 mm. 17, 10, 30, 9, 19; Goodman, *John of Gaunt*, 151–2, 171 nn. 38–9.

59 Both are after the marriage of Jane Beaufort in March 1392 as she is referred to as Jane Ferrers.

60 Armitage-Smith, *John of Gaunt*, 349; Goodman, *John of Gaunt*, 154.

61 The duke's will made provision for an obit yearly for the duchess on 24 March: Armitage-Smith, *John of Gaunt*, 435.

August 1383, when the household was at Kenilworth, and 30 August–6 September 1383 when the household moved from Banbury, to Henley, Maidenhead, and Westminster.[62] The numbers of meals and horses provide some idea of figures that would have appeared on the attendance rolls for the same time, but unfortunately records of both kinds do not survive for the same period. The expenses of the traditional household departments, *Paneteria*, *Butelaria*, *Garderoba*, *Coquina*, *Pulleteria*, *Scutillaria*, *Salseria*, *Aula &c*, *Stabulum*, *Vadia &c*, are entered daily. In the margins other expenses are recorded: on the left the cost of bread, wax and wines, numbers for *cena* and *prandium*, and sometimes the number of horses present. On the right-hand there are expenses with a total for *frumentum*, from time to time followed by miscellaneous expenses and payments to servants of the household travelling on errands. The numbers of meals recorded may give some indication of the number present in the household at the time, but it is not possible to know whether any sort of check-roll was kept while the household was on the move and at a different place each day (as opposed to when part of the household was away, but recorded in residence at another location even if only for a few days, such as in London in X/9).

Some false impressions which have survived for centuries can be dispelled by the check-rolls. Constance is sometimes thought to have lived apart from the duke;[63] she is present throughout the time of the accounts. Much is made of the duke's repudiation of his mistress, Katherine Swynford. Despite the events of 1381, during the duke's absence in Spain in 1386–9 she seems to have been in the household of Henry of Derby, or closely associated with it, as she and her daughter Jane were given livery for Christmas 1388.[64] By November 1391 (VI/6) she was once more established in the duke's household, with all four Beaufort children, now young adults in their late and middle teens.[65]

Although the survival of these membranes is random, and together they present the character of an old-fashioned school register, they nonetheless cover a cross-section of the duke's activities. Danger and drama are experienced in the summer of 1381;[66] in January 1394 there were the tensions of parliament[67] – at this gathering the duke accused the earl of Arundel of collusion in the Cheshire rebellion of the previous autumn, while Arundel's counter-attack resulted in his having to seek the duke's

62 In early July 1383 the duke was in Scotland negotiating a truce (Goodman, *John of Gaunt*, 96). He then travelled south again and presumably joined the household at Kenilworth then went on to London, with others meeting him *en route*. There were six horses listed at Kenilworth on 1 August, by 31 August at Banbury there were 58, and the number increased daily until 80 arrived at Westminster on 4 September. (XIX/19 and XX/20. There is no surviving record for 2–29 August.)

63 Armitage-Smith, *John of Gaunt*, 358.

64 DL 28/1/2 mm. 21, 24, Wardrobe Account of Mary of Derby, 1387–8. They were given two *baldekins* of blue and white with miniver for trimming, *pro liberatione suis*, rather than *de dono* as others in the list. John Beaufort received half a *baldekin* of gold and red *de dono domini*. The names of Alice Tynneslowe and Aimie de Melbourne, Constance's *demoiselles* in the 1381 and 1391 check-rolls, also appear in these accounts as Mary's *domicelle*. They receive livery of *panno taune* with squirrel trimming.

65 The Glynde stable lists clarify the order of birth of the Beauforts of whom Jane has always been assumed to be the youngest. The order is consistent: John, Henry, Jane, Thomas; the number of horses reflects this, John has the most and Thomas the least. There can be no reason for Thomas being last in the list other than he is youngest.

66 I/1–V/5.

67 XV/13, XVI/14.

pardon in public.[68] In 1392 we observe members of the household on a diplomatic mission to France;[69] and in 1391–2[70] and 1393–4[71] we eavesdrop on the celebrations of Christmas and New Year, when the duke, surrounded by his family,[72] must have distributed gifts at least as lavish as those described in the *Register* of 1379–83.[73] Throughout these events the work of the household continued, each member going about his or her business, their individual comings and goings recorded in the check-rolls. Much valuable research has been done by Simon Walker on those members of the duke's affinity of the rank of knight and esquire.[74] Further work, which took as its focus combining the information in these check-rolls with the range of biographical information available in Duchy of Lancaster records and elsewhere, would give a much fuller picture of a major household and its members as a community involved in the most important events of the late fourteenth century.

68 Goodman, *John of Gaunt*, 153–4.
69 XI/10.
70 VII/11, VIII/7.
71 XV/13.
72 Several of those present in 1393–4 were to be among the *dramatis personae* of the events five years later following the duke's death.
73 *Register II*, 327, 556, 715.
74 Walker, *The Lancastrian Affinity*.

TABLE. Numbers of Household Members and Horses in the Check-rolls GLY 3469 (1–17)

Daily allowance	I/1: 1–31 Jan. 1381 Leicester	II/4: 1–21+ Apr. 1381 Leicester	III/3: 4–30 Jun. 1381 Knaresborough	IV/2: 1–31 Jul. 1381 Pontefract	V/5: 1–31 Sep. 1381 Pontefract?	VI/6: 1–29+ Nov. 1391 Hertford	VII/11: 1–31 Dec. 1391 Hertford	VIII/7: 1–31 Jan. 1392 Hertford	IX/8: 1–23 Feb. 1392 Hertford	X/9: 1–4 Dec. 1391, 15–16, 23–30 Jan., 11–15 Feb. 1392 London	XI/10: 23 Feb. – 30 Mar. 1392 en route for Amiens	XII/17: 13–30 Sep. 1392 Leicester	XIII/12: possibly includes 7–15 Oct. and 7–16 Nov. 1393	XIV/15: 1–30 Nov. 1393 Hertford	XV/13: 1–31 Dec. 1393, 1–8 Jan. 1394 Hertford	XVI/14: possibly includes 1–2 Dec. 1393 and 4–8 Jan. 1394	XVII/16: 1–28 Feb., 1–24 Mar. 1394
Household list												Names cut away		Names cut away			Names cut away
Knights *ad xij d*	18	18	2+	18	18	16	16	14+	15	16	15	—	20	—	(20)	(13) 7	—
Confessor *ad x d ob*	1	1	1	1	1	1	1	1	1	1	1	—	1	—	(1)	1	—
Esquires *ad vij d ob*	22	24	1+	24	23	35	36	35	36	36	35	—	39	—	37+	38	—
Valets *ad iiij d ob*	9	9	0+	9	9	—	—	—	—	—	—	—	—	—	—	—	—
Valets *ad iiij d*	28	28	3+	29	29	37	37	37	36	36	38	—	38	—	42	39	—
Valets *ad iij d*	2	1	0+	2	2	—	—	—	—	—	—	—	—	—	—	1	—
Grooms, *demoiselles* &c *ad ij d*	22	20	15+	19	32	48	48	48	48	42	37	—	39	—	38+	30	—
Clerks *ad j d ob*	4	4	1+	3	3	2	3	2	2	2	1	—	0+	—	2	1	—
Pages *ad j d*	8	12+	7+	1+	15	17	17	18	18	12	12	—	12+	—	16	8	—
Sub-total	114	117+	30+	106+	132	156	158	155	156	145	139	—	149+	—	156+*	138*	—
H/h members named in Stable list only	44	51	14+	51	33	23	25	28	24	24	—	—	25	—	19	4	—
Total Household	158	168+	44+	157+	165	179	183	183	180	169	139	—	174+	—	175+*	142*	—
Stable list																	
Total Horses	132	138	34+	128	121	184	187	213	214	201	*none*	—	199	—	202	151	—

Figures give no indication whether those named are present or not. Where entries are cut away, if it is possible to conjecture a figure from similar entries at a near date, this is given in brackets and totals including such figures are marked *; where part of an entry for a group has been cut away figures which remain are given with a plus sign to indicate the number is incomplete.

APPENDIX. John of Gaunt's Household Attendance Rolls: GLY 3469
Proposed re-ordering of some dates suggested by Dell

Dates which seem secure are in bold. The new order is in capital roman numerals, with the number given by Dell following. Roll numbers are the original order in which the membranes were used as backing for the two rolls of the Waleys Cartulary.[1]

I/1 *Dated by Dell:* **Tuesday 1 – Thursday 31 January 1381**. *Roll B.10.*
W 12 x L 30 in (30.5 x 76 cm).[2]
Recto: sub-heading *J[ovis] iij* to *Mer[curii] xxx* (cut away before *iij* and after *xxx*) and from *p[rim]o* to *u[ltimo]* (31st); entries for 31 days.
Verso: sub-heading for days of week and month, *Mart[is] p[rim]o* to *Jov[is] ult[imo]*; entries for 31 days.
The duke was at Leicester from the end of December 1380 to the end of January 1381.[3]

II/4 *Dated by Dell: Monday 1 – 31 [July 1381]. Roll A.7.*
W 11½ x L 29 in (29 x 73.5 cm).
Recto: headings cut away; entries for 30 days.
Verso: sub-heading *Lune* to *Martis*, with *Mercurii* crossed through, no dates; entries for 30 days.
Two months in 1381 began on Monday: April (a 30-day month) and July (31 days). Although II/4 has a sub-heading for 31 days, the last day, *Mercurii*, is crossed through and the entries beneath are for a 30-day month, i.e. April. The membranes numbered 2 and 4 by Dell should be transposed.
Suggested date **Monday 1 – Tuesday 31 April 1381**. *Register II* entries show the duke was at The Savoy at the beginning and end of April, visiting Leicester in the middle of the month.[4]

III/3 *Dated by Dell*: **Tuesday 4 June – Sunday 30 June 1381**. *Roll A.5.*
W 19 x L 12 in (48.25 x 30.5 cm).
Recto: sub-heading *Martis quarto* to *Dominica ultimo* (30th); entries for 27 days.
Verso: headings cut away; entries for 27 days.
The duke was in Scotland.[5] This roll may be for Knaresborough.[6]

1 Glynde Archive MS 1139. Dell, *Glynde Place Archives*, 97.

2 Measurements are very approximate. Due to the irregularity of the cutting, the measurements of top and bottom of the same membrane can differ as can those of each side.

3 Entries in *Register II* are dated from 2 January (970) to 21 January (503, 979) 1381. On 29 January a letter is dated at The Savoy (1165).

4 *Register II*, 497–8, 977 for Leicester, Goodman, *John of Gaunt*, 78, and *Register II*, 519, for The Savoy.

5 *Register II*, 22 June, Melrose Abbey (1186) – 10 July, Edinburgh (564); and Goodman, *John of Gaunt*, 80–3.

6 When the duke returned to Edinburgh after the earl of Northumberland's refusal to admit him to

IV/2 *Dated by Dell: Monday 1 – 21 [April 1381]. 4 [Ric.II, 1381]. Roll A.7.*
W 11 x L 30 in (28 x 76 cm).
Recto: partial heading *Julij anno quarto* above, sub-heading *Lune primo* to *Dominica xxj*, then cut away; entries for 21+ days.
Verso: headings cut away; entries for 21+ days.
IV/2 is the only membrane with part of a main heading to survive: *Julij anno quarto* (not mentioned by Dell). See II/4 above.
Suggested date **Monday 1 – Sunday 21 July 1381** (see II/4, above). The duke had ordered the household to assemble at Pontefract.[7]

V/5 *Dated by Dell: Sunday 1 – [? September or December 1381]. Roll B.5.*
W 12 x L 33 in (84 x 30.5 cm).
Recto: sub-heading from *Dominica primo* to *Lune viij*, then cut away; entries for 30 days.
Verso: sub-heading from *Dominica primo* to *Lune viij*, then cut away; entries for 29 days.
There is a more settled pattern of attendances on this roll which better fits September, when the duke was in York,[8] rather than December, when the duke travelled from Fulham, to Dover, then to Leeds Castle.[9] Indirect support for September is that the falconers are absent: they spent from late April to October away from court with mewing (moulting) falcons.[10]
Suggested date **Sunday 1 – Tuesday 31 September 1381**.

*

VI/6 *Dated by Dell: Wednesday 1 – 29 or after, March or November 1391. Roll B.6.*
W 12 x L 27 in (30.5 x 68.5 cm).
Recto: headings cut away; entries for 28+ days.
Verso: sub-heading from *Mercurii primo* to *Dominica xvj*, then illegible, then cut away; entries for 28+ days.
The last two or three days of VI/6 are cut away or illegible, but a comparison name by name of household members and horses in the last days of VI/6 with the first days of VII/11, gives a convincing a match of all names appearing on both rolls. The duke attended parliament at Westminster from 3 November to 2 December[11] and this roll shows that the duke's knights, all but half a dozen esquires, and about half the valets (but not the duchess, her servants, or any clerks) left on Thursday 2 November and were absent for the rest of the month. On VII/11 there are corresponding arrivals on 5 December.

Alnwick, he believed Constance to be still at Knaresborough: Goodman, *John of Gaunt*, 83.

7 *Register II*, 541.

8 Goodman, *John of Gaunt*, 89.

9 Goodman, *John of Gaunt*, 91, *Westminster Chronicle*, 23.

10 DL 28/3/5 m. 10. Information about special payments to falconers taking mewing falconers away from court appears in the Receiver General's account for 1396/7 but this would have happened at the same time in any year. Where rolls survive for the months between October and March, falconers are present.

11 Goodman, *John of Gaunt*, 149.

Suggested date **Wednesday 1 – Wednesday 29+ November 1391.** This is roll seems likely to be for Hertford.[12]

VII/11 *Dated by Dell: [Days cut away at top, before March 1392.] Roll A.1.*
W 11.5 x L 26 in (29 x 66 cm).
Recto: sub-heading with some dates: *primo*, *secundo*, cut away, *x* to *xx*, cut away; entries for 31 days.
Verso: headings cut away; entries for 30+ days.
This is a 31-day month and there is an entry against William Hagh, a clerk with the rank of esquire, '*allocatus pro vadiis suis a primo Decembris usque xvj dies eisdem mens utroque die computato per xvj dies*'; he is then listed as present from the seventeenth. See also X/9a where entries for those present on 1–4 December match those absent on the same dates on this membrane.
Suggested date: **Friday 1 – Sunday 31 December 1391**. The duke was at Hertford for Christmas and New Year.[13]

VIII/7 *Dated by Dell: Monday 1 – 31 [August 1390, May 1391 or January 1392]. Roll A.9.*
W 11½ x L 28 in (29 x 71 cm).
Recto: headings cut away then sub-heading from *Martis ix* to *Mercurii, ultimo* (31st), initials of the days cut through but some identifiable, and days of the month from *iv* to *ultimo* (31st), sub-heading cut away before *iv*; entries for 30+ days.
Verso: sub-heading *Lune primo* to *Martis*, only *primo* of dates visible; some initials of days indistinct; entries for 29+ days.
There is an entry against John Brytwell, a valet, '*allocatus pro vadiis suis a primo [die Octrobris] ad xviij [die] Januarii utroque die computato per xc dies per diem ij d xvij s iiij d*' and he is then listed as present from the 19th. Entries for those absent on 15–16 and 23–30 January match those present on X/9b and X/9c.
Suggested date: **Monday 1 – Wednesday 31 January 1392**. The household spent the New Year at Hertford.[14]

IX/8 *Dated by Dell:* **Thursday 1 – Friday 23 February 1392**. *Roll B.4.*
W 12 x L 34½ in (30.5 x 87.5 cm).
Recto: sub-heading from *Jovis primo* to *Veneris xxiij*; entries for 23 days.
Verso: sub-heading from *Jovis primo* to *Veneris xxiij*; entries for 23 days.
Entries for absences for 11–15 February match those present on these dates in X/9d.
The household was presumably still at Hertford.

[12] An indenture was dated at Hertford on 2 November, N. B. Lewis (ed.), *Indentures of Retinue with John of Gaunt, Duke of Lancaster, enrolled in Chancery, 1367–1399* (Camden Society, 4th Series, 22, 1964), no. 24.

[13] Goodman, *John of Gaunt*, 149.

[14] Ibid.

X/9 *Dated by Dell: Friday 1 – 4 December, Monday 15 – 22 January, Sunday 11 – 15 February [1391/2]. Roll B.9.*
W 11½ x L 30 in (29 x 76 cm).
Recto: headings and names of two knights cut away, four (not three as given by Dell) columns with entries for 4, 2, 8 and 5 days.
Verso: four columns, X/9a sub-heading *December*, *Veneris primo* to *Lune iiij*; entries for 4 days; those present match absences on VII/11; X/9b sub-heading *Januari*, *Lune xv* to *Martis xvj*; entries for 2 days; those present match absences on VIII/7; X/9c sub-heading *Martis xxiij* to *Martis xxx*,[15] entries for 8 days; those present match absences on VIII/7; X/9d sub-heading *Februari*, *Dominica xj* to *Jovis xv*; entries for 5 days; those present match absences on IX/8.
Dates are therefore: X/9a **Friday 1 – Monday 4 December 1391**; X/9b **Monday 15 – Tuesday 16 January 1392**; X/9c **Tuesday 23 – Tuesday 30 January 1392**; X/9d **Sunday 11 – Thursday 15 February 1392**.
X/9 appears to be an attendance roll for the household while in London. The duke was at Westminster for the Parliament which closed on 2 December 1391,[16] and a reference in the Receiver General's account for 1392–3 cites a warrant dated 22 January 1392 at London.[17] There were meetings of the king's great council at London from 12–16 February, which the duke attended.[18]

XI/10 *Dated by Dell:* **Friday 23 [February] – Saturday 30 [March 1392]**. *Roll B.1.*
W 12 x L 29 in (30.5 x 73.75 cm).
Recto: sub-heading *Veneris xxiij* to *Jovis xxix*, *Veneris primo* to *Jovis xxviij*, then cut away; entries for 34+ days.
Verso: sub-heading *Veneris xxiij* to *Jovis xxix*, *Veneris primo* to *Mercurii xxvij*, then cut away; entries for 33+ days.
This roll, for part of February and the first 28 days of March 1392, appears to be for a party of nearly 120 members of the household forming a retinue to accompany the duke via Dover and Calais to meet Charles VI at Amiens.[19] There are no horses. On 7 March, the date on or close to which the duke crossed to Calais,[20] about 30 of the party, mostly household officials and servants of the duchess, left. It seems that this is a check-roll for the retinue accompanying the duke to France, with Constance and her servants going as far as Dover.
See also X/9d above. Entries in the Receiver General's account for 1392–3 place the duke at Hertford at the beginning of February then in London to the end of the month.[21]

15 There is a lacuna in the membrane, and some of the letters in the heading of the third column are indistinct but match dates on VIII/7.
16 Goodman, *John of Gaunt*, 149.
17 DL 28/3/2 m. 14r.
18 Goodman, *John of Gaunt*, 149.
19 Goodman, *John of Gaunt*, 150–1.
20 DL 28/3/2 m. 16 cites a warrant dated at Calais on 7 March.
21 DL 28/3/2 m. 16.

XII/17 *Dated by Dell: Friday 13 – Monday 30 [November 1394]. Roll A.3. September 1392 or April 1393 are possible alternatives.* Names cut away.

W 11½ x L 31 in (29 x 78.75 cm).

Recto: sub-heading *Veneris xiij* to *Lune ultimo* (30th) with names and daily entries up to Thursday 12th cut away; then entries for 18 days.

Verso: sub-heading *Martis xvij* to *Lune ultimo* (30th) with names and daily entries up to Monday 17 cut away; then entries for 15 days. The verso is identified from the recto by entries for the stables.

Although names are cut away, there are two incomplete entries in the daily record: … *ultimo die Septembris utroque die computato per cv dies iiij d xxxv s*, and … *[ultimo] die Septembris utroque die computato per cv dies per diem ijd xvij s vj d.* which when compared with similar entries indicates this is for September.

Suggested date: **Friday 13 – Monday 30 September, 1392**. There are no Register entries for this month, but the Receiver General's account for 1392–3 cites a warrant dated 28 September 1392 at Leicester.[22]

*

XIII/12 *Dated by Dell: [Days mutilated, between March 1392 and March 1393.] Roll A.2.*

W 11½ x L 30 in (29 x 76 cm).

Recto: five columns, XIII/12a sub-heading: *primo*; entries for 1 day; XIII/12b sub-heading: *vij* to *xv*, perhaps with a tail of the initials of *Jovis* over *ix* and *Martis* over *xiiij*; entries for 9 days. Possibly May 1392, January, or October 1393; XIII/12c sub-heading cut away; entries for 6 days; XIII/12d sub-heading cut away; entries for 4 days; XIII/12e sub-heading: *Veneris vij* to *Dominica xvj*; entries for 9+ days. Possibly June 1392, February, March or November 1393.

Verso: five columns, headings cut away.

The date is after March 1392, when Jane Beaufort married and became Jane Ferrers,[23] and before November 1393, when John Deincourt died.[24] XIII/12d fits with XIV/15, November 1393.

XIII/12 and XVI/14[25] are similar in format to X/9 for London in 1391–2. On both only one of the four or five columns have surviving sub-headings for day and date. XIII/12d has a sub-heading *Veneris vij* to *Dominica xvj*, which matches absences on 7–16 November 1393 in XIV/15, and although no names remain, the pattern of attendance is plain (in which case XIII/12b, with a sub-heading *Jovis vij* to *Veneris xv*, could be for 7–15 October 1393). XIII/12d has a sub-heading *Veneris vij* to *Dominica xvj* (then cut away).

Possible dates: columns XIII/12a and XIII/12c not yet identified; column XIII/12d fits with absences on XIV/15 for November 1393; therefore

22 DL 28/3/2 m 10.

23 MS GLY 1139; Dell, *Glynde Place Archives*, 261.

24 *CIPM, XVII, 15–23 Richard II* (London 1904–), 142–4.

25 Both are after the marriage of Jane Beaufort in March 1392 as she is referred to as Jane Ferrers.

XIII/12b could be for **7 – 15 October 1393**, as XIII/12d is for **7 – 16 November 1393**.

XIV/15 *Dated by Dell:* **Saturday 1 – Sunday 30 November 1393**. *Roll B.7.*
Names cut away.
W 11½ x L 32 in (29 x 81.25 cm).
Recto: sub-heading cut away or indistinct then legible from *xxvj* to *ultimo* (30th); entries for 30 days.
Verso: sub-heading *Novembris Sabbati primo* to *Dominica ultimo*; entries for 30 days.
Names are cut away but daily entries for a 30-day month remain and the pattern of presence and absence on this roll closely fits entries for XIII/12c: sub-heading *Veneris vij* to *Dominica xvj*; entries for 9+ days. At the bottom of the dorse, cut away at the left an inscription remains: ... *myn/ ... rr/ ... j c/* with *Willi' Eyr' Thes' &c* to the right.

XV/13 *Dated by Dell: Monday 1 – 31, Thursday 1 – 8 [July–August 1392, or December–January 1393/4]. Roll A.4.*
W 11½ x L 27 in (29 x 68.5 cm).
Recto: headings and names of all knights, the confessor, and possibly three esquires are cut away; entries for 31 and 8+ days.
Verso: sub-headings *Lune primo* to *Mercurii ultimo*, and *Jovis primo* to *Jovis viij* and names and entries for 31 and 8+ days are complete.
Throughout July and August 1392 the duke dated warrants at Leicester, London, Tutbury, London and Leicester again, and then Pontefract in early August,[26] but there is no comparable activity on this roll. People arrived throughout the first month, everyone was in residence at the latest by the twenty-fourth, and no one left before the third day of the second month; the pattern of movement in XV/13 must be for December and January 1393–1394.
Suggested dates: **Monday 1 – Wednesday 31 December 1393, Thursday 1 – Thursday 8 January 1394**. The duke and Henry of Derby spent Christmas 1393 at Hertford.[27]

XVI/14 *Dated by Dell: [Days cut away, after March 1392.] Roll A.6.*
W 11¼ x L 27 in (28.5 x 68.5 cm).
Recto: headings cut away, four columns, XVI/14a entries for 2 days; XVI/14b entries for 5 days; XVI/14c entries for 5 days; XVI/14d entries for 13+ days.
Verso: four columns: XVI/14a headings cut away; entries for 2 days; XVI/14b headings cut away; entries for 5 days; XVI/14c headings cut away; entries for 5 days; XVI/14d sub-heading *Dominica j* to *Veneris xiij*; entries for 13+ days.
XVI/14a is a loose match for 1 and 2 December 1393 in XV/13.[28] XVI/14b has no headings but entries match those on XV/13 for *Dominica*

26 DL 23/3/2 mm. 17, 10, 30, 9, 19; Goodman, *John of Gaunt*, 151–2, 171 nn. 38–9.
27 Goodman, *John of Gaunt*, 153.
28 XVI/14a has more negative matches than positive, i.e. people are away on both rolls.

iv to *Jovis viij*, 4–8 January 1394.[29] XVI/14d sub-heading *Dominica j* to *Dominica xv* (then cut away). Possible dates for XVI/14d are September or December 1392, or June 1393. But the Master of the Leopard is listed as a visitor and this roll is therefore likely to be after Henry of Derby's return from the Holy Land in July 1393.[30] After 1 June 1393 Sunday next falls on the first of February, March, and November 1394. The duke left for France in mid-March 1394, returned to England in mid-June,[31] then went to Gascony at the end of September to deal with discontent there, and remained away from England, possibly until December 1395.[32] February or March 1394 therefore seem the most likely date for this membrane but it is not possible to attempt a match as no names survive on XVII/16. See also XIII/12, above.

XVII/16 *Dated by Dell:* **Sunday 1 – Saturday 28 February, Sunday 1 – Tuesday 24 March 1394**. *Roll B.8.* Names cut away.
W 11½ x L 30 in (29x 76 cm).
Recto: headings cut away; entries for 26 and 23+ days.
Verso: sub-headings from *Mercurii iiij* to *Sabbati ultimo* (28th), and *Dominica primo* to *Martis xxiiij*; entries for 26 and 27+ days.
The duke left England for France soon after 10 March.[33] A large group assembles on 10 March, most of whom leave on 17 March. The duchess Constance is thought to have died on 24 March[34] but there is no activity around this date which might be related to this event.

*

Journal of the household

XVIII/18 Sunday 5 – 19 July [1383]. Roll B.3. 30 x 11½ in (76 x 29 cm). At Kenilworth.

XIX/19 Monday 20 July – 1 August [1383]. Roll A.10. 28 x 11 in (71 x 28 cm). At Kenilworth.

XX/20 Sunday 30 August – 6 September [1383]. Roll B.2. 29 x 11¼ in (73.75 x 28.5 cm). The household moves from Banbury, to Henley, Maidenhead, and Westminster.

29 Although there are no headings, of 192 people (and horses) named in both lists, all those absent on XVI/14b match those present on XV/13 from *Dominica iv* to *Jovis viij*, 4 – 8 January 1394.

30 The leopard was possibly a gift to Henry of Derby from the King of Cyprus, and expenses for the leopard and its keeper feature regularly in the accounts for Henry's travels in 1392–3 (Toulmin Smith, *Expeditions to Prussia*, lxv, 256). Horses of the 'Meistre del Leopard' appear in check-rolls XIII/12, XV/13 and XVI/14.

31 Armitage-Smith, *John of Gaunt*, 349.

32 Armitage-Smith, *John of Gaunt*, 386, says 'for a few months his movements cannot be traced'.

33 Armitage-Smith, *John of Gaunt*, 349.

34 In the duke's will there is provision for a yearly obit for the duchess Constance on 24 March, see n. 61, above.

'WITH MY LIFE, HIS JOYES BEGAN AND ENDED':[1] PIERS GAVESTON AND KING EDWARD II OF ENGLAND REVISITED

Jochen Burgtorf

The relationship between the Gascon noble Piers Gaveston (*c.* 1282–1312) and King Edward II of England (1284–1327) has long been the subject of debate.[2] Fourteenth- and fifteenth-century gossip, the works of Renaissance writers, particularly Christopher Marlowe's *Edward the Second* (1592) and Derek Jarman's silver-screen adaptation of the same (1992), Hollywood's distortion of English medieval history in the form of Mel Gibson's *Braveheart* (1995), and a number of recent works of popular fiction have shaped the public perception of this relationship.[3]

The story of Edward and Gaveston is quickly told. When Edward was prince of Wales, Gaveston joined his household, and the two became friends. Shortly before the death of King Edward I in 1307, Gaveston was banished from England. When young Edward became king, he recalled Gaveston from exile, appointed him earl of Cornwall, and gave him his niece, Margaret de Clare, in marriage. Early in 1308, while Edward II celebrated his wedding to Isabella of France on the continent, Gaveston briefly served as *custos regni* (keeper of the realm).[4] Later that same year, baronial opposition pressured the king to send Gaveston into exile for a second time, and Edward appointed Gaveston his lieutenant in Ireland. This second exile was accompanied by a sentence of excommunication levelled against the earl by the prelates of England but later revoked by Pope Clement V. Gaveston returned to

1 M. Drayton [1563–1631], 'Piers Gaueston Earle of Cornwall', in *The Works of Michael Drayton*, i, ed. J. W. Hebel (Oxford, 1931), 157–203, here 164.

2 J. S. Hamilton, *Piers Gaveston, Earl of Cornwall, 1307–1312: Politics and Patronage in the Reign of Edward II* (Detroit, 1988) remains the best comprehensive treatment to date, since P. Chaplais' work, *Piers Gaveston: Edward II's Adoptive Brother* (Oxford, 1994), is an analysis of the relationship between Edward and Gaveston, but not a full biography of either individual. The historiography from the fourteenth century to the present is discussed at length in J. T. Prock, 'The Historiography of Edward II and Piers Gaveston' (M.A. thesis, Arizona State University, 1995). For Edward, see now R. M. Haines' authoritative study, *King Edward II (Edward of Caernarfon: His Life, his Reign, and its Aftermath), 1284–1330* (Montreal, 2003).

3 J. Parks, 'History, Tragedy, and Truth in Christopher Marlowe's *Edward II*', *Studies in English Literature, 1500–1900*, 39 (1999), 275–90; T. Prasch, 'Edward II' [review of Derek Jarman's film], *American Historical Review*, 98 (1993), 1164–6; J. Aberth, *A Knight at the Movies: Medieval History on Film* (New York, 2003), 303–5 (on *Braveheart*). Some recent novels reduce the relationship to 'gay pornography'; cf. J. C. Penford, *The Gascon* (New York, 1984), and C. Hunt, *Gaveston* (London, 1992). For a transfer of the plot into the world of twentieth-century media, see S. Merritt, *Gaveston* (London, 2002). For a useful discussion of the portrayal of medieval England in modern popular fiction, see S. Alexander, 'Through a Glass Darkly: Medieval England as it is Perceived in Fictional Mirrors' (M.A. thesis, Wichita State University, 1997).

4 For Isabella, see now P. C. Doherty, *Isabella and the Strange Death of Edward II* (New York, 2003), and A. Weir, *Queen Isabella: Treachery, Adultery, and Murder in Medieval England* (New York, 2005).

England in 1309, but was banished again in 1311 as a result of the Ordinances which the barons had forced upon the king. After a few months, the king recalled Gaveston once more, and from then on the Gascon was a fugitive within the kingdom. In 1312, the year in which a son was born to Edward's wife and in which Gaveston's wife gave birth to a daughter, the barons were able to seize Gaveston and had him executed. Edward was inconsolable and mourned the loss of his friend. The quantity and the quality of the attention that Edward bestowed on Gaveston have led to considerable speculation regarding the relationship between the two men.

This essay will not join the debate on whether or not, or to what extent, medieval men or women were aware of their sexual preferences. Rather, it intends to ask: What were the themes of the relationship between Edward and Gaveston? And why did the barons oppose this relationship? While Edward and Gaveston did cross the line – on various levels – with regard to what their contemporaries deemed acceptable, the author of this essay doubts that sexuality was one of these levels.[5] Also, reservations are in order with regard to a fairly recent re-interpretation of the two men's relationship, namely the idea that Gaveston was Edward's adoptive brother.[6]

The sources for this investigation are the familiar ones. Apart from the charter evidence which sheds some light on the two men's relationship, it is fourteenth-century historical writing which offers the most insights.[7] Particularly important are the contemporary texts: the *Vita Edwardi Secundi*,[8] the *Annales Paulini*,[9] and Robert of Reading's continuation (1307–25) of the *Flores Historiarum*.[10] Where appropriate, a few later texts – such as Ralph Higden's *Polychronicon*[11] and Thomas Burton's share of the chronicle of Meaux[12] – will be brought into the discussion as well. However, before the main issues are discussed, it is necessary to review existing writing on this matter, skipping over the various literary, propagandistic, and antiquarian works written between the sixteenth and the nineteenth century.[13]

5 For some of the scholarship regarding this interpretation, see C. Sponsler, 'The King's Boyfriend: Froissart's Political Theater of 1326', in G. Burger and S. F. Kruger (eds.), *Queering the Middle Ages* (Minneapolis, 2001), 143–67; P. Hammond, *Figuring Sex between Men from Shakespeare to Rochester* (Oxford, 2002), 117–28.

6 For this interpretation, see Chaplais, *Piers Gaveston*.

7 For the historiography of this time period, see A. Gransden, *Historical Writing in England, II: c.1307 to the Early Sixteenth Century* (London, 1982), 1–57.

8 This essay will utilize the widely available 1957 edition/translation: N. Denholm-Young (ed.), *Vita Edwardi Secundi monachi cuiusdam Malmesberiensis* (London, 1957); I will, however, refer to the new edition/translation in a few instances as well: Wendy R. Childs (ed.), *Vita Edwardi Secundi* (Oxford, 2005).

9 W. Stubbs (ed.), *Annales Paulini* (Rolls Series, 76, 1882), i, 253–370.

10 H. R. Luard (ed.), *Flores Historiarum* (Rolls Series, 95, 1890), iii, 137–348.

11 C. Babington and J. R. Lumby (eds.), *Polychronicon Ranulphi Higden monachi Cestrensis* (Rolls Series, 41, 1865–86).

12 E. A. Bond (ed.), *Chronica monasterii de Melsa, a fundatione usque ad annum 1396, auctore Thoma de Burton, abbate, accedit continuatio ad annum 1406, a monacho quodam ipsius domus* (Rolls Series, 43, 1867).

13 I have already cited or mentioned respectively the works of M. Drayton (1563–1631), see above note 1, and C. Marlowe (1564–93), see above note 3. Other works are, to name but a few, J. Boucher, *Histoire tragique et memorable de Pierre de Gaverston, gentilhomme Gascon, jadis mignon d'Edoüard II, roy d'Angleterre, tirée des Chroniques de Thomas Valsingham, et tournée de Latin en François* (Paris, 1588), which could have significantly influenced Drayton and Marlowe who both published their works within five years of this compilation; F. Hubert, *The historie of Edward the Second, surnamed Carnarvan, one of our English kings, together with the fatall down-fall of his two vnfortu-*

In 1898 M. Dimitresco published the first modern biography of Piers Gaveston.[14] The strength of Dimitresco's work is its extensive use of charters with chronicle evidence playing only a secondary role. Dimitresco states that 'l'influence occulte de cet étranger' (this foreigner's secret influence), namely Gaveston's sway over Edward, explains the chroniclers' attitude, but claims that the documents set the record straight – figuratively speaking.[15] Dimitresco's work leaves the reader with the impression that Gaveston was, above all, a capable administrator, and it refrains from any further comments on the nature of the relationship between the two men. However, if Gaveston's influence had indeed been a secret one his life probably would have lasted beyond 1312.

While Dimitresco's book can be considered a product of academic historical writing – the author had connections to the Parisian École pratique des Hautes Études –, Gaveston's next biographer, W. P. Dodge, who published his work only one year after Dimitresco, was a barrister-at-law and an amateur historian.[16] He was also somewhat more direct. With regard to the events following the death of King Edward I, namely the installation of Gaveston as earl of Cornwall, he comments that to 'the careless minds of both [i.e. Edward and Gaveston], England was not a kingdom to be governed, but merely a place where their intimacy could run its course unchecked', and later concludes that Edward's 'sturdy regard for Gaveston is the one saving feature of his erratic and affectionate nature'.[17]

Probably because of Victorian propriety, Dodge declined to elaborate further on 'intimacy' and 'sturdy regard'. In the following years, historians seemed content to state that Edward's and Gaveston's contemporaries believed that the relationship was a homosexual one. In an article for the 1910 issue of the well established *American Journal of Insanity*, C. Robinson concluded that 'the proof of the fact is doubtful, yet ... it was a matter of common report in Europe'.[18] One of the early twentieth century's most eminent English constitutional historians, T. F. Tout, then discarded the idea that the relationship could have been a homosexual one: 'Of the graver charges, which have taken classic shape in Marlowe's powerful but unhistorical tragedy, there is no more evidence than the gossip of several prejudiced chroniclers.'[19] In 1918 J. C. Davies weighed in on the issue and declared that, despite 'the king's liberal grants to Gaveston and the undue attentions which he paid him, the worst word that

nate favorites Gaveston and Spencer (London, 1629); N. N., *Histoire remarquable de la vie et mort d'un favory – Pierre de Gabaston – du roy d'Angleterre* (Paris, 1649); E. Cary, *The History of the most unfortunate prince King Edward II with choice political observations on him and his unhappy favorites, Gaveston and Spencer* (London, 1680); J. Adamson, *The reigns of King Edward II and so far of King Edward III as relates to the lives and actions of Piers Gaveston, Hugh de Spencer, and Roger, Lord Mortimer* (London, 1732); N. N., *The Life and Death of Pierce Gaveston, Earl of Cornwal, Grand Favorite and Prime Minister to that Unfortunate Prince, Edward II, King of England* (London, 1740); E. E. C., *Piers Gaveston* (2 vols., London, 1838).

14 M. Dimitresco, *Pierre de Gavaston, comte de Cornouailles, sa biographie et son rôle pendant le commencement du règne d'Édouard II, 1307–1314* (Paris, 1898).

15 Ibid., 1.

16 W. P. Dodge, *Piers Gaveston: A Chapter of Early Constitutional History* (London, 1899).

17 Ibid., 50 and 193.

18 C. Robinson, 'Was King Edward the Second a Degenerate? A Consideration of His Reign from that Point of View', *American Journal of Insanity*, 66 (1910), 445–64, here 454.

19 T. F. Tout, *The Place of the Reign of Edward II in English History* (Manchester, 1914), 13; see also T. F. Tout, *The History of England: From the Accession of Henry III to the Death of Edward III, 1216–1377* (London, 1905), 240.

can be applied to the king's attitude is "ill-advised"'.[20] By 1939, when A. A. Taylor completed an M.A. thesis on Gaveston at the University of London, the prevalent interest in legal history dominated the analysis,[21] and H. Johnstone's 1947 study of Edward's life prior to his accession to the throne largely echoed Tout's gossip *dictum*.[22]

In the next four decades, scholars presented a number of studies on Edward and Gaveston respectively, but it was not until the 1970s and 1980s that the debate regarding their relationship returned in full force, and the pendulum began to swing towards the interpretation of the relationship as a homosexual one.[23] In 1970, J. R. Maddicott published his biography of Thomas, earl of Lancaster (Edward's cousin and one of the king's most prominent opponents), in which he asserts that there was a 'homosexual relationship between Edward and Gaveston' and that 'despite all that has been said in Gaveston's defence the chronicle evidence makes it very difficult to doubt that such a relationship did exist'.[24] This statement is not followed by a reference citing the so-called 'chronicle evidence'. Later in the same paragraph, Maddicott does offer some corroboration by mentioning that Edward sent his wedding presents to Gaveston and that the king spent much time on Gaveston's couch at his coronation banquet.[25] Both incidents are related in the *Annales Paulini*[26] and will be returned to later. By 1989, when Maddicott's article on Gaveston appeared in the *Lexikon des Mittelalters*, the 'very difficult to doubt ... homosexual relationship' of 1970 had become a 'close, undoubtedly homosexually marked friendship'.[27]

In his 1972 biography of Aymer de Valence, earl of Pembroke, J. R. S. Phillips discussed Edward's favourites and referred to 'the homosexual attachment which some of them at least had with the king'.[28] Gaveston is not mentioned in this context,

20 J. C. Davies, *The Baronial Opposition to Edward II: Its Character and Policy. A Study in Administrative History* (Cambridge, 1918), 86.

21 A. A. Taylor, 'The Career of Peter of Gavaston and his Place in History' (M.A. thesis, University of London, 1939). For an assessment of this unpublished thesis, see Hamilton, *Piers Gaveston*, 16.

22 H. Johnstone, *Edward of Carnarvon, 1284–1307* (Manchester, 1946).

23 H. F. Hutchison, *Edward II: The Pliant King* (New York, 1971), seems to be convinced that the relationship was a homosexual one; see also H. F. Hutchison, 'Edward II and his Minions', *History Today*, 21 (1971), 542–9. C. Bingham, *The Life and Times of Edward II* (London, 1973), 54, states that 'of the precise nature of his [i.e. Edward's] relations with Gaveston there is no evidence at all'. M. Keen, *England in the Later Middle Ages* (London, 1973), 52, uses the phrase 'probably homosexual'. N. Fryde, *The Tyranny and Fall of Edward II, 1321–1326* (Cambridge, 1979), 14, argues that Edward's problem (in the eyes of his contemporaries) was his 'infatuation with individuals' and does not suggest anything specific about the king's relationship to Gaveston. M. Prestwich, *The Three Edwards: War and State in England, 1272–1377* (New York, 1980), 80, states that 'it is hard to doubt a sexual element in his [i.e. Edward's] friendship with Gaveston'; in the second edition of this work (London, 2003), 72, Prestwich acknowledges P. Chaplais' suggestion (1994), which will be addressed below, that there could have been an adoptive brotherhood between Edward and Gaveston, but then continues that such an adoptive brotherhood 'does not exclude the possibility that their [i.e. Edward's and Gaveston's] relationship was a homosexual one'. E. Hallam and H. Trevor-Roper (eds.), *Chronicles of the Age of Chivalry* (London, 1987), 177, describe the relationship as 'undoubtedly homosexual'.

24 J. R. Maddicott, *Thomas of Lancaster, 1307–1322: A Study in the Reign of Edward II* (London, 1970), 83.

25 Ibid., 83.

26 *Annales Paulini*, 258 and 262 (discussed below).

27 J. R. Maddicott, 'Gaveston, Piers', in *Lexikon des Mittelalters*, 4 (Munich, 1989), col. 1147 [translation mine].

28 J. R. S. Phillips, *Aymer de Valence, Earl of Pembroke, 1307–1324: Baronial Politics in the Reign of Edward II* (Oxford, 1972), 290.

and there is no reference listing evidence to back up this statement. The fact that both Maddicott's and Phillips's books are devoted to two of Gaveston's most outspoken enemies might explain what in the early 1970s would still have been a 'verdict' of homosexuality. Methodologically, neither work offers a comprehensive and systematic assessment of the relationship. By 2004, Phillips had moved to a more cautious interpretation and stated that 'too many of them [i.e. the chroniclers' remarks] are either much later in date or the product of hostility, or a combination of the two, and thus not acceptable at face value ... But whatever the actual nature of their relationship – sexual, a formal bond, or simply a very close friendship – Gaveston was perceived as wielding a degree of influence over the king that excluded others who considered they had a right to be consulted.'[29]

In 1988, J. S. Hamilton published his still authoritative Gaveston biography which, early on, declares that 'there is no question that the king and his favourite were lovers'.[30] What follows is a one-page *tour de force* regarding the late medieval understanding of 'sodomy'. The only source pertaining to Edward cited in this discourse is the chronicle of Meaux which states that Edward indulged too much in the *vitium sodomiticum* (vice of sodomy).[31] However, apart from the fact that Gaveston is not mentioned in this passage of the chronicle, the text was not written until approximately 1400,[32] and, according to K. van Eickels, this statement has to be seen as merely a quantifying hint at Edward's overall depravity, not as a qualifying statement concerning the king's sexual orientation.[33] Later on, Hamilton analyzes the outburst of anger that, according to Walter of Guisborough (who is the sole source for this incident), Edward I had during the winter of 1306/7, after his son had asked him to entrust the county of Ponthieu to Gaveston (allegedly causing the king to send Gaveston into his first exile).[34] Hamilton argues that 'this exile was most likely the result of the prince's inappropriate behaviour ... But what was the nature of this inappropriate behaviour? Had the prince and his favourite become homosexual lovers? Perhaps, even though this is not explicitly stated in any of the chronicles at this time.'[35] In his Gaveston article for the *Oxford Dictionary of National Biography* (2004), Hamilton maintains that 'it has been generally assumed that the two men developed a homosexual relationship. Recently, however, it has been suggested that they entered into a compact of adoptive brotherhood. The extant records will bear either interpretation, although neither can be proved.'[36]

In his 1994 study of Gaveston, P. Chaplais first of all attempted, in a way reminiscent of Tout, to dismiss any argument in support of the two men's homosexuality. He points out that, while there is 'malicious gossip' in the later chronicles, one of the principal contemporary sources, the *Vita Edwardi Secundi*, does not suggest

29 J. R. S. Phillips, 'Edward II', in H. C. G. Matthew and B. Harrison (eds.), *Oxford Dictionary of National Biography* (hereafter *ODNB*), 17 (Oxford, 2004), 824–37, here 826.

30 Hamilton, *Piers Gaveston*, 16–17.

31 *Chronica monasterii de Melsa*, ii, 355: 'Ipse quidem Edwardus in vitio sodomitico nimium delectabat.'

32 Gransden, *Historical Writing in England*, 355–71.

33 K. van Eickels, *Vom inszenierten Konsens zum systematisierten Konflikt: Die englisch-französischen Beziehungen und ihre Wahrnehmung an der Wende vom Hoch- zum Spätmittelalter* (Stuttgart, 2002), 196.

34 H. Rothwell (ed.), *Cronica Walteri de Gyseburne (Hemingburghe/Hemingforde) de gestis regum Angliae* (Camden Society, 3rd series, 89, 1957), 382–3.

35 Hamilton, *Piers Gaveston*, 35.

36 J. S. Hamilton, 'Gaveston, Piers', in *ODNB*, 21, 654–6, here 654.

anywhere 'that anything improper of a physical nature ever took place between Edward and Gaveston'; secondly, according to Chaplais, there is ample evidence that 'Edward's attitude towards women does not appear to have been very different from that of other men of his time'; thirdly, Chaplais finds it 'difficult to believe that Philip the Fair [i.e. the king of France] would have given away his twelve-year-old daughter in marriage to a man [i.e. Edward II] whose ethics in love did not conform to the high standards which he expected of a son-in-law'.[37] Chaplais then breaks new ground and investigates the aforementioned possibility of an adoptive brotherhood between Edward and Gaveston, which will be discussed below.

R. M. Haines' 604-page biography, *King Edward II*, published in 2003, devotes two pages to the 'question of Edward's sexual orientation'. Haines explains that 'the king was clearly capable of sustained heterosexual relationships' (as evidenced by his four legitimate children and at least one illegitimate son), mentions Chaplais' thesis without explicitly endorsing or refuting it, and concludes: 'Whether Edward was a homosexual or not is of less importance than the fact that what can certainly be interpreted as inordinate affection regularly served as the mainspring of his actions.'[38]

This historiographical overview concludes with two essays published in 2006. W. M. Ormrod, in 'The Sexualities of Edward II', discards the positivist debate of the 'last few generations' over Edward II's sexuality as 'anachronistic and futile', asking instead 'why some people in the fourteenth century found it appropriate and necessary to include issues about sexuality in their construction of this king's character and reign', and suggests that this discourse was part of a contemporary effort to show that Edward II was acting 'outside the boundaries of normative behaviour' – an effort intended to lead to the king's deposition.[39] In 'Sermons of Sodomy', I. Mortimer points out that 'the earliest specific accusation that Edward was a sodomite' surfaced in a 1326 sermon preached by Adam Orleton, the bishop of Hereford, intended to undermine the king's position; and that the sodomy allegations of the sermon should be seen in the context of other early fourteenth-century sodomy accusations, namely those against Pope Boniface VIII and the Templars, which were also intended to undermine the accused's moral integrity and to bring about their downfall.[40] Thus, recent studies have moved away from the debate over the nature of Edward's and Gaveston's relationship. Yet, how can we understand the baronial opposition against Edward and Gaveston without addressing the nature – or the themes – of the two men's relationship? It is to four of these themes that we now turn, namely familiarity, friendship, brotherhood, and love.

To take familiarity first. The *Vita Edwardi Secundi* acknowledges that the baronial hatred for Gaveston was very surprising in light of the fact that, 'at that time, it was the case in the houses of almost all magnates that one from the *familia* [i.e. one from the group of household dependants] would enjoy the prerogative of the

[37] Chaplais, *Piers Gaveston*, 8–9. The same can be said of Gilbert de Clare, earl of Gloucester, who would certainly not have consented to the marriage of his sister Margaret to Gaveston if he had been convinced that Gaveston was more interested in men; see Phillips, 'Edward II', 826.

[38] Haines, *King Edward II*, 42–3.

[39] W. M. Ormrod, 'The Sexualities of Edward II', in G. Dodd and A. Musson (eds.), *The Reign of Edward II: New Perspectives* (Woodbridge, 2006), 22–47.

[40] I. Mortimer, 'Sermons of Sodomy: A Reconsideration of Edward II's Sodomitical Reputation', in Dodd and Musson (eds.), *The Reign of Edward II*, 48–60.

lord's esteem'.[41] According to the *Vita*, Gaveston's father was a Gascon knight and a *familiaris* of King Edward I. Gaveston himself, when he was a young squire, was received as a *familiaris* into the household of young Edward, prince of Wales. There, within a short time, he reached the apex of the highest favour with his Lord 'because of the pleasing performance of [his] duties'.[42] Thus, the author of the *Vita* suggests that Gaveston worked his way up. It is, of course, only a small step from *familiaritas* to *singularis familiaritas*, from familiarity to extraordinary familiarity, and while the former might be acceptable, the latter was not, as shall be shown below.

At this point, however, it should be noted that the chronicle evidence has to be read with a healthy dose of suspicion. For example, with regard to Christmas of 1307, the *Annales Paulini* mention that the king celebrated 'his Christmas' (i.e. 25 December) with Gaveston at Wye, a manor of Battle Abbey, located southwest of Canterbury.[43] The phrase *Nathale suum*, 'his Christmas', may suggest that the king retreated with his friend to a private setting. Wye, was, however, not a cosy country house. It was an important *manerium*, a place frequently used by medieval English kings to hold court. What is more problematic here, however, is that according to the charter evidence, which is generally more reliable than the chronicles, Edward and Gaveston were at Westminster on 26 December.[44] In fact, upon close scrutiny, it can be established that Edward was in Westminster from 10 December on, and that, after a brief trip to King's Langley (18 December) and Byfleet (19–22 December), he was back at Westminster for Christmas (24–26 December), that he then moved to Canterbury (30 December–4 January), and only afterwards spent a few days, including the feast of *Epiphania Domini*, at Wye (5–11 January 1308).[45] By then, Edward was on his way to his wedding, and his entourage must have been considerable. Fourteenth-century logistics, let alone court protocol and the liturgy of the religious holiday, would not have allowed for travelling back and forth between Westminster and Wye in a matter of hours on Christmas day. Edward and Gaveston did not spend a single Christmas together at Wye. Just because a chronicler claims the king did something does not mean that the king did, in fact, do it.

Secondly, we turn to the theme of friendship. There can be no doubt that Edward and Gaveston were friends. In 1309, according to the *Vita*, Edward was overjoyed when Gaveston returned from Ireland, and received him like 'a friend returning from a long pilgrimage'.[46] Two years after Gaveston's death, at Christmas of 1314, Edward had Gaveston's body transferred from Oxford to King's Langley. In this context, the author of the *Vita* refers to Gaveston as the king's *specialis amicus*,

41 Denholm-Young (ed.), *Vita Edwardi Secundi*, 14: 'in omnium fere magnatum domibus optentum sit hodie ut unus aliquis de familia dominice dilectionis gaudeat prerogatiua'.

42 Ibid.: 'Hic Petrus a Wasconia oriundus filius fuit cuiusdam militis regis Edwardi senioris quondam familiaris. Dum autem Edwardus iunior adhuc esset princeps Wallie, dictus Petrus armiger iuvenis in familiarem domus eius assumptus est, et grata exhibitione obsequiorum apud dominum suum summi fauoris apicem optinuit in breui'; see M. Prestwich, 'The Unreliability of Royal Household Knights in the Early Fourteenth Century', *Fourteenth Century England*, 2 (2002), 1–11, here 3.

43 *Annales Paulini*, 258: 'Hoc anno rex Edwardus tenuit Nathale suum cum Petro de Gavastone apud Wy, manerium abbatis de Bello.'

44 T. Rymer, *Fœdera, conventiones, literæ*, ed. G. Holmes (10 vols., The Hague, 1739; reprint Westmead, Eng., 1967), i. 4, 106.

45 *CPR 1307–12*, 25–31; *CCR 1307–13*, 12–16. See also C. H. Hartshorne, 'An Itinerary of Edward II', *Collectanea Archaeologica*, i (1861), 113–44, here 114.

46 Denholm-Young (ed.), *Vita Edwardi Secundi*, 8: 'quasi qui recepit amicum ex longa peregrinatione reuertentem'.

i.e. his 'confidential' friend.[47] Both N. Denholm-Young and W. R. Childs translate this phrase as 'intimate friend'.[48] To modern ears, other possible translations of *specialis*, for example 'confidential',[49] are probably less suggestive of physical action than 'intimate'.

Towards the end of his life, Edward himself wrote a poem in which he remembered his friends fondly, but without referring directly to Gaveston: 'Mercy, I trow, I needs shall reap/ From precious gifts and kindly deeds/ Which oft upon my friends and kin,/ Within my power I did bestow./ If I have erred, it grieveth me:/ But to their counsel was I sworn.'[50] Gaveston's circle of friends initially included even some of his later archenemies. According to the *Vita Edwardi Secundi*, Henry de Lacy, earl of Lincoln, had originally through his 'favour and friendship' (*fauore et amicitia*) encouraged and especially esteemed Gaveston.[51] This suggests that Gaveston must have been at least somewhat likable. After Gaveston's return from his Irish exile, it was Lincoln who even encouraged John de Warenne, earl of Surrey, then one of Gaveston's enemies, to befriend Gaveston, and according to the *Vita*, Warenne became Gaveston's *necessarius amicus ... et fidelis adiutor* (his indispensable friend and faithful helper).[52] This did not last long, though, and the *chassé-croisé* between the barons caused the author of the *Vita* to exclaim: 'The love of magnates is as a game of dice.'[53] If the friendship among nobles was a rather volatile phenomenon it is not surprising that the terms *amicus* and *amicitia* appear so rarely in the sources to describe Edward's and Gaveston's relationship which was far from volatile.

The third theme of this relationship to be addressed here is brotherhood. Much has been made of Edward calling Gaveston – in public – his 'brother' (*frater*), first mentioned by the *Vita Edwardi Secundi* in the context of Gaveston's return from his Irish exile in 1309: 'Knowing that Piers had already returned, the king travelled in the direction of Chester to meet him, and there, delighting in his return, very gratefully received him in an honourable way just like his brother. In fact, he had always named him his brother.'[54] In 1311, when Edward was asked to agree to the expulsion and exile of Gaveston, he responded: 'Truly, you shall desist from the persecution of my brother Piers, and you shall allow him to have the earldom of Cornwall.'[55] With regard to the events of 1312, the *Vita* states that the barons, when

47 Ibid., 58: 'dominus rex corpus Petri de Gauestone, sui quondam specialis amici, ab Oxonia ad Langeleye fecit transferri'.

48 Ibid.; Childs (ed.), *Vita Edwardi Secundi*, 100–1.

49 J. F. Niermeyer, *Mediae Latinitatis Lexicon Minus* (Leiden, 1984), 982, s.v. 'specialis.'

50 P. Studer, 'An Anglo-Norman Poem by Edward II, King of England', *Modern Language Review*, 16 (1921), 34–46, here 41: 'Merci me ert si com(e) je croy/ [Et] les honurs et les bontez/ Qe a mon poair sovent fesoy/ A mes amys et mes privetz./ Si je ey(e) mesfet, ceo poise moy:/ A lor consayl estoie jurez.' For the English translation, see ibid., 44.

51 Denholm-Young (ed.), *Vita Edwardi Secundi*, 4: 'Ille vero [sc. Henricus de Lacy comes Lyncolnie] qui Petrum prius fauore et amicitia pre ceteris excepto rege fouerat et dilexerat, inter omnes barones maximus eius inimicus factus est et persecutor.'

52 Ibid., 7–8: 'comes de Warenna, qui ... hilarem uultum Petro nunquam exhibuit, necessarius amicus iam factus est et fidelis adiutor'.

53 Ibid., 8: 'Amor magnatum quasi ludus in alea'; see A. King, 'Thomas of Lancaster's First Quarrel with Edward II', *Fourteenth Century England*, 3 (2004), 31–45, here 31.

54 Denholm-Young (ed.), *Vita Edwardi Secundi*, 7: 'Rex itaque, sciens Petrum iam rediisse, obuiam illi uenit ad Cestriam, ibique de reditu suo letus grataner ualde eum tamquam fratrem suum honorifice suscepit. Reuera fratrem suum semper appellauerat.'

55 Ibid., 17: 'Verum a persecutione fratris mei Petri desistatis, et comitatum Cornubie habere permittatis.'

they executed Gaveston, had 'killed a great earl whom the king had accepted as a brother, whom the king esteemed like a son, and whom the king had as a companion and friend'.[56] The Latin sentence here sounds almost liturgical: ... *in fratrem, ... ut filium, ... in socium et amicum*.[57] Maybe the author was trying to show that Gaveston was, at least to Edward, as perfect and complete as the Holy Trinity. It is worth noting that the verb *adoptare*, which appears here, has multiple meanings, namely 'adopting', 'accepting', 'wishing', and 'aiming at',[58] and only 'adopting' suggests a legal process of some sort.

To P. Chaplais, this phrase in the *Vita*, namely *quem rex adoptauerat in fratrem* (whom the king had accepted/adopted as a brother), characterizes the essence of the relationship between Edward and Gaveston.[59] Similarly, the *Annales Paulini* refer to Gaveston as *adoptivus frater suus* (Edward's adoptive brother),[60] and the so-called 'Chronicle of the Civil Wars of Edward II' mentions that Edward, when he was still prince of Wales, had entered into a *foedus* (a pact) with Gaveston.[61] The 'Chronicle of the Civil Wars of Edward II' is, however, an anti-Edwardian piece, written around 1327,[62] and should be used with caution. According to Chaplais, the 'pact of brotherhood' between David and Jonathan was the biblical precedent for the *foedus* between Edward and Gaveston.[63] This argument is not without flaw. While David did refer to Jonathan as a 'brother' (2 Samuel 1:26), the 'pact' between them is not defined as a 'pact of brotherhood' but simply as a 'pact' (1 Samuel 18:3).

Yet, David had good reason to call Jonathan 'brother' because he was, in fact, Jonathan's brother-in-law as a result of his marriage to Jonathan's sister Michal.[64] One could argue that Edward tried something similar, namely to establish family bonds, when he arranged the marriage between Gaveston and his own niece, Margaret de Clare, but, strangely enough, Chaplais does not make that connection. He concedes that there is no conclusive evidence for an adoptive brotherhood, but points out that there is 'a great deal of circumstantial evidence' for it: 'The grant to Gaveston of the earldom of Cornwall, his appointment as keeper of the realm, as royal lieutenant in Ireland, and as royal chamberlain, as well as the special part he played in the coronation ceremony, all these favours were consistent with adoptive brotherhood.'[65] The theory is interesting, but there are so many parallels between the Edward-Gaveston and David-Jonathan stories in the chronicles that one must wonder to what extent the idea of an adoptive brotherhood might have originated in the chroniclers' imagination. Maybe the language of brotherhood in connection with Edward and Gaveston does not refer to a flesh-and-blood or spiritual relation

56 Ibid., 28: 'Occiderunt enim magnum comitem quem rex adoptauerat in fratrem, quem rex dilexit ut filium, quem rex habuit in socium et amicum.'

57 Ibid.

58 Niermeyer, *Mediae Latinitatis Lexicon Minus*, 22, s.v. 'adoptare.'

59 Denholm-Young (ed.), *Vita Edwardi Secundi*, 28; see Chaplais, *Piers Gaveston*, 12–13.

60 *Annales Paulini*, 263: 'Rex quidem adoptivi fratris sui Petri de Gavastone personam exulare seu honorem ejus minuendum non potuit sustinere.'

61 G. L. Haskins, 'A Chronicle of the Civil Wars of Edward II', *Speculum*, 14 (1939), 73–81, here 75: 'cum eo firmitatis fedus iniit'. Chaplais, *Piers Gaveston*, 12–13 provides the more convincing reading: 'cum eo fraternitatis fedus iniit'.

62 Haskins, 'Chronicle of the Civil Wars', 73–4.

63 1 Samuel 18:3: 'inierunt autem Ionathan et David foedus'; 2 Samuel 1:26 (David mourning): 'doleo super te frater mi Ionathan'. See Chaplais, *Piers Gaveston*, 13–14.

64 1 Samuel 18:27: 'dedit itaque ei [sc. David] Saul Michol filiam suam uxorem'.

65 Chaplais, *Piers Gaveston*, 109.

or proximity at all.[66] Maybe it refers to the idea of brotherly equality. Kings called other kings 'brother' to express just that.[67] Gaveston, however, was not a king, and that made the king's treatment of him as an equal problematic, as shall be shown below.

The fourth theme of the two men's relationship is that of love. According to the *Annales Paulini*, Edward's father had Gaveston banished 'when he realized that his son, the prince of Wales, loved (*adamaret*) a certain Gascon knight beyond measure'.[68] The verb *adamare* can mean 'to fall in love with someone' as well as 'to grow very fond of someone'. While the verb *amare* is used to express the state of being in love with someone or being fond of someone, *adamare* is used primarily to express the dynamic process of an increasing sentiment, namely falling in love with someone or growing fond of someone.[69] It is conceivable that King Edward I had been observing this process between young Edward and Gaveston, and that he saw danger. According to the *Vita Edwardi Secundi*, after Edward II's accession to the throne, the barons were not able to divert the goodwill (*uoluntas*) of the king from Gaveston; rather, the more the king heard that they were trying to extinguish his, i.e. Edward's, favour, the more his love (*amor*) grew and his affection (*affectio*) towards Gaveston thrived.[70] While *amor* can certainly imply physical desire (especially in classical Latin), it can also, at least since the thirteenth century, mean the 'favour of a sovereign'.[71]

Three chroniclers refer to Gaveston as Edward's *amasius* (lover).[72] The term *amasius* is strong and can have physical connotations; in fact, the female form *amasia* stands for 'concubine'.[73] What is important to note, however, is that this term is not used in any contemporary writing: Ralph Higden wrote in the second quarter of the fourteenth century, and Henry Knighton, who plagiarized Higden's work extensively, as well as Thomas Burton of Meaux wrote in the last quarter of the fourteenth century.[74] Neither the *Vita* nor the *Annales Paulini* use the term *amasius*. Thus, it is likely that it should be considered gossip. However, even the contemporary chroniclers disapproved of the strong bonds between Edward and Gaveston.

[66] C. du Fresne, seigneur du Cange, *Glossarium mediae et infimae Latinitatis* (10 vols., Niort, 1883–7), iii, 594–8, s.v. 'frater', here 594: 'Nomen consanguinitatis vel propinquitatis sive carnalis sive spiritualis'.

[67] Du Cange, *Glossarium*, iii, 600, s.v. 'fraternitas' (7): 'Titulus honorarius, quo utebantur Reges, cum ad alios reges scribebant: fratres enim sese vulgo appellant.'

[68] *Annales Paulini*, 255: 'Sub illo quoque tempore cernens rex Angliae quod filius suus, princeps Walliae, adamaret quendam Vasconiensem militem ultra modum.'

[69] *Thesaurus linguae Latinae*, ed. auctoritate et consilio Academiarum quinque Germanicarum (10 vols. to date, Leipzig, 1900–82), i, 567, s.v. 'adamo'.

[70] Denholm-Young (ed.), *Vita Edwardi Secundi*, 1–2: 'Nec tamen uoluntatem regis a Petro poterant separare, quin etiam quanto plura audiret rex que gratiam eius conarentur extinguere, tanto magis inualescebat amor et crescebat affectio regis erga Petrum.'

[71] Niermeyer, *Mediae Latinitatis Lexicon Minus*, 41, s.v. 'amor'.

[72] *Chronica monasterii de Melsa*, ii, 279: 'Qui statim revocavit de partibus transmarinis praescriptum Petrum de Gavestona Vasconiensem, amasium suum, cujus consortium paterno jussu abjuraverat.' That Gaveston was Edward's 'amasius' is also mentioned in *Polychronicon Ranulphi Higden*, viii, 296: 'Qui statim revocavit amasium suum Petrum de Gavestoun.' See also J. R. Lumby (ed.), *Chronicon Henrici Knighton* (Rolls Series, 92, 1889–95), i, 405, which repeats verbatim the statement from the *Polychronicon Ranulphi Higden*.

[73] Niermeyer, *Mediae Latinitatis Lexicon Minus*, 39, s.v. 'amasia'.

[74] Gransden, *Historical Writing in England*, 44, 159, 355–71.

According to the *Annales Paulini*, 'the king called Piers, because of much love, his brother; the rabble, however, usually called him the king's idol (*ydolum*), whom Edward feared to displease like one would fear a father, and whom Edward strove to please like one would please a superior'.[75] Both the *Vita* and the *Annales Paulini* report that, according to rumors, some considered Gaveston a sorcerer (*maleficus*), i.e. someone who had the king bound with an evil spell,[76] because the king seemed to love Gaveston more than his queen and 'without measure'.[77] We may now turn to the other question, namely why the barons opposed the relationship between Edward and Gaveston.

The contemporary chronicles are unanimous in their charge that the relationship between Edward and Gaveston lacked 'measure' or 'moderation'. The *Vita Edwardi Secundi* claims that Edward, with regard to Gaveston, was 'incapable of moderate favour' (*modum autem dilectionis ... habere non potuit*).[78] According to the *Annales Paulini*, Edward, while he was still prince of Wales, loved Gaveston 'beyond measure' (*adamaret quendam Vasconiensem militem ultra modum*).[79] Robert of Reading's continuation of the *Flores Historiarum* explains the barons' opposition against Edward with the 'magnitude of immoderate love' that the king had shown towards Gaveston (*ob immoderati magnitudinem amoris quem erga ipsum Petrum gesserat*).[80] In the following, we shall discuss four areas of Edward's and Gaveston's relationship where violations of measure were clearly visible, namely social mobility, political trust, public conduct, and, once again, familiarity.

To begin with social mobility. It is noteworthy that modern historians usually refer to Edward's favourite as Piers Gaveston, not as Piers of Gaveston,[81] even though the medieval sources, both chronicles and charters, usually call him *Petrus de Gavastone*, i.e. they include *de* (of), the preposition of origin or nobility. J. S. Hamilton has shown that Piers Gaveston's nobility was of a much higher quality than fourteenth-century writers were willing to concede.[82] Despite his noble background, the *Annales Paulini* claim that Gaveston had been *de pulvere elevatus* (raised from

75 *Annales Paulini*, 259: 'Rex vocavit Petrum, prae amore nimio, fratrem suum; vulgus vero eum regis ydolum vocitabat, cui displicere ut patri timuit, et ut superiori studuit complacere.'

76 While 'magus' is a more or less neutral term, even used in the Gospel of Saint Matthew for the wise men who came to Bethlehem to adore the newborn Christ (Matthew 2:1: 'cum ergo natus esset Iesus in Bethleem Iudaeae in diebus Herodis regis ecce magi ab oriente venerunt Hierosolymam'), the word 'maleficus' definitely has negative connotations (Du Cange, *Glossarium*, v, 193–4, s.v. 'maleficium' and 'maleficus').

77 *Annales Paulini*, 262: 'Karolus et Lodowicus patrui reginæ, cernentes quod rex plus exerceret Petri triclinium quam reginæ, cum indignatione ad Franciam remigarunt. In omnem igitur terram exiit rumor iste, quod rex plus amaret hominem magum et maleficum quam sponsam suam elegantissimam dominam et pulcherrimam mulierem.' Denholm-Young (ed.), *Vita Edwardi Secundi*, 15: 'Modum autem dilectionis rex noster habere non potuit, et propter eum sui oblitus esse diceretur, et ob hoc Petrus malificus putaretur esse.'

78 Denholm-Young (ed.), *Vita Edwardi Secundi*, 15.

79 *Annales Paulini*, 255.

80 *Flores Historiarum*, iii, 146. Ibid., iii, 331: 'prædictus novus rex eum ultra modum et rationem amavit'.

81 Cf. the titles of his biographies, namely Dodge, *Piers Gaveston*; Hamilton, *Piers Gaveston*; Chaplais, *Piers Gaveston*. The exception is Dimitresco, *Pierre de Gavaston*, above, n. 14.

82 Hamilton, *Piers Gaveston*, 19–28.

the dust),[83] and according to Walter of Guisborough the Gascon had come *quasi ex nihilo* (so-to-speak out of nothing).[84] Those claims are unreal.

On 6 August 1307 seven earls gave their consent by witnessing the charter that put Gaveston in charge of the earldom of Cornwall.[85] Thus, the claim of the Middle English *Brut* chronicle that Edward I had, before his death, demanded an oath from his barons that they would refuse Gaveston's return to England[86] has to be discarded as fiction – or would the barons have broken an oath they had given to a dying king? According to the 1307 charter by which Edward I had sent Gaveston into his first exile, there was every possibility that Gaveston could be recalled,[87] and yet the Ordinances of 1311 claim that Edward I had made his son abjure Gaveston's company forever.[88] The *Vita Edwardi Secundi* firmly denies the earls' consent to Gaveston's elevation to the earldom of Cornwall and states that 'the greater part of the barons did not give their consent, in some cases because Gaveston was a foreigner, in other cases because of envy, the reasons for this envy being that Gaveston alone had favour in the eyes of the king and ruled as if he were a second king to whom all were subordinate and to whom no one was equal.'[89]

On 16 June 1308, Edward wrote to his father-in-law, King Philip IV of France, to inform him of what had been going on from his, i.e. Edward's, perspective: 'Indeed, after the government of the kingdom and of our lands had, God willing, been received by us, and after we had considered the virtues of the manifold valor that we had, since long ago, clearly seen in the noble man Peter of Gaveston, earl of Cornwall, we gratefully decided to bestow on him that earldom – with the will, the counsel, and the consent, and at the instigation of the earls, barons, and nobles of the said kingdom, while he himself was absent and unknowing. But then the same earls, barons, and nobles turned [their] will, counsel, and consent into the contrary

83 *Annales Paulini*, 258: 'Porro Petrus de Gavastone, dictus comes Cornubiæ, de pulvere elevatus, cœpit Anglicos detestari.'

84 *Cronica Walteri de Gyseburne*, 382: 'In vita patris sui habuit rex quemdam militem sibi familiarissimum de Wasconia oriundum quem cum esset princeps Wallie quasi ex nihilo suscitauerat.'

85 *Fœdera*, i. 4, 88–9. The charter was witnessed by Henry de Lacy, earl of Lincoln, Thomas, earl of Lancaster, John de Warenne, earl of Surrey, Humphrey of Bohun, earl of Hereford and Essex as well as constable of England, Edmund, earl of Arundel, John of Brittany, earl of Richmond, and Aymer de Valence, earl of Pembroke. The earldom of Cornwall carried considerable prestige; see G. L. Harriss, *King, Parliament, and Public Finance in Medieval England to 1369* (Oxford, 1975), 156: King Richard I had conferred it on his younger brother John (d. 1216); Henry III had given it to his younger brother Richard (d. 1272); in 1337, Edward III reserved it *in perpetuum* for the oldest son of the royal family, and this practice continues into the twenty-first century. Gaveston's elevation, however, occurred thirty years prior to 1337.

86 F. W. D. Brie (ed.), *The Brut or the Chronicles of England* (Early English Text Society, original series, 131, 1906), 202–203: Edward I allegedly has the earls of Lincoln, Warwick, and Pembroke swear 'that thai shulde nought suffre Piers of Gauaston come ageyn into Engeland forto make his son vse ryaute'.

87 *Fœdera*, i. 4, 70.

88 *The Statutes of the Realm*, printed by command of His Majesty King George the Third in pursuance of an address of the House of Commons of Great Britain (London, 1810), i, 162: 'e voleit que n[ost]re seign[eu]r le Roi son fiz forsjurast a touz jou la compaignie de luy [sc. lavantdit Pierres]'.

89 Denholm-Young (ed.), *Vita Edwardi Secundi*, 1: 'Maior tamen pars baronum terre non consensit, tum quia Petrus alienigena erat a Vasconia oriundus, tum propter inuidiam. Inuidebant enim ei magnates terre, quia ipse solus haberet gratiam in oculis regis et quasi secundus rex dominaretur, cui subessent omnes et par nullus'; *Cronica Walteri de Gyseburne*, 383: 'Mortuo autem rege et nondum adhuc sepulto misit ipse filius nouus rex celeres nuncios et reuocauit Petrum. Deditque ei, irrequisitus magnatibus suis, comitatum Cornubie et exaltauit eum super omnes propinquos eius et parentes.'

in this manner, and they themselves, as well as certain inhabitants of the kingdom and of their lands, rose up against us in a grave fashion, that they had no qualms to present themselves to us many times as enemies and complainers; and from this one truly fears scandals and even graver dangers could arise in the kingdom and these lands.'[90] The barons may have wanted to forget their assent to Gaveston's appointment, but the king had the charter to prove it.

On the same day, Edward sent a letter to Pope Clement V asking him to revoke the sentence of excommunication that the prelates of England had issued against Gaveston: 'Indeed, then – against justice – the aforementioned archbishop and bishops promulgated against the aforementioned earl, who had not been admonished, cited, confessed, or convicted of any crime, the sentence of excommunication, should he fail to leave the confines of the aforementioned kingdom of England by the day following the next [Feast of] Saint John the Baptist [i.e. 25 June 1308].'[91] The sentence was eventually revoked;[92] however, the pope, at least initially, seems to have sided with the barons. On 13 August 1308, Clement V wrote a letter (*Zelus comedit nos*) to Edward II, in which he encouraged the king to seek an agreement with the barons in their ongoing controversies. While Gaveston was not mentioned in this letter, the pope took the opportunity to remind Edward of his father's example: 'And it would not be inappropriate for your Highness to hold firm to the memory and to consider through diligent meditation in the confines of your bosom how your father Edward, of shining memory, directed his deeds through healthy counsel, how he always presented the barons with royal favours, always embraced [them] with arms of esteem, always obliged them with honours, always attracted [them] with presents and favours, always saw to their advantages, and continually increased [their] status through appropriate and useful encouragement.'[93] This letter shows what was really at stake: Edward was not paying sufficient attention to his barons (according to Ralph Higden, the king even preferred the company of carters, ditchers, rowers, and the like over the barons' company).[94] The barons, in turn, were glorifying the

90 *Fœdera*, i. 4, 122: 'Sane, post Regni & terrarum nostrorum gubernacula, per nos, Deo volente, suscepta, consideratis multæ probitatis virtutibus, quas ab olim in Nobili viro Petro de Gavaston, Comite Cornubiæ, vigere percepimus, Comitatum ipsum de voluntate, consilio, & consensu, & ad procurationem Comitum, Baronum, & Procerum Regni prædicti, sibi absenti & ignoranti, gratiose duximus concedendum. Sed demum iidem Comites, Barones ac Proceres, hujusmodi voluntatem, consilium, & consensum in contrarium immutantes, ac ipsi, & quidam Regni & terrarum ipsorum Incolæ, contra nos graviter insurgentes, nobis infestos multipliciter & molestos se reddere non verentur; ex quo scandala & pericula graviora suboriri posse in Regno & terris eisdem verisimiliter formidantur.'

91 Ibid., 123: 'Demum vero præfati, Archiepiscopus & Episcopi, in memoratum Comitem, non monitum, non citatum, non confessum, nec super aliqua fraude convictum, excommunicationis sententiam, nisi, infra Crastinum Sancti Johannis Baptistæ proximo futurum, dicti Regni Angliæ fines exiret, contra justitiam promulgarunt.'

92 W. W. Capes (ed.), *Registrum Ricardi de Swinfield, Episcopi Herefordensis, 1283–1317* (London, 1909), 451–2.

93 *Fœdera*, i. 4, 126: 'Nec indigne tuam oportet Celsitudinem tenaciter habere memoria, & infra claustra tui pectoris diligenti meditatione resolvere, qualiter, claræ memoriæ, Edvardus Genitor tuus, salubri consilio dirigens actus suos, eosdem Barones semper fuit Regiis favoribus prosecutus, semper dilectionis brachiis amplexatus, semper eos prævenit honoribus, semper donis et muneribus allexit magnificis, semper commoda procuravit ipsorum, & auxit statum condignis & utilibus incrementis.'

94 *Polychronicon Ranulphi Higden*, viii, 298; see A. Richardson, '"Hedging, Ditching, and Other Improper Occupations": Royal Landscapes and their Meaning under Edward II and Edward III', *Fourteenth Century England*, 4 (2006), 26–42, here 31.

memory of the king's father who had most certainly not been as accommodating as presented here in the pope's letter.

However, it seems that the barons' version of history would prevail. In the Ordinances of 1311, they claimed that Gaveston's return from his first exile 'was never by common assent, but only by the assent of some persons, who, under condition that he should well demean himself after his return, assented thereto'.[95] Strangely enough, this 'condition' is nowhere to be found in the charters of 1307.

Envy seems to have been the key reason for the barons' opposition. In 1311, when the barons demanded Gaveston's permanent exile, they accused Edward of having preferred 'unknown over known, stranger over brother, foreigner over inhabitant'.[96] However, Gaveston had not been 'unknown' at court when he was recalled from his first exile in 1307, he was neither a stranger to Edward nor to the court, and – given the fact that Gascony was at least technically still under English rule (which Edward I had fought to preserve) and that Gaveston was married to the king's niece – the label of 'foreigner' was not altogether fair either, and one should note that in the Ordinances of 1311 Gaveston was not accused of 'being' a foreigner but, rather, of 'favouring' foreigners.[97] As an aside, if there was an adoptive brotherhood between Edward and Gaveston, the abovementioned passage from the *Vita Edwardi Secundi* suggests that the barons were not aware of it. It seems that the barons mainly disapproved of the king's overly active role in Gaveston's social advancement, and the king's insisting on this social advancement probably did not help things. In time, the author of the *Vita* found himself ridiculing that 'Edward's continuous "love" towards Gaveston expressed itself in a public order issued from the king's court, that no one should call him [i.e. Gaveston] by his own name, namely "Sir Piers of Gaveston", but "Earl of Cornwall" instead'.[98] Was Gaveston's rank being ignored? If that was the case Edward would have had to issue such an edict to uphold the public order, which was, undoubtedly, one of the duties of a king.

We now turn to the second area of Edward's and Gaveston's relationship where violations of measure were visible, namely political trust. The political songs of Edward II's reign make fun of the notion that, while Gaveston was alive, there were two kings in England, rather than one[99] – or, to quote the *Annales Paulini*, that there were *duos reges in uno regno; istum verbaliter, istum realiter* (two kings in one kingdom; one in name and one in reality).[100] The top charge levelled against Gaveston in the Ordinances of 1311 was that Gaveston had 'evil[ly] led and evil[ly] coun-

[95] *Statutes of the Realm*, i, 162: '& qe son retourner nestoit unqes p[er] comun assent, mes solement p[er] assent dasqunes p[er]sones qe soutz condicion si bien se portast apres son retorner a ceo se assentirent'.

[96] Denholm-Young (ed.), *Vita Edwardi Secundi*, 15–16: 'quia ignotum noto, extraneum germano, et aduenam incole conabatur preferre'.

[97] *Statutes of the Realm*, i, 162: '[Pierres de Gavaston] ostant les bones ministres, mettant ceux de sa covine, auxi bien aliens com autres'. That did not, of course, stop the chroniclers from referring to Gaveston as a foreigner; see *Flores Historiarum*, iii, 331: 'causa cujusdam alienigenæ, videlicet cujusdam de Vasconia nomine Petro de Gavarestone'.

[98] Denholm-Young (ed.), *Vita Edwardi Secundi*, 3: 'Rex autem continuum amorem erga eum habebat, in tantum ut exiret a curia regis preceptum publicum ne quis eum nomine proprio uocaret, uidelicet dominum Petrum de Gauestone, sed comitem Cornubie nominaret.'

[99] L. Kendrick, 'On Reading Medieval Political Verse: Two Partisan Poems from the Reign of Edward II', *Mediaevalia*, 5 (1979), 183–204, here 192.

[100] *Annales Paulini*, 259: 'Unde indignatus est populus universus, duos reges in uno regno, istum verbaliter, istum realiter conregnare.'

seled our Lord the King, and … [had] enticed him to do evil in divers and deceitful manners'.[101] This is reminiscent of the accusation mentioned above that the king was under Gaveston's evil spell. Yet J. S. Hamilton has shown on the basis of the charter evidence that 'Gaveston seems to have taken little interest in political affairs'; he certainly was the recipient of numerous grants and favours, but compared to the other earls he witnessed rather few royal charters.[102]

Nonetheless, Edward's trust in Gaveston was obviously far-reaching. When he named him as *custos regni* before leaving for the continent to marry Isabella of France, his appointment charter spelled out rather clearly just how much he trusted his friend: 'Since we are especially confident concerning the circumspection, industriousness, and faithfulness of our esteemed and faithful Peter of Gaveston, Earl of Cornwall, we, through these present letters, install this earl as our keeper of the said kingdom, to hold our place in this same kingdom, [and] to better conserve the peace and tranquility of the people of the said kingdom.'[103] There is, however, nothing extraordinary about the wording here. Edward had cited a very similar rationale on 6 November 1307, when appointing the earls of Lincoln and Pembroke as proctors to arrange his marriage with Isabella of France.[104] It was in his capacity as *custos regni* that Gaveston received the king's wedding presents which Edward sent to him – without passing them on to him as presents.[105]

The barons may have seen Edward's trust for Gaveston as a sign of distrust for them. This raises the question whether Edward had reason for such distrust. At least one chronicler suggests that the barons had advised Edward's father to banish Gaveston in the first place.[106] According to John of Trokelowe's *Annales*, the barons saw themselves despised when Gaveston was appointed *custos regni*, and they grumbled quite a bit.[107] There were, after all, several earls who were older than Gaveston. At the coronation, Gaveston carried the crown and appeared in the procession as the

[101] *Statutes of the Realm*, i, 162: 'qe Pierres de Gavaston ad malmenez & malconseiles n[ost]re Seign[eu]r le Roi & lad entice a malfair en d[i]verses maners & deceivantes'.

[102] J. S. Hamilton, 'Charter Witness Lists for the Reign of Edward II', *Fourteenth Century England*, 1 (2000), 1–20, here 5; J. S. Hamilton, *The Royal Charter Witness Lists of Edward II (1307–1326) from the Charter Rolls in the Public Record Office*, List and Index Society, 288 (Chippenham, 2001), x.

[103] *Fœdera*, i. 4, 106: 'Nos, de circumspectione, industria, & fidelitate dilecti & fidelis nostri Petri de Gavastone, Comitis Cornubiæ, specialiter confidentes, ipsum Comitem Custodem nostrum dicti Regni, ac locum nostrum in eodem Regno tenentem, pro pace & tranquilitate populi dicti Regni melius conservanda, constituimus per præsentes.'

[104] Ibid., 95–6: 'de circumspecta industria & fidelitate probata … ac nobilium virorum dilectorum & fidelium nostrorum'.

[105] *Annales Paulini*, 258: 'Quæ omnia [sc. donaria] rex Angliæ concito Petro misit.' While the verb 'mittere,' in medieval Latin, can mean 'to donate,' it is not its primary meaning, and the chronicler could have used a stronger verb, such as 'donare' (to give) if it had been his intention to be unequivocal here. See also E. A. R. Brown, 'The Political Repercussions of Family Ties in the Early Fourteenth Century: The Marriage of Edward II of England and Isabelle of France', *Speculum*, 63 (1988), 573–95, here 582, who translates 'misit' as 'bestowed' and, thus, suggests the formal donation which, in my opinion, did not take place.

[106] *Annales Paulini*, 255: 'ex consilio comitum et baronum suorum compulit rex ipsum militem abjurare quoad viveret regnum suum.'

[107] H. T. Riley (ed.), *Johannis de Trokelowe Annales, 1307–1323 (Chronica monasterii Sancti Albani)* (Rolls Series, 28, 1866), iii, 61–127, here 65: 'Unde magnates Angliae, videntes se despectos, non minimum murmurabant.'

last one of the earls right before the king himself.[108] One chronicler suggests that Gaveston's hands should be considered 'unclean' or 'unworthy', and that the people and the clergy were displeased with the king's decision to let Gaveston carry the crown.[109] The *Annales Paulini* state that Edward, after recalling Gaveston from his first exile, discarded the advice given by his elders – just as Solomon's son Reheboam had done[110] – and instead clung to the counsel of those young ones with whom he had been raised, especially Gaveston.[111] This is another hint of just how strongly the chroniclers measured their kings against biblical characters, and the Reheboam reference has yet to be appreciated in its fullness.[112]

Since the Bible was one of the key normative texts for a fourteenth-century chronicler, one has to consider the suggestive discourse that comes with a Reheboam reference that may elude readers today but that a fourteenth-century audience would have picked up on right away. The reign of the Old Testament King Reheboam was one of the worst, and it was not just associated with inappropriate advisers, but also with male cult prostitutes (the Vulgate calls them *effeminati*, but the technical term may be *hierodules*).[113] Thus, if the chroniclers saw Edward's reign in light of the reigns of the first kings of Israel the interpretation of the relationship between the king and Gaveston as a homosexual one comes as no surprise.

The third area of the two men's relationship where violations of measure were visible was that of public conduct. Several chroniclers mention the emotional greetings between Edward and Gaveston.[114] Yet 'gestures of physical intimacy were a self-understood element of noble and courtly communication and public interaction; embraces and kisses on the lips signalled friendly welcomes and good-byes.'[115] In the case of Edward and Gaveston, John of Trokelowe asserts that 'the king honoured Peter – through the kisses he gave him and through repeated embraces – with extraordinary familiarity' (*familiaritate ... singulari*).[116] It needs to be emphasized that the kisses and embraces as such would not have upset the barons; they were

108 The order of the coronation procession is indicative of Gaveston's status. For brevity's sake, I only list the earls in the order in which they walked: Hereford carried the royal scepter; Lancaster, Lincoln and Warwick carried swords; Arundel, assisted by the son of Oxford and other nobles, carried the royal vestments; Cornwall carried the crown and was followed by the king himself ('Deinde venit Petrus de Gavaston Comes Cornubiæ, portans Coronam Regalem; Deinde sequebatur ipse Coronandus'). *Fœdera*, i. 4, 112.

109 *Annales Paulini*, 261: 'sed coronam Sancti Edwardi [sc. rex] tradidit Petro ad portandum manibus inquinatis. Ex quo non immerito indignati sunt populus atque clerus.'

110 1 Kings 12:8: 'qui [sc. Reoboam] dereliquit consilium senum quod dederant ei et adhibuit adulescentes qui nutriti fuerant cum eo'.

111 *Annales Paulini*, 257: 'Hic [sc. rex] statim Petrum de Gavastone ab exilio in Angliam revocavit. Quo habito, statim spreto consilio senum, sicut Roboam, adhæsit consilio juvenum qui secum ab adolescentia fuerant conversati, et præcipue et super omnia consilio Petri de Gavastone.'

112 The various Reheboam references are mentioned, but not further explored, in Haines, *King Edward II*, 39, 49, 67, 385 note 10.

113 1 Kings 14:24: 'sed et effeminati fuerunt in terra feceruntque omnes abominationes gentium quas adtrivit Dominus ante faciem filiorum Israhel'.

114 *Flores Historiarum*, iii, 139: 'et ab ipso rege lætitia geminata receptus est'; *Johannis de Trokelowe Annales*, iii, 65: 'Inter quos Petrum, datis osculis et ingeminatis amplexibus, familiaritate venerabatur singulari'; *Vita Edwardi Secundi*, ed. Denholm-Young, 15: 'solus Petrus gratiam et uultum hilarem regis habuit et fauorem'.

115 Van Eickels, *Vom inszenierten Konsens zum systematisierten Konflikt*, 342 [translation mine].

116 *Johannis de Trokelowe Annales*, iii, 65: 'Inter quos Petrum, datis osculis et ingeminatis amplexibus, familiaritate venerabatur singulari.'

part of the protocol. It just seems that Gaveston received more kisses and embraces than they did, and that caused them grief.

Robert of Reading was probably correct in his assessment that the king's love 'from all sides' (*regisque amore undique circumvallatum*) made Gaveston arrogant.[117] The author of the *Vita Edwardi Secundi* states that the arrogance which Gaveston displayed would have been sufficiently intolerable if he had been the son of a king – which he was not.[118] Gaveston certainly should have refrained from wearing royal purple at Edward's coronation.[119] The king, however, did his part of the damage. Within a year of his accession to the throne, Edward made several appointments.[120] The *Annales Paulini* report that Edward made Gaveston 'the kingdom's highest secretary and chamberlain'.[121] This does not mean that Gaveston received a formal office at court; rather, he became the most trusted man at court, and he was closest to the king.[122] According to the *Vita*, 'Edward showed favour and a friendly face to no one but Piers, and when Piers was around, no earl or baron entering the king's chamber was even spoken to directly by the king, and that was a cause for envy.'[123] The barons cannot have been pleased when they asked for certain royal favours and the king referred them to Gaveston, whom he had entrusted with these decisions.[124]

By 1311, the king feared the barons' envy to the extent that he claimed to have incarcerated Gaveston at Bamburgh Castle (Northumberland), even though he had merely sent him there for his own protection.[125] On 30 November 1311, Edward issued a rather strange order. According to the Ordinances of the same year, Gaveston had been banished, but there were rumors that he was still around and wandering from place to place (*adhuc latitat, discurrit, & vagatur de loco in locum, de Castro in Castrum, de Fortiletia in Fortiletium*) in Cornwall, Devonshire, Somerset, and Dorset. Therefore, the barons had asked the king (*Nobis, per Comites & Barones*

117 *Flores Historiarum*, iii, 139: 'Cernens igitur idem Petrus se, ut favilla regi, erectum in sullime, regisque amore undique circumvallatum, ita ut nulli in regno videretur esse secundus, noluit alicui dominorum pacificari, sic extollens se supra se cunctis proceribus procellere, ipsosque contemptui habere et aliquando regiam dignitatem transcendere disposuit plena voluntate.'

118 Denholm-Young (ed.), *Vita Edwardi Secundi*, 16: 'Et certe in filio regis satis esset intollerabile supercilium quod pretendit. Publice tamen scitur quod non erat filius regis nec regalem prosapiam quicquid attingens.'

119 *Annales Paulini*, 262: 'ipse in purpura'. The earls were wearing golden cloth, and among the guests were those who would have had a lot more reasons to wear purple than Gaveston, particularly the two brothers of King Philip IV of France (Count Charles of Valois and Count Louis of Evreux).

120 On 12 March 1308, Nicholas de Segrave was appointed marshal (*Fœdera*, i. 4, 113–14); on 8 May 1308, Thomas, earl of Lancaster, was made seneschal (*Fœdera*, i. 4, 118).

121 *Annales Paulini*, 258: 'Petrum vero de Gavastone fecit secretarium et camerarium regni summum.'

122 Davies, *Baronial Opposition*, 100; T. F. Tout, *Chapters in the Administrative History of Medieval England* (Manchester, 1920–33), ii, 224; Tout, *Place of the Reign*, 152.

123 Denholm-Young (ed.), *Vita Edwardi Secundi*, 15: 'Erat enim causa odii secundaria [sc. erat … fastus eius intollerabilis … prima causa odii] hec, quod cum ab antiquo omnibus desiderabile exstiterit habere gratiam in oculis regum, solus Petrus gratiam et uultum hilarem regis habuit et fauorem, in tantum ut, si comes vel baro colloquium habiturus cum rege cameram regis intraret, in presentia Petri nulli rex uerba dirigebat, nulli faciem hilarem ostendebat, nisi soli Petro.'

124 *Annales Paulini*, 259: 'Nam si quis ex comitibus aut ex magnatibus haberet requirire specialem gratiam regis super aliquo negotio expediendo, rex eum mitteret ad Petrum; et quod ille diceret aut præciperet, mox fieret; et rex etiam acceptaret.'

125 Ibid., 269: 'Eodem anno rex, timens invidiam et odium majorem regni erga dominum Petrum de Gavastone, posuit eum in castro de Bamborkh pro sua securitate, asserens prælatis et magnatibus regni se misisse eum ibidem in carcerem ut placeret eisdem.'

prædictos, fuerit supplicatum) to search for Gaveston and, if the latter could be apprehended, to punish him in accordance with the Ordinances. The king, in turn, ordered Hugh Courtenay and William Martin to search for Gaveston and, if they should be able to find him, deal with him in accordance with the Ordinances.[126] One may wonder whether the king merely issued this order *pro forma* while Gaveston was safe somewhere. On 20 January 1312, Edward informed the sheriff of York that, since 'the order of exile against the aforementioned Peter had been promulgated against the law and custom of our kingdom, which we are forced to observe by oath, the earl [i.e. Gaveston], following our order, has come to us into our kingdom, prepared to stand trial before us in all matters according to the aforementioned law and custom, wherefore we have received him to our peace and trust'.[127] It is conceivable that Edward issued the original search warrant to appease the barons, thereby facilitating Gaveston's secret travel to the royal court. Once Gaveston was safe in the king's presence, there was no more need for pretence.

We now return to familiarity, the area of the two men's relationship where violations of measure were the most evident. Familiarity and proximity go hand in hand.[128] According to the chronicle evidence, only Gaveston truly enjoyed the king's *familiaritas*. It had troubled Edward I that his son's fondness of Piers Gaveston was growing beyond measure.[129] Was Edward concerned that *familiaritas* would turn into *familiaritas singularis*, or that Gaveston would become *familiarissimus*, the most familiar one?[130] Did Edward I want to halt a process that, in his opinion, could get out of hand? It is conceivable that Edward I foresaw that the English peers would not be too excited about a clear favourite emerging in the court of the prince of Wales. The good measure, the *ordo*, was in danger. It is, of course, also possible that the chroniclers endowed Edward I with this remarkable foresight. According to the *Vita Edwardi Secundi*, one of the reasons why the barons wanted Gaveston banished was so that he would no longer remain *in familiaritate regis*, which both N. Denholm-Young and W. R. Childs once again translate as 'intimate with the king'.[131] While this translation is not impossible, it has, at least to twenty-first-century ears, sexual connotations, and it has to be pointed out that *familiaritas* has much more to do with the relationship of trust between a lord and a dependant[132] than with physical, let alone sexual intimacy.

Does this *familiaritas* mean that either Edward or Gaveston neglected their wives, apart from the fact that Edward II was the father of four children and of at

126 *Fœdera*, i. 4, 201–2.

127 *Fœdera*, i. 4, 203: 'Quia tamen idem exilium in prædictum Petrum, contra legem & consuetudinem Regni nostri, ad quarum observationem vinculo juramenti sumus astricti, fuit promulgatum: Idemque Comes, de mandato nostro, ad nos in Regnum prædictum jam accessit, paratus coram nobis in omnibus stare juri, secundum legem & consuetudinem prædictas; Per quod ipsum Comitem ad pacem & fidem nostram admisimus.'

128 Du Cange, *Glossarium*, iii, 409–10: s.v. 'familia', 'familiares' (including 'familiaritas'), and 'familiarius'.

129 *Annales Paulini*, 255: 'Sub illo quoque tempore cernens rex Angliae quod filius suus, princeps Walliae, adamaret quendam Vasconiensem militem ultra modum.'

130 *Cronica Walteri de Gyseburne*, 382: 'In vita patris sui habuit rex quemdam militem sibi familiarissimum de Wasconia oriundum quem cum esset princeps Wallie quasi ex nihilo suscitauerat.'

131 Denholm-Young (ed.), *Vita Edwardi Secundi*, 6: 'Voluissent certe comites quod Petrus Anglia recessit, ita quod amplius in familiaritate regis non permansisset'; *Vita Edwardi Secundi*, ed. Childs, 12–13.

132 Niermeyer, *Mediae Latinitatis Lexicon Minus*, 22, s.v. 'familiaritas'.

least one illegitimate son, and that Gaveston was apparently the father of two daughters?[133] Later chroniclers accused the king of neglecting his wife.[134] One repeatedly cited example for such negligence, the 'couch-incident after the coronation', comes from the *Annales Paulini*. They report that 'Charles and Louis, Isabella's uncles and brothers of King Philip IV, when they perceived that Edward visited Piers' dining couch more than that of the queen, returned to France with indignation.'[135] It does not say, as has been stated elsewhere, that the uncles 'left the banquet in indignation'.[136] That would have been an open affront to which Edward would have had to respond. One must remember that Isabella was a young teenager of probably twelve years when she got married,[137] and that Edward was a good ten years her senior. It has been pointed out that the reason for the indignation of the uncles may be found in fundamental differences between the French and English coronation festivities: until the late twelfth century, the English coronation banquet was held without the presence of women (who, in fact, dined separately).[138] Another question that could be asked is why Edward abandoned his pregnant queen when he was fleeing with Gaveston in 1312. Here, the answer is obvious: the queen was pregnant, the life of a potential heir to the throne was at stake, and Isabella's joining of the hectic flight was too much of a risk.

The attention that Edward devoted to Gaveston infuriated the barons, who, in early 1310, refused to come to the scheduled session of parliament.[139] According to the *Vita*, they were upset that their mortal enemy, who had thrown the kingdom and themselves into confusion, was lurking (or hiding) in the royal chamber (*regio lateret in thalamo*).[140] This accusation could be seen to weigh somewhat more heavily, considering that the word used for chamber, namely *thalamus* (from the Greek *θάλαμος*), does have the prominent meaning 'bedchamber'.[141] Yet, K. van Eickels has shown that this may not have been nearly as unusual as it may seem to us today:[142] the sharing of the bed by two men was considered a 'peace-and-friendship ritual' from medieval to early modern times, and the list of prominent examples

133 Joan and Amie: Hamilton, 'Gaveston, Piers', 656; J. S. Hamilton, 'Another Daughter for Piers Gaveston? Amie de Gaveston, Damsel of the Queen's Chamber', *Medieval Prosopography*, 19 (1998), 177–86.

134 J. Maitland (ed.), *Chronicon de Lanercost MCCI–MCCCXLVI* (Edinburgh, 1839), 217: 'rex Angliæ, qui duxerat filiam ejus [sc. regis Franciæ] uxorem, minus eam dilexit propter Petrum prædictum'; *Polychronicon Ranulphi Higden*, viii, 300: 'ejusque [sc. Petri] contemplatione [sc. rex] Isabellam reginam suam neglexit'.

135 *Annales Paulini*, 262: 'Karolus et Lodowicus patrui reginae cernentes, quod rex plus exerceret Petri triclinium quam reginae, cum indignatione ad Franciam remigrarunt.'

136 Hamilton, *Piers Gaveston*, 48.

137 Chaplais, *Piers Gaveston*, 8 with note 14, and 9.

138 Van Eickels, *Vom inszenierten Konsens zum systematisierten Konflikt*, 193 with note 35.

139 Denholm-Young (ed.), *Vita Edwardi Secundi*, 8: 'barones uniuersi … ad locum consuetum parliamenti nostri uenire differrent'.

140 Ibid., 9: 'dicentes … dum capitalis inimicus eorum, qui regnum turbauerat et ipsos, regio lateret in thalamo, accessum eorum non fore securum'.

141 H. Frisk, *Griechisches etymologisches Wörterbuch* (Heidelberg, 1960–73), iii, 648; H. Estienne, *Thesaurus linguae Graecae, nova editio auctior et emendatior* (Paris, 1831–65), iv, 230.

142 Van Eickels, *Vom inszenierten Konsens zum systematisierten Konflikt*, 341–93, suggess that the joint eating from one bowl and sleeping in a shared bed may have been an equivalent of the *homagium* in the discourse of friendship.

is impressive.[143] Thus, it was not compromising to be the 'bedfellow' of the king, rather, it was the apex of royal favour, especially if it was witnessed by many.[144] It seems safe to assume that the barons were jealous.

The actions of the barons after the Ordinances of 1311 reveal that they had issues with the entire *familia* of Edward II. To them, the banishment of Gaveston was only the beginning. They now wanted Gaveston's accomplices and supporters banished from the court of the king. According to the *Vita Edwardi Secundi*, it aggravated the king so much that he was not to be allowed to retain even one *familiaris* according to his own wish, that he decided to recall Gaveston.[145] It was ultimately in the issue of *familiaritas* that the king's and the barons' sense of measure and *ordo* collided.

It has not been the intention of this essay to discard the valuable scholarship that has been produced on Piers Gaveston and King Edward II of England. However, there are – figuratively speaking – stones that have yet to be turned, connections that have yet to be made, and wordings which have yet to be studied in a broader context. An attempt has been made here to identify and analyze four themes of Edward's and Gaveston's relationship, namely familiarity, friendship, brotherhood and love. In the light of the revised and diminished value of the old *vitium sodomiticum* claim, as well as in the light of the now plausible explanation for Gaveston's presence in Edward's *thalamus*, it seems that the evidence does not bear the interpretation that there was sexual intimacy between the king of England and the earl of Cornwall. Furthermore, if one looks beyond the explicit David-Jonathan allusions and begins to consider the entire suggestive discourse on the early kings of Israel found in the fourteenth-century chronicles, the adoptive brotherhood argument becomes highly unlikely as well, and the 'homosexual undertones' can be seen for what they are, namely biblically inspired fiction.

Secondly, this essay has discussed four areas of Edward's and Gaveston's relationship where violations of measure were clearly visible. The reasons for the baronial opposition to Edward's and Gaveston's relationship can be found in the obvious lack of measure with regard to Gaveston's social mobility, the political trust Edward placed in him, the public conduct of both, and, once again, the familiarity between the two which angered the barons because they were not admitted to this familiarity. The barons' envy then inspired fourteenth-century chroniclers to paint Edward's reign and the king's connection to Gaveston in the darkest possible colors. It may be true that Edward was not cut out to be king – and being measured against the legacy of his father cannot have helped him very much – but the barons' envy which culminated in the killing of Gaveston did not show them in a favourable light either, and it certainly did have the proportions of a deadly sin.

Thus, we now return to the title of this paper which is taken from the poem 'Piers Gaueston' by Michael Drayton, a contemporary of Christopher Marlowe and William Shakespeare. While Drayton's portrayal of Edward's and Gaveston's rela-

143 Ibid., 368–93; for example, Louis the German and Charles the Bald (842); King Lothar of West-Francia and Duke Henry (early tenth century); Philip II and Richard Lionheart (1187); Louis the Bavarian and Frederick the Fair (1313); John the Fearless of Burgundy and Louis of Orléans (1405); the Duke of Somerset and King Edward IV of England (1463).

144 Ibid., 388.

145 Denholm-Young (ed.), *Vita Edwardi Secundi*, 21: 'Ad hec rex ultra modum commotus, quod nec unum familiarem iuxta proprium uotum retinere sibi liceret, sed sicut prouidetur fatuo, totius domus sue ordinatio ex alieno dependeret arbitrio, in odio comitum reuocauit Petrum, per animan Dei iurans ex solito quod libere proprio uteretur arbitrio.'

tionship has clear 'homosexual undertones', Drayton has Gaveston say a short line in the thirty-fourth verse which is actually in accordance with the fourteenth-century evidence and may very well capture the true essence of this relationship: *With my life, his joyes began and ended.*[146] While the close friendship between the Gascon noble Piers Gaveston and King Edward II of England will probably continue to be debated, there can be no doubt that Edward was joyful in the company of Gaveston, and that this joy ended in 1312 when Gaveston lost his life on Blacklow Hill.

146 Drayton, 'Piers Gaueston', 164.

CLERICAL RECRUITMENT IN ENGLAND, 1282–1348

David Robinson

Ordination set a mediaeval clerk apart from his contemporaries. As a 'literate' youth he was tonsured by the bishop and might thereafter in time proceed to the order of acolyte. He might after that move swiftly to the first of the higher, or 'holy', orders, the subdiaconate, or delay for a few years before taking this step. Alternatively, he might not progress to holy orders but prefer to remain free to marry and pursue a non-ecclesiastical career. Once ordained subdeacon, he would probably progress within a year or two to diaconate and priesthood.[1] Although a few subdeacons' and deacons' posts existed in cathedral, collegiate and some other churches, there was usually little benefit in suffering the restrictions imposed by a clerical life-style without enjoying the spiritual and pecuniary benefits of being able to celebrate Mass. No doubt a few subdeacons and deacons died or suffered serious disability or for some other reason failed to proceed to the priesthood.

Ordinands who gathered at the embertides to be examined and, unless rejected, to be ordained subdeacon, deacon or priest fall into three categories: members of religious orders; secular clerks who had already obtained a rectory or other benefice before committing themselves to the higher orders; and unbeneficed secular clerks. In some ordination lists they appear under separate headings, 'religiosi', 'beneficiati', and 'non beneficiati', and in many other lists ordinands are in practice grouped in this way.[2]

The present study is concerned only with unbeneficed secular ordinands being ordained to the three higher orders in the period up to 1348. There are some borderline cases, notably chantry chaplains who seem, where we can see the distinction being made, normally to have been treated as unbeneficed even when their chantry is described as perpetual. A small number of unbeneficed ordinands were on the point of obtaining a benefice, or were members of the bishop's *familia* and would expect to obtain one fairly soon. Gilbert de la Thorne was ordained subdeacon in the diocese of Exeter on Easter Eve 1318 'ad graciam specialem domini episcopi' and deacon in September 1319 'ad graciam domini'. As clerk, Thorne had been active in the bishop's service for a number of years. A year later, when the bishop collated the rectory of Bradstone to him, he was described as 'familiaris episcopi' and, as rector, he was ordained priest in September 1320.[3] Thomas de Marwell was ordained

1 For minimum ages and other qualifications see V. Davis, *Clergy in London in the Late Middle Ages* (London, 2000), 5,11. For ordination lists as evidence of clerical mobility see V. Davis, 'Episcopal Ordination Lists as a Source for Clerical Mobility in England in the Fourteenth Century', in N. Rogers (ed.), *England in the Fourteenth Century* (Stamford, 1993), 152–70.

2 See, for example, R. M. T. Hill (ed.), *The Rolls and Register of Bishop Oliver Sutton* (Lincoln Record Society, iii, 48, 1954; iv, 52, 1958; v, 60, 1965; vi, 64, 1969; vii, 69, 1975). The ordinations are in volume vii and letters dimissory are among the memoranda in volumes iii–vi.

3 F. C. Hingeston-Randolph (ed.), *Register of Walter de Stapeldon, Bishop of Exeter* (London and Exeter, 1892), 516, 524, 193, 387, 530. Names found in published registers are usually given in the

subdeacon in 1312 and deacon in 1314 in the diocese of Winchester by grace of the bishop, Henry Woodlock, who came from Marwell. In March 1315 Marwell was instituted rector of St Roald, Winchester, resigning his deacon's office in St Elizabeth's chapel, Winchester, which was in the bishop's gift, and in May 1315 was ordained priest on the title of his rectory.[4] These men have more in common with the well-connected administrators, academics and members of wealthy families who appear in the ordination lists already in possession of benefices than with the general run of unbeneficed ordinands. Most unbeneficed ordinands would look forward to a future in which they would say Masses as required and might aspire to become a parochial chaplain or, with very good fortune, to attain in due course a chantry, vicarage or even one of the less valuable rectories. These men, sometimes described as the 'clerical proletariat', formed the great majority of the secular priestly workforce.

Lists of ordinands are to be found in bishops' registers. The earliest registers are primarily records of institutions to benefices, important not only for recording the name of the rector or vicar instituted but for the identity of the patron of the benefice, which was of longer-term importance for the bishop and his successors. To this core might be added a variety of entries sufficiently important to justify at least medium-term preservation.[5] Ordination lists are first found in the 1260s and their creation and preservation are no doubt related to increasing concern for maintaining the standard of the clerical profession, which included the examination of candidates as to their freedom, legitimacy, age and abilities. In addition, to avoid pauper clergy bringing the priesthood into disrepute, each ordinand must possess a title, a secure income on which he could depend. A bishop ordaining a man without a title was responsible for his maintenance if he fell into poverty. Ordination lists in episcopal registers provide the names of men ordained and their titles. The most common titles were the ordinand's own patrimony, a title provided by a lay man or woman, or one provided by a religious house.

Sometimes lists of ordinands on loose folios were inserted when quires were bound into registers; in other cases the lists were copied into the quires. There is sometimes reason to question how systematically they were entered. Increasingly the lists were compiled as separate quires and either bound into the register or bound separately as a register of ordinations. In the latter case there was a risk that the register would later be discarded as being of no permanent utility: the ordination register of Archbishop Melton of York (1317–40) was recorded in the fifteenth century but has not survived, and ordination registers of bishops Droxford (1309–29) and Shrewsbury (1329–63) of Bath and Wells are known to have existed. Early lists may well have been initially compiled a few days before the ordination itself, when the ordinands were examined, and Dr Dohar has drawn attention to evidence indicating that some men listed were not in fact ordained but may have been excluded at examination. He also draws attention to errors – men included in

form in which they appear in the edition; names found in unpublished registers are usually given as they appear in the manuscript.

4 A. W. Goodman (ed.), *Registrum Henrici Woodlock diocesis Wintoniensis* (Canterbury and York Society, xliii, xliv, 1940, 1941), vi, 576, 742, 848, 865, 876; *VCH Hampshire*, ii, 212.

5 For a comprehensive bibliography of published bishops' registers and a catalogue of unpublished ones to 1640, see D. M. Smith, *Guide to Bishops' Registers of England and Wales* (Royal Historical Society, 1981) and *Supplement* (Canterbury and York Society, 2004).

lists for two separate orders on the same day or apparently ordained to the same order at successive ordinations. Sometimes the scribe noticed an error or duplication at the time; sometimes an apparent error can be explained, for example by the existence of two men bearing the same name.[6] In general, errors seem to be most frequent in the earlier years. Overall, where the series of lists appears complete, and ordinations were held frequently in a diocese, most men can be traced as they progressed through each of the higher orders in turn. Lists of acolytes are less regularly entered and the conferring of the first tonsure is recorded only rarely and in a few dioceses.

The earliest lengthy series of ordination lists begin in 1282. The register of John Pecham, archbishop of Canterbury, first records the names of men ordained on Trinity eve 1282, and the register of Godfrey Giffard, bishop of Worcester, first records names of men ordained three months later, on Saturday following the Exaltation of the Holy Cross. Between 1282 and 1348 the diocesan coverage is: Carlisle 1294–1324, 1332 onwards; Durham 1334 onwards; York 1342 onwards; Coventry and Lichfield 1300 onwards; Lincoln 1290–99, 1345 onwards; Ely 1338 onwards; Worcester 1282 onwards; Hereford 1328 onwards; Exeter 1308–21; Winchester 1305–33, 1346 onwards; Canterbury 1282–92, 1295–1305, 1314–28; Rochester 1320 onwards. Only Worcester, Coventry and Lichfield and, with a short gap, Carlisle, therefore cover the whole of the first half of the fourteenth century but coverage increases until in the later 1340s evidence survives for ten of the seventeen English dioceses. No bishops' registers survive for Chichester during this period, and the surviving contemporary registers for London, Norwich, Bath and Wells and Salisbury do not include ordination lists. In some instances there are gaps in the record, for example in Winchester in 1319–20 and in Worcester during parts of the 1340s. No record of the York diocesan ordination in Thirsk parish church on Whit Saturday 1347 survives beyond the heading and the names of twenty-eight men who produced proof of their orders to the archiepiscopal clerks, together with two rough inserted sheets; the suffragan bishop who celebrated the ordination failed to return the names. Only the list of unbeneficed priests survives for a Lincoln ordination in the second half of 1347. Incompleteness may be suspected in a number of other cases. On the other hand, the Worcester register of Walter Reynolds includes ordinations which he undertook in the diocese of London on behalf of the bishop in December 1308, February 1309 and June 1311. The register of John Kirkby, bishop of Carlisle, includes ordinations which he celebrated for the bishops of Lincoln, Durham, York, Coventry and Lichfield and London, for which only the Durham and two of the York ordinations are also recorded in the registers of the host bishops: the evidence of his London ordination is especially valuable.[7] Gaps in the holding,

[6] Davis, *Clergy in London*; W. J. Dohar, 'Medieval Ordination Lists: the Origins of a Record', *Archives*, 20 (1992), 17–35. D. M. Smith, 'Lost Archiepiscopal Registers of York: the Evidence of Five Medieval Inventories', *Borthwick Institute Bulletin*, I, i, 31–7. For Bath and Wells, see D. M. Smith, *Guide*, 30–2.

[7] York, Register of Archbishop Zouche, Borthwick Institute of Historical Research, Register 10A fol. 18; Lincoln, Register of Bishop Gynwell, Lincoln Archives Office, Episcopal Register IXD fol. 1; R. A. Wilson (ed.), *Register of Walter Reynolds, Bishop of Worcester, 1308–1313* (Worcestershire Historical Society, 1927), 102–4, 123–9; R. L. Storey (ed.), *Register of John Kirkby, Bishop of Carlisle, 1332–1352, and the Register of John Ross, Bishop of Carlisle, 1325–32* (Canterbury and York Society, lxxix, 1993), 28–9, 38–9, 45–6, 47–55, 65–7, 95, 100–7, 108 (beneficed clergy only), 109–10, 147–54, 169–75.

as opposed to the recording, of ordinations, occur during the vacancy of a see, although there are examples of ordinations being held at these times by authority of the archbishop of Canterbury or other keepers of the spiritualities.[8] There might also be periods when the bishop was otherwise engaged, for example on royal business, or indisposed, in which case he might commission another bishop. This might be another English diocesan such as Reynolds and Kirkby but more often an Irish or Welsh bishop or a suffragan with a nominal see *in partibus* was commissioned, in which case the names of men ordained were usually entered into the diocesan bishop's register and were probably in many cases compiled by the diocesan staff.

The days assigned by canon law for ordinations were the Saturdays of the four embertides – Saturday following the first Sunday in Lent, Saturday after Whitsunday, and the Saturdays of the embertides following Holy Cross Day and the feast of St Lucy. In addition, ordinations of small numbers of men, usually restricted to beneficed clergy and the religious but occasionally including one or two unbeneficed men, were sometimes held on the Saturday before Passion Sunday, on Holy Saturday or, exceptionally, at other times. The frequency of ordinations varied from diocese to diocese and bishop to bishop. In Ely, between 1338 and 1347, Simon Montacute (1337–45) and Thomas de Lisle (1345–61) held major ordinations once a year, except in 1338, when Montacute, newly arrived from Worcester, ordained in March and September. In Coventry and Lichfield, Roger Northburgh (1322–58) held ordinations in the 1320s and 1330s three or four times in most years.[9]

Completeness and accuracy can be gauged by the format and appearance of the register, the absence of unexplained gaps and the proportion of men who can be traced through all three orders. Where the York and Durham registers can be compared with Kirkby's Carlisle register there are a few differences which seem to reflect scribal errors but most of the variations are the result of policy decisions as to the inclusion or exclusion of certain categories of ordinand. Acolytes or members of religious orders may be omitted from Kirkby's own register but included in the register of the host diocese. In some instances Kirkby omits men from the host diocese, who are included in the registers of their own dioceses, and, conversely, Carlisle men are omitted from two lists in the Durham registers.[10]

The diocese is a natural basis for the study of ordinations and there have been several studies of individual dioceses. The present study relates to the geographical pattern of clerical recruitment before the Black Death and covers all the dioceses for which systematic evidence survives between 1282 and 1348. The evidence varies to some extent from diocese to diocese and between the earlier and later parts of the period but the evidence from different dioceses is often complementary even though at times frustrating in its *lacunae.*

A man must be ordained by, or with the authority of, his diocesan bishop. He might be ordained in a diocese other than his own by obtaining letters dimissory from his diocesan bishop or, in the bishop's absence, his vicar-general. When the see

[8] See, for example, J. W. Willis Bund (ed.), *Register of the Diocese of Worcester during the vacancy of the see, usually called "Registrum Sede Vacante"* (Worcestershire Historical Society, 1897), xl–lii, 21–6, 153–169.

[9] Ely, Register of Bishop Montacute and Bishop de Lisle, Cambridge University Library, EDR G1/1 fols. (first series) 97–119, (second series) 91–101; Lichfield Record Office, B/A/1/1 fols. 143–216.

[10] As shown by the editor, R.L. Storey, *Reg. Kirkby*, 38–9, 45, 109–10, 147, 174–5.

was vacant the keeper of the spiritualities would issue letters dimissory. In general, letters dimissory are less systematically recorded than ordinations in bishops' registers, and it is more difficult to judge whether the records are complete.[11] Receipt of letters dimissory is not proof that a man was in fact ordained elsewhere: there are many instances in which a man obtained them, presumably as a precaution, and then proceeded to ordination in his own diocese. Also, a grant made to a 'clerk' for promotion 'to minor and all holy orders' may not be evidence that the man had already decided to proceed to holy orders. In the ordination lists men from other dioceses ordained with letters dimissory are almost always identified as such and can easily be excluded from calculations of the number of men of a diocese who were ordained in that diocese.[12] The more difficult question is the extent to which ordinands from a diocese might escape our eye, and thereby corrupt our statistics, by being ordained to all three orders in other dioceses with letters dimissory. In practice it appears that relatively few men obtained all their orders outside their native diocese unless there was a lengthy gap in the holding of ordinations. In Ely, for example, 124 men received letters dimissory to higher orders between March 1338, Bishop Montacute's first ordination, and June 1348. Ninety-seven of these 124 appear in at least one of the Ely ordination lists during this period out of a total of 415 men who appear in the list. Although, therefore, 97 (23%) of the 415 Ely men ordained in the diocese also received letters dimissory, the total number of Ely men ordained is increased by only the 27 who never, up to 1348, appear in any Ely list of ordinations: more than half of these occur between December 1347 and June 1348. Because of the lack of ordination lists for some of the other dioceses, and in particular the neighbouring dioceses of London and Norwich, we cannot determine how many of these Ely men were actually ordained elsewhere. In larger dioceses the picture is usually similar, although with a rather higher percentage of 'missing' men. In Worcester under Bishops Adam Orleton (1327–33) and Simon Montacute (1334–7) it seems that men receiving letters dimissory may add 10–15% to the number of men ordained by those bishops.[13] Used with care, letters dimissory entered in a general register and the recording in ordination lists of men ordained with letters dimissory can reveal valuable information about ordinands in dioceses for which ordination lists have not survived.

Dioceses varied considerably in size, wealth and population. For comparative purposes the 1334 lay subsidy provides a measure of wealth for the greater part

[11] For example, for Lincoln in *Register of Bishop Sutton* and Register of Bishop Dalderby, Lincoln Archives Office, Episcopal Register III, they appear in chronological order in general memoranda registers; in the register of Dalderby's successor, Burghersh, Lincoln Archives Office, Episcopal Register V, almost the whole period is covered by a single 64-folio section of the register: *Register of Bishop Sutton,* iii–vi; Reg. Burghersh fols. 84–147, 156–9. The letters dimissory of Burghersh's successor, Thomas Bek, also form a single section, Lincoln Archives Office, Episcopal Register VII fols. 141–158.

[12] As with any general statements as to the accuracy of registration there are exceptions but these appear to be few.

[13] For letters dimissory: Ely, Register of Bishop Montacute and de Lisle, fols. (first series) 96–7, (second series) 85–6; R. M. Haines (ed.), *Calendar of the Register of Adam de Orleton, Bishop of Worcester, 1327–1333* (Worcestershire Historical Society and Historical Manuscripts Commission Joint Publication, 27, 1979), 221–6; R. M. Haines (ed.), *Calendar of the Register of Simon de Montacute, Bishop of Worcester, 1334–1337* (Worcestershire Historical Society, new series 15, 1996), 307–23.

of the country. Glasscock demonstrates its general acceptability as a comparative measure of lay wealth and Schofield shows by use of the *Taxatio Ecclesiastica* of 1291 that the pattern of relative prosperity and poverty is not seriously altered, at least at county level, if clerical property is taken into account. Clerical wealth and the vagaries of assessment may produce misleading results for smaller areas. More serious is the omission of Cheshire, County Durham, the Cinque Ports and western parts of the diocese of Hereford, and also the exemption of the Devon and Cornwall tinners. Cumberland, Westmorland and Northumberland were excused the 1334 subsidy because of the effects of Scottish incursions and their assessments date from 1336. The lay subsidy may also be taken as a reasonable surrogate for population. At county level there is a broad correlation between assessment in 1334/1336 and population recorded in the 1377 poll tax, despite the chronological interval and intervening demographic disaster, although most of the northern and western counties with highland terrain, Cumberland surprisingly excepted, rank lower in 1334/1336 than in 1377.[14]

One complicating factor is the existence of detached portions of dioceses and of 'peculiar' jurisdictions within dioceses. The archbishop of Canterbury exercised immediate jurisdiction over the deanery of Shoreham in west Kent, the deaneries of South Malling, Pagham and Tarring in Sussex, the deanery of Bocking in Suffolk and Essex, the deanery of Croydon in Surrey and Middlesex, the deanery of Risborough in Buckinghamshire and the deanery of Arches in London, which lay geographically in the dioceses of Rochester, Chichester, Norwich, Winchester, Lincoln and London. Men from these places are recorded as ordinands in the archbishop's register and, if they are ordained in another diocese, bear the archbishop's letters dimissory. The bishop of Rochester exercised a similar jurisdiction in the parishes of Freckenham (Suffolk) and Isleham (Cambridgeshire) and there were other examples, including the archbishop of York's jurisdictions of Hexhamshire in Northumberland and Churchdown near Gloucester. Because of the complex intertwining of Canterbury and Rochester in west Kent our analyses will treat these dioceses, including their detached parts, as a single entity.[15]

Within dioceses there were peculiar jurisdictions in which the bishop's authority was curtailed to a greater or lesser degree. These exemptions seem rarely to have extended to the exclusion of the diocesan bishop's control over secular ordinands. The two heads of exempt jurisdictions who appear to have consistently maintained the power to grant their own letters dimissory were the abbots of St Albans, with an extensive jurisdiction mainly in Hertfordshire, and the abbot of Bury St Edmunds for men of that town. The abbots of Evesham appear, unless the Worcester registers mislead us, to have maintained this aspect of their peculiar jurisdiction only fitfully, and men from other peculiar jurisdictions appear, with very few, mostly

[14] R. E. Glasscock (ed.), *The Lay Subsidy of 1334* (London, 1975); C. C. Fenwick (ed.), *The Poll Taxes of 1377, 1379 and 1381* (3 vols., London, 1998, 2001, 2005); R. S. Schofield, 'The Geographical Distribution of Wealth in England, 1334–1649', *Economic History Review*, 2nd series, 18 (1965), 483–510.

[15] I. J. Churchill, *Canterbury Administration I* (London, 1933), especially 63–4; Smith, *Guide*, 1, 171, 232. The Ordnance Survey maps, *Monastic Britain, North Sheet* and *South Sheet* (Chessington, 1955), show diocesan boundaries, including detached parts of dioceses.

early, exceptions, as ordinands in their own dioceses without letters dimissory or, if ordained elsewhere, bearing the letters dimissory of their diocesan bishop.[16]

There are two possible ways of counting numbers of ordinands. If all men passed through the orders of subdeacon, deacon and priest in their own diocese we could take the number of men ordained priest as the total. Numbers of subdeacons and deacons would be only slightly higher. Because of the men ordained outside their native diocese with letters dimissory this calculation gives an under-estimate of the number of ordinands, and the extent of the under-estimate will differ from diocese to diocese and from time to time. Dioceses with frequent ordinations are likely to be used for all three ordinations by a high proportion of ordinands whereas in a diocese with less frequent ordinations a higher proportion of men would use a neighbouring bishop for at least one order. It might also be the case that men on the borders of a large diocese would be more likely to obtain letters dimissory in order to be ordained in a neighbouring diocese. A diocese with several vacancies of see would also 'lose' a significant proportion of men for at least one ordination, as in Worcester in 1333–4 and 1337 when some subdeacons and deacons delayed promotion to higher orders but many are found in the Hereford registers and some in other dioceses. The number of different men appearing for ordination provides a more accurate figure for comparative purposes. There are two difficulties with this. By omitting men who received all three orders outside their diocese it, like the alternative method but to a much lesser extent, gives us an under-estimate. The other problem is that occasionally we may fail to distinguish between two different men with the same name but we may on the other hand make a false distinction when one man appears at different ordinations bearing different names.

Ordinands' names may take a number of forms but most men are named in one of three ways. In the diocese of Hereford Roger Broun of Yarpole was ordained subdeacon in May 1328, Roger Broun was ordained deacon in December 1328 and Roger of Yarpole was ordained priest in September 1329.[17] In this case, the three forms of the name in the Hereford register clearly relate to the same man. In other cases we cannot make a certain identification and by counting a man twice might over-estimate the number of different men being ordained. John Mogge was ordained subdeacon in Exeter diocese in March 1314 to a title provided by sir Robert de Horton. John de Nymeton was ordained deacon in December 1314 and priest in September 1315 to the same title. Because the title was the same we are alerted to the possibility of John Mogge and John de Nymeton being identical but the link is only established in the London episcopal register when John Mugge of Bishops Nympton was instituted as rector of St Clement Danes in 1325.[18] The danger of identifying two men with the same name as a single individual is greatest in the

[16] For some of the main peculiar jurisdictions see the Ordnance Survey maps cited above. Dalderby made at least one grant of letters dimissory to a man who appears to have come from St Albans: 'Adam dictus atte Sterte of St Albans', clerk, who received letters dimissory for all minor and holy orders on 14 December 1309 (Register of Bishop Dalderby fol. 171v); but at this time the newly elected abbot was still seeking papal confirmation.

[17] W. W. Capes (ed.), *Registrum Thome de Charlton, Episcopi Herefordensis A.D. MCCCXXVII–MCCCXLIV* (Cantilupe Society, 1912, Canterbury and York Society, ix, 1913), 99, 103, 107.

[18] *Register of Bishop Stapeldon*, 496, 501, 505; R. C. Fowler (ed.), *Registrum Radulphi Baldock, Gilberti Segrave, Ricardi Newport, et Stephani Gravesend, episcoporum Londoniensium A.D. MCCCIV–MCCCXXXVIII* (Canterbury and York Society, vii, 1911), 276.

earlier registers where the simple forms of name, often with common Christian name and surname, such as John de Staunton or Robert de Preston, are more often found and when titles are often omitted. In later registers the more complex form becomes more common and when in many dioceses titles from religious houses replace patrimonial titles it is often possible to identify ordinands by means of their titles.

At diocesan level it is desirable to adopt both approaches as counterchecks on each other, although in practice the differences are not very great, and for analysis at more local levels it is best simply to use the number of different men. Because counting individuals includes men who appear as deacons and priests at the beginning of a series of lists and also men who appear as subdeacons and deacons at the end of a series the effective period being studied under this approach is approximately two years greater than the period covered by the lists and if there is a significant gap, as in Carlisle, Winchester and Canterbury, the period should be increased by two more years (four in the case of Canterbury which has two gaps). Where the series covers only a short period we need to be aware that numbers of ordinands tend to be particularly high at the first ordination after a vacancy. This is not seriously misleading if we have a long series of lists but it tends to magnify numbers if we have records for only a few years. For all these reasons there are dangers in drawing over-precise conclusions from the evidence.

In dioceses with comprehensive records for a reasonable period and with regular ordinations we may expect the number of ordinations to be over twice the number of separate individuals recorded: Carlisle, Ely, Exeter, Coventry and Lichfield, Rochester, Hereford, and Lincoln in the 1290s. York, Durham, Worcester, Winchester and Canterbury are a little below this level but, except for Durham, these include periods with minor but significant gaps in the holding or recording of ordinations. Lincoln in the 1340s is well below, but the period is a short one and includes an incomplete list.

Comparing numbers of ordinands with wealth we find that a number of dioceses show a ratio of one ordinand per annum to £300–400 taxable wealth, or one 'act of ordination' to £140–170. York, Coventry and Lichfield, Worcester, Ely and Exeter, and Lincoln in the 1340s, are all in this range. Hereford seems to have produced a greater number of ordinands, perhaps one ordinand to less than £200 or one 'act of ordination' to less than £100. The Hereford subsidy assessment excludes parts of the diocese, for which we have needed to make a speculative allowance, but there is no room to doubt that the diocese was producing a remarkably high number of ordinands. Durham and, especially, Carlisle, produce significantly fewer ordinands. This may suggest that the 1336 assessment made too little allowance for the ravages of the Scots, and may well also reflect the very approximate valuation suggested for County Durham. The other dioceses which produced relatively low numbers of ordinands were those in the south-east: Canterbury and Rochester, and Winchester. They appear to have produced only one ordinand per annum to £1,100–1,400 or one 'act of ordination' to £600.

The diocese of Lincoln presents conflicting evidence. In the 1290s it appears nearer to the Winchester figure, whereas in the 1340s it produced a number of ordinands similar *pro rata* to the norm. The large dioceses for which long series of lists survive, Worcester and Coventry and Lichfield, show fluctuations during the period but no dramatic changes, and numbers of Winchester ordinands in 1346–8 are similar to those earlier in the century. Numbers of letters dimissory issued by Bishop

TABLE 1. Dioceses, Ordinands and Movable Wealth (£)

Diocese	Ordinands	Ordinations	Movable wealth 1334/6	Years of Ordinations	Movable wealth x Years*	Movable wealth x Years/Ordinands*	Movable wealth x Years	Movable wealth x Years/Ordinations
Carlisle	367	763	8,730	46	436,500	1189	401,580	526
Durham	291	491	10,246	14	163,936	563	143,444	292
York	1136	2150	50,000	6	400,000	352	300,000	140
Ely	415	845	13,810	10	165,720	399	138,100	163
Winchester	655	1247	26,764	30	909,976	1389	802,920	644
Canterbury and Rochester	1042	1845	32,239	33	1,225,082	1176	1,063,887	577
Exeter	751	1732	19,784	13	296,760	395	257,192	148
Coventry and Lichfield	5956	13,047	39,875	48	1,993,750	335	1,914,000	147
Lincoln 1290s	916	1880	128,267	9	1,410,937	1540	1,154,403	614
Lincoln 1340s	1963	3207	128,267	4	769,602	392	513,068	160
Worcester	6548	12,554	32,400	66	2,203,200	336	2,138,400	170
Hereford	1596	3229	13,500	20	297,000	186	270,000	84

*In columns 6 and 7 the number of years is increased by 2 for the reasons explained on p. 59; for Carlisle, Winchester, Canterbury and Rochester, see below.

The table should be taken as indicative of orders of magnitude; there are many detailed caveats as to the evidence and in particular the figures for those dioceses for which evidence survives only for short periods need to be treated with caution. The Lincoln 1340s period (1345–8) includes major ordinations in both 1345 and 1348: because of the short overall period of time covered the calculations treat the period as covering four years.

Carlisle: col. 6 has 50 as divisor to cover the break 1324–32.

Durham: Co. Durham was not included in the Lay Subsidy. Its movable wealth has been taken as approximately £4 per square mile, similar to the North Riding, rather less than Cumberland but greater than Northumberland and Westmorland, and giving a value of £4,000. This may somewhat exaggerate its lay wealth because of the high proportion of ecclesiastical property.

York: there is a small degree of estimation because of the difficulty of aligning the north-western boundary and the detached jurisdictions with the Lay Subsidy units.

Winchester: col. 6 has 34 as divisor because of the break 1333–46.

Canterbury and Rochester: cols. 4 and 6 have 33 and 38 years as divisors based on Canterbury lists covering 34 years with two gaps and Rochester, a much smaller diocese, covering 28 years. The detached parts of both dioceses are included, except for the Deanery of Arches, for which no meaningful estimate can be made in view of the artificially low fine paid by London in 1334.

Coventry and Lichfield: Cheshire was not included in the Lay Subsidy. Its movable wealth has been taken as approximately £11 per square mile, similar *pro rata* to Derbyshire and Staffordshire, and greater than Lancashire south of the Ribble, and giving a value of £7,000.

Worcester: col. 1 uses the figures given by Simon Towneley for Bishop Gifford, 'Unbeneficed Clergy in the Thirteenth Century: Two English Dioceses' in *Studies in Clergy and Ministry in Medieval England* (York, 1991), pp. 47, 51; the published edition is somewhat confused.

Hereford: the hundred of Clun and those parts of the diocese which were in Wales were excluded from the Lay Subsidy and a significant part of western Herefordshire seems also not to have been included; £1,500 has been added to the value of the diocese to allow for this. The published edition of Bishop Charlton's register does not appear to distinguish between religious ordinands and seculars ordained with religious house titles. The ordinand's status is usually clear from the context and the numbers involved are small: Dr Dohar, who worked from the original register, gives a total for priests which is similar to my own calculation but does not give separate figures for subdeacons and deacons (W. J. Dohar, *The Black Death and Pastoral Leadership: the diocese of Hereford in the Fourteenth Century* (Philadelphia, 1995), tables 4.1, 4.2; figures 4.2, 4.3).

Burghersh (1320–40) suggest that Lincoln ordinands may well have reached 3–400 per annum by the 1330s, which is the level reached in the 1340s.[19] The low number of ordinands in Lincoln in the 1290s may be explained by Bishop Sutton's exercising tight control over the standard of ordinands. In 1292 his letter stating his intention to hold an ordination at Whitsun stressed the need to ensure that candidates' manner of life was satisfactory and that each had a title which was true and not feigned. While statements of this kind are not uncommon, there is specific evidence of Sutton acting against men with feigned titles or committing other breaches of ordination canon law. He was not only, like any other reforming bishop concerned for observance of canon law and his own rights, opposed to men being ordained by other bishops without letters dimissory but was manifestly suspicious of their qualifications. He suspended Walter of Brackley for five years for being given the first tonsure by the bishop of Glasgow and the other minor orders by the bishop of Worcester without letters dimissory and for being ordained subdeacon and deacon by 'the bishop of Lincoln' (presumably himself) on a false title and priest by the same bishop on a title obtained from a religious house on condition that its use was to be purely formal. Robert of Warmington, ordained acolyte and subdeacon by the bishop of Moray and deacon and priest by the bishop of Ross without letters dimissory, was required to minister as deacon and study grammar and other things necessary for the priesthood for a year, after which he was to return to the bishop for 'promotion'. A year later he returned and was dispensed. Richard Challen of Theddlethorpe was dispensed for ministering in the holy orders which he had received from the bishop of Dunblane without letters dimissory and permitted to minister in the orders for a year but was also to study grammar and other things necessary to the priesthood. A year later he was examined in grammar and licensed to minister indefinitely subject to good behaviour. Lincoln was precocious in its very high proportion of ordinands with titles from religious houses, which may reflect an attempt to ensure that titles were genuine and not fictitious or collusive, and Sutton's registrar carefully records archidiaconal testimony to lay and patrimonial titles.[20] It may be significant that numbers of ordinands in Coventry and Lichfield diocese are lower by about 40% in 1324–7, when that diocese moved sharply from patrimonial and lay to religious house titles. Sutton's register is also noteworthy for the high proportion of letters dimissory granted to men who do not appear to have been ordained to any order in their native diocese. Out of 307 men given letters dimissory to higher orders, approximately 258 do not appear in the Lincoln ordination lists, so that we may need to add over 25% to our number of Lincoln ordinands.

The overall pattern appears to be that there was a broadly similar level of ordinations in relation to wealth in a swathe of dioceses from York to Exeter. The exceptions are Carlisle and Durham in the north, impoverished by border warfare, and the south-eastern dioceses, which were wealthy and presented many opportunities for alternative employment.

Analysis at diocesan level provides a very broad picture and we need, if possible, to examine the evidence at a more local level. The evidence of ordinands' origins

[19] Lincoln, Register of Bishop Burghersh; and Bishop Bek, Lincoln Archives Office, Episcopal Register VIIB fols. 2–16; Lincoln, Register of Bishop Gynwell, Lincoln Archives Office, Episcopal Register IXD.

[20] *Register of Bishop Sutton*, iv, 6–7, cf. vii, 55; for Walter of Brackley, iii, 192; for Robert of Warmington, vi, 31–2, 111; for Richard Challen, vi, 111.

derives principally from their names. Here we are faced with three problems: whether we can identify the place to which an ordinand's name refers; whether the ordinand actually came from that place; and the origin of those ordinands who lack a place-name surname. The forms by which ordinands' names are recorded vary from diocese to diocese and from period to period. In general the form 'Roger Broun of Yarpole' becomes increasingly common by the 1330s and 1340s but it is common throughout our period for men from larger towns and cities: the diocesan registry staff recognised the need to distinguish men with the same Christian name from these places at an early date. The form 'Roger Broun' is never very common and tends in most dioceses to decline. 'Roger of Yarpole' is the normal form in the earlier part of our period but is superseded by the longer form in a number of dioceses by the 1330s and 1340s. When a place-name is in the form 'Roger Broun of Yarpole' it is reasonable to assume that the ordinand came from Yarpole. When it is in the form 'Roger of Yarpole' it is probable but by no means certain that the man actually came from that place. John de Croume, ordained subdeacon in 1321 in the diocese of Worcester, was ordained deacon in 1322 and priest in 1323 as John Crumme/Cromme of Bengeworth.[21] Toponymic surnames were often acquired when a man moved to another place and although it appears that the episcopal scribes, when they described a man as being 'of' a place, were normally at this time identifying one who came from that place and would have borne another surname locally, this is not always the case. In particular, townsmen frequently used as surnames the names of the places from which they or their parents had come. We are therefore on safer ground when the 'full form' of name is given.

Titles provide useful evidence for the origins of many ordinands when there is more than one place of a particular name. Although there are a number of factors influencing the giving of titles, geographical proximity was an important one. Religious houses generally gave titles to men from within about fifteen miles of the house; some restricted themselves to a much closer radius and only a few, in less populous areas or giving large numbers of titles, gave titles to many men from further afield. Lay titles may be even more closely geographically focused and in Durham, where the location of the property on which the title was given is often stated, we may, for example, work on the assumption that William de Elwick, ordained 1335–7 with a title from Hugh de Burden in Grindon, came from Elwick in south-east Durham, six miles from Grindon, and not Elwick in Northumberland.[22] If a diocese is small and is in a part of the country where there are not many place names common to more than one place there may be few instances where we cannot be certain of the place to which a name relates. In Ely, we can be reasonably sure of the origins of over 95% of ordinands; we sometimes need to treat adjacent places such as the Swaffhams or the Eversdons as one although the Ely clerks normally give place names in full including modifiers. In a large diocese with a number of common place names we have more difficulty. In York, for example, with its multiple examples of names such as Bolton, Burton, Kir(k)by, Middleton and Thornton, we are uncertain of the origins of about 35% of ordinands. Lincoln presents two problems. Because of its size there are duplications even of uncommon place names: Ashwell

21 E. H. Pearce (ed.), *Register of Thomas de Cobham, Bishop of Worcester, 1317–1327* (Worcestershire Historical Society, 1930), 115, 144, 160.

22 T. D. Hardy (ed.), *Registrum Palatinum Dunelmense*, iii (Rolls Series, 1875), 170.

in Hertfordshire and Rutland; Wing in Buckinghamshire and Rutland. In these cases we can often identify the probable origin from the title: John son of John the Clerk of Ashwell, ordained subdeacon in June 1348 with a title from Sempringham priory, was probably from Rutland, whereas Thomas of Ashwell, ordained in 1291 with a title from Newnham priory, Bedfordshire, and William Ingold of Ashwell, ordained deacon in March 1348 with a title from Caldwell priory, also Bedfordshire, were probably from Hertfordshire.[23] Also, in Lincolnshire and to a lesser extent Leicestershire there are a number of common names of Danish origin, such as Somer(s)by, Normanby, Osgodby and Claxby. In many of these cases we can identify the county of origin but cannot safely give a more precise place of origin. We can with reasonable probability identify more than 85% of place names borne by Lincoln diocese ordinands and in the 1340s we have the added security that almost all of the ordinands are recorded with both surname and place of origin.

At sub-diocesan level and beginning in the north we find that in Carlisle and Durham the origin of ordinands reflects in general the distribution of population. In Carlisle the city itself and the towns of Penrith and Appleby provide at least 68 of the 367 ordinands, and most of the others come from the low-lying area in the north of the diocese stretching south-west from Carlisle to the diocesan boundary near Workington or from the valleys of the Eden, Petterill and Lowther towards the south-east. In Durham, ordinands come mainly from the eastern side of the diocese. Newcastle (eight men at least) and Durham City (nine men) predominate. In Northumberland the towns of Alnwick and Morpeth produced three and four men respectively. In County Durham, the main sources of ordinands other than Durham City seem to have been mainly those towns which were still the largest ones in the sixteenth century; Darlington and the Aucklands produced six men each, Barnard Castle five and Staindrop four, although Brancepeth seems only to have produced one. Hartlepool, a port and market town, produced four ordinands.[24] Outside the towns there is a strong concentration of ordinands from County Durham south-east of a line between Wearmouth and Barnard Castle. The influence of Newcastle was greater than is indicated by the eight ordinands whose names identify them as coming from there. Thirty-seven men obtained titles based on property in Newcastle or from laymen identifiable as Newcastle residents, and many of these ordinands, whether without a place-name surname or with a place-name surname from elsewhere, may have been Newcastle men. The diocese of York covered virtually the whole of Yorkshire and Nottinghamshire together with Lancashire north of the Ribble and south Cumberland and Westmorland. Despite the problems caused by common place names it seems fairly clear that south Nottinghamshire produced a higher proportion of ordinands than its wealth would suggest. In Yorkshire the East and West Ridings seem to produce more ordinands than the North Riding, even in proportion to wealth. The north-western parts of the diocese produced significantly fewer.

The pattern in the diocese of Lincoln is especially interesting. Between the 1290s and 1340s the number of men ordained per annum increased between three- and fourfold. The increase seems not to have been quite evenly distributed across the diocese but differences may reflect casual factors, especially given the short

23 *Register of Bishop Sutton*, vii,19; Register of Bishop Gynwell, fols. 3, 6.
24 *An Historical Atlas of County Durham* (Durham, 1992), 24, 40.

period covered in the 1340s. What is significant, and common to both periods, is the difference between different parts of the diocese. Bedfordshire, Buckinghamshire, Huntingdonshire and Rutland in the 1340s produced numbers of ordinands roughly comparable with the overall averages for York, Ely, Exeter, Coventry and Lichfield and Worcester. Northamptonshire produced 50% more and Leicestershire twice as many whereas Lincolnshire produced only two-thirds as many ordinands, Hertfordshire less than half as many and Oxfordshire less than one-third as many. Although Lincolnshire may be affected by the higher proportion of men whose origin cannot be identified, it is clear that relatively few men were coming forward for ordination from Hertfordshire and Oxfordshire. Although the absolute numbers are much smaller the pattern is equally recognisable in the 1290s. When we examine the pattern more closely we see that south and east of a line running immediately south of Stevenage, Dunstable and Bicester and then south-west to the Thames near Eynsham the number of ordinands reduces sharply.

Hundreds and wapentakes, or groups of these units, are a convenient basis for more detailed examination. As we focus on smaller areas we are more subject to the effects of misleading subsidy assessments or the exceptional production of ordinands in one or two parishes at particular dates. The presence of a town or large village with a common name may render analysis impossible. Also, hundreds and wapentakes are not necessarily coherent geographical entities. Nevertheless, grouped together if necessary, they reveal interesting patterns.

In Buckinghamshire the southern and central hundreds – Burnham, Stoke, Desborough, Risborough, Stone, Aylesbury, Ixhill, Waddesdon, Ashenden, Yardley and Cottesloe – assessed at £5,341 produced a mere handful of ordinands.[25] Only seven men in the 1290s and seven in the 1340s can be definitely attributed to these hundreds. Some men who cannot be located with certainty may derive from this area although it is striking that the men whose names associate them with an Eton or Eaton have titles which do not suggest Eton in Buckinghamshire as their probable origin. The towns of Aylesbury (£127), Wendover (£95), High Wycombe (£90), Amersham (£25) and Marlow (£23) provided four ordinands in the 1290s and nine in the 1340s. The northern hundreds – Buckingham, Seckloe, Moulsoe, Rowley, Stodfold, Bunsty and Mursley – assessed at £3,930 produced at least 31 men in the 1290s and 86 (one ordinand per annum for £274) in the 1340s. There is a similar pattern in eastern Oxfordshire. The south-eastern hundreds – Binfield, Langtree, Ewelme, Lewknor, Thame, Pyrton and Dorchester (£3,764) – produced five ordinands in the 1290s and four in the 1340s.The northern hundreds – Bloxham and Banbury (£1,937) – produced four in the 1290s and 25 in the 1340s, and the northern parts of Ploughley and Wotton together with, in the 1340s, the western hundreds of Chadlington and Bampton, provided most of the others. Only one ordinand in the 1290s and two in the 1340s are named as 'of Oxford' (£914) and none 'of Henley' (£60). In the part of Hertfordshire which lay within the diocese of Lincoln the picture is similar. The northern hundreds of Odsey and Hitchin and the northern part of Broadwater provide most of the ordinands. Dacorum and Hertford hundreds produce few. The other counties in the diocese do not in general show such sharp contrasts although some areas seem to show higher or lower levels than their neigh-

25 These assessments are recalculated, where necessary, to exclude areas outside the bishop's jurisdiction and are rounded to the nearest pound.

bours. Kesteven in Lincolnshire seems rather low but the only major exception is the Parts of Holland which, with more than one-fifth of the wealth of Lincolnshire, produced only one-fifteenth of the Lincolnshire ordinands.

Although relatively few men from the diocese of Lincoln in 1345–7 proceeded to all three orders outside the diocese, it is reasonable to ask whether in as large a diocese as Lincoln there might be a tendency for ordinands in the distant corners of the diocese to seek the convenience of ordination in a neighbouring diocese and for the southern part of the diocese to be under-represented in the Lincoln lists for that reason. The men who obtained letters dimissory in the 1290s and in 1345–7 who do not appear in the Lincoln ordination lists largely reflect the pattern of the Lincoln lists. They show a rather higher proportion of men from the far south of the diocese but not sufficient to alter the overall pattern. A longer timespan is provided by the 432-folio miscellaneous register of John Dalderby (1300–20), in which letters dimissory are entered in chronological order among the other entries, and the 64-folio section of the register of Henry Burghersh which is devoted to letters dimissory. These are not a complete record – men appear in the ordination lists of other dioceses with Lincoln letters dimissory who do not appear in Burghersh's register – but they provide us with over 4,000 names, not necessarily typical of the whole body of ordinands in their geographical spread but with the potential to support or qualify the evidence of the ordination lists. For the early part of Dalderby's episcopate numbers are small and probably represent only a small proportion of Lincoln ordinands but in 1311 over two hundred men received letters dimissory and although the number fell thereafter it was again around or over 150 in 1316–18. Numbers are again low in the early years of Burghersh's episcopate but from July 1329 until his death there are more than 100 names in every year except 1333 and the number rises to approximately 293 in 1335, 414 in 1336, 398 in 1337 and 247 in 1338, a period in which it seems probable that all Lincoln ordinands needed letters dimissory because of the bishop's administrative commitments.[26] Because titles are hardly ever given in Burghersh's register and are frequently not given in Dalderby's, we cannot identify the probable origins of as high a proportion of men as in the ordination lists but increasingly over the period names are in the extended form so that we can assume that, provided that we can identify the place, the ordinand actually came from there.

In Burghersh and Dalderby's registers the southern and central hundreds of Buckinghamshire provide at least 80 ordinands, although they came preponderantly from the more central hundreds. Only eleven of them came from the Thamesside hundreds of Burnham, Desborough and Stoke (£1,757). Aylesbury (11), Wendover (9), High Wycombe (11), Marlow (5) and Amersham (1) added thirty-seven men. The northern hundreds produced 143 ordinands, which is still a significantly higher proportion in relation to wealth. In Oxfordshire Bloxham and Banbury produced 59 men, whereas the western hundreds of Chadlington and Bampton (£5,513) produced 92, still a lower rate but higher than the ordination lists would have suggested; the Worcester registers show many men from these hundreds being ordained in that diocese. Wootton, Ploughley and Bullingdon (£7,042) produced 60, Dorchester, Thame, Pyrton and Lewknor (£2,080) add 19, and the eastern Thamesside hundreds

26 Lincoln Reg. Burghersh: there are some duplications of entries and some instances in which the same man either certainly or probably appears in more than one entry.

of Binfield, Langtree and Ewelme(£1,684) may have produced as few as five men. Twenty men 'of Oxford' and seven 'of Henley' appear. The pattern in Hertfordshire is similar, with one exception. Hertford itself produced eight men who obtained letters dimissory from Dalderby and eleven from Burghersh, but nine of the latter (eight 'clerks' and one man whose order is not stated) were granted letters dimissory to minor as well as holy orders, and it is possible that not all of them advanced to higher orders. The overall picture in the other counties is of a fairly level pattern of production, with Huntingdonshire and Hertfordshire producing proportionately more men, perhaps because of the proximity of Ely and London dioceses, and Kesteven fewer, but Holland again stands out for the low number of ordinands produced. In particular, Boston was assessed at £1,100 and can only be shown to have produced two ordinands between 1345 and 1348. Including the 1290s and the letters dimissory from 1290 to 1347 we can find only seven ordinands whose names indicate that they came from Boston, although we need as always to be careful in drawing negative conclusions.

Whatever the weaknesses of the evidence to support precise analysis, at least without very detailed examination of each locality, the broad outlines are clear. These are given a measure of support from the relatively low attendances at ordinations held at Wycombe by Bishops Sutton and Gynwell, and at Hertford and Dorchester by Bishop Sutton, although these were all held in December and may reflect a more general tendency for December ordinations in this diocese to be less well attended. The evidence of Lincoln men with letters dimissory ordained in other dioceses is in accordance with the overall geographical pattern and, in providing an even earlier date for its inception, extends it backwards into the 1280s. In Canterbury diocese, a number of north Buckinghamshire men were ordained in that period: Richard of Olney in 1284, Ralph of Olney in 1289, John clerk of Olney in 1287–8, William of Great Linford in 1288, William of Newport Pagnell, 1287–8, John of Lavendon, 1287–8, Hugh of Lathbury, 1288, Martin of Newport Pagnell, 1288–9, William of Olney, 1288, and Walter of Lathbury, 1288–9. This small area of north Buckinghamshire provided ten of at most 34 unbeneficed Lincoln men ordained in Canterbury under Pecham.[27]

To the east of Lincoln diocese, ordinands in Ely were fairly evenly distributed but with rather higher numbers from Armingford hundred and neighbouring parishes in south-western Cambridgeshire. Ely provided twenty-eight men and Cambridge fourteen.

The most striking feature in the diocese of Worcester is the large number of ordinands from eastern Gloucestershire, in and around the Cotswolds. In the sixty-six years of Worcester lists Salmonsbury hundred between Stow on the Wold and the Oxfordshire border, valued at £872, produced almost 500 ordinands. To its south Brightwells-Barrow hundred (£989), bordering Oxfordshire and Wiltshire and including Lechlade and Fairford, produced almost 300. These amount to one ordinand per annum to £120 (Salmonsbury) and £210 (Brightwells-Barrow). The hundreds to the north, Kiftsgate (£1,688) bordering south-west Warwickshire and south-east Worcestershire, and Holford and Greston (£888) bordering south-east Worcestershire, produced about 300 and 160 respectively, or one ordinand per

27 F. N. Davis (ed.), *The Register of John Pecham Archbishop of Canterbury 1279–1292* (Canterbury and York Society, lxiv, lxv, 1968, 1969), i, 215, 246, 249, 253; ii, 3, 5, 6, 8–9, 12–13, 18, 20–22.

annum to £360–370. Bradley to the west and Crowthorne to the south also produced about one ordinand to £350–400 value. Some additions may need to be made for men of uncertain origin and for possibly misleading names, but most of the major place-names in these hundreds are unique in the diocese and the pattern is similar throughout the period covered by the lists. By contrast the hundreds of the Vale of Severn produced fewer ordinands. Henbury, Grumbalds Ash, Pucklechurch, Thornbury, Berkeley, Langley and Swinestead, Bisley, and Cleeve, valued at over £5,000, may have produced as few as 300 men. There are rather more common place-names in these hundreds and in the early period there are many men without place-name surnames so that the totals are probably under-estimates but the overall pattern is unmistakable. The southern and lower Severn hundreds – Berkeley, Thornbury, Henbury, Swinestead and Langley and Pucklechurch, together with the liberty of Barton Regis – produced particularly low numbers. Outside the taxation hundreds, Gloucester (£541) produced 118 men whereas Cirencester (£250) and Winchcombe (£107), in and just under the Cotswolds respectively, produced 92 and 58 respectively. Bristol (£2,200) is only recorded as producing 69 men. It is quite possible that some men without place names, or with different topographical names, may have come from Bristol, but what is striking is the apparent decline in Bristol ordinands over the period: 37 in 1282–1302; 32 in 1303–48. The later periods see an increasing proportion of men with both surname and place name, so that it is less likely that Bristol men would be concealed under other names, and although some lists are missing in the 1340s this cannot explain the extent of the decline. Worcestershire and south-west Warwickshire produced ordinands at the same level as the neighbouring Kiftsgate and Holford and Greston hundreds, Worcestershire perhaps producing slightly more than south-west Warwickshire. Worcester (£200) produced 81 men, Warwick (£195) 68 and Stratford upon Avon (£131) 56. Droitwich (£107) appears to have produced 89 ordinands but it is possible that some 'Wych' placenames attributed to Droitwich may relate to other places. Overall the Gloucestershire average is close to the average for the northern part of the diocese but the distribution is much more uneven.

The diocese of Coventry and Lichfield covered a wider range of terrain than any other: from the Ribble in Lancashire to south Warwickshire a few miles north of Banbury. We are handicapped by the large proportion of men whom we cannot attribute with confidence to a specific place. With this caveat, which may affect the north of the diocese in particular, the Lancashire parishes seem to have a very low rate of production of clergy. This conclusion is supported by the small number of men receiving titles from houses in and near that part of the diocese. Also, although the main sponsoring house in Lancashire, Whalley, was on the Ribble in the far north of the diocese, the men it sponsored, when their places of origin can be located, are predominantly from south Lancashire near Manchester. The Warwickshire parishes produced ordinands at about the normal rate of one per annum to £400, as did the neighbouring hundred of Offlow in Staffordshire and Appletree hundred in Lower Dovedale in Derbyshire. Pirehill hundred in north-west Staffordshire is a little below this level. Three south-east Derbyshire hundreds – Repton, Litchurch and Morleyston – appear to have produced almost twice as many. The north-east Derbyshire hundred of Scarsdale and the other three Staffordshire hundreds, Seisdon and Cuttlestone in the south-west and Totmonslow in the northern dales, produced fewer men. North Shropshire seems to have produced fewer still. Cheshire was not taxed in 1334, but produced about one-third the number of Derbyshire ordinands and two-fifths the number of Staffordshire ordinands. This, for an area similar to that of Derbyshire and almost 90% that of Staffordshire, suggests a pattern of production which may be intermediate between Lancashire and the south-eastern parts of the diocese, and similar to that of High Peak in north Derbyshire.

It is not easy to analyse the distribution of ordinands in Hereford diocese because of the absence of Clun, the Welsh parishes and parts of western Herefordshire from the Lay Subsidy, but the area centred on Hereford and extending between Leominster and Ross on Wye, especially on the western side, predominates.

South of the Thames, the combination of Canterbury and Rochester because of the intermingling in west Kent and the very small size of Rochester leaves us working with figures for 34 years between 1282 and 1326 for Canterbury and 28 for Rochester, 1320–48. This, together with the absence of the Cinque Ports from the 1334 subsidy, presents us with problems of comparability. Nevertheless we can see a clear distinction between east and mid-Kent on the one hand and west Kent on the other which does not align with the diocesan boundaries. In the north-east of the county the lathe of St Augustine (£7,245) produced 189 ordinands and the adjacent lathe of Scray (£5,183) produced 131. Canterbury (£599) produced 95 ordinands and Dover forty. The lathe of Aylesford (£5,631), which included the western part of Canterbury and the eastern part of Rochester diocese, produced 123. By contrast the westernmost lathe of Sutton (£3,832) produced only 59 men. In particular the five north-western hundreds, nearest to London (Blackheath, Lesnes, Beckenham, Bromley and Ruxley (£1,944)), which included parishes in Rochester diocese and in the exempt Canterbury deanery of Shoreham, may have produced as few as seven ordinands. The southern lathe of Shipway (£3701) seems to have produced only 46 men. Like Holland in Lincolnshire it was an area of marsh and sheep-rearing. In the immediate jurisdictions Hadleigh in the deanery of Bocking sent 26 men for ordination, thirteen of them in 1314–15, Archbishop Reynolds's first two years. Only eight men can be identified by their names as coming from London although there may have been others among those ordinands who do not have place name surnames.

In the diocese of Winchester the relatively small total is made up to a remarkable extent of men from a small number of places. In Hampshire, 36 men from Winchester are joined by fifteen men from Basingstoke (all with both surname and place-name), twelve from Alton (nine with surname and place name), eight from Selborne (six with surname and place name) and fourteen perhaps from Micheldever (although only five of them had both surname and place name, so this may have been a surname in some cases); these amount to almost one-third of the number of men definitely attributable to the county. With the usual caveats as to the reliability of the crude evidence for individual places we may note that Southampton appears to have produced only seven ordinands and Portsmouth six. Surrey produced rather fewer ordinands *pro rata* than Hampshire, even allowing for the large number from Winchester itself which swells the Hampshire total, and its provision is dominated by Guildford (twelve men, nine with surname and place name) and the adjacent parish of Merrow (six, but only two with surnames).

For Exeter we have the advantage that at the first ordination, a large one at Crediton in Devon, the candidates were listed by archdeaconry. Of 243 unbeneficed ordinands, 102 were from the archdeaconry of Cornwall, 55 from Exeter, 44 from Totnes and 17 from Barnstaple, together with 25 from the peculiar jurisdictions of whom a number clearly came from Cornwall. As Devon was assessed at £13,101 and Cornwall at £6,684, Cornwall produced proportionately more ordinands than Devon. The only other ordination for which archdeaconries were identified was a small one in 1310 from which the evidence is inconclusive.[28] The evidence of place names suggests that Cornwall produced proportionately more ordinands in 1308–21 as a whole but the number of men of uncertain origin is high.

Comparisons across dioceses are difficult. The periods covered differ, there may be differences in completeness of recording and there are differences in the proportion of men with place-name surnames which can be attributed unequivocally to a particular place. The high levels of production of clergy in south-west Cambridgeshire seem to surpass the levels in neighbouring parts of Hertfordshire, Bedfordshire and Huntingdonshire, although this may in part reflect the high proportion of identifiable place names in Ely diocese. Chadlington and Bampton hundreds in Oxfordshire, although producing more ordinands than their neighbours to the south-east, are low producers compared with the west Gloucestershire hundreds, even allowing for their having higher levels of men with letters dimissory. Holland in Lincoln diocese produced far fewer ordinands than Wisbech hundred in Ely. In other areas there appear to be tempting similarities. The south-eastern Derbyshire hundreds, the south-western Nottinghamshire hundreds of Broxtowe and Rushcliffe and the neighbouring Leicestershire hundred of Goscote all seem to have produced in the region of one ordinand to £180–200 per year. There are other cases which would repay further detailed investigation.

We can take our examination of the low numbers being ordained from south-eastern dioceses further. The register of the bishops of London from 1304 to 1338, the only one surviving before 1362, does not include ordination lists or letters dimissory but we have lists of men ordained in the diocese by bishops Reynolds of Worcester and Kirkby of Carlisle. The men ordained in 1340 by Kirkby in St Paul's cathedral show a distinctive pattern. Of 51 London diocese men ordained, 20 are from the four northern Essex hundreds – Uttlesford and Freshwell, Hinckford, Lexden and Tendring – bordering Suffolk and Cambridgeshire, ten from elsewhere in Essex (two of them from Thaxted in the northern tip of Dunmow hundred), one from Hertfordshire and one from Middlesex. Eleven have only a surname and may come from London. Eight men have surnames apparently derived from places outside the diocese and these may also be London men. The earlier evidence from Reynolds' ordinations is less conclusive; the twenty-two men he ordained include one 'of London' and seven with surnames only. Four appear to come from north Essex, five from elsewhere in Essex and two from Middlesex, with three bearing place names apparently from outside the diocese who may have come from London.[29] The evidence of men from London diocese ordained in the dioceses of Canterbury, Rochester and Winchester supports that of the 1340 ordination. We might expect a preponderance of men from London and the south of the diocese; many of the Winchester ordinations took place at Southwark. In fact we find that, out of 116 men, 30 are from the four northern hundreds, 23 from other parts of Essex, ten

[28] *Register of Bishop Stapeldon*, 446–51, 469–71. The subsidy assessments given in this case are for the counties and do not allow for peculiar jurisdictions and the slight discrepancies between the diocesan and county boundaries.

[29] *Register of Bishop Kirkby*, 101–7; *Register of Bishop Reynolds*, 102–4, the names of London diocese ordinands are missing from the record of the ordination of 1311 on pp. 123–9.

from Hertfordshire, nine from Middlesex and eighteen from London, with fourteen whose place name cannot be conclusively identified and twelve without place names. The four northern Essex hundreds were assessed at £6,374 out of a total Essex assessment of £17,950, so that they are considerably over-represented. The Thamesside hundreds – Becontree, Chafford, Barstable and Rochford – assessed at £4,218 appear to have produced no ordinands in 1340, possibly one in Reynolds' register and four with letters dimissory (three from the easternmost hundred, Rochford). Nine of the Hertfordshire men are from its more northerly hundreds, Odsey, Edwinstree and Braughing. Middlesex, assessed at £4,920, had a *pro rata* production of ordinands with south and mid-Essex. London, which fined for 1,100 marks [£733 6s. 8d.] representing movable wealth of £11,000, escaped lightly in the 1334 assessment. Unless we include all the men whom we cannot attribute elsewhere to London and treat London's payment as a genuine fifteenth we have, even allowing for that part of London which was in the archbishop of Canterbury's immediate jurisdiction, a much lower proportion of ordinands than in northern Essex. The dividing line between the high-producing north of Essex and the rest of the county forms an eastern extension of the line we have seen in Lincoln diocese. The preponderance of ordinands from northern Essex is particularly notable because men from that part of the diocese were particularly likely to be ordained in the diocese of Ely: sixteen of the 39 London diocese men ordained there were from those four hundreds, together with eight from northern Hertfordshire. Salisbury provides some evidence for an east-west divide reflecting proximity to the south-east. The register of Simon of Ghent (1297–1315) suggests that relatively more letters dimissory were granted to men from western than eastern Berkshire, a conclusion which is supported by ordinations of Salisbury men in Winchester diocese, but not in those of Canterbury and Rochester, although in all these cases the numbers are small.[30] North Wiltshire and west Berkshire have a particularly high number of men with letters dimissory and many of them were ordained in Gloucester and Hereford dioceses. This may be an extension of the south-east Gloucestershire area of high production of ordinands, although we cannot be sure of how high a proportion of the total number of Salisbury ordinands they represent.

One final piece of evidence comes from the Hertfordshire parishes in the peculiar jurisdiction of St Albans. This extended north-south across Hertfordshire, with outliers in Buckinghamshire. We have evidence of men ordained with letters dimissory of the abbot in Lincoln, Winchester, Canterbury, Rochester and Ely. These show at least twelve men from St Albans itself – another seven have no place-name and may well come from there – and ten from north of it but only six from the southern parishes in the peculiar which accounted for almost 40% of its subsidy assessment. We cannot compare overall figures because we do not know how many men in total were ordained and in particular how many were ordained in London, but the low figures for the wealthy southern parishes accord with the other evidence.

What are the reasons for this pattern? There are three possible explanations: the evidence may be misleading; factors such as the nature of lordship and ecclesiastical patronage, the existence of religious houses willing to grant titles or the availability of chantries as sources of employment may have been significant; or the social and

[30] C. T. Flower and M. C. B. Dawes (eds.), *Registrum Simonis de Gandavo, diocesis Saresbiriensis A.D. 1297–1315* (Canterbury and York Society, xl, xli, 1934).

economic character of the south-east, and in particular the importance of London as the metropolis, may have influenced the career decisions of young men away from seeking ordination.

There are two possible weaknesses in the evidence. A high proportion of men from south-eastern dioceses may have been ordained away from their dioceses with letters dimissory. This does not appear to be the case. In the surviving London lists, Lincoln and Norwich provide more ordinands than Canterbury, Rochester and Winchester, and in the 1340 list 69 unbeneficed Norwich men and 47 Lincoln men were ordained against 51 London men, eleven from Canterbury, three from Rochester (of whom one was from Isleham) and none from Winchester. The Winchester ordinations also show a dominance of Lincoln and Norwich men and relatively few London, Canterbury and Rochester ordinands. Rochester lists include a considerable number of Canterbury ordinands but for at least the period 1320–26, for which we also have Canterbury ordination lists, a majority of these men received at least one of their orders in their own diocese. Lincoln and Norwich were of course large and populous dioceses but the numbers of their men being ordained in the south-east cannot be explained by their size alone.

The other possible weakness in the evidence would occur if ordinands' names provided misleading evidence as to their places of origin but the pattern which we see in Lincoln diocese is as evident in the 1340s, when we are almost always given both surname and place name, as it is in the 1290s, when names are mostly in the simpler form, and the evidence of Canterbury, Rochester and Winchester includes many men whose names are given in the more detailed form.

Turning to other possible reasons, the geographical pattern does not appear to be affected by the availability of religious houses willing to provide large numbers of titles for men coming forward for ordination. In the two large dioceses with long runs of ordination lists – Worcester and Coventry and Lichfield – the geographical pattern of ordinands covers both the early period when patrimonial titles predominate and the later period dominated by religious house titles. Among the dioceses for which we have only shorter periods of evidence, lay and patrimonial titles predominated in Carlisle and Durham, which produced low numbers of ordinands, in Exeter under Bishop Stapledon and, until 1347, in York which were about average, and until the 1340s in Hereford, which was well above the average. Religious house titles became predominant in the low-producing dioceses of Canterbury and Winchester from the 1320s and predominate in Rochester from at least that period. South-eastern England was not lacking in religious houses which might have given titles. It is true that Thamesside Essex and Buckinghamshire were rather thinly provided with religious houses but houses which gave titles were rarely the great and wealthy ones and there was no obvious reason why, if there had been a demand for titles, the small houses in the area or a little further afield could not have provided them. Medmenham abbey, for example, a small house near the Thames with endowments largely restricted to Medmenham itself, gave few titles and those it gave went mostly to men from further north.[31] London itself was not lacking in religious houses. They provided titles but not in great numbers and often to men from outside the south-east.

The pattern does not appear to be affected by the nature of local lordship, the

31 *VCH Buckinghamshire*, i, 376.

patronage of parish churches or whether a high proportion of local churches were appropriated to a religious house and served by resident vicars. Further analysis might show a degree of correlation between one or more of these factors and the numbers of men being ordained from particular places but the broad areas of high and low clergy production show a mixture of lordship, patronage and appropriation.

Wealth and poverty, sources of wealth and changes of economic fortune do not seem to be significant in any systematic way. One possible explanation for the high number of ordinands from the Cotswolds might have been the lack of employment provided by sheep-farming but the lathe of Shipway in Kent and the Parts of Holland in Lincolnshire which produced few ordinands were also sheep-rearing areas. Poverty in the north may have resulted in particularly low numbers of men being ordained in Carlisle and Durham dioceses but Devon and Cornwall, also counties with relatively low assessed wealth in relation to their area and population, produced average numbers and the diocese of Hereford, not exceptional for wealth, produced high numbers. The agrarian crisis of the second decade of the century does not seem to have affected numbers. In the south midlands, population and agricultural decline seem to have affected both extreme north and south-western, but not central, Buckinghamshire and the higher parts of north-west and south-west Bedfordshire by the early 1340s, but the pattern of production of clergy was common to the 1290s and the 1340s. The lay subsidy shows a filigree pattern of wealth per square mile in the Thames valley which does not accord with the relatively simple pattern of production of clergy, whereas Essex shows a largely uniform level of wealth, near to the national average and similar to, for example, most of Surrey and west Kent, which does not reflect the pattern seen in the ordination lists. The pattern north of the Thames shows some similarity to, but no precise correlation with, the London hinterland for transport, as shown by the cost of carriage of wheat. South of the Thames there is no division between east and west Kent in the mapping of transport costs similar to that for the production of ordinands.[32]

The foundation and endowment of chantries in a church provides an obvious reason for men coming forward for ordination from a particular place. William de Yaxley, abbot of Thorney, founded a chantry in Yaxley church (Huntingdonshire) in 1292, which may help to date the large amount of ambitious late thirteenth-century work in the church.[33] It is tempting to ascribe the ordination of five Yaxley men in the 1290s to this foundation, although the men's titles were not given by Thorney abbey. A number of the leading citizens of Newcastle who gave titles to men in the 1330s and 1340s were founders of chantries in St Nicholas' and All Saints' churches there, but there is no evidence of a direct link between titles and foundations. One probable example of such a link relates to Newcastle under Lyme in the diocese of Coventry and Lichfield. William son of Thomas of Newcastle granted a title to John Lycoris of Newcastle for ordination as subdeacon at Trinity 1317. Lycoris was

32 *The Lay Subsidy of 1334*, xxvii; A. R. H. Baker, 'Evidence in the "Nonarum Inquisitiones" of Contracting Arable Lands in England during the Early Fourteenth Century', *Economic History Review*, 2nd Series, 19 (1966), 518–32; B. M. S. Campbell, T. A. Galloway, D. J. Keene and M. Murphy, *A Medieval Capital and its Grain Supply* (Historical Geography Research Series, 30, 1993), 61.

33 N. Pevsner, *Bedfordshire and the County of Huntingdon and Peterborough* (Harmondsworth, 1968), 369–71; *VCH Huntingdonshire*, iii, 247.

ordained deacon in December of that year and priest the following Trinity, in both cases to a patrimonial title. In August 1318 William was granted a licence to endow a chantry in the chapel of St Katherine in Newcastle church and in 1323 Lycoris was instituted as its first chaplain on William's presentation.[34] The foundation of chantries may explain why men came forward for ordination from certain parishes. It cannot explain the low numbers coming forward from London and its environs. London was famous, or notorious, for the large number of chantries at St Paul's cathedral and elsewhere in the city. There was priestly employment available for the young men of London and the south-east if they had been willing to seek ordination. It seems reasonable to conclude that it was the existence of more attractive forms of employment which influenced them.

How does the pattern of ordinations relate to the pattern of later employment? The best, although incomplete and late, evidence for the geographical distribution of clergy is in the clerical poll taxes of 1377, 1379 and 1381. It seems reasonable to assume that the distribution, although not the actual numbers, of unbeneficed clergy in that period would not be seriously different from that of the period before the Black Death. The poll taxes show that the city of London gave employment to large numbers of unbeneficed clergy. With a taxed lay population in 1377 of 23,314, there were in 1377–81 approximately 500 chaplains serving in parishes and 150 in non-parochial establishments. By comparison, Bedfordshire, excluding the deanery of Bedford for which evidence does not survive, contained 207 chaplains in 1379. The population of Bedfordshire in 1377 was 20,339, and the deanery of Bedford probably accounted for about one-sixth of this. There were, therefore, fewer than half as many unbeneficed clergy *pro rata* in Bedfordshire than in London. It is interesting to compare the poll-tax evidence for the Parts of Holland, another area notable for low numbers of ordinands. In Holland, excluding Boston, with a taxed lay population of 18,592 in 1377 there were 162 unbeneficed clergy in 1381. This is fewer than Bedfordshire but of a similar order of magnitude. The two significant differences were that Holland produced far fewer ordinands and that, the parishes in Holland being much larger and wealthier, there were many more clergy per parish. In Boston, with a taxed lay population of 2,871 in 1377, there were 58 chaplains in 1381, a total which is lower than that of London in relation to population, but much closer to London than to its own rural hinterland. The evidence of London and Boston, at least, suggests that cities and large towns, whether they provided employment in many small parishes or predominantly in one large one and whether or not they included a cathedral or other major non-parochial establishment, offered employment to disproportionately high numbers of clergy but that some of them produced very few.[35]

[34] *Registrum Palatinum Dunelmense*, iii, 153, 159 (Richard de Emeldon); 200 (John Shapacap); 126, 170, 188 (Alan Pulhore); H. L. Honeyman, 'The Cathedral Church of St Nicholas', *Archaeologia Aeliana*, 4th series, 9 (1932), 159, 161; J. B. Hughes (ed.), *Register of Walter Langton, Bishop of Coventry and Lichfield, 1296–1321* (Canterbury and York Society, xci, xcvii, 2001, 2007), nos. 1318, 1319, 1320; Register of Bishop Northburgh, Lichfield Record Office B/A/1/2 fol. 138v; *CPR 1317–21*,197. William is identified as William Swanild and William son of Thomas Swanild in the institution entries, as William son of Thomas in the patent roll entry and as William son of Thomas, burgess of Newcastle, in the ordination list.

[35] The evidence is not complete for any of the years but it appears that the returns for the three taxes are very broadly compatible where returns survive for more than one. For London: A. K. McHardy (ed.), *The Church in London, 1375–1392* (London Record Society, 1977); A. K. McHardy, 'The Churchmen of Chaucer's London: The Seculars', *Medieval Prosopography*, 16 (1995), 57–87. For Lincoln: A. K.

Movement to the south-east might take place before ordination or afterwards. The high numbers of men with letters dimissory ordained in the south-eastern dioceses, with the partial exception of Canterbury, might in itself be an indication of the intention of those ordained to work in the south-east although in most cases their titles are from their own localities. In Rochester one-quarter and in Winchester less than one-fifth of the ordinands from outside the south-east with religious house titles obtained their titles from houses in the south-east.

In some cases we may infer residence from the place where the letters were granted combined with the title. Thomas de Folkesworth, subdeacon, was granted letters dimissory to deacon and priest in June 1300 by Bishop Dalderby of Lincoln at Melton by Canterbury at the request of M Thomas de Upton, canon of Wingham and clerk of the archbishop of Canterbury, who promised to provide a title, and was ordained deacon in September and priest in December in that diocese. Henry son of Simon de Butmeswell, who was granted letters dimissory to all holy orders by Dalderby in November 1301 at the request of John of Foderingeye, clerk of the archbishop, and ordained subdeacon in December 1301 and deacon in June 1302 in Canterbury diocese, possessed thirty acres of land in Kent and ten 'in patria sua', which may suggest that he had moved from Lincoln diocese to Kent, although he received the letters at Canons Ashby in Northamptonshire.[36] These men were exceptional in enjoying the patronage of archiepiscopal clerks. Although some men ordained with letters dimissory obtained all their orders in a non-local diocese, most, even of those ordained in the south-east, were quite as likely to return to their native diocese for ordination as priest; there is no simple pattern of movement to the south-east as a man passes through the orders.

We can find examples of movement to the south-east reflected in the names of men obtaining benefices there. We need to exclude the 'privileged' clerks holding rich benefices. It is in chantries, vicarages and the poorer rectories, and many of the City of London rectories were not valuable, that we may find evidence to indicate the origin of clergy who may have served without a benefice for years. In some cases the reason for a non-local man obtaining a London benefice may reflect the identity of the patron: William of Wixford, presented by the abbot of Evesham to St Michael Cornhill, a rectory worth only £5, came from a village seven miles from Evesham. On the other hand there is no obvious reason for John le Kyng, citizen of London, presenting in succession to a chantry in St Olave, Old Jewry, Roger of Lavendon (north Buckinghamshire) in 1329, Roger son of Edmund of Little

McHardy (ed.), *Clerical Poll-taxes of the Diocese of Lincoln, 1377–1381* (Lincoln Record Society, 1992); A. K. McHardy, 'The Lincolnshire Clergy in the Late Fourteenth Century', in W. M. Ormrod (ed.), *England in the Fourteenth Century* (Woodbridge, 1986), 145–51. See also idem, 'Ecclesiastics and Economics: Poor Priests, Prosperous Laymen and Proud Prelates in the Reign of Richard II', in W. J. Sheils and D. Wood (eds.), *The Church and Wealth* (Studies in Church History, 24, 1987), 29–137; A. K. McHardy, 'Careers and Disappointments in the Late-Medieval Church: Some English Evidence', in W. J. Sheils and D. Wood (eds.), *The Ministry: Clerical and Lay* (Studies in Church History, 26, 1989), 111–30. The figures given here are primarily my own, based on the editions, but depend on Dr McHardy's analysis of the evidence.

36 Lincoln, Register of Bishop Dalderby, fols. 9, 39; R. Graham (ed.), *Registrum Roberti Winchelsey, Cantuariensis Archiepiscopi, A.D. 1294–1313* (Canterbury and York Society, li, lii, 1952, 1956), 937, 942, 952, 955.

Abington (Cambridgeshire) in 1330 on Roger of Lavendon's death, and in 1333 Henry de Pirneye of Emberton in north Buckinghamshire.[37]

Vicarages in the diocese of Winchester, and especially in Surrey, seem frequently to have attracted men whose origins were in the midlands. Under Bishop Woodlock, who was a Hampshire man and former prior of Winchester and therefore had no reason to encourage the promotion of men from further afield, Merton priory presented Walter of Walsoken (Norfolk) as vicar of Carshalton in 1310 and Southwark priory presented Nicholas of Seckington (Warwickshire) as vicar of Mitcham in 1314. This continued in the following episcopates. William of Daglingworth (Gloucestershire) was presented to the vicarage of Horley in 1316 by Chertsey abbey and ultimately collated by bishop Sandale, in 1320 Gilbert of Swalcliffe (Oxfordshire, near Banbury) was presented to the vicarage of Battersea by Westminster abbey and ultimately collated by bishop Asserio, and in 1321 Thomas son of William Faber of Offord (Huntingdonshire) was presented to the vicarage of Effingham by Merton priory.[38] Men from the diocese of Worcester seem to have been particularly successful in obtaining benefices in the diocese of Winchester during the episcopate of John Stratford (1323–33). Although Stratford came from the diocese of Worcester these men were not the privileged clergy who would naturally look for employment and patronage from a successful clerk from their native place. So far we have only provided examples and this is no substitute for detailed analysis but there appear to have been few examples of movement by non-privileged clergy in the opposite direction. The Worcester registers show that most vicarages were served by men of that diocese. Dr Bennett has shown that in the three north-eastern deaneries of Lincolnshire, 40% of the men who held livings between 1290 and 1340 and whose provenance can be established came from the three deaneries, 73% from Lincolnshire and 79% from within the diocese; these figures include the 'plum' benefices most likely to be held by non-local clergy.[39]

To sum up, it seems that the attractiveness of London to clergy from far afield was as true of the first half of the fourteenth century as it was of the second half when Chaucer and Langland referred to it. The cause was not only the large number of posts available for priests in London but the reluctance of young men from London and the south-east to seek ordination. This is presumably because secular sources of employment were available which were more attractive than becoming a clerical casual worker. There may be similar explanations for other areas of low production of clergy, notably south-western Gloucestershire in the shadow of Bristol and Gloucester, and Holland in Lincolnshire, perhaps in the shadow of Boston and Kings Lynn. Dr McHardy observes: 'Put in crudely materialistic terms, the unbeneficed were providing goods and services which the customers wanted, at prices which many could afford and were prepared to pay. Both their high numbers, and the considerable mobility which at least some of them demonstrated, showed the unbeneficed – the mass-priests above all – as a class highly responsive to consumer

37 *Register of Bishop Baldock etc.*, 289, 293, 301.

38 *Registrum Henrici Woodlock*, 733, 742; F. J. Baigent (ed.), *Registers of John de Sandale and Rigaud de Asserio, Bishops of Winchester (A.D. 1316–1323)* (Hampshire Record Society, 1897),12, 127–8, 438–9, 444–5.

39 N. Bennett, 'Pastors and Masters: The Beneficed Clergy of North-East Lincolnshire, 1290–1340', in P. Hoskin, C. Brooke, B. Dobson (eds.), *The Foundations of Medieval Ecclesiastical History: Studies Presented to David Smith* (Woodbridge, 2005), 47.

demand.'[40] It is reasonable to conclude that economic factors influenced their recruitment and their mobility before they obtained priestly employment as well as afterwards. Detailed work on individual dioceses will no doubt refine and may amend the picture outlined here and allow for the presentation of more comprehensive statistics together with the detailed commentary and qualifications they require.

40 A. K. McHardy, 'Ecclesiastics and Economics', 136.

SECULAR PATRONAGE AND RELIGIOUS DEVOTION: THE DESPENSERS AND ST MARY'S ABBEY, TEWKESBURY

Martyn Lawrence

The abbey church of St Mary at Tewkesbury, seven miles north of Gloucester, is the burial place of one of the fourteenth century's most reviled families, the Despensers.[1] From the twelfth century, successive Clare earls of Gloucester were laid to rest in the choir of Tewkesbury, establishing it as a mausoleum of some importance. Following in their wake, six generations of the Despenser family were buried in the abbey, and lavish improvements – modelled on the changes made by Henry III at Westminster – were made in an extravagant attempt to emulate the work of the previous patronal family. This article looks at the Despensers' patronage of the abbey and the evidence of their spirituality, devotion and piety (and showmanship) over six generations, and suggests that by using a more informed chronology than has been employed previously, specific motivation for secular patronage can be identified. It argues that Tewkesbury Abbey served the Despensers in two capacities. First, it was their spiritual home, a place for worship, devotion and burial;[2] other magnate families acted similarly, the Beauchamps at Warwick, the FitzAlans at Arundel, and the de Veres at Colne Priory (Essex) affording striking examples. But, second, in an age of display, when an upwardly mobile family needed to 'market' themselves to the crown, Tewkesbury was also a place in which the Despensers drew attention to their illustrious heritage-by-marriage. Throughout the fourteenth and early

1 *The* most reviled, if we follow *The Independent*, 27 December 2005, in which Hugh Despenser the younger was noted as the 'worst Briton' of the fourteenth century.

2 The concept of Tewkesbury as a 'Despenser mausoleum' was first mooted by R. K. Morris, 'Tewkesbury Abbey – the Despenser Mausoleum', *Bristol and Gloucester Archaeological Society Transactions* [hereafter *BGAST*], 93 (1974 for 1975), 142–55; updated by R. K. Morris with M. Thurlby, 'The Gothic Church: Architectural History', in R. K. Morris and R. Shoesmith (eds.), *Tewkesbury Abbey: History, Art and Architecture* (Almeley, 2003), 109–30. One voice dissenting from Morris's earlier conclusions is J. P. McAleer, 'Tewkesbury Abbey in the Later Twelfth and Thirteenth Centuries', *BGAST*, 110 (1992), 78. Other comments may be found in A. Hartshorne, 'Observations upon Certain Monumental Effigies in the West of England, and particularly in the Neighbourhood of Cheltenham', *BGAST*, 4 (1879–80), 231–47; D. H. Dean, 'The Despencers and their Chantries', *Westminster Cathedral Chronicle*, 41 (1947), 212–13; N. E. Saul, '"Forget-me-nots": Patronage in Gothic England', *History Today*, 37 (1987), 19–21, reprinted in his *Age of Chivalry: Art and Society in Late Medieval England* (London, 1992), 36–47; T. A. Heslop and V. A. Sekules (eds.), *Medieval Art and Architecture at Gloucester and Tewkesbury* (British Archaeological Association Conference Transactions, 7, 1985), passim; and more generally in J. T. Rosenthal, *The Purchase of Paradise: Gift-Giving and the Aristocracy, 1307–1485* (London, 1972); B. Golding, 'Burials and Benefactions: an Aspect of Monastic Patronage in Thirteenth-Century England', in W. M. Ormrod (ed.), *England in the Thirteenth Century: Proceedings of the 1984 Harlaxton Symposium* (Woodbridge, 1984), 64–75; A. M. Morganstern, *Gothic Tombs of Kinship in France, the Low Countries and England* (Philadelphia, 2000), esp. 103–16; B. and M. Gittos, 'Motivation and Choice: the Selection of Medieval Secular Effigies', in P. R. Coss and M. H. Keen (eds.), *Heraldry, Pageantry and Social Display in Medieval England* (Woodbridge, 2002), 143–67.

fifteenth centuries, they made extensive alterations to the fabric of the building, and their continuing endowment made Tewkesbury one of the richest and most gloriously decorated of all Benedictine abbeys.[3] The tombs and chantry chapels of six generations of Despensers ring the high altar and their images in stained glass look down from above. There is no better place to search for the significance of powerful physical statements of ancestry and political might in the life of a baronial family than at Tewkesbury.

The death of the last de Clare earl at Bannockburn in 1314 and the subsequent partition of the de Clare estates marked the beginning of the Despensers' tenure as lords of Glamorgan (and thus as lords of Tewkesbury).[4] Hugh the younger had married Eleanor, the last earl's eldest daughter, in 1306, and on entering his Tewkesbury lordship evidently had serious ambitions for the abbey. He not only wanted it to outshine the burial places of other Marcher lords at Bristol and Wigmore; he also sought in it reinforcement for his recently acquired aristocratic connections.[5] In the short term, however, his and his family's plans for the abbey were to go seriously awry. His and his father's close association with Edward II's regime was to lead to their downfall following the king's overthrow in the autumn of 1326. Hugh's father, the elder Hugh, was never given burial at all, his body being fed to a pack of dogs at Bristol in October. The younger Hugh himself was to die a traitor's death at Hereford a few weeks later, and his mutilated remains were not reclaimed by his widow until after December 1330.[6] It is a mark of the intense hatred felt for the younger Hugh that he was not merely executed with such savagery, but that his head was displayed for almost four years above London Bridge. When his body was finally interred, his tomb was notable for its understated appearance: no effigy was included (although there is space for one in the tomb recess) and there are none of the soaring arches and intricate details that mark out the other Tewkesbury tombs. Facing away from the high altar and looking south-east, it gives the impression of work done quickly. It is hard to avoid the conclusion that Hugh the younger was

3 See in particular the essays in Morris and Shoesmith (eds.), *Tewkesbury Abbey*; and J. M. Luxford, *The Art and Architecture of English Benedictine Monasteries, 1300–1540* (Woodbridge, 2005), passim.

4 TNA:PRO, C 47/9/24 (the partition of the English de Clare estates in 1317, although Tewkesbury was part of the late earl of Gloucester's widow's dower and did not fall to Despenser until 1320); G. T. Clarke (ed.), *Cartae et alia munimenta quae ad dominium de Glamorgancia pertinent* (Cardiff, 1910), iii, 1048–56. The abbey held extensive lands of the lords of Glamorgan (W. Rees, 'The Possessions of the Abbot of Tewkesbury in Glamorgan', *South Wales and Monmouthshire Record Society*, 2 (1950), 139–52), and the Despensers also held court in the town, which in May 1327 was valued at £132 (TNA:PRO, SC 11/Roll 249; *Calendar of Charter Rolls 1300–26*, 463; *CPR 1324–27*, 206).

5 See J. Brown, '"Peut-on assez louer cet excellent ministre?" Imagery of the Favourite in England, France and Spain', in J. H. Elliot and L. W. B. Brockliss (eds.), *The World of the Favourite* (New Haven, 1999), 223–35, which outlines the use of imagery by three later royal favourites, Buckingham, Olivares and Richelieu, and argues that the excessive power they wielded led to a need for their rule to be defended, not merely immortalised. Despenser's own plans for Tewkesbury may also be read in the same light – that he intended to use the abbey as a canvas for apologetics (i.e. the justification of his position ahead of other members of the upper nobility), and not merely for display.

6 She petitioned the crown on 15 December 1330 (T. Rymer (ed.), *Foedera, Conventiones, Literae et Cujuscunque Generis Acta*, Record Commission (London, 1816–30), II(ii), 804), after which 'one of the quarters of hym was buried by the lavatory of the high altare in Twekesbyry' (L. Toulmin Smith (ed.), *The Itinerary of John Leland in or about the years 1535–1543* (London, 1964), iv, 140), and long afterwards, the rest of his limbs were brought there (W. Dugdale, *The Baronage of England* (London, 1676), i, 394). A transcript of the order to the Mayor of London to this effect is in London, Inner Temple Library, MS Petyt 533, xxii, fol. 349.

Plate 1. Tewkesbury Abbey: the choir looking east

buried with little ceremony as a political expedient.[7] Nor should this be a surprise: the last thing that his recently rehabilitated son, Hugh Despenser III, and Tewkesbury's new abbot, John Coles (1328–47), would have wished to do was draw attention to a disgraced man. The matter of awareness is important. Seventy years later, Thomas, Lord Despenser's burial was equally modest: following his execution in January 1400, his head was removed from London Bridge on his mother's request, and his remains were buried 'beside his father'[8] in the choir 'beneath a lamp that burns before the host'.[9] In stark contrast with the splendid chantries of Thomas's father and great-uncle, not even a brass inscription was laid. For the sake of the next generation, in times of forfeiture and disgrace it made good political sense to avoid too much exposure.

Richard Morris has suggested that the Despenser building work at Tewkesbury took place in four phases, albeit with breaks and temporary suspensions.[10] These phases correspond roughly to the domination of the younger Hugh (*c.* 1315–28); the Despenser disgrace, coupled with the later life of Eleanor Despenser (*c.* 1327–37); the rehabilitation and career of Hugh III (*c.* 1335–49); and the early career of Edward (*c.* 1350s–60s). Morris, however, admits that it is difficult to be certain of the strength of individual influence on early changes to the abbey design. This article, amongst other things, contends that more attention should be paid to Hugh Despenser III as a source of inspiration for the work, and that we should be hesitant in supplying too much architectural acumen to the younger Hugh. The younger Despenser was a man who threw caution to the wind, paying little heed to the material foundations of his power, and more concerned with making money than with the establishment of a legacy. Furthermore, despite his enormous ambition, there is no documentation showing any involvement on his part in the work; and an apparent break in building at the end of the 1320s may be due as much to the death of Abbot Kempsey (1282–1328) as to the execution of the two Despensers. Purely in motivational terms, Hugh III's concern to strengthen his position after 1331 supplies a more appealing reason for major structural developments at Tewkesbury. This third Hugh needed to portray his ancestors in an appropriate and sympathetic light to facilitate his own political restoration. It was around this time that the choir and ambulatory were substantially remodelled and a series of enormous traceried windows erected in the clerestory (plate 1). Hugh III's influence on this work has not received enough attention from students of Tewkesbury, who have traditionally attributed the initiative largely to Eleanor Despenser.[11] Eleanor's marriage to Sir William Zouche in 1329 was to lead to the latter's own inclusion in a window on

7 Perhaps as an ultimate insult, Despenser did not even get to keep his tomb to himself. He shares his burial place with Abbot John Coles, whose coffin was later placed over his own.

8 G. B. Stow (ed.), *Historia Vitae et Regni Ricardi Secundi* (Philadelphia, 1977), 165.

9 Quoted from the monastic *Chronica de Theokesburie*: Oxford, Bodleian Library, MS Top. Glouc. d.2, fol. 26r. This (the so-called 'Founders' Book') is the only full version of three copies of the rather mechanical *Chronica*; the others are Oxford, Bodleian Library, MS Lat. misc. b.2 (R), dorse, and London, BL, Cotton MS Cleopatra C.III, fols. 220r–234v. The Top. Glouc. MS is discussed in J. M. Luxford, 'The Founders' Book', in Morris and Shoesmith (eds.), *Tewkesbury Abbey*, 53–64, and the Cottonian MS is printed in R. Dodsworth and W. Dugdale, *Monasticon Anglicanum* (London, 1655–73), ii, 59–65.

10 Morris, 'Despenser Mausoleum', 145–6; Morris with Thurlby, 'Architectural History', 117–19.

11 Until, that is, the publication of Luxford, *Art and Architecture*, 172–8, 182, where a case is made for more active involvement by the monastic superiors. I find Luxford's argument eminently plausible, but have chosen to focus this article on the secular impetus, as I remain convinced that setting the

Plate 2. Tewkesbury Abbey, the choir: stained glass window on the north side of the choir showing the Lords of Tewkesbury

the south side. The match between Eleanor and this relatively obscure Herefordshire knight was the sequel to her dramatic abduction by him from the family's manor of Hanley Castle (Worcs.). It is not clear how far Zouche saw himself as assimilated into the Despenser family identity. However, his assumption of the title of lord of Glamorgan (and thereby lord of Tewkesbury) and subsequent inclusion in the stained glass roll of honour implies that he was well aware of the significance of Tewkesbury as a forum of public display. Sarah Brown argues that Zouche could not have been included in the window scheme before his death in 1337;[12] and since Eleanor only briefly outlived him, it must have been Hugh III who was instrumental in finalising the gallery of figures. However, the *Chronica de Theokesburie*, which includes an illustration of every lord of Glamorgan, has no depiction of Zouche. The cloistered monk who compiled the *Chronica* rightly or wrongly considered him unworthy of inclusion. Perhaps he was viewed as an 'intruder' into the lineage or, more probably, was left out because he made no material contributions to the fabric. Hugh III, by contrast, is depicted in the *Chronica* holding a miniature church building in his hand (probably the parish church of Llantrisant (Glamorgan), which he had appropriated to the abbey in 1343),[13] and in 1347 was described as 'patron of the abbey of St Mary's'.[14]

There are seven clerestory windows, five of which, above and either side of the altar, have religious designs. The remaining two, north and south, above the site of the choir screen (denoted NIV and SIV by the *Corpus Vitrearum Medii Aevi*) contain secular figures who were instrumental in the life of the abbey (plate 2). In SIV, three Clare earls stand beside William Zouche. NIV is more potent as it contains the founder, Robert FitzHamon, beside two Clare earls and the younger Despenser. Most of the glass dates from the second quarter of the fourteenth century, which was a critical time for the Despensers, and an attempt to draw attention to the Conqueror's kin is deeply symbolic. FitzHamon was a favourite of William Rufus and from him received the great estate which would become known as the honour of Gloucester, the abbey church at Tewkesbury part of it. Both windows NIV and SIV are on the outermost ends of the series, and are designed to lead the eye from founder to earl to Despenser and thence to the figures of prophets and Old Testament kings.[15] Ultimately, the observer arrives in the east window at the Last Judgement, where Christ rewards the faithful and delivers the unjust to eternal death. The entire series of windows is important, for it supplies a chronology in glass of successive lords of Glamorgan. There is an inherent legitimacy writ large in the design – a deliberate statement of succession vital in the aftermath of Edward II's deposition. The heraldry suggests a date before 1340,[16] and it is possible to pinpoint the imme-

work at Tewkesbury in the context of the Despensers' experiences is the best way to determine their motivation for patronage.

12 S. Brown, 'The Medieval Stained Glass', in Morris and Shoesmith (eds.), *Tewkesbury Abbey*, 190.

13 Oxford, Bodleian Library, MS Top. Glouc. d.2, fol. 22v; *CPR 1343–45*, 118.

14 *VCH Gloucester*, ii, 63.

15 A kneeling figure in the corner of the east window has often been identified as Eleanor Despenser, although more recent studies indicate the difficulty of this: Brown, 'Medieval Stained Glass', 187–8.

16 Brown, 'Medieval Stained Glass', 190. See also P. R. Coss, 'Knighthood, Heraldry and Social Exclusion in Edwardian England', in Coss and Keen (eds.), *Heraldry, Pageantry and Social Display*, 39–68, esp. 48–9, which differs from some of the dates suggested here but maintains the importance of Tewkesbury as 'an excellent example of an aristocratic tendency to project their values back into a pre-heraldic past, in the interests of lineage' (p. 49).

diate cause in the decision of Edward III to raise Hugh Audley to the earldom of Gloucester in 1337. Audley never held the honour of Tewkesbury but his elevation automatically associated him with the de Clares. The perceived threat to Despenser ambitions may well have led to the design of the glazing scheme, either to compete with Audley, or to attract the king's attention. Perhaps the glazing scheme needs to be rooted more firmly in the secular – and, particularly, the political – world in which the Despensers operated. The years 1337 and 1338 were, after all, ones of pivotal importance in the rehabilitation of the Despensers. Having faced disgrace after the fall of Edward II, Hugh III was to spend the remainder of his life rebuilding his family's reputation.[17] After three years incarceration in Bristol Castle, he emerged to fight in the English victory at Halidon Hill (1333), and rode to Scotland in 1336 under the banner of the king's brother, John of Eltham, earl of Cornwall.[18] By the time that the French war broke out in 1337, he was well on his way to recognition as a capable soldier. Remaining on the northern border for a time, he won his spurs in the retinue of the earl of Warwick in the summer of 1337;[19] he then served independently in the winter of 1337–38 with the earls of Gloucester, Arundel and Salisbury.[20] An indication of how far Edward III was prepared to promote reconciliation with sons of his old enemies was afforded by his summons to Despenser to attend the Great Council in 1338.[21] A still greater sign of favour came in 1338 when Edward awarded him the hand in marriage of Elizabeth, daughter of his friend William Montagu, earl of Salisbury. Coming hard on the heels of Eleanor Despenser's death in 1337, when all the Despenser lands had passed to Hugh, it marked a whirlwind change in the family fortunes. Such a dramatic period for the family was played out amidst the spires and pinnacles of Tewkesbury Abbey.

The suggestion is substantiated by the heraldic scheme which forms such a prominent feature of the stained glass.[22] Since the Despensers were so deeply preoccupied with self-aggrandisement, it is only natural that they should have made great play with heraldry. In the great windows of the choir they included the arms of many powerful kinsfolk and allies, some of them earls and members of the royal family. This was one obvious way in which they could proclaim power and status through the witness of association. A number of the arms were those of families locally important in Gloucestershire and the Marches. Among these were the arms of Bradeston, Mowbray, Berkeley, d'Amory and Audley. A number of the other coats of arms, however, were of families with which the Despensers were connected by marriage or in other ways. These included the arms of Warenne, Hastings, FitzAlan, Grandison and Montagu – all of them to be numbered among the richest and most well

[17] M. J. Lawrence, 'Power, Ambition and Political Rehabilitation: the Despensers, *c.*1281–1400' (University of York, unpublished Ph.D. thesis, 2005), 82–5.

[18] TNA:PRO 101/19/36, m. 1. Eltham had been a ward of the Despensers in the 1320s and held some of their confiscated estates: TNA:PRO, E 101/382/12; J. S. Bothwell, 'Edward III, The English Peerage, and the 1337 Earls: Estate Redistribution in Fourteenth-Century England', in J. S. Bothwell (ed.), *The Age of Edward III* (Woodbridge, 2001).

[19] TNA:PRO, E 101/20/17, m. 7d; BL, Cotton MS Nero C.VIII, fol. 284v.

[20] *Rotuli Scotiae*, I, 508a; *CPR 1334–38*, 550; *CCR 1337–39*, 403.

[21] Lawrence, 'Despensers', 205.

[22] For positioning, see G. McN. Rushforth, 'The Glass in the Quire Clerestory of Tewkesbury Abbey', *BGAST*, 46 (1924), 315–16; Brown, 'Medieval Stained Glass', 188–9.

connected dynasties in the land.[23] Some of these families – the Hastings's, FitzAlans and Grandisons – held Marcher estates. The fact that they were magnates, however, lent their inclusion an additional significance. Three coats of arms of members of the royal family were included: those of John of Eltham, earl of Cornwall (d. 1336), Thomas of Brotherton, earl of Norfolk (d. 1338), and Edmund Woodstock, earl of Kent (d. 1330). Eltham, as we have seen, was Eleanor Despenser's ward and Hugh III's patron, and Brotherton held many of the Despenser estates after forfeiture.[24] Woodstock's inclusion is the most interesting. He had been one of the younger Despenser's closest allies, but was implicated in a plot against Mortimer and Isabella and executed for treason in March 1330, making him an unlikely candidate. Yet the presence of his arms suggests that the Despensers intended to convey a sense of empathy, perhaps even of solidarity. The events of 1326–30 not only instilled in Hugh III a need to be image-conscious, making him acutely aware of the fine line between success and failure at the highest level; it left him with a lasting sense of family tragedy, which found its expression in the Tewkesbury stained glass.

Hugh III was the first Despenser lord to be buried with honour, interred on the right (i.e., the north) side of the high altar, where his wife Elizabeth was to join him ten years later. Such a position – 'set down at the right hand of the throne of God' – must be seen as a deliberate statement about the Despensers' recovery. It not only marked a move away from the burial place of the de Clare earls, who had all been buried before the altar, but also began a process of surrounding the altar with substantial monuments, something which would continue for the next ninety years. L. L. Gee has argued that the Despensers observed a strict code of decorum at Tewkesbury by allowing the de Clares pride of place before the altar and reserving the space around the side of the choir for themselves.[25] While there is no doubt that the Despensers' contributions to the abbey were designed in part to honour their ancestors – and notwithstanding the fact that only the area under the arches offered sufficient physical space for tombs of this sort – it is surely more likely that the soaring pinnacles and imposing chapels were intended to eclipse everything that had gone before. Hugh III died suddenly from plague in the spring of 1349, having made few burial arrangements, and it is unsurprising that the *Chronica de Theokesburie* only makes reference to the couple's alabaster tomb after Elizabeth's death in 1359.[26] It was presumably constructed in the early 1350s (plate 3). The mourners on the base of the tomb have long disappeared, but it is tempting to search for parallels with Sir Hugh Hastings' brass at Elsing (Norfolk), upon which Hugh III had been commemorated together with King Edward III and his companions-in-

23 In addition to Hugh III's own marriage to Elizabeth Montagu, his eldest sister Isabel married Richard FitzAlan, earl of Arundel (a marriage that was later annulled, but not before their eldest son Edmund married another Montagu, Sibyl); another sister, Eleanor, married Laurence Hastings, earl of Pembroke. Hugh III's aunt Isabel, sister to Hugh the younger, married John Hastings senior. (Full genealogies may be found in Lawrence, 'Despensers', 7–8.) A similar heraldic scheme to that at Tewkesbury has been identified in Etchingham Church, Sussex: N. E. Saul, *Scenes from Provincial Life: Knightly Families in Sussex, 1280–1400* (Oxford, 1986), 148–52.

24 *Calendar of Charter Rolls 1327–41*, 3–4.

25 L. L. Gee, *Women, Art and Patronage from Henry III to Edward III: 1216–1377* (Woodbridge, 2002), 88.

26 Oxford, Bodleian Library, MS Top. Glouc. d.2, fol. 23r: 'she was buried with her husband from her first [*sic* – actually her second] marriage in a tomb made of beautiful white marble'.

Plate 3. Tewkesbury Abbey: tomb of Sir Guy Brian (d. 1390) with, behind it, the tomb of Sir Hugh Despenser III (d. 1349) and his wife

arms from Crécy and other French campaigns.[27] The window of the Lady Chapel at St Augustine's, Bristol (now Bristol Cathedral), which also dates from the 1340s, contains a host of heraldic devices belonging to families whose military experience was rooted in the wars of Edward III.[28] But most significantly, Hugh III's three-tiered canopy also bears similarities to the tomb of Edward II at Gloucester. Nigel Saul has remarked upon the considerable irony that more than twenty years after the turmoil of the 1320s, a memorial to a murdered monarch should have been the template for Hugh and Elizabeth.[29] But this can be taken a step further. In emulating the murdered king's burial, the Despensers were making a deliberate attempt to demonstrate the family's loyalty to the crown. It was a message to all onlookers that they were loyal servants of Edward III (and by extension, fully supported the method of Edward's assumption of the throne), and that the horrors of 1326 were relegated to the past. Such a suggestion is entirely in keeping with Richard Morris's suggestion that by his interment on the north of the altar, Hugh III was being shown to be the second founder of Tewkesbury Abbey.[30]

Moving on a generation, other influences can be sought for the Trinity Chapel, the chantry tomb of Edward Despenser. After his death in 1375, Edward was buried on the south side of the sanctuary before the door of the vestry, his chapel possibly providing a thoroughfare from the vestry to the high altar for chantry priests.[31] His will stressed the need to be buried 'near to the bodies of my ancestors', emphasising the importance of dynastic continuity in death.[32] On top of the Trinity Chapel Edward's figure kneels in perpetual prayer, a rare English example of the devotional image known as the *priant*.[33] His wife Elizabeth, a widow for thirty-four years until her own death in 1409, chose to be buried beneath the sanctuary floor rather than in the chapel with Edward.[34] Both, however, are depicted within the chapel in a series of devotional wall paintings. Angels flank the Trinity, which is housed in a painted niche, besides which Edward and Elizabeth pray towards the image. Edward's will makes no mention of the chapel or the paintings, but it is likely that the artwork was influenced by time spent in Italy. In the mid-1360s, Edward served as steward to Lionel of Clarence, third son of King Edward III, and in 1368 accompanied Lionel to Milan for his marriage to Violante, daughter of the Milanese duke Galeazzo Visconti. When Lionel died just three months after the wedding, suspicions were rife that he had been poisoned, and Despenser took up arms against the Milanese,

27 The best discussion is M. W. Norris, *Monumental Brasses: The Memorials*, 2 vols. (London, 1977), i, 18–19; see also N. E. Saul, 'Bold as Brass: Secular Display in English Medieval Brasses', in Coss and Keen (eds.), *Heraldry, Pageantry and Social Display*, 169–94.

28 A. Sabin, 'The Fourteenth-century Heraldic Glass in the Eastern Lady Chapel of Bristol Cathedral', *Antiquaries Journal*, 37 (1957), 54–70.

29 Saul, '"Forget-me-nots"', 20; also D. C. Welander, *The History, Art and Architecture of Gloucester Cathedral* (Stroud, 1991), 147–50. In addition, the tomb of Pope John XXII at Avignon is similar to (although smaller, and heavier in design than) Edward II's Gloucester tomb: see J. J. G. Alexander and P. Binski (eds.), *Age of Chivalry: Art in Plantagenet England 1200–1400* (London, 1987), no. 497; Morganstern, *Gothic Tombs of Kinship*, 82–91. I am grateful to Seymour Phillips for pointing out to me the significance of this connection.

30 Morris with Thurlby, 'Architectural History', 125; also Luxford, *Art and Architecture*, 182.

31 P. Lindley, 'The Later Medieval Monuments and Chantry Chapels', in Morris and Shoesmith (eds.), *Tewkesbury Abbey*, 170.

32 Lambeth Palace Library, Reg. Sudbury, fol. 89v.

33 See references in Luxford, *Art and Architecture*, 174 note 163.

34 Lambeth Palace Library, Reg. Arundel, ii, fol. 108v.

eventually joining the papal armies in their crusades against the Visconti where he remained until 1372.[35] The inclusion of the Trinity may possibly be traced to the particular devotion of Edward, the Black Prince, in whose retinue Despenser fought at Poitiers on his first expedition abroad. The prince lies on a tomb chest at Canterbury looking up at an image of the Trinity, and contemporary chroniclers paid ample witness to his devotion to the cult which was growing in popularity during the fourteenth century. David Green has identified a number of the prince's friends and retinue members who founded institutions or gave patronage to buildings with links to the Trinity, and it is possible that Despenser also saw it as a fashionable symbol of devotion.[36] Nevertheless, the entire Tewkesbury structure speaks of considerable effort and devotion, hinting at a husband and wife whose religious conviction and appreciation of the arts, perhaps developed together, outranked many others.

Further evidence of Edward's piety may be found in his bequests to the abbey. The *Chronica de Theokesburie* states that he gave 'a costly chalice of purest gold and a most precious jewel made with surpassing craftsmanship', while according to his will he bequeathed 'two whole sets of my best clothes, two gilt chalices, a gilt hanaper *ove le treippe*, and a ewer, given to me by the French king, in which the body of Christ should be placed on Corpus Christi day'.[37] Like the wall paintings in his chapel, the ewer echoes Edward's successful career. He must have received the gift either during the brokering of the Treaty of Brétigny (1360) or during the time when King John was at the English court.[38] He also made a series of smaller gifts to local priories, requesting that they say alms for his soul: £10 each to Llanthony, Neath, Little Marlow and Canons Leigh.[39]

At the end of the fourteenth century, the decision was made to re-inter the abbey's founder, Robert FitzHamon. The motive for reburial is usually attributed solely to Abbot Parker or the monks,[40] but it is highly probable that Elizabeth Despenser was involved. FitzHamon's Founder's Chapel bears striking similarities to the Trinity Chapel, and as Lindley suggests, may be a critique of the earlier structure. The two

35 For further details, see Lawrence, 'Despensers', 32, 87–8, 155–8; T. B. Pugh, 'Despenser, Edward, first Lord Despenser (1336–1375)', *Oxford Dictionary of National Biography* (Oxford, 2004) [http://www.oxforddnb.com/view/article/7550, accessed 16 June 2007]; and for a recent account of the fighting, W. Caferro, *John Hawkwood: an English Mercenary in Fourteenth-Century Italy* (Baltimore, MD, 2006), 134–43.

36 D. S. Green, *The Black Prince* (Stroud, 2001), 121; also R. Barber, *Edward, Prince of Wales and Aquitaine* (London, 1978), 236–7, 240–41; C. Wilson, 'The Medieval Monuments', in P. Collinson, N. Ramsay and M. Sparks (eds.), *A History of Canterbury Cathedral* (Oxford, 1995), 494–7.

37 Oxford, Bodleian Library, MS Top. Glouc. d.2, fol. 25r; Lambeth Palace Library, Reg. Sudbury, fol. 89v. Edward patronised the London goldsmith, Nicholas Twyford, from whom a number of gifts were bought for visiting envoys between 1378 and 1384, and just before his death had commissioned a gold seal for the lordship of Glamorgan and Morgannwg: F. Devon (ed.), *Issues of the Exchequer, Henry III to Henry VI* (London, 1847), 201; C. M. Barron, 'Richard II and London', in A. Goodman and J. L. Gillespie (eds.), *Richard II: the Art of Kingship* (Oxford, 1999), 139 note 46.

38 Lawrence, 'Despensers', 205, indicates Edward's regular summons to parliament at the beginning of the 1360s, and thus, one presumes, time spent at court. He witnessed 56 of the 130 great charters issued between 1362 and 1368 (ibid., 66).

39 Lambeth Palace Library, Reg. Sudbury, fol. 89v.

40 M. A. Hicks, *Warwick the Kingmaker* (Oxford, 1998), 60; Morris with Thurlby, 'Architectural History', 129; Lindley, 'Medieval Monuments and Chantry Chapels', 171; Luxford, *Art and Architecture*, 174.

sit in perfect symmetry on the north and south sides of the sanctuary. Since Elizabeth had organised the erection of the Trinity Chapel,[41] it is not unlikely that she was involved in this equally major work. It would certainly account for the similarities between the two chapels, at the same time attesting a remarkable level of interaction between the secular and ecclesiastical authorities at the abbey. The plans for the new chapel were laid during Thomas Despenser's formative years and, according to the *Chronica*, it was completed in 1397.[42] This, of course, was an auspicious year for the Despensers when Thomas was raised to the earldom of Gloucester. Whether it was coincidence or otherwise, it certainly represented the fruition of all that Elizabeth had worked for. Little wonder Tewkesbury played an enormous part in the consciousness of the lords of Glamorgan. It became the means of displaying their elevation in status for all to see.

The building of the Fitzhamon chapel affords an interesting perspective on the motivation behind Thomas's burial. As we have seen, Thomas had no chantry chapel of his own and was buried inconspicuously beneath the choir floor. However, physically less may be symbolically more. Whilst the visual 'minimalism' involved is undeniable, Thomas's tomb lies amongst those of the former earls of Gloucester. Could this have been deliberate? Thomas, his son Richard (d. 1414), and his two daughters Isabel and Elizabeth all lie between the de Clares and the high altar.[43] The return to the original burial place of the earls may well have been largely a matter of convenience and aesthetics – after all, space was at a premium in the abbey – but once again it is tempting to see it as an intentional statement. The Despensers clearly saw Gloucester as 'their' earldom, and by slotting in these four tombs they now surrounded the altar entirely.[44] Perhaps Isabel was trying to capture this mood when she buried her first husband, Richard Beauchamp of Worcester, at Tewkesbury and arrayed his chapel (the Beauchamp Chapel, on the north side of the choir) with twelve mourners. She chose statues of de Clare earls (including Gilbert, the last earl), Hugh Despenser the younger and Thomas Despenser. The fact that it was considered politically expedient to include the latter two says much about the family's private influence in the abbey, but also about the legacy that Isabel, as the last surviving Despenser, wished to leave.

This leads into a consideration of the role of the Despenser women, whose patronage of the abbey is the best evidence we have of their cultural and religious lives. Their piety was not merely restricted to widowhood. Many noblewomen possessed relics, books of hours and psalters, and showed devotion to particular saints. Isabel Beauchamp, daughter of Thomas Despenser, made lavish bequests to shrines of the Virgin Mary at Tewkesbury, Caversham, Worcester and Walsingham, and made pilgrimage to Canterbury on her way home from France in 1431.[45] She was also a great patron of the arts, commissioning John Lydgate to translate 'Fifteen

41 Oxford, Bodleian Library, MS Top. Glouc. d.2, fol. 25r: 'his wife raised a stone chapel constructed with remarkable skill, which is dedicated in honour of the Holy Trinity'.

42 Oxford, Bodleian Library, MS Top. Glouc. d.2, fol. 14r.

43 I have relied on Figure 13.1 in Lindley, 'Medieval Monuments and Chantry Chapels', 162, for the tomb placements.

44 For the Despensers' claim to the earldom of Gloucester, see M. J. Lawrence, 'Edward II and the earldom of Winchester', *Historical Research* (forthcoming).

45 J. C. Ward, *English Noblewomen in the Later Middle Ages* (Harlow, 1992), 145–6.

Joys of Our Lady', a rosary poem of devotion to the Virgin.[46] When she died, she requested burial at Tewkesbury with her family and her first husband, rather than at Warwick with her second husband.[47] Isabel's funeral arrangements were extensive: she ordained six new monks at the abbey and bequeathed jewels and dresses of silk and gold valuing 300 marks.[48] Within a year a rare style of effigy was installed over her tomb. She requested a cadaver effigy, representing her body as a corpse, with the burial shroud pulled back to reveal her naked decaying body. Her head was to be bare, with hair pulled backwards from her face, the whole intended to convey in death a deliberate contrast from the richness she had enjoyed in life. Around her were mourners, griffins and statues of the poor. Effigies of this kind were most often commissioned by clergy, and Isabel's will contains genuine concern for the reaction of the abbey and convent: her jewels were to be sold for the highest possible price and the money delivered to the monks 'that they are not grudged with my burial there or anything I have done about my body'.[49] Her effigy was dramatic, intended to shock the viewer into reflection and prayer.[50]

Other Despenser women made substantial contributions to the abbey fabric. Eleanor's role as a sponsor of monastic building in the 1320s and 1330s was eclipsed only by that elsewhere of her sister, Elizabeth de Burgh, one of the most generous patrons of her time.[51] Elizabeth's foundations of Clare College, Cambridge, the Greyfriars at Walsingham, and her gifts to Denny Abbey, Anglesey Abbey and Clare Priory all came about during a lengthy period of widowhood. This patronage makes for an interesting comparison in cultural taste with that of Edward Despenser's widow Elizabeth. As has been suggested elsewhere,[52] the two Elizabeths were alike in the careful management of their estates. In their other interests, however, they differed significantly. Elizabeth de Burgh's widowhood was marked by open-handed generosity, whereas in Elizabeth Despenser's case it is single-minded devotion to family interests which stands out. Unlike other women of high status, Elizabeth founded no monasteries, colleges or hospitals. We know of no particular saint to whom she was attached, and her involvement at Tewkesbury is the most prominent 'cultural' feature of her widowhood. It seems that promotion of Tewkesbury, its architecture, heritage

46 It was dedicated to 'the worshipfull Pryncesse Isabelle nowe Countasse of Warr lady Despenser': K. K. Jambeck, 'Patterns of Women's Literary Patronage: England, 1200–ca.1475', in J. H. McCash (ed.), *The Cultural Patronage of Medieval Women* (Athens, GA, 1996), 246; D. Pearsall, *John Lydgate* (London, 1970), 168, 274; D. Brindley, *Richard Beauchamp: Medieval England's Greatest Knight* (Stroud, 2001), 110, 129. See also D. D. Egbert, 'The "Tewkesbury" Psalter', *Speculum*, 10 (1935), 377.

47 Oxford, Bodleian Library, MS Top. Glouc. d.2, fol. 31r. Her first husband was Richard Beauchamp, earl of Worcester (d. 1422); her second Richard Beauchamp, earl of Warwick (d. 1439).

48 Oxford, Bodleian Library, MS Top. Glouc. d.2, fols. 31r, 32r.

49 Lindley, 'Medieval Monuments and Chantry Chapels', 176–8; N. H. Nicolas (ed.), *Testamenta Vetusta* (London, 1826), i, 239; F. J. Furnivall, *The Fifty Earliest English Wills* (Early English Text Society, original series, 78, 1882), 116–17.

50 On this theme, see S. Oosterwijk, 'Food for Worms – Food for Thought: the Appearance and Interpretation of the "Verminous" Cadaver in Britain and Europe', *Church Monuments*, 20 (2005), 40–80.

51 Gee, *Women, Art and Patronage*, 29; Ward, *English Noblewomen*, 153; F. A. Underhill, *For her Good Estate: the Life of Elizabeth de Burgh* (New York, 1999), 135–48; idem, 'Elizabeth de Burgh: Connoisseur and Patron', in McCash (ed.), *Cultural Patronage*, 266–87.

52 For Elizabeth Despenser, see Lawrence, 'Despensers', 135–8; for Elizabeth de Burgh, see Underhill, *For her Good Estate*, passim; J. C. Ward, 'Elizabeth de Burgh, Lady of Clare (d. 1360)', in C. M. Barron and A. F. Sutton (eds.), *Medieval London Widows* (London, 1994), 29–46.

and ownership, was more important to her than any purely religious motivation. Her will – where she styled herself Elizabeth Burghersh, Lady Despenser – echoed her life. It differs from those of Elizabeth de Burgh and her own grand-daughter Isabel because it is concerned essentially with her family. There is no mention of any doles to the poor, unlike – for example – Beatrice, Lady Roos, who died in 1414 and left a litany of gifts to her tenants and the convents and lazar-houses of York.[53] Instead, Elizabeth pardoned her son-in-law Sir Thomas Morley for monies owed to her, and left a series of gifts to her daughters Anne and Margaret, and to several retainers.[54] She requested interment 'between my lord and husband, Edward Lord Despenser, and my son, Thomas':

> I desire that I be buried within three days after my decease, and that a black cloth with a white cross be laid over my body, with five tapers about it, and no more, during the office of burial. Likewise that a stone of marble should be placed over my grave, with my portraiture thereon. Also I will that seven of the most honest priests that can be found sing for me for one whole year next after my death and that each of them for so doing receive one hundred shillings; and I desire that one thousand masses should be sung for my soul.[55]

Regrettably it is very difficult to establish genuine motivation or piety on the evidence of wills alone.[56] Outward signs of devotion may or may not be indications of internal conviction; similarly, omissions, like those above, may be misconstrued. Only occasionally is it possible to get behind the source, as we can with Thomas Despenser's sister Elizabeth, Lady Zouche, who died in 1408.[57] This lady left £20 to the abbey in her will and requested burial 'where the bodies of my brothers are buried'.[58] This seemingly inconsequential statement refers to two other children of Edward and Elizabeth who were buried at Tewkesbury: their eldest son Edward, who died aged twelve at Cardiff, and second son Hugh, who died in infancy. Although the dates of the boys' deaths are unknown, they probably died in the 1360s, the fourth period of construction identified by Richard Morris. The loss of two potential male heirs was a hereditary and personal tragedy, made worse by the death of their third child and first daughter Cecile shortly afterwards. Three surviving daughters preceded Thomas's birth in 1373. The dedication shown by Elizabeth Despenser to her son's cause should be viewed with this in mind; Edward's death in 1375 must have ushered in a time of great concern over the likelihood of dynastic survival. It is small wonder Lady Zouche, having witnessed this, wished to spend eternity with her family. Her decision explains how the abbey was not merely a place for the family to display their greatness, but also a haven of peace in an age when so many

53 York, Borthwick Institute for Archives, Archiepiscopal Register 18, fol. 358r–v.

54 Lambeth Palace Library, Reg. Arundel, ii, fols. 108v–109r.

55 Lambeth Palace Library, Reg. Arundel, ii, fol. 108v; cf. Oxford, Bodleian Library, MS Top. Glouc. d.2, fol. 25r. No trace of the marble stone (possibly a brass) or of the grave has been discovered (Lindley, 'Medieval Monuments and Chantry Chapels', 170).

56 R. C. Swanson, *Church and Society in Late Medieval England* (Oxford, 1989), 265–8.

57 A similar attempt is made in M. A. Hicks, 'Piety and Lineage in the Wars of the Roses: the Hungerford Experience', in R. A. Griffiths and J. W. Sherborne (eds.), *Kings & Nobles in the Later Middle Ages: a Tribute to Charles Ross* (Gloucester, 1986), 90–108.

58 Nicholas (ed.), *Testamenta Vetusta*, i, 172. See also P. Payne and C. M. Barron, 'The Letters and Life of Elizabeth Despenser, Lady Zouche (d. 1408)', *Nottingham Medieval Studies*, 41 (1997), 126–56.

children died young. Tewkesbury for the Despensers was more than a sacred space. It was a sanctuary of rest.

Tewkesbury exerted a magnetic force over its benefactors. Not only were consecutive Despenser lords interred in the abbey along with their wives, various second husbands or spouses chose to be buried there too. Sir William Zouche was buried in the now-destroyed Lady Chapel and his image appears in the south clerestory window.[59] A generation later, Elizabeth Montagu, wife of Hugh III, chose to be buried beside him rather than beside her first husband, Giles Badlesmere (d. 1338), or her third, Guy Brian (d. 1390). Sir Guy himself is buried beneath a freestone effigy across the aisle from Hugh and Elizabeth's twin alabaster effigies, and his tomb canopy is closely modelled on theirs – despite the fact that his death occurred over thirty years later (plate 3). Richard Beauchamp of Worcester, Isabel Despenser's first husband, also desired burial at Tewkesbury, and the chapel which Isabel constructed for him is an extravagant illustration of their wealth and appreciation of grandeur.[60] It sits beside the Founder's Chapel on the north side of the sanctuary and at the west end is constructed on two vertical levels, on the model of William Wykeham's chantry in Winchester Cathedral.[61] The lower section has extravagant fan vaulting and a tiny face on the underside of the roof amidst the vaulting may be that of Isabel herself. As we have seen, Isabel was commemorated by a cadaver monument within the chapel.[62] Her second husband Richard Beauchamp of Warwick was interred at Warwick, but desired the Tewkesbury priests to say a mass for him every day and an obit every year 'for ever more'.[63] Their son Duke Henry (d. 1446) was buried at Tewkesbury between the choir stalls under the great central tower. Constance Despenser (d. 1416), wife of Thomas, in fact affords the only notable exception to the family preference for burial at Tewkesbury. She chose to be buried at Reading Abbey. A granddaughter of Edward III and thus a member of the royal family, she was the first principal family member not to be buried at Tewkesbury in almost a century.[64]

Tewkesbury was a place for public display and private piety, a locus for a dynasty proud of its noble or comital rank. Burial within the abbey walls associated the Despenser family with the great families which had gone before. The building programme and burial arrangements together show the Despensers' vibrant use of the visual to reclaim and reinforce their status and lineage – and, in some cases, to express their religious devotion. Such ideas were already in the air in January 1324, when Edward II visited Tewkesbury and placed a cloth of bright green and gold

59 The absence of any tomb for Eleanor had led to suggestions that she and Zouche were buried together in the Lady Chapel (J. H. Blunt, *Tewkesbury Abbey and its Associations* (London and Tewkesbury, 1875), 66; Gee, *Women, Art and Patronage*, 21), but there is no hard evidence for this.

60 Oxford, Bodleian Library, MS Top. Glouc. d.2, fol. 28r: 'Isabel his wife arranged for a beautiful chapel which was constructed with remarkable skill'.

61 Lindley, 'Medieval Monuments and Chantry Chapels', 173.

62 Though she was actually buried just outside it.

63 'My desire is that [the mass] may be the first mass, if it may be, or else I would it were the last': 'The Last Will and Testament of Richard Beauchamp, Earle of Warwicke and Aumarle …', in T. Hearne (ed.), *Historia Vitae et Regni Ricardi II. Angliae Regis* (Oxford, 1729), 242–3.

64 Oxford, Bodleian Library, MS Top. Glouc. d.2, fols. 27r–v. Tewkesbury was also chosen as their burial place by some of the Despensers' retainers. Hugh Mortimer of Weldon was one: E. F. Jacob (ed.), *Register of Henry Chichele, Archbishop of Canterbury, 1414–1443* (4 vols., Canterbury and York Society, 1936–45), ii, 287.

upon Gilbert de Clare's tomb.[65] The king's visit was in all probability arranged by the Despensers themselves to draw the widest attention to their ancestral heritage. In contrast to the Hungerfords, whose experience in the fifteenth century was of tension between family interest and the religious obligations imposed by ancestors,[66] the Despensers experienced no conflict between the imperatives of spiritual and dynastic obligation. Indeed, their particular fusion of devotion with heritage gave rise to some of the most dramatic church architecture of the late Middle Ages.

65 BL, Add. MS 35114, fol. 7v.

66 Hicks, 'Piety and Lineage', 97–100.

THE 'CALCULUS OF FACTION' AND RICHARD II'S DUCHY OF IRELAND, *c.* 1382–9

Peter Crooks

During the penultimate decade of the fourteenth century, a long-standing factional struggle between the two most powerful comital houses in English Ireland became markedly more intense.[1] The nobles in question were Gerald fitz Maurice (d. 1398), third earl of Desmond, head of the Munster branch of the famous Geraldine family; and James Butler, third earl of Ormond (d. 1405).[2] On two occasions – in the autumn of 1384 and again in the spring of 1387 – the records of the Irish chancery laconically report the outbreak of 'great discords' between these earls.[3] The royal administration in Ireland deemed it prudent to intervene. Among those it entrusted with the task of mediation were some of the most distinguished political figures in Ireland, including Maurice, fourth earl of Kildare (d. 1390) – whose career of over four decades may have marked him out as something of an elder-statesman[4] – and two experienced bishops.[5] The dispute was not easily composed. The negotiations in 1384 lasted well over a week.[6] One of the mediators grandly claimed that his efforts

The following abbreviations are used in this article:

COD	*Calendar of Ormond Deeds, 1172–1603*, ed. E. Curtis (6 vols., Dublin, 1932–43)
HBC	*Handbook of British Chronology*, ed. E. B. Fryde, D. E. Greenaway, S. Porter and I. Roy (3rd edn, Cambridge, 1996)
IExP	*Irish Exchequer Payments, 1270–1446*, ed. P. Connolly (Dublin, 1998)
IHS	*Irish Historical Studies*
NAI	National Archives of Ireland, Dublin
NHI	*A New History of Ireland*, ed. T. W. Moody, F. X. Martin and F. J. Byrne
NLI	National Library of Ireland, Dublin
ODNB	*Oxford Dictionary of National Biography*
PRIA	*Proceedings of the Royal Irish Academy*
PKCI	*A Roll of the Proceedings of the King's Council in Ireland* […], ed. J. Graves (London, 1877)
PROME	*The Parliament Rolls of Medieval England*, ed. C. Given-Wilson et al.
RCH	*Rotulorum Patentium et Clausorum Cancellariae Hiberniae Calendarium, Hen. II – Hen. VII*, ed. E. Tresham (Dublin, 1828)

1 For the development of the Desmond–Ormond antagonism, see P. Crooks, '"Hobbes", "Dogs" and Politics in the Ireland of Lionel of Antwerp, *c.* 1361–6', *Haskins Society Journal*, 16 (2005), 138–44.

2 For whom, see G. Mac Niocaill, 'Fitzgerald, Gerald fitz Maurice, Third Earl of Desmond', in *ODNB*, xix, 811–12; C. A. Empey, 'Butler, James, Third Earl of Ormond', ibid., ix, 146–7.

3 *RCH*, 121, no. 77; ibid., 137, no. 220.

4 R. Frame, 'Fitzgerald, Maurice fitz Thomas, Fourth Earl of Kildare', in *ODNB*, xix, 838–9.

5 They were Alexander Petit, *alias* 'Balscot', bishop of Ossory (1371–86) and later of Meath (1386–1400); and Thomas le Reve, bishop of Lismore and Waterford (1363–94). See *NHI*, ix: *Maps, Genealogies, Lists – A Companion to Irish History, Part II* (Oxford, 1984), 286, 304, 317.

6 Sir Patrick Freigne laboured for fifteen days upon this arbitration, but this included the time it took him to travel from the town of Kilkenny to Clonmel and back again: TNA:PRO, E 101/246/6, no. 33 (*RCH*, 122, no. 28).

had helped restore the king's lieges in Munster to tranquillity.[7] If so, peace was ephemeral. Early in 1387, the earl of Kildare was again commissioned to intervene and treat between the two earls.[8]

The antagonism between the Geraldine and Butler families was to become perhaps the most notorious, and certainly the most enduring, magnate rivalry in Irish history.[9] It is sobering, then, to realise how little we know of its crucial early phases. The foregoing summary represents almost the sum-total of our present knowledge of the conflict as it unfolded in the 1380s.[10] In part, this stems from the obduracy of the evidence.[11] But our ignorance is also the result of the choices and assumptions of historians, who have concentrated their efforts on delineating royal policy and tracing the doings of the king's chief governors.[12] By contrast, the private concerns of the 'unreliable' resident nobility of Ireland, including their 'internecine quarrels and private wars', tend to dismissed brusquely as disruptive to the colony's political life.[13] A despondent Professor Watt captures the mood with his characterisation of the 1380s as a 'particularly drab phase of [colonial] history, with a dreary succession of [chief governors]', who were 'as unable to ward off the hostile Gaelic Irish as to suppress Anglo-Irish marauding and the debilitating feuds among the magnates, of which that between Ormond and Desmond is the most scandalous'.[14]

Drabness and dreariness are, of course, in the eye of the beholder; yet Professor Watt's bleak depiction is puzzling given that, by any standards, the 1380s was a memorable period in colonial affairs. This was due primarily to Richard II's contentious experiment in devolution. On 12 October 1385 the king announced his intention of granting Ireland as a palatinate to his favourite, Robert de Vere, ninth earl of Oxford (d. 1392), who was to bear the title marquess of Dublin.[15] This was the most dramatic constitutional departure in 'Anglo-Irish relations' since 1254, when Henry III had granted Ireland (together with a string of other lands) to his son, the future Edward I, on the understanding that 'the above-mentioned lands and castles

7 TNA:PRO, E 101/246/6, no. 32.

8 *RCH*, 137, no. 220.

9 For the conflict in the early modern period, see, most recently, A. M. McCormack, *The Earldom of Desmond, 1463–1583: The Decline and Crisis of a Feudal Lordship* (Dublin, 2005), 88–108.

10 The conflict escalated further in the 1390s, but those events are better documented: P. Crooks, 'Factionalism and Noble Power in English Ireland, *c.* 1361–1423' (University of Dublin Ph.D. thesis, 2007), 165, 201–43.

11 Most significantly, the Irish chancery rolls are no longer extant. Where possible, I have attempted to compensate for the inadequacies of the calendar published in 1828 by the Irish Record Commission (*RCH*) by providing references to superior transcripts of the original rolls. In such cases, I have placed the corresponding entry from *RCH* in parentheses.

12 See, e.g., A. J. Otway-Ruthven, *A History of Medieval Ireland*, 2nd edn (London, 1980), 317–22; A. Tuck, 'Anglo-Irish Relations, 1382–1393', *PRIA*, 69 (1970), C, no. 2, 15–31; D. Johnston, 'Chief Governors and Treasurers of Ireland in the Reign of Richard II', in T. B. Barry, R. F. Frame and K. Simms (eds.), *Colony and Frontier in Medieval Ireland: Essays Presented to J. F. Lydon* (London, 1995), 97–115.

13 Tuck, 'Anglo-Irish Relations', 17. Similar language is employed in R. Halliday, 'Robert de Vere, Ninth Earl of Oxford', *Medieval History*, 3 (1993), 76.

14 J. A. Watt, 'The Anglo-Irish Colony under Strain, 1327–99', in A. Cosgrove (ed.), *NHI*, ii: *Medieval Ireland, 1169–1534* (Oxford, 1987), 390–91. This historiographical argument is further elaborated in P. Crooks, 'Factions, Feuds and Noble Power in the Lordship of Ireland, *c.* 1356–1496', *IHS* 35, no. 140, 2007).

15 *CPR 1385–9*, 115. On de Vere, see A. Tuck, 'Vere, Robert de, Ninth Earl of Oxford, Marquess of Dublin, and Duke of Ireland', in *ODNB*, lvi, 312–15; Halliday, 'Robert de Vere, Ninth Earl of Oxford', 71–95.

shall never be separated from the crown of England, but shall ever remain to the kings of that country'.[16] De Vere's elevation attracted widespread notice and resentment.[17] The title of marquess was previously 'unknown in England',[18] such that the monk of Westminster had to explain that it signified a dignity, 'superior to an earl and less than a duke; so that the king caused him to be seated in parliament above the earls'.[19] On 13 October 1386, the king honoured de Vere still further by creating him duke of Ireland.[20] Although de Vere himself never crossed the Irish Sea, his involvement clawed the English colony in Ireland to the centre of the most dramatic episode of the decade, the Appellant crisis of 1387–8. Such was the efficiency with which the Lords Appellant aborted the embryonic duchy of Ireland that it is easy to forget that even more grandiose designs may have been in the making. More than one rumour had it that Richard intended to elevate Ireland to the dignity of a kingdom.[21] The claim cannot be lightly dismissed. Previous kings – most recently Edward III – had conceived of Ireland as a forum for the activities of their sons.[22] A royal protégé such as Robert de Vere may then have served as a surrogate for the childless Richard. To be sure, the alienation of Ireland from the English crown would have been a novelty; but in this field of endeavour, novelty was the distinctive mark of Richard II.[23] Groundless or not, the gossip conveys the urgency with which Ireland was impinging on the English political consciousness.[24]

Since Michael Bennett's important study of Richard II's 'wider realm', students of English history are unlikely to overlook the important place of Ireland in the reign

16 *Calendar of Documents Relating to Ireland Preserved in Her Majesty's Public Record Office, London*, ed. H. S. Sweetman and G. F. Handcock (5 vols., London, 1875–86), ii, nos. 326, 335. James Lydon terms this the 'doctrine of inalienability': Lydon, 'Ireland and the English Crown, 1171–1541', *IHS*, 29 (1995), 282. In 1388, the breach of this 'doctrine' provided the Lords Appellant with ammunition against Robert de Vere: *The Westminster Chronicle, 1381–1394*, ed. L. C. Hector and B. F. Harvey (Oxford, 1982), 246–9; C. Given-Wilson (ed.), 'Richard II: Parliament of February 1388, Text and Translation', in *PROME*, pt 2, 'Appeal of Treason', article 11 [CD-ROM, Scholarly Digital Editions (Leicester, 2005)].

17 The official creation was made in parliament on 1 December 1385: Given-Wilson (ed.), 'Richard II: Parliament of October 1385, Text and Translation', in *PROME*, item 17; *Calendar of Charter Rolls 1341–1417*, 301.

18 *The St Albans Chronicle: The* Chronica Maiora *of Thomas Walsingham*, i: *1376–1394*, ed. J. Taylor, W. Childs and L. Watkiss (Oxford, 2003), 780–1.

19 *Westminster Chronicle*, 145. For the history of this 'foreign' title, see D. Crouch, *The Image of Aristocracy in Britain, 1000–1300* (London and New York, 1992), 98–100.

20 *Calendar of Charter Rolls 1341–1417*, 307.

21 *Thomae Walsingham, Quondam Monachi S. Albani, Historia Anglicana*, ed. H. T. Riley (2 vols., Rolls Series, 1863–4), ii, 148; *Chronicon Angliae* […], ed. E. M. Thompson (London, 1874), 372; *Westminster Chronicle*, 248–9; Given-Wilson (ed.), 'Richard II: Parliament of February 1388, Text and Translation', in *PROME*, pt 2, 'Appeal of Treason', article 11. Adam Usk makes a similar claim in respect of Thomas Holand in 1399: *The Chronicle of Adam Usk, 1377–1421*, ed. C. Given-Wilson (Oxford, 1997), 76–7.

22 See, for instance, M. T. Flanagan, *Irish Society, Anglo-Norman Settlers, Angevin Kingship: Interactions in Ireland in the Late Twelfth Century* (Oxford, 1989), 276–81; J. R. Studd, 'The Lord Edward and King Henry III', *BIHR*, 50 (1977), 4–19; P. Connolly, 'Lionel of Clarence and Ireland, 1361–1366' (University of Dublin Ph.D. thesis, 1977). Henry IV likewise appointed his son, Thomas, as lieutenant of Ireland in 1401: *CPR 1399–1401*, 507.

23 For Richard's new creations in England, see C. Given-Wilson, *The English Nobility in the Late Middle Ages: The Fourteenth-Century Political Community* (London and New York, 1987), 47–53.

24 The monk of Westminster reports that Richard conferred the duchy of Ireland on his uncle, Thomas of Woodstock, in 1389. This is untrue, but the persistence of such rumours is instructive in itself: *Westminster Chronicle*, 378–9.

of Richard II.[25] Irish historians, however, have not yet exhausted the implications of this for political dynamics within the colony. This may be due to the lingering assumption that at the rotten core of factionalism lurked the problem of noble disengagement from the affairs of the central government. Of course, there is much to be said about the local causes of the Geraldine–Butler dispute: where the shifting boundaries of lordship over men and land converged or intersected in the south of Ireland, friction was the inevitable result.[26] Yet the issues at stake transcended the provincial and had a relevance in much broader contexts – the Dublin administration and the English court to name but two. The present essay is an attempt to draw the resident lords of English Ireland in from the historiographical margins. Rather than examining the Geraldine–Butler antagonism simply in terms of local tensions, it shifts the emphasis and explores two political patterns illustrated by the records describing the interactions between the nobility and the central government. In doing so, it seeks to contribute to our understanding of political society in colonial Ireland.

A first pattern concerns the influence of colonial faction on attitudes to the king's representative in Ireland. A recent comment on this period colourfully describes how a newly appointed king's lieutenant may have viewed his commission, 'with all the trepidation of an Englishman venturing among not only the "wild Irish", but into the Byzantine factionalism of colonial Anglo-Ireland'.[27] If so, this was partly because the resident nobles of Ireland were adept at championing the grievances of the colony's political community in the pursuit of private ends. Sophisticated political manoeuvres, rather than magnates on the rampage, posed the principal threat to those unfortunate chief governors who found themselves mired in factional controversy. Indeed, the events of these years would have been familiar to the beleaguered chief governors of the Tudor age, who discovered that the colony's response to their programmes of reform was informed not by suspicion of royal government, but by what Professor Ciaran Brady has described as the 'complex and delicate calculus of faction'.[28] This evocative phrase is, however, equally useful when its sense is inverted and we examine the 'calculus of faction' at the court of Richard II. Given the entanglement of Ireland in English politics during these years, metropolitan developments must surely have had some bearing upon the fate of rival parties in the colony. This essay takes each of these political patterns in turn in the period *c*. 1382–9, dividing roughly with the creation of the duchy of Ireland in 1386.

25 M. J. Bennett, 'Richard II and the Wider Realm', in A. Goodman and J. Gillespie (eds.), *Richard II: The Art of Kingship* (Oxford, 1999), 187–204.

26 The local causes of the conflict are examined in detail in Crooks, 'Factionalism and Noble Power', 129–36.

27 K. Kerby-Fulton and R. Horie (eds.), 'The French Version of the *Modus Tenendi Parliamentum* in the Courtenay Cartulary: A Transcription and Introduction', in K. Kerby-Fulton and M. Hilmo (eds.), *The Medieval Reader: Reception and Cultural History in the Late Medieval Manuscript* (Studies in Medieval and Renaissance History, 3rd ser., i, New York, 2001), 227.

28 C. Brady, *The Chief Governors: The Rise and Fall of Reform Government in Ireland, 1536–88* (Cambridge, 1994), 176. See also idem, 'Court, Castle and Country: The Framework of Government', in C. Brady and R. Gillespie (eds.), *Natives and Newcomers: Essays on the Making of Irish Colonial Society, 1534–1641* (Dublin, 1986), 29–30; idem, 'England's Defence and Ireland's Reform: The Dilemma of the Irish Viceroys, 1541–1641', in B. Bradshaw and J. Morillo (eds.), *The British Problem,* c. *1534–1707: State Formation in the Atlantic Archipelago* (Basingstoke and London, 1996), 90.

I

The years 1382–6 were stormy ones in colonial politics, witness not only to the discord between the Geraldines and Butlers, but also to trenchant criticism of the king's ministers in Ireland, in particular the chief governor from 1383 to 1386, Sir Philip Courtenay (d. 1406).[29] Courtenay's appointment as king's lieutenant in 1383 was a belated response to a power vacuum that had developed in Ireland during 1381–2. On the night of 26–7 December 1381 Edmund Mortimer, earl of March and Ulster, died at Cork while holding the office of king's lieutenant.[30] He was followed to the grave within a year by the man who had dominated much of the colony's political life for some three decades: James Butler, second earl of Ormond.[31] The passing of Edmund Mortimer had provoked consternation within the English administration in Ireland.[32] Fortunately, when the second earl of Ormond died, he left a mature and capable heir. His son, James III Butler (d. 1405), was at least twenty-two years old in 1382.[33] In the late 1370s, he had acted as his father's deputy in the office of chief governor of Ireland,[34] and he had also been a beneficiary of royal patronage.[35] He was, then, well able to assume the mantle of his father. In this, the royal administration seems to have been eager to facilitate him. James III was granted livery of his estates with minimal delay on 2 March 1383.[36] His two mainpernors were a former chief governor of Ireland, Sir Robert Ashton (d. 1384) of Pitney, Somerset;[37] and the archbishop of Canterbury, William Courtenay (1381–96).[38]

The involvement of Archbishop Courtenay may be significant in terms of the court's long-term plans both for Ormond and colonial security generally. Three months later, on 20 June 1383, the archbishop's nephew, Sir Philip Courtenay,[39] uncle of Edward Courtenay, earl of Devon, entered into an indenture with the king to become the king's lieutenant of Ireland for a period of ten years.[40] During the

29 For Sir Philip Courtenay, see J. S. Roskell, L. Clark and C. Rawcliffe (eds.), *The House of Commons, 1386–1421* (4 vols., Stroud, 1992), ii, 670–73; Tuck, 'Anglo-Irish Relations', 21.

30 *Chartulary of Saint Mary's Abbey, Dublin* [...], ed. J. T. Gilbert, (2 vols., London, 1884–6), ii, 285; *Westminster Chronicle*, 22–3; *St Albans Chronicle, 1376–94*, 580–81; W. Dugdale, *Monasticon Anglicanum* [...], ed. J. Caley, H. Ellis and B. Bandinel (6 vols., London, 1817–30), vi, 353; *Usk*, 46–7.

31 There is a discrepancy between the date for his death given in the annals (18 October) and the date of 6 November given in the inquisitions *post mortem* conducted in England: *Chartulary of St Mary's Abbey*, ii, 285–6; *CIPM 1377–84*, 281–4, nos. 696–709. However, an exchequer record dated 23 October 1382 refers to the death of the second earl of Ormond: TNA:PRO, E 101/246/2, no. 27. This suggests that the earlier date of 18 October is correct.

32 *Parliaments and Councils of Mediaeval Ireland*, ed. H. G. Richardson and G. O. Sayles (Dublin, 1947), 115–20, no. 66 (*RCH*, 111, no. 39).

33 *CIPM 1377–84*, 281, no. 696.

34 TNA:PRO, E 101/246/5, nos. 44, 70, 120, 180, 231; *Parliaments & Councils*, 108–9, no. 60 (B).

35 *CFR 1377–83*, 103.

36 *CFR 1377–83*, 352.

37 *NHI*, ix, 474; *VCH Somerset*, iii, 15. Sir Robert Ashton held the manor of Brean, Somerset, by demise of the second earl of Ormond: *CCR 1381–5*, 459; *CCR 1385–9*, 209.

38 For whom, see J. Dahmus, *William Courtenay, Archbishop of Canterbury, 1381–1396* (Philadelphia, 1966).

39 On the Courtenay family in this period, see M. Cherry, 'The Courtenay Earls of Devon: The Formation and Disintegration of a Late Medieval Aristocratic Affinity', *Southern History*, 1 (1979), 71–97.

40 TNA:PRO, E 101/68/9/221. Courtenay's appointment followed on 1 July 1383: *CPR 1381–5*, 291. An earlier patent of appointment, dated 23 June 1383, was later vacated: *CPR 1381–5*, 293.

spring, the appointment of the king's favoured candidate to serve as lieutenant – his half-brother, Sir John Holand (d. 1400) – had been cancelled.[41] Sir Philip Courtenay, evidently, was hit upon as Holand's replacement. He was, however, a far less exalted figure than the English of Ireland had come to expect since the lieutenancy of Edward III's son, Lionel of Antwerp (1361–6). Difficulties in persuading the colonial community to accept Courtenay were anticipated,[42] and it may have been envisaged that the influence of the new earl of Ormond could help overcome any such obstacles. For Ormond, the potential value of the arrangement lay in having the ear of the king's representative in Ireland.

Ormond acted as chief governor of Ireland from 20 August 1383 until Courtenay landed at Waterford on 11 September 1383,[43] and after the latter's arrival the two men did indeed collaborate.[44] Courtenay's obligations as the king's lieutenant were, however, multiple. While he seems to have been generally amenable to Butler interests, he could not afford to antagonise Ormond's rivals, the Desmond Geraldines. The lieutenant's circumspection is clear from a document dated 3 February 1384, by virtue of which Ormond received custody of lands at Knockgraffon, Tipperary, that were then in royal hands.[45] The grant contains the proviso that should Ormond lease these lands to 'any one of the nation of the Burkeyns', they would automatically revert to the crown.[46] The 'Burkeyns' in question were the Burghs of Clanwilliam, descended from Richard Burgh, the 'red' earl of Ulster (d. 1326).[47] Their territory lay in west Tipperary and east Limerick between the supremacies of the earls of Ormond and Desmond. In 1377, Sir Richard Burgh of Clanwilliam had been embroiled in a struggle with Gerald, third earl of Desmond, and there had been further upheaval in 1381.[48] Their conflict was complicated by the fact that the head of the Clanwilliam lineage, Sir Richard Burgh, had been retained for life by James, second earl of Ormond.[49] Consequently there was a danger that Burgh's conflict with Desmond could escalate into a major confrontation between the two comital houses. Courtenay's desire to avoid this demonstrates some sensitivity on his part to the subtleties of the colony's internal politics.

That sensitivity notwithstanding, the Geraldines and Butlers clashed in the autumn

41 See Johnston, 'Chief Governors', 103 note 32; Tuck, 'Anglo-Irish Relations', 20. Holand was later earl of Huntingdon (1388) and duke of Exeter (1397–9): G. E. C[okayne], *The Complete Peerage of England, Scotland, Ireland, Great Britain, and the United Kingdom, Extant, Extinct, or Dormant*, new edn by Vicary Gibbs et al. (12 vols., London, 1910–59), v, 195–200; vi, 653–4.

42 His indenture stipulates that accusations against him would be heard before the king: TNA:PRO, E 101/68/9/221. Note also the suggestion that Courtenay took the precaution of carrying to Ireland a French rendition of the English version of the *Modus tenendi parliamentum*, because he 'wanted a copy of … a treatise on parliamentary procedure in order to start his new position': Kerby-Fulton and Horie, 'French Version of the *Modus*', 227.

43 TNA:PRO, E 101/246/7, nos. 76–7; E 101/246/6, no. 100; 'Lord Chancellor Gerrard's Notes of his Report on Ireland […]', ed. C. McNeill, *Analecta Hibernica*, 2 (1931), 200.

44 Crooks, 'Factionalism and Noble Power', 174–81.

45 Knockgraffon (barony of Middlethird, co. Tipperary) was in the medieval cantred of Moyenen: C. A. Empey, 'The Cantreds of Medieval Tipperary', *North Munster Antiquarian Journal*, 13 (1970), 27.

46 NLI, D 1299 (*COD*, ii, no. 271).

47 For the Clanwilliam Burghs, see D. G. Marnane, *Land and Settlement: A History of West Tipperary to 1660* (Tipperary, 2003), 217–20.

48 *RCH*, 103, no. 91; ibid., 108, no. 46.

49 NLI, D 1012 ('Private Indentures for Life Service in Peace and War, 1278–1476', ed. M. Jones and S. Walker, *Camden Miscellany XXXII*, Camden Society, 5th ser., 3 (1994), 76–7, no. 44; cf. *COD*, ii, no. 37). See also a second agreement dating from 1360: NLI, D 1037 (*COD*, ii, no. 61).

of 1384. The immediate spark for their quarrel is unknown, but it is likely that it was somehow connected with the efforts of the third earl of Ormond to establish himself. In August 1383 James III, 'now earl of Ormond', concluded an agreement with his mother, Elizabeth, and her new husband, Sir Robert Herford. Under its terms, Elizabeth was to surrender to her son all the Irish estates she held as dower, with the exception of some manors in north county Dublin, four hundred marks, and one third of the prisage of wines in Ireland.[50] By November 1383 Ormond had solicited a writ from England granting him permission to travel to court in order to render his homage to the king.[51] The young earl did not set out for Westminster immediately. Nonetheless, he was already associating himself indirectly with some of Richard II's intimates. One broker of patronage was the king's half-brother, John Holand, whose appointment as lieutenant of Ireland had been cancelled in 1383. Although Holand fell from grace in July 1385 after murdering Ralph, son of the second earl of Stafford, he had previously been a great favourite of the king.[52] In July 1384 John Holand petitioned on behalf of 'Robert de Hereford *alias* Robert Lovekyn, knight, who is busy in the said John's service', for a pardon in the latter's account as the king's seneschal of Tipperary for the period between the death of the second earl of Ormond and the release of the Butler estates to Earl James III.[53] This Sir Robert Herford was the same man who had recently married Elizabeth, dowager countess of Ormond. Herford was later to return to Ireland and become closely associated with Butler fortunes.

These glimpses of Ormond's activities lend the impression of a young man in a hurry. Doubtless, that drive and ambition was replicated at a local level in the south of Ireland, where the Butler lordship rubbed shoulders with the territorial concerns of the Munster Geraldines. Against this background, the fact that Ormond came to blows with Gerald, third earl of Desmond, during 1384 should occasion little surprise.[54] The significant point for this discussion is that, although Sir Philip Courtenay found it necessary to dispatch mediators to Clonmel in Tipperary to restore peace, the outbreak of discord did little to shake the lieutenant's confidence in Ormond. In late November 1384 Courtenay was preparing to return to England. On the eve of his departure, he went to considerable lengths to bolster Ormond's position. On 26 November 1384 he issued Ormond with a general pardon.[55] The same day, a payment of one hundred shillings was authorised to Sir Patrick Freigne, a close supporter of the Butler family, for his travails earlier that month attempting to arbitrate between the Butler and Geraldine factions.[56] Two days later, on 28 November, Courtenay nominated Ormond as chief governor.[57] Ormond took

50 *COD*, ii, no. 265. The original deed (NLI, D 1292) is missing at present from NLI. On 30 March 1384 Elizabeth was pardoned for marrying Sir Robert Herford and was granted livery of her lands in England and the march of Wales: *CPR 1381–5*, 403; *CCR 1381–5*, 372.

51 *CPR 1381–5*, 330; NLI, D 1293 (*COD*, ii, no. 266).

52 N. E. Saul, *Richard II* (New Haven and London, 1997), 120, 243–4; Tuck, *Richard II*, 79–80.

53 *CPR 1381–5*, 453 (quotation); *CCR 1381–5*, 467. Sir Robert Herford had previously served the second earl of Ormond as seneschal of Tipperary in 1381–2: NLI, D 1279–80 (*COD*, ii, nos. 254–5). For a catalogue of his career, see T. Blake Butler, 'Seneschals of the Liberty of Tipperary', *The Irish Genealogist*, 2 (1943–55), 332–3.

54 *RCH*, 121, no. 77.

55 *RCH*, 121, no. 8.

56 TNA:PRO, E 101/246/6, no. 33 (*RCH*, 122, no. 28).

57 Oxford, Bodleian Library, MS Rawlinson B 502, fol. 95r (*RCH*, 122, no. 1).

up office as justiciar of Ireland on 30 November 1384 and served in that capacity until Courtenay's return in May 1385.[58]

One man who may have helped drive the interests of Courtenay and Ormond together in the last months of 1384 was Robert Wikeford, archbishop of Dublin (1376–90).[59] On 10 September 1384 Wikeford had received an English-seal appointment as chancellor of Ireland.[60] He had arrived in the colony by 8 November, when the out-going chancellor, Sir Ralph Cheyne, was instructed to release to him the great seal of Ireland.[61] Wikeford immediately began to foment trouble against Courtenay. Within a matter of weeks, the lieutenant had resolved to remonstrate personally at Westminster against the new chancellor. Having appointed Ormond as chief governor of Ireland, Courtenay travelled to England and informed the king that Wikeford had summoned councils and parliaments without permission, had laid imposts upon the people, and had taken fines and granted pardons for his own use. Outraged, the king wrote to Wikeford on 30 December, 'marvelling not a little, that by colour of his office the chancellor after his last coming to Ireland has done all those things, for which he had no such authority'.[62] By the time Courtenay returned to Ireland in the early summer, the archbishop had been superseded in office.[63] Wikeford's motives need not detain us here longer than to suggest that the explanation may be located in the events in the late 1370s, when Wikeford had agitated against the authority of Ormond's father, Earl James II, then chief governor of Ireland.[64] The revival of that controversy in 1384 helps to explain the trust that Courtenay placed in James, third earl of Ormond, despite the latter's recent embroilment with the Desmond Geraldines. Archbishop Wikeford of Dublin was a mutual enemy.

On 6 May 1385 Sir Philip Courtenay disembarked at Dalkey, county Dublin, bearing a new appointment as lieutenant of Ireland.[65] It would be reasonable to

58 TNA:PRO, E 101/246/6, no. 97. On 30 November Ormond issued Courtenay with a protection: Oxford, Bodleian Library, MS Rawlinson B 502, fol. 95r. The justiciary rolls, which are no longer extant, showed that Ormond held pleas from 1 December 1384 until 28 April 1385: H. Wood, 'The Office of Chief Governor of Ireland, 1172–1509', *PRIA*, 36 (1923), C, no. 12, 230.

59 For whom, see D. B. Johnston, 'Wikeford, Robert (*d.* 1390)', in *ODNB*, lviii, 864–5.

60 *CPR 1381–5*, 455 (*RCH*, 120, no. 41).

61 Oxford, Bodleian Library, MS Rawlinson B 502, fol. 95r (*RCH*, 120, no. 43). On 10 November 1384 Sir Philip Courtenay ordered that payment be made to Cheyne of arrears of his fee as chancellor from 26 June to 7 November 1384: TNA:PRO, E 101/246/6, no. 92 (*RCH*, 122, no. 2). On 22 November, Cheyne was handsomely compensated for his ejection from office with a grant of the wardship of the liberty of Wexford for the sum of £160: *RCH*, 119, no. 22; *CPR 1385–9*, 523. A point of interface between Cheyne and James, third earl of Ormond, was Sir Robert Ashton, one of Ormond's mainpernors in 1383. Ashton had served as justiciar of Ireland 1372–3 and, at his departure, he had appointed his cousin, Sir Ralph Cheyne, as his deputy. After Ashton's death in January 1384, some of his estates descended to Cheyne: *NHI*, ix, 474; *House of Commons*, ii, 555.

62 *CCR 1381–5*, 500.

63 Wikeford's replacement as chancellor of Ireland was Bishop Alexander Balscot of Ossory, who took up office on 12 April 1385: *CPR 1381–5*, 532; *RCH*, 129, no. 21.

64 TNA:PRO, C 49/75, m. 27–27v; *CPR 1377–81*, 271; *CCR 1377–81*, 171–2, 225. Wikeford's opposition to Ormond may have been connected with the fact that in 1378, while Ormond was justiciar, the archiepiscopal manor of Swords, co. Dublin, was seized into the king's hands: *Documents on the Affairs of Ireland before the King's Council*, ed. G. O. Sayles (Dublin, 1979), 250–3, no. 264. For discussion, see Crooks, 'Factionalism and Noble Power', 146–8, 152–3, 176–81. On Swords, see R. Stalley, 'The Archbishop's Residence at Swords: Castle or Country Retreat?', in *Medieval Dublin VII*, ed. S. Duffy (Dublin, 2006), 152–76.

65 *RCH*, 128, no. 15; *CPR 1381–5*, 540.

expect that Courtenay's return would usher in a second period of cooperation with Ormond. In fact, the relationship between the two men quickly soured. It is not easy to account for this change, but it is possible that Ormond's hostility was aroused by the belief that the lieutenant was insufficiently devoted to Butler interests. After his return, Courtenay seems to have attempted to establish greater parity between the Geraldines and Butlers. In doing so, he may have been attempting to redress an imbalance caused by Ormond's recent tenure as justiciar of Ireland. Ormond had not exercised that office with great tact. At almost his very first opportunity, 1 December 1384, he had appointed a panel of justices to inquire into seditions in the south of Ireland.[66] Two of the areas to be covered by the investigation, Kilkenny and Tipperary, lay within Butler country and so were not contentious. The commission, however, also embraced counties Waterford and Limerick. These were areas of keen Geraldine interest. Still more provocative was the fact that a number of the commissioners – Sir Patrick and Sir Robert Freigne, and John Lumbard – were Ormond's adherents.[67] Coming so soon after the settlement of strife in Munster the previous autumn, this challenge to the authority of the earl of Desmond must have been deeply disquieting to the Geraldines of Munster. Courtenay may also have viewed Ormond's actions with dismay. The fact that the lieutenant now favoured an even-handed approach was signalled by his appointment of Desmond and Ormond to act *jointly* as his deputies at a great council that was to convene at Kilkenny on 17 July 1385. Courtenay could not attend this assembly because he was campaigning against the Irish of Leinster.[68] For Ormond, the appointment of Desmond as co-deputy may have been particularly galling given that the council was to be held at Kilkenny, a town at the heart of Butler interests.[69]

Ormond's antipathy towards his former ally became entwined with a more general anti-ministerial sentiment that was expressed at great councils held at Kilkenny and Dublin in the latter half of 1385.[70] In the course of these assemblies, the ills besetting the colony were discussed, in particular the 'great power of the Irish enemies and English rebels' who, rather ominously, were said to be confederating with the king's 'other enemies of Scotland and Spain', such that 'at this next season, as is likely,

66 *RCH*, 121, no. 86.

67 For indentures between the Freignes and James, second earl of Ormond, see NLI, D 1223–5, 1272 (*COD*, ii, nos. 205 (i–iii), 247; 'Private Indentures', 98–9, no. 68). Lumbard is named as Ormond's servant in 1388: *RCH*, 141, no. 195. All three men appear as witnesses in *COD*, ii, no. 265. Another commissioner, Walter Coterel, was soon to be appointed a justice of pleas before the seneschal of Kilkenny: *RCH*, 127, no. 236.

68 *RCH*, 123, no. 1. Bishop Alexander of Ossory (chancellor of Ireland) and Bishop Thomas of Lismore–Waterford were also commissioned to deputise for Courtenay. One biography of Courtenay misdates this nomination of deputies to July 1384 and states that the lieutenant was in England at the time: *House of Commons*, ii, 671. Possibly there is some confusion with Sir Philip's brother, Sir Peter Courtenay, who attended the Salisbury parliament of April 1384 and was one of those who tortured the unfortunate friar, John Latimer. See *Westminster Chronicle*, 68–75; T. F. Tout, *Chapters in the Administrative History of Mediaeval England* (6 vols., Manchester, 1920–33), iii, 392–3, note 1.

69 For the growth of Butler influence in co. Kilkenny – described by one historian as the 'Butler *Drang nach Osten*' – see C. A. Empey, 'County Kilkenny in the Anglo-Norman Period', in W. Nolan and K. Whelan (eds.), *Kilkenny History and Society: Interdisciplinary Essays on the History of an Irish County* (Dublin, 1990), 88.

70 For the subtle distinction between great councils and parliaments in late fourteenth-century Ireland, see H. G. Richardson and G. O. Sayles, *The Irish Parliament in the Middle Ages* (2nd edn, Philadelphia, 1964), 104–10.

there will be made a general conquest of the greater part of Ireland'.[71] It was decided that the only remedy was the personal presence of the king in Ireland. Two envoys – Bishop Alexander Balscot of Ossory and Archbishop Robert Wikeford of Dublin – were elected to travel to England to solicit a royal expedition or, failing that, the appointment of 'le plus graunt et plus foiable seigneur dengleterre'.[72] Ormond's contribution to this movement has left only a shadowy impression in the records. A first step towards demonstrating his involvement is to re-examine the chronology. It has generally been assumed that the complaints against Courtenay date from a session of the great council of Ireland that convened at Dublin in October 1385.[73] Yet, the records state that grievances were voiced at councils held both at Dublin *and* Kilkenny. The only council held at Kilkenny in 1385 was that summoned for 17 July, which Courtenay did not attend. This indicates that it was in July, and not October, that the idea of electing emissaries to travel to England was first mooted. The delegation did not finally set out for court until early 1386, but traces of their earlier preparations survive. In September 1385 one Robert Crull, prebendary of Swords, was granted a licence to absent himself from Ireland.[74] Crull was later named as a member of the company of the envoys of the colonial community and it is stated that he had travelled to England at their request, 'to transact with the Council business relating to Ireland'.[75] The preparations of Bishop Alexander Balscot of Ossory for a journey to Westminster also predate the Dublin great council of October 1385. As chancellor of Ireland, he had to nominate a deputy to act in his absence. On 20 September 1385 William fitz William was appointed keeper of the great seal.[76] If the envoys were indeed first chosen in July, this may lend an added significance to their remonstrations about the danger posed by the king's 'enemys descoce'.[77] Early in June 1385 writs were issued in England for what was to be the last summons of the English feudal host. The army, which was to march upon Scotland, met at Newcastle at the end of July and campaigned in Scotland during August.[78] The threat of incursions along the coast of Ireland was by no means groundless.[79] Nevertheless, the exhumation of Scottish skeletons at the precise moment that the king was

71 *Statutes and Ordinances and Acts of the Parliament of Ireland, King John to Henry V*, ed. H. F. Berry, 484–5 (*RCH*, 128, no. 18).

72 *Statutes ... of the Parliament of Ireland*, 486–7 (*RCH*, 128, no. 18).

73 Otway-Ruthven, *History of Medieval Ireland*, 318; Halliday, 'Robert de Vere, Ninth Earl of Oxford', 76; cf. Tuck, *Richard II*, 81.

74 *RCH*, 123, no. 20. For Crull, see H. Cotton, *Fasti Ecclesiae Hibernicae: The Succession of the Prelates and Members of the Cathedral Bodies in Ireland*, ii: *The Province of Leinster* (Dublin, 1848), 136.

75 *CPR 1385–9*, 91.

76 *RCH*, 123, no. 26. It is not clear if the appointment was effective. Later, on 13 November, Bishop Alexander of Ossory appointed Robert Sutton as his lieutenant in the office of chancellor because he was about to set out for England. On 20 January 1386, Sutton was superseded by Thomas Everdon: *RCH*, 125, no. 136; ibid., 124, nos. 78, 80–81.

77 *Statutes ... of the Parliament of Ireland*, 484.

78 Saul, *Richard II*, 144–5; N. B. Lewis, 'The Last Summons of the English Feudal Levy, 13 June 1385', *EHR*, 73 (1958), 1–26; J. J. N. Palmer, 'The Last Summons of the Feudal Army in England (1385)', *EHR*, 83 (1968), 771–5; N. B. Lewis, 'The Feudal Summons of 1385', *EHR*, 100 (1985), 729–43, with comment by J. J. N. Palmer, ibid., 743–6.

79 *RCH*, 127, no. 243; NLI, MS 4 [Harris], fol. 29; *The Original Chronicle of Andrew of Wyntoun*, ed. F. J. Armours (6 vols., Edinburgh and London, 1902–14), vi, 320–25. The colony also suffered attacks from Spanish and French fleets: *CPR 1385–9*, 492 (*RCH*, 138, no. 33); *St Albans Chronicle, 1376–94*, 368–71.

marching northwards may, in part, have been a contrivance intended to attract the attention of the court.[80]

It is against this background that we must set the actions of the earl of Ormond in the second half of 1385. The Kilkenny great council of 17 July, during which grievances were first expressed against the king's lieutenant, was the same assembly over which the earls of Desmond and Ormond were appointed jointly to deputise for Sir Philip Courtenay. As we have seen, Ormond may have taken umbrage at this acknowledgement of Desmond's status. Courtenay's absence, of course, would have been a prime opportunity for Ormond to vent his spleen, not least because the earl could presumably dominate a great council held in his home territory. Almost immediately after the great council, there are signs that Ormond was preparing to set out for court.[81] He had reached England by the autumn. There he rendered his homage to the king and attended the Westminster parliament that convened on 20 October.[82] He took the opportunity to voice complaints about Courtenay and sought to forestall any reprisals upon his return. On 28 October, the king expressly ordered Courtenay, 'not to impeach or trouble the earl, his men or servants' for travelling to court, as 'he [Ormond] fears that the lieutenant … may impeach him'.[83]

Ormond's visit to England coincided with the creation of Robert de Vere as marquess of Dublin. It is tempting to relate this to the desire expressed by the colonial community for either a royal expedition to Ireland or the appointment of 'the greatest and most trustworthy lord of England'.[84] It seems almost inconceivable that, with the premier magnate of English Ireland to hand, the king would have neglected to take his counsel on such a significant matter. This is not to suggest that the idea of creating a marquessate for de Vere originated with Ormond; but the earl's serendipitous arrival at court may well have impressed on Richard II that Ireland could serve as a land of opportunities in terms of providing a fit reward for a royal favourite.[85] In this respect, the episode is reminiscent of the diplomatic coup of Ormond's father, Earl James II, in soliciting the expedition of Lionel of Antwerp in 1361.[86] Unfortunately, there is little beyond the timing to prove Ormond's involvement. What is indisputable, however, is that Richard II looked on Ormond with affection. The young earl was knighted by the king himself in full parliament, and he cut a fine enough figure at court to attract the attention of the monk of Westminster, who linked Ormond's name with some of the most illustrious men in England,

[80] For the Scottish invasions of Ireland earlier in the fourteenth century, see R. Frame, 'The Bruces in Ireland, 1315–18', *Ireland and Britain, 1170–1450* (London and Rio Grande, 1998), 71–98, first printed in *IHS*, 19 (1974), 3–37; S. Duffy (ed.), *Robert the Bruce's Irish Wars: The Invasions of Ireland, 1306–29* (Stroud, 2002).

[81] *RCH*, 127, nos. 196, 204, 225, 235–7.

[82] *HBC*, 565.

[83] *CCR 1385–9*, 14.

[84] *Statutes … of the Parliament of Ireland*, 487.

[85] Cf. the situation in thirteenth-century Ireland, when it has been suggested that John fitz Geoffrey (d. 1258) may have encouraged King Henry III to view Ireland, 'as a place where the demands of *curiales* might be satisfied': R. Frame, 'Henry III and Ireland: The Shaping of a Peripheral Lordship', in *Ireland and Britain*, 52, first printed in P. R. Coss and S. Lloyd (eds.), *Thirteenth Century England IV* (Woodbridge, 1992), 179–202.

[86] See the petition of 1360 requesting 'un bone chiefteyn suffisant, estoffés et efforcéz de gentz et tresore': *Parliaments & Councils*, 19–22, no. 16 (quotation at 21). For the involvement of James, second earl of Ormond, see Crooks, '"Hobbes"', 134–7.

including three of the king's surviving uncles. This remarkable extract, which seems to have escaped the notice of Irish historians,[87] is worth quoting:

> On 9 November in full parliament at Westminster, the king raised two of his uncles to the rank of duke, advancing Edmund of Langley, earl of Cambridge, to duke of York and elevating Thomas of Woodstock, earl of Buckingham, to the dukedom of Gloucester[88] ... On the same day also James earl of Ormond received the belt of knighthood from the king. The ceremonies over, the king and queen joined the newly invested great ones and the other nobles present in attending a banquet arranged for the occasion with great taste and brilliance by the duke of Lancaster.[89]

Ormond was subsequently showered with gifts. Sometime before June 1386, he married Anne, daughter of John, late fourth lord Welles (d. 1361).[90] The Welles family may not have been of the first rank, but the marriage was by no means a poor match. Anne's brother, John, fifth lord Welles (d. 1421), married Eleanor, sister of Thomas Mowbray (d. 1399), earl of Nottingham (1383) and later duke of Norfolk (1397). Although Mowbray later defected to the Appellants, in 1386 he was still a great favourite of the king, who made him Earl Marshal of England during that year.[91] Ormond, therefore, was moving in illustrious circles. As if this were not enough, he was also given material support. On 30 November, the city of Waterford was ordered to pay him forty pounds annually from the farm of the city as Ormond's father, the second earl, had been accustomed to receive.[92] The timing of the grant may be significant. The following day, 1 December 1385, Robert de Vere was created marquess of Dublin.

Ormond's tactic of abandoning a chief governor lukewarm to his interests in order to seek the greater rewards that could be won at court had proved extremely effective. Across the water in Ireland, Sir Philip Courtenay was attempting to prevent further muck from being raked against him. At the great council held at Dublin on 23 October he challenged anyone who felt aggrieved, 'by reason of any extortion, oppression, unjust seizure, or imprisonment by the said lieutenant ... [to] speak, confess or show it, and he would immediately amend and remedy it'. The assembled prelates, magnates and commons were presumably intimidated into submissiveness rather than overcome by sycophancy. They at once, 'declared, confessed

87 It is noticed, however, in J. L. Gillespie, 'Richard II's Knights: Chivalry and Patronage', *Journal of Medieval History*, 13 (1987), 148–9; idem, 'Richard II: Chivalry and Kingship', in J. L. Gillespie (ed.), *The Age of Richard II* (Stroud, 1997), 126.

88 These were the king's uncles, sons of Edward III. On Thomas of Woodstock (d. 1397), see A. Goodman, *The Loyal Conspiracy: The Lords Appellant under Richard II* (London, 1971), 74–104.

89 *Westminster Chronicle*, 140–41. Knighton notes that Richard II created an 'incomparable number of knights', and connects the event with the creation of the marquess of Dublin: *Knighton's Chronicle, 1337–1396*, ed. G. H. Martin (Oxford, 1995), 338–9. For discussion, see J. J. N. Palmer, 'The Parliament of 1385 and the Constitutional Crisis of 1386', *Speculum*, 46 (1971), 477–90; C. Given-Wilson, 'Richard II and the Higher Nobility', in *Richard II: The Art of Kingship*, 117–19. The duke of Lancaster was, of course, John of Gaunt (d. 1399).

90 His new wife first appears in the records on 17 June 1386: *CPR 1385–9*, 163. For the Welles family, see *Complete Peerage*, xii, pt 2, 441–3.

91 Goodman, *Loyal Conspiracy*, 163; Saul, *Richard II*, 121–3; *Complete Peerage*, xii, pt 2, 442–3.

92 *CCR 1385–9*, 22; *CPR 1385–9*, 68.

and said that they were aggrieved in none of the premises'.[93] Having received the all clear, Courtenay had the record of his exoneration enrolled in the Irish chancery, no doubt in anticipation of future attacks on him.[94] This precaution did him little good. In January, the two envoys who had been elected 'at the councils at Dublin and Kilkenny' set out for England. They travelled separately. The archbishop of Dublin landed in England on 14 January 1386.[95] Bishop Alexander Balscot of Ossory set sail on 20 January,[96] probably taking with him a copy of the grievances presented at the assemblies held at Kilkenny and Dublin.[97] Balscot's aim was clearly to petition for Courtenay's dismissal. In this he was successful. The lieutenant was accused of 'intolerable oppressions, duresses [and] excesses', and on 26 March 1386 Balscot was issued with a strict order to place Courtenay under arrest.[98]

Like Ormond, Bishop Alexander Balscot was rewarded for travelling to England. On 10 March 1386 he was translated from his diocese of Ossory to Meath, a move that would certainly have been considered a promotion.[99] Balscot's associate, Robert Crull, was appointed treasurer of Ireland.[100] These complainants against Courtenay seem to have crystallised to form the colonial element in the expedition that Robert de Vere was to have led to Ireland. All three – Earl James III of Ormond, Bishop Alexander of Meath (chancellor of Ireland) and Robert Crull (the newly appointed treasurer) – were soon consorting with the officials of the marquess of Dublin, in particular the man de Vere appointed as his lieutenant in Ireland, Sir John Stanley.[101] During the spring of 1386, shipping was arrested along the west coast of England for de Vere's army and protections were issued to his men.[102] On 12 February the admirals were ordered to release a ship called *le Gabriel* of Waterford, captained by Walter Spence, for the use of the earl of Ormond.[103] Ormond was retained by the marquess, his company consisting of twenty-six men-at-arms and eighty archers.[104] Another member of Sir John Stanley's retinue was Ormond's step-father, Sir Robert

[93] A similarly 'curious comedy' was played out in the Westminster parliament of January 1390, when the majority of the king's ministers asked to be discharged from office. They then demanded that anyone who wished to accuse them of any offence or official impropriety should declare it publicly in parliament. The challenge went unanswered, and the ministers were reappointed: Given-Wilson (ed.), 'Richard II: Parliament of January 1390, Text and Translation', in *PROME*, item 6. The phrase quoted is that of Tout, *Chapters*, iii, 460.

[94] *Statutes ... of the Parliament of Ireland*, 486–7 (*RCH*, 128, no. 9).

[95] *CPR 1388–92*, 88.

[96] *RCH*, 124, nos. 79, 82.

[97] *Statutes ... of the Parliament of Ireland*, 484–7 (*RCH*, 128, no. 18). These complaints were exemplified on 14 January, the very same day that the chancellor, Bishop Alexander Balscot, nominated a series of attorneys. The next day, 15 January, Balscot appointed Thomas Everdon as his deputy during his absence: *RCH*, 124, nos. 80–81, 96; ibid., 126, nos. 161–2.

[98] T. Rymer, *Foedera, Conventiones, Litterae, etc.*, ed. G. Holmes (20 vols., London, 1704–13), vii, 504–5; NLI, MS 4 [Harris], fol. 15–15v; *CCR 1385–9*, 49.

[99] *NHI*, ix, 286. He was addressed by his new title on 26 March, when the king ordered him to arrest Courtenay, 'late the king's lieutenant': *CCR 1385–9*, 49.

[100] For Crull's account as treasurer, see *IExP*, 544–5.

[101] Stanley was appointed by de Vere at London on 20 March 1386, but his indenture (which was later enrolled in the Irish chancery) is dated 8 June at Kennington: TNA:PRO, C 47/10/24/8 (*RCH*, 131, no. 31). De Vere had been granted Kennington for eight years without rent on 4 February 1386: *CPR 1385–9*, 115. For Stanley, see M. J. Bennett, *Community, Class and Careerism: Cheshire and Lancashire Society in the Age of* Sir Gawain and the Green Knight (Cambridge, 1983), 215–23.

[102] *CPR 1385–9*, 125–6, 128, 130–31, 156.

[103] Ibid., 107.

[104] Ibid., 157.

Herford.[105] In June, Alexander Balscot and Robert Crull likewise brought small companies to the general muster of Stanley's army in the West Country.[106] The king himself displayed an interest in the arrangements and spent some time with de Vere at Bristol in mid-July.[107]

One final aspect of this episode adds weight to the suggestion that Ormond's involvement in engineering Sir Philip Courtenay's fall from grace in 1385–6 was motivated by his private concerns, in particular his acrimonious relationship with the Desmond Geraldines. Early in 1386, just as the complainants against Courtenay were setting out for England, Sir Philip Courtenay issued Gerald, third of Desmond, with significant governmental commissions. On 4 January 1386 Courtenay nominated Desmond as his deputy, 'for the defence of Munster'.[108] The appointment gave Desmond authority across much of the south of Ireland, in Geraldine as well as Butler territories. A further sign of Courtenay's confidence came when he appointed Desmond and his adherent, Patrick Fox, as justices to take assizes in the crosslands of county Kerry.[109] By the time these grants were made, Courtenay was well aware of the actions being taken against him. With Ormond lobbying at Westminster, it is scarcely surprising that the lieutenant should have chosen this moment to grace the Desmond Geraldines with his favour.

II

As James, third earl of Ormond, set sail for Ireland in the summer of 1386, his affiliation to a royalist party surrounding the new marquess of Dublin was quite distinct. He was returning with a knighthood, a wife, and pecuniary reward; he had banqueted with the royal family and entered the service of the king's favourite; and letters had been issued ordering the arrest of Sir Philip Courtenay. All this seemed set to guarantee Ormond's pre-eminence. It was to be a transient victory. The turn of events in England in the autumn of 1386 conveyed an important lesson. To be the king's friend was not always a blessing; indeed, at times it was decidedly a predicament. We turn now to the ramifications across the Irish Sea of factional politics in England.

The 'Wonderful' parliament, which was in session from 1 October to 28 November 1386, was extremely hostile to the king and his ministers.[110] Amid this charged

105 Ibid., 130. Herford had been disadvantaged during Courtenay's lieutenancy. The lands and tenements he held with his wife, Elizabeth, widow of Earl James II of Ormond, were seized into the king's hands due to his past debts and his absence from Ireland. On 21 September 1386, Sir John Stanley, in his capacity as lieutenant of the marquess of Dublin, ordered restoration of these lands: NLI, MS 4 [Harris], fol. 23.

106 *CPR 1385–9*, 163. Crull nominated attorneys on 12 June 1386: ibid., 155. One of Crull's attorneys, William Rikhill, also served as attorney for the earl of Ormond: ibid., 152.

107 Saul, *Richard II*, 155, 471.

108 NAI, Lodge MSS, xvii, fol. 149 (*RCH*, 127, no. 238). A grant to Desmond of forty pounds from the fee farm of the city of Cork – issued as a reward 'for certain great expenses which the said earl sustained in the parts of Munster' – may also date from this time. The grant was made 'in the time of the Marquis [*sic*] of Dublin', which might refer to any time between 1 December 1385 and 13 October 1386; but, in light of Desmond's recent appointment 'for the defence of Munster', it is conceivable that it predates Courtenay's flight from Ireland in April 1386: *PKCI*, 126–8, no. 113.

109 *RCH*, 127, no. 242.

110 *HBC*, 565.

environment the king acted to inflame feeling by creating Robert de Vere duke of Ireland.[111] This act of bravado on the king's part was followed by an extended period during which his power was constrained. From 19 November, the government of England was vested in a commission that was to hold office for a year. While the commission was not altogether inimical to the king's interests, some members – notably Archbishop Courtenay of Canterbury – were likely to be extremely hostile to the duke of Ireland and his supporters.[112] The shift in the balance of power was quite distinct. The court, which had been so willing to indulge complaints against Sir Philip Courtenay, suddenly began to support the former lieutenant. Courtenay had remained in office in Ireland until Easter 1386.[113] In late April, being aware of the 'danger of arrest and imprisonment', he fled Ireland with his family and 'with great difficulty and danger escaped and came into England with great trouble'.[114] He later sat as a knight in the 'Wonderful' parliament.[115] The appointment of the commission of government in November 1386 provided him with an opportunity to recoup his losses. Courtenay petitioned that he had been thrust out of office contrary to the terms of his indenture. He accused de Vere's officers of seizing all his goods and chattels, as well as the revenues and profits of Ireland which should rightfully have been at his disposal. The ministers of the duke of Ireland were now ordered to restore these, while de Vere himself was instructed to pay Courtenay one thousand marks in compensation.[116]

This anxiety to ensure that Courtenay would receive justice doubtless stemmed from hostility to the new duke of Ireland. A side-effect was that the authority of de Vere's administration in Ireland, which should have bolstered Ormond's power, was undermined. It took a number of months for the impact of this reversal of fortune to be felt across the Irish Sea. Early in 1387, the sheriffs of Meath, Kildare, Dublin and Louth received instructions to investigate the 'oppressions and extortions' perpetrated by Sir Philip Courtenay.[117] Seemingly the party hostile to Courtenay still held

111 *Calendar of Charter Rolls 1341–1417*, 307; *Complete Peerage*, vii, 70. For the reaction to this promotion, see Given-Wilson (ed.), 'Richard II: Parliament of October 1386, Introduction', in *PROME*.

112 Palmer, 'Parliament of 1385 and Constitutional Crisis of 1386', 488–9; W. M. Ormrod, 'Government by Commission: The Continual Council of 1386 and the English Royal Administration', *Peritia*, 10 (1996), 303–21.

113 He made a grant under the Irish seal on 14 April 1386, recorded in an *inspeximus* of 18 April 1388: *CPR 1385–9*, 432. A document enrolled in the Irish chancery states that Ireland came into the hands of the marquess of Dublin on 19 April 1386: *RCH*, 134, no. 125. Prior Richard White of the hospital of St John of Jerusalem was appointed as justiciar of Ireland by de Vere's council in England; he was sworn into that office on 19 April 1386: NLI, MS 4 [Harris], fols. 21, 31–31v. He served in that capacity until the arrival of Sir John Stanley on 30 August at Dalkey, co. Dublin. On 18 September in the Great Hall of Dublin Castle, Stanley displayed his patent of appointment to the king's council in Ireland: Bodleian Library, MS Rawl. B 502, fols. 95v–96r (*RCH*, 131, no. 31).

114 *Issues of the Exchequer* […], ed. F. Devon (London, 1837), 241. It has twice been stated incorrectly that Courtenay was arrested in Ireland in 1390: N. Pronay and J. Taylor, *Parliamentary Texts of the Later Middle Ages* (Oxford, 1980), 122; Kerby-Fulton and Horie, 'French Version of the *Modus*', 226–7, 229 note 5. In both cases, the document cited in support of this assertion is an order dated 27 October 1390 to investigate the 'goods and chattels of Philip de Courtenay there [in Ireland] arrested by the king's authority': *CPR 1388–92*, 349.

115 Tuck, 'Anglo-Irish Relations', 26; *House of Commons*, ii, 671–2.

116 *CCR 1385–9*, 232; Saul, *Richard II*, 165.

117 *RCH*, 136, nos. 205–6. Orders to take inquisitions concerning Courtenay's goods had been issued on 20 September 1386, shortly after Stanley assumed office as lieutenant of the marquess: *RCH*, 136, no. 184.

sway. A new mood soon became discernible. On 12 February 1387 Gerald, third earl of Desmond, was granted custody of the lands of his kinsman, Sir John Roche of Fermoy, during the minority of the latter's son and heir, Maurice (d. 1448).[118] The Roche estates lay in county Cork, one of the regions in which Butler and Geraldine influence intersected. Ormond's later involvement with these Cork lands suggests that he was disgruntled the favour shown to his rival. In December 1390, the year after Richard II had declared himself fully of age, custody of the Roche lands was transferred to John Elyngham, a sergeant-at-arms of the king. Later, in 1397, Ormond along with the treasurer of Ireland from de Vere's period, Robert Crull, came to Elyngham's aid by swearing that the latter did not receive a penny from his grant until 20 August 1393.[119] Ormond's support for Elyngham is significant. It suggests that he was gratified by the Geraldines's loss of the custody in 1390, and – stretching the evidence further back again – it tends to confirm that he considered the original grant of 1387 inimical to his interests. The grant to Desmond of the Roche inheritance predates by just one month the report of 14 March 1387 that great discords had once again broken out between Desmond and Ormond. The Roche wardship, of course, was hardly the sole cause of the conflict. Nonetheless, the preferment shown to Desmond is indicative of the uncertain atmosphere in which the conflict arose. At one moment Ormond's fortunes were in the ascendant, bolstered by the favour of the king and his favourite; the next, his support base had collapsed and his adversary was being cultivated.

The result of the arbitration in 1387 is not recorded, but it is relatively clear that Desmond continued to hold the confidence of the central government. In the next few years, during which Richard II's authority became increasingly uncertain, he was to receive a series of commissions bolstering his authority in the south of Ireland.[120] A less conventional show of support came on 8 December 1388, when Desmond was issued with a licence to foster his son, James (d. 1463), later seventh earl of Desmond, with Conchobhar Ó Briain, brother of Brian *Sreamach* Ó Briain of Thomond.[121] The letter granting this licence speaks of the good place that Earl Gerald of Desmond daily held for the king in the parts of Munster.[122] The wider Geraldine affinity also felt the warm glow of favour. On 3 February 1389 Patrick Fox – who was later to serve with Desmond as a keeper of the peace – was granted, in conjunction with the mayor and community of Limerick city, the keeping of the royal fishery in the city for seven years.[123] A decade previously, James III Butler (as he then was) had himself been granted the 'keeping of the weirs, issues and profits belonging to the king's fishery of Lymeryk' for ten years.[124] The ten-year term had only recently elapsed at Michaelmas 1388. The fact that the fishery should have

118 *RCH*, 133, no. 92; NAI, Ferguson Repertory, i, fol. 84. See *The Pipe Roll of Cloyne (Rotulus Pipae Clonensis)*, ed. P. MacCotter and K. W. Nicholls (Cloyne, 1996), 183; E. Donnelly, 'The Roches, Lords of Fermoy: The History of a Norman-Irish Family', *Journal of the Cork Historical and Archaeological Society*, 40 (1935), 38.

119 *CCR 1396–9*, 119.

120 R. Frame, 'Commissions of the Peace in Ireland, 1302–1461', *Analecta Hibernica*, 35 (1992), nos. 58, 107.

121 I have followed the numbering of the earls of Desmond in *NHI*, ix, 233; cf. *Complete Peerage*, iv, 246–7.

122 NAI, Lodge MSS, xxi, fol. 39 (*RCH*, 139, no. 88 [misprinted as no. 82]).

123 *RCH*, 140, no. 124; Frame, 'Commissions of the Peace in Ireland', nos. 58–9, 108.

124 *CFR 1377–83*, 103.

passed so soon into the hands of a Geraldine supporter must truly have been an affront to Ormond.

Meanwhile, the conflict in England had intensified. As the crisis approached its most furious point in the winter of 1387, Sir John Stanley returned to England leaving Alexander, bishop of Meath, as justiciar of Ireland.[125] Robert de Vere, duke of Ireland, fled to the continent after losing the battle of Radcot Bridge in December 1387. During the 'Merciless' parliament, which convened at Westminster on 3 February 1388, he was sentenced in his absence to death and forfeiture.[126] The duchy of Ireland – now in its last days – was not isolated from the furore. On 6 March the king's confessor, Bishop Thomas Russhok of Chichester, and six royal justices were banished from England and condemned to live out their lives in the Irish coastal towns of Dublin, Cork, Waterford and Drogheda.[127] Shortly afterwards, on 20 March, parliament was prorogued until 13 April.[128] During the hiatus, letters were sent to Ireland commanding the justiciar to cease using the duke of Ireland's seal, banners and pennons, 'as the king is informed that the bishop in error used the seal of the said Robert [de Vere, late duke of Ireland] … after common knowledge that by reason of a judgement rendered against him in this parliament he forfeited to the king all his lordships, manors, lands and goods, likewise causing the said Robert's banners etc. to be raised against attacks of the [king's Irish] enemies, to the dishonour of the king'.[129] The traffic to and fro across the Irish Sea was clearly swift.[130] De Vere had been condemned early in February 1388.[131] Tidings of his fate had been carried to Ireland and news of the justiciar's recalcitrance borne back to Westminster, all within the space of two months.

Ormond's attitude to this activity is difficult to assess. We cannot assume that he was entirely hostile to the Appellant movement. Like most of the English nobility, he probably had no desire to have his 'head broken for the duke of Ireland'.[132] There is no evidence that he offered de Vere any support, military or otherwise, in 1387–8. Rather, he seems to have spent this time sitting out the storm in Ireland.[133] Ormond may even have sympathised with the Appellants. One of their leading supporters was Sir Thomas Mortimer, a former chief governor of Ireland and half-brother of Edmund, earl of March (d. 1381), with whom Ormond's father had been on friendly terms.[134] Sir Thomas Mortimer slew the constable of Chester, Sir Thomas Molineux,

125 Stanley's last recorded pleas were held on 4 November 1387; the bishop of Meath held pleas on 13 November. See Wood, 'Office of Chief Governor', 230.

126 J. N. L. Myres, 'The Campaign of Radcot Bridge in December 1387', *EHR*, 42 (1927), 20–33; *HBC*, 565.

127 Given-Wilson (ed.), 'Richard II: Parliament of February 1388, Text and Translation', *PROME*, pt 3, 'Attainders'. See also *CCR 1385–9*, 509–10, 515–16; *Knighton's Chronicle*, 502–5; *Westminster Chronicle*, 336–7; *Usk*, 12–13; Bibliothèque Municipale de Troyes, MS 1316, fol. 49v.

128 *HBC*, 565.

129 *Foedera*, vii, 577; *CCR 1385–9*, 388 (quotation); *PKCI*, xiii–xiv, no. 3.

130 For communications across the Irish Sea, see Frame, *English Lordship in Ireland*, 114–19.

131 Saul, *Richard II*, 193.

132 A comment attributed to Ralph, Lord Basset: *Knighton's Chronicle*, 407. See also C. Given-Wilson's comment that most lords 'were more concerned to avoid trouble than to take a stand': 'Richard II and the Higher Nobility', in *Richard II: The Art of Kingship*, 116.

133 NLI, D 1314 (*COD*, ii, no. 285); *PKCI*, xii, no. 2.

134 *NHI*, ix, 474; Crooks, 'Factionalism and Noble Power', 139–41, 154–7.

at the battle of Radcot Bridge, a fact recorded by several English chroniclers.[135] Its contemporary significance in Ireland is suggested by the fact that Henry Marlborough noted in his Irish chronicle that Thomas Molineux had been killed 'apud Rotcotebrigg' in 1387.[136]

Ormond's private feelings may be unknowable, but the adverse effect of the Appellant crisis on his career is all too apparent. In contrast to Earl Gerald of Desmond, Ormond virtually disappears from the records after 1387. His interests had been closely tied to the party surrounding Robert de Vere.[137] The careers of such men were in jeopardy in 1388. The general antipathy that was directed towards the king's justices in England during the Appellant crisis also flared up in Ireland at this time.[138] One royal justice, Edmund Clay, had been commissioned to arrest Sir Philip Courtenay in 1386 and had later served de Vere as chief justice of Ireland.[139] Shortly after the fall of the duke of Ireland, Clay was accused at court of 'various extortions, damages, grievances and excesses against the king and people [in Ireland]', and, in April 1388, mandates for his arrest were issued.[140] By that summer, messengers acting on behalf of the Appellants had reached the colony. In July 1388 one John Horwelle, a sergeant-at-arms, attended a great council held at Clonmel, where he furnished the assembly with the names of those king's knights who had been put 'beyond the protection of the lord king at the last parliament held in England'.[141] His little list included Robert de Vere's chamberlain, Sir John Lancaster, who had served alongside Ormond as a commander in the expedition that de Vere was supposed to have led to Ireland in 1386.[142] Another man who was closely associated with the Butler family and who had been arrested earlier in 1388 was Richard II's chamber knight, Sir Nicholas Dagworth.[143] Like these men, Ormond seems to have been considered part of a political out-group. Consequently, he was not entrusted with the task of seizing offices granted by de Vere or dismantling the symbols of his administration.[144]

Association with the duke of Ireland had, therefore, proved embarrassing for Ormond. The atmosphere in Ireland in 1388 did not seem propitious for a recovery of his former status. By the late summer of that year, the earl had decided to travel

135 *Westminster Chronicle*, 222–3; *Knighton's Chronicle*, 422–3. See J. L. Gillespie, 'Thomas Mortimer and Thomas Molineux: Radcot Bridge and the Appeal of 1397', *Albion*, 7 (1975), 161–73, especially 163–5; Myres, 'The Campaign of Radcot Bridge', 20–33; A. Dunn, 'Richard II and the Mortimer Inheritance', in C. Given-Wilson (ed.), *Fourteenth Century England II* (Woodbridge, 2002), 161–3.

136 Bibliothèque Municipale de Troyes, MS 1316, fol. 49v.

137 Ormond served, for instance, as justiciar 'of the marquess [of Dublin] in Ireland': *IExP*, 545.

138 For that hostility in England, see J. R. Maddicott, *Law and Lordship: Royal Justices as Retainers in Thirteenth- and Fourteenth-Century England*, Past and Present Supplement 4 (1978), 66–8.

139 *Foedera*, vii, 504; *CCR 1385–9*, 49. Clay was appointed chief justice of the lieutenant's bench on 20 September 1386, shortly after the arrival of Sir John Stanley: *RCH*, 132, no. 49; NLI, MS 4 [Harris], fol. 24. See F. E. Ball, *The Judges in Ireland, 1222–1922* (2 vols., New York, 1927), i, 166.

140 *CCR 1385–9*, 411.

141 *Parliaments & Councils*, 125–7, no. 71.

142 Sir John Lancaster brought twenty men-at-arms and sixty archers to a muster of de Vere's army in the summer of 1386: *CPR 1385–9*, 163. On Lancaster, see Tuck, *Richard II*, 61, 80.

143 *Issues of the Exchequer*, 235; *Westminster Chronicle*, 228–9; C. Given-Wilson, *The Royal Household and the King's Affinity: Service, Politics, and Finance in England, 1360–1413* (New Haven and London, 1986), 162. For the Ormond–Dagworth connection, see Crooks, 'Factionalism and Noble Power', 113–14, 137–48.

144 *CPR 1385–9*, 436.

to England.[145] His visit was well-timed. It coincided with Richard II's wooing of the commons at the Cambridge parliament of September 1388, which gained the king support from a political community that was increasingly disenchanted with the Appellant coalition.[146] Early the next year, the king won over the two least committed Appellants, the earls of Nottingham and Derby.[147] Ormond had returned to Ireland by this time. A change in official attitudes to him is detectable by mid-February 1389, when he was appointed 'keeper and governor' of Kilkenny and Tipperary.[148] This was no great concession. The Butlers were, after all, lords of the liberty of Tipperary, while Kilkenny was at the centre of their interests. But the appointment is indicative of a slight warming in the political climate. The thaw truly arrived after 3 May 1389, the day Richard II assumed the governance of his realm.[149] The monk of Westminster, who had previously made note of Ormond's career, records that Richard removed 'all officers, both greater and less, even those beyond the sea'.[150] And indeed, Richard II was soon attending to the business of making appointments in Ireland. On 31 July, Sir John Stanley entered into an indenture with the king to serve as justiciar of Ireland for three years.[151] On 1 August the patent of his appointment was issued.[152] His powers of patronage were clarified on 13 August,[153] and a week later the appointment was discussed and ratified by the king's council in England.[154] With Stanley's appointment confirmed, the two other principal ministers were slotted into place. Bishop Alexander Balscot of Meath was appointed as chancellor of Ireland;[155] and Robert Crull was once again admitted as treasurer.[156] The intention was clearly to reconstitute the Irish administration as it had existed in the time of the duke of Ireland, when Stanley, Balscot, and Crull had held the three senior posts in the Irish administration.

Even before this reorganisation at the pinnacle of the royal administration, Richard II's assumption of power had affected the distribution of authority at a local level in the colony. At the end of May 1389 Thomas Butler, brother of Earl James III of Ormond, together with Nicholas White of Clonmel, was appointed to investigate seditions in county Cork.[157] Here was a clear sign that Ormond was once again flexing his muscles in the south of Ireland. Other appointments to investigate

145 *RCH*, 138, no. 32; ibid., 141, no. 195.

146 A. Tuck, 'The Cambridge Parliament, 1388', *EHR*, 84 (1969), 225–43; Saul, *Richard II*, 200–2; Saul, 'The Commons and the Abolition of Badges', *Parliamentary History*, 9 (1990), 302–15.

147 Saul, *Richard II*, 203.

148 NAI, Lodge MSS, xvii, fol. 149 (*RCH*, 142, no. 226).

149 *Foedera*, vii, 618–19; *CCR 1385–9*, 671.

150 *Westminster Chronicle*, 390–92; Tout, *Chapters*, iii, 456–7.

151 TNA:PRO, E 101/68/11/265 (*RCH*, 145, no. 136).

152 *CPR 1388–92*, 91 (*RCH*, 144, no. 77).

153 *CPR 1388–92*, 99. Stanley was granted Blackcastle, co. Meath, on 23 August 1389: *CPR 1388–92*, 106; *RCH*, 144, no. 81; *COD*, ii, no. 291; NAI, Ferguson Repertory, i, fol. 144; BL, Add. MS 4798, fol. 19.

154 *Proceedings and Ordinances of the Privy Council of England*, ed. N. H. Nicolas (7 vols., London, 1834–7), i, 7.

155 *CPR 1388–92*, 109 (*RCH*, 144, no. 78). He was sworn into office as chancellor on 25 October: *RCH*, 144, no. 79.

156 *CPR 1388–92*, 103. Crull had been removed from the treasurership on 27 May 1388. He did not, in fact, resume the office until 1391. In the mean time, Richard White, prior of the hospital of St John of Jerusalem in Ireland, served as treasurer: *IExP*, 545–6.

157 *RCH*, 142, no. 242. The commission was repeated on 1 June: NAI, Lodge MSS, xvii, fol. 149 (*RCH*, 141, no. 185).

seditions in counties Kilkenny, Waterford and Wexford provide further evidence of Ormond's rehabilitation. The Kilkenny commission, for instance, was to be headed by Ormond's retainer, Sir Patrick Freigne.[158] Meanwhile, Ormond's step-father, Sir Robert Herford – who had crisscrossed the Irish Sea during 1388–9, probably representing Butler interests – received an English-seal appointment as chancellor of the green wax of the Irish exchequer.[159] Richard II's assertion of authority in 1389, therefore, seems to have led to an immediate improvement in Ormond's standing in Ireland. Royal favour was, once again, demonstrating its capacity to further careers.

III

This review of the events of 1382–9 serves, in the first place, as a corrective to the traditional portrayal of the nobles of English Ireland in the late fourteenth century as disengaged from workings of the central government. The royal administration – far from being 'ineffectual' and unable to suppress the violence of a disharmonious nobility[160] – was in fact a cardinal feature of the factional struggle between the Geraldines and Butlers, whether as a vehicle for the promotion of private fortunes or as a forum for vigorous politicking with the intention of subverting the interests of rivals. Since high office and proximity to court were primary constituents of power, it follows that internal political alignments played a central role in determining colonial attitudes to the king's ministers. By the same token, political waves generated at the factious court of Richard II had the power to rock Irish boats.

Recognition of this interdependence allows us to decipher the otherwise bewildering politics of late fourteenth-century Ireland; but a point of wider significance emerges when Ireland is placed in a framework of colonialism more generally. Irish historians of an earlier generation might well have depicted the political patterns reviewed in this essay in terms of J. C. Beckett's 'Anglo-Irish Tradition'.[161] Such fond insularism has since fallen by the wayside. 'Greater Britain' and (for some early modernists) the 'Atlantic World' are now the paradigms of choice.[162] The gusto with which scholars have opened up the borders between old national historiographies has rarely, however, been matched by a desire step out from behind chronological barricades.[163] One historian has recently stated that '[a]sserting an on-going continuity between the Norman [*sic*] colonization of Ireland and Britain's early modern imperial Atlantic adventures is … implausible'.[164] Yet the utility of a longer view is strongly suggested by Keith Stringer's reflections on another modish topic

158 *RCH*, 141, no. 182.

159 *CPR 1388–92*, 49. For his movements, see *CPR 1385–9*, 505; *RCH*, 141, no. 202.

160 Watt, 'Anglo-Irish Colony under Strain, 1327–99', in *NHI*, ii, 390–91.

161 J. C. Beckett, *The Anglo-Irish Tradition* (London, 1976), especially 24–5.

162 The literature is vast, but for a useful entrypoint into the debate, see D. Armitage, 'Greater Britain: A Useful Category of Historical Analysis?', *American Historical Review*, 104 (1999), 427–45; J. Ohlmeyer, 'Seventeenth-Century Ireland and the New British and Atlantic Histories', ibid., 446–62.

163 Although see A. F. McC. Madden, '1066, 1776 and All That: The Relevance of English Medieval Experience of "Empire" to Later Imperial Constitutional Issues', in J. E. Flint and G. Williams (eds.), *Perspectives of Empire: Essays Presented to Gerald S. Graham* (London, 1973), 16–18.

164 K. Kenny, 'Ireland and the British Empire: An Introduction', in K. Kenny (ed.), *Ireland and the British Empire* (Oxford, 2004), 6.

– nationalism – and his conclusion that 'medievalists and modernists have more to learn from each other than has often been thought'.[165]

This essay could be thought of as an attempt to bring a medieval Irish dimension to the growing portfolio of work which describes how the distribution of power in colonies – in many times and many places – was typically the result of a 'bargaining process' between settler elites and the agents of the metropolitan government.[166] Further work exploring points of contrast with other colonial societies would naturally be instructive.[167] But, in many respects, it is the continuities that are the most striking. The exasperation of the sixteenth-century chief governor, Sir Henry Sidney (d. 1586),[168] could perhaps stand for the mindset of some of his counterparts two centuries before:

> This [divided] composition of a Council I thought convenient, for the primitive reformation of so old a cancered faction as was and yet is between the two earls [of Desmond and Ormond], who albeit they would inveigh against each other, yet if any sentence passed for the advancement of the Queen's[169] prerogative, or suppression of either of their tyrannies, straightways it was cried out of, and complained to the Queen, specially by the Earl of Ormond, as injustice and oppression.[170]

Of course, the king's lieutenants of the medieval period did not write memoirs, so historians must scavenge elsewhere for juicy titbits. One such is Sir Philip Courtenay's effort – which sprang from a similar feeling of personal insecurity in a factious environment – to gain vindication from the great council held at Dublin in October 1385.[171] Nor need the parallels end in the Tudor era, for the theme of this essay touches on the eternal dilemma of colonial administrators. At the turn of the twentieth century, the political novelist, Rev. James Owen Hannay (1865–1950), memorably captured the gulf between the theoretical powers of a chief governor and the practical limitations imposed by indigenous interest groups:

> The Right Honourable George Chesney was a Cabinet Minister, and was popularly supposed to govern Ireland. In reality, his position was like that of a football in a tightly-packed scrimmage. Vigorous forwards impelled him, more by kicking than persuasion, in opposite directions. The equilibrium which might have resulted was continually being interfered with by adroit players, who

165 K. Stringer, 'Social and Political Communities in European History: Some Reflections on Recent Studies', in C. Björn, A. Grant and K. Stringer (eds.), *Nations, Nationalism and Patriotism in the European Past* (Copenhagen, 1994), 9–34 (quotation at 23).

166 J. P. Greene, 'Negotiated Authorities: The Problem of Governance in the Extended Polities of the Early Modern Atlantic World', *Negotiated Authorities: Essays in Colonial Political and Constitutional History* (Charlottesville and London, 1994), 14–16; J. L. Phelan, 'Authority and Flexibility in the Spanish Imperial Bureaucracy', *Administrative Science Quarterly*, 5 (1960), 47–65.

167 S. Reynolds has demonstrated the value of such an approach: 'Empires: A Problem of Comparative History', *BIHR*, 79 (2006), 151–65. For some preliminary remarks contrasting medieval and early modern states and their capacity to pursue colonial projects, see J. Ohlmeyer, 'A Laboratory for Empire?: Early Modern Ireland and English Imperialism', in Kenny (ed.), *Ireland and the British Empire*, 28.

168 For whom, see W. T. MacCaffrey, 'Sidney, Sir Henry', in *ODNB,* l, 545–50.

169 Elizabeth I (1558–1603).

170 C. Brady (ed.), *A Viceroy's Vindication? Sir Henry Sidney's Memoir of Service in Ireland, 1556–78* (Cork, 2002), 52.

171 *Statutes ... of the Parliament of Ireland*, 486–7 (*RCH*, 128, no. 9).

> shoved him sideways or heeled him out backwards … He was never without the consciousness that alert half-backs were lurking in Westminster, eager for a chance of picking him up and whisking him away. It speaks for the toughness of the leather in which he was encased that the Right Honourable Mr. Chesney not only enjoyed life, but continued fully distended with that wind which is the prime necessity of politicians who make many speeches.[172]

Few chief governors in late medieval Ireland could boast such leathery resilience!

[172] George A. Birmingham [pseud.], *The Seething Pot* (London, 1905), 95–6. On Hannay, see B. Taylor, *The Life and Writings of James Owen Hannay (George A. Birmingham), 1865–1950* (Lewiston [NY], 1995); and for a sketch of Hannay's mental world, see A. Gailey, 'An Irishman's World', *The Irish Review*, 13 (1992–3), 31–9. My thanks to Dr Gailey for bringing my attention to this passage.

RICHARD II IN THE *CONTINUATIO EULOGII*: YET ANOTHER ALLEGED HISTORICAL INCIDENT?

G. B. Stow

A well known passage in the continuation of the *Eulogium Historiarum* has been very influential in assessments of Richard II and his policies. In its account of events in the year 1398 the *Eulogium* describes a rather bizarre scene in Richard's chamber:

> After this, on solemn festival days, which were set aside for royal display, the king ordered a throne to be set up in his chamber, on which he often sat in full view from dinner until vespers, speaking to no one but overlooking all men, and if his gaze fell upon anyone, no matter what his rank, that person had to genuflect toward the king.[1]

This celebrated passage has been consistently cited in support of the view that near the end of his reign Richard II had adopted innovative, tyrannical, and perhaps even insane policies that played a part in his deposition from the throne in 1399. Kenneth A. Vickers says that the king might well have gotten away with his tyrannical behavior 'had not Richard himself drawn attention to his despotism [when] he emphasised his power by increasing the solemnity of Court ceremonial'.[2] Anthony Steel interprets the *Eulogium*'s account as attesting 'the last stage of his illness; the regality had grown until it had swallowed the entire world and as Richard looked around him he saw nothing but the mirror of his royal personality, inhabited by

1 F. S. Haydon (ed.), *Eulogium Historiarum sive Temporis* (3 vols., Rolls Series, 1858–63), iii, 378. For a good part of the twentieth century a sensational passage in the Westminster Chronicle was interpreted as indicating that Richard II suffered from some sort of mental illness. According to the usual reading, when he was informed in 1384 by a Carmelite friar of a plot against his life, supposedly hatched by John of Gaunt, Richard 'burst into hysterical fury, threw his cap and slippers out of the window, and flung himself about the room like a madman': G. M. Trevelyan, *England in the Age of Wycliffe* (London and New York, 1909), 276. The passage was first published in C. Babington and J. R. Lumby (eds.), *Polychronicon Ranulphi Higden* (9 vols., Rolls Series, 1865–86), ix, 33. This account was subsequently discredited by L. C. Hector, who proved that the chronicler's editors had misread a critical marginal sign inserted by the author of the text, which when taken into account showed that it was the *friar* – and not the king – who tore off his clothes, threw them out the window, and carried on like a madman: 'An Alleged Hysterical Outburst of Richard II', *EHR*, 68 (1953), 62–5.

2 K. A. Vickers, *England in the Later Middle Ages* (London, 1914), 293. So far as can be determined, the earliest interpretation of the *Eulogium* reference as indicative of an alteration of Richard II's court policy was that of J. H. Ramsay: 'The development of an almost Oriental etiquette at court marked the new social relations of the King to his subjects …': *The Genesis of Lancaster 1397–1399* (2 vols., Oxford, 1913), ii, 343–4. T. F. Tout interprets the *Eulogium* reference as an example of Richard's 'love of the externals of monarchy and neglect of its substance': *Chapters in the Administrative History of Mediaeval England* (6 vols., Manchester, 1920–33), iv, 33.

flickering shades whose movements could be governed by a glance'.[3] Nigel Saul observes that the *Eulogium* reference marks a decided turning point in the closing years of Richard's reign; 'in the summer of 1397 Richard II's kingship suddenly changed its character. The king's behaviour became more tyrannical ... At the same time Richard began to cultivate a loftier and more exalted image of himself as king. According to the *Eulogium* chronicler, one of the few writers to give us a picture of his court in these years ...'[4]

Its wide acceptance notwithstanding, it is curious that Ricardian scholars have accepted the *Eulogium*'s reference at face value, especially in light of its dubious reputation. The *Eulogium* is well known as a problematic text, most notably for its inaccurate chronologies and its plethora of textual interpolations.[5] Furthermore, the *Eulogium* has long been considered a glaring example of anti-Ricardian and pro-Lancastrian biases; Chris Given-Wilson describes its tone as 'thoroughly inimical to the king', reflecting 'bitter hostility towards Richard'.[6]

In light of these inherent flaws, and in accordance with L. C. Hector's admonition that 'there should be as little disagreement as possible about the admissibility of the evidence upon which are to be founded assessments and re-assessments of Richard's personality',[7] it is worth reconsidering the authenticity of the *Eulogium*'s celebrated crown-wearing reference. It will be demonstrated at the end that this passage represents a later textual interpolation on the part of an ardent Lancastrian sympathizer, whose purpose was to blacken Richard II's character.

The first thing to point out in support of this notion is that there is something suspicious about the celebrated passage when considered within its full textual context:

> Eodem anno Rex scripsit ad papam ut quemdam laicum literatum asserens, ut quidam dicebant, Thomam esse mortuum; fecitque parliamentum hoc compromittere in xii. personas, quae continuando parliamentum ubicunque et quandocunque regi placeret statuta sibi placita secum ordinarent. Quibus omnibus peractis in partes Occidentales est reversus. Nuntius festinanter rediens de Curia Romana portavit bullas, et rex fecit Rogerum consecrari; et cito post idem Rogerus celebravit ingressum suum Cantuariae sumptuose. *Et post hoc rex in diebus solennibus in quibus utebatur de more regalibus jussit sibi in*

3 *Richard II* (Cambridge, 1941), 178–9.

4 N. E. Saul, *Richard II* (New Haven and London, 1997), 339. See also Saul's 'Richard II and the Vocabulary of Kingship', *EHR*, 110 (1995), 875. Cf. M. McKisack, *The Fourteenth Century, 1307–1399* (Oxford, 1959), 490, who says that during the unfolding of events in 1398, '... and all the time, the king's megalomania grew. The continuator of the *Eulogium* tells how on feast-days ...': 490.

5 T. F. Tout dismisses the *Eulogium* as 'a mass of gross errors': *Chapters in the Administrative History of Mediaeval England*, iii, 396 note 1. C. Given-Wilson describes the *Eulogium* as 'a somewhat puzzling chronicle': idem, 'The Manner of King Richard's Renunciation: A "Lancastrian Narrative"?', *EHR*, 118 (1993), 366.

6 C. Given-Wilson (ed.), *Chronicles of the Revolution, 1397–1400* (Manchester, 1993), 5–6, 64. In the words of G. O. Sayles, monastic chronicles 'could be hopelessly biased and indulge in character assassination. Thus under Richard II they became a vehicle of propaganda that was purposively devised and disseminated in order to denigrate the king and to put Henry of Lancaster's usurpation of the throne in a favorable light: idem, 'King Richard II of England: A Fresh Look', *Proceedings of the American Philosophical Society*, 115 (1971), 28. See also his 'Richard II in 1381 and 1399', *EHR*, 94 (1979), 820, and 'The Deposition of Richard II: Three Lancastrian Narratives', *BIHR*, 54 (1981), 257–70.

7 'An Alleged Hysterical Outburst', 62.

camera parari thronum, in quo post prandium se ostentans sedere solebat usque ad vesperas nulli loquens sed singulos apsiciens. Et cum aliquem respiceret, cuiuscumque gradus fuerit, oportuit ipsum genuflectere. Rex autem apud Notyngham convocatis archiepiscopo et episcopis ac consiliariis suis, dixit se non posse secure equitare per regnum propter odium Londoniensium et septemdecim comitatuum adjacentium, et ideo voluit eos collecto exercitu exstirpare nisi signum securitatis sibi praestarent.[8]

[In the same year the king wrote to the pope concerning a certain learned layman, stating, as they say, that Thomas had died; he then made twelve men agree to the continuation of parliament that wherever and whenever it was agreeable to the king they should produce statutes in accordance with their bills. When all of this was accomplished he set out for the west parts of the realm. A messenger then returned hastily from the Roman curia with a papal bull, and so the king made arrangements for the consecration of Roger; and shortly afterwards Roger celebrated his consecration as archbishop of Canterbury. After this, on solemn festival days, which were set aside for royal display, the king ordered a throne to be set up in his chamber, on which he often sat in full view from dinner until vespers, speaking to no one but overlooking all men, and if his gaze fell upon anyone, no matter what his rank, that person had to genuflect toward the king. The king then called together his councillors, the archbishop and other bishops, at Nottingham, saying that he did not feel secure to travel freely about the realm on account of the hostility of Londoners and of the seventeen adjacent counties, and that therefore he hoped to gather a great army in order to destroy them unless they could give him assurance of his safety.]

When read within its full textual context, the passage in question seems oddly out of place in relation to the subject matter on either end of its appearance. Leading up to the entry we are informed about events attending the appointment and subsequent consecration of Roger Walden as archbishop of Canterbury. Immediately following the crown-wearing passage the narrative returns to matters of church and crown with an account of Richard's gathering together the newly minted archbishop and others at a council at Nottingham. Clearly, therefore, the crown-wearing reference bears all the hallmarks of a later textual interpolation.[9]

Further support for this interpretation emerges in the form of newly discovered manuscript evidence. In the text of a chronicle that in many ways resembles the *Eulogium*, the so-called *Southern Chronicle* – and at precisely the point where we would expect to discover the crown-wearing reference – we encounter instead a distinct textual lacuna:

Quidam clericus regis thesaurariis Rogerus Walden' factus est episcopus Cant' missa ad curiam magna summa pecuniae *ut quidam dicebant.*] [*Rex autem Notyngham* convocatis episcopis ac consiliariis suis, dixit se non posse secure equitare per regnum propter odium Londoniensium et septemdecim comitatuum, ...[10]

[8] *Eulogium Historiarum*, iii, 378.
[9] An additional problem concerns inconsistencies in chronology: see below, 128.
[10] BL, Add. MS 11714, fol. 12r.

[A certain clerk of the king's treasury, Roger Walden, was made archbishop of Canterbury, and was sent to the curia with a great sum of money, as they say. The king then convened his bishops and councillors at Nottingham, because he said that he did not feel secure to travel freely about the realm on account of the hostility of Londoners and of the seventeen adjacent counties, ...]

Why does the crown-wearing passage appear in the *Eulogium*, but not in the *Southern Chronicle*? What is needed in order to clarify this matter is a careful analysis of the manuscript traditions behind both narratives, along with a consideration of the relationship between them.[11]

Let us begin with the *Eulogium*. Our chronicle should more properly be labeled the *Continuatio*, since its narrative presents a continuation of the *Eulogium Historiarum*, whose text concludes with its coverage of events in 1366.[12] The text of the *Continuatio*, on the other hand, covers the years 1364 to 1413, and survives in a single manuscript, BL, MS Cotton, Galba E. VII. According to F. S. Haydon the *Continuatio* as it now stands is a late composite text, pulled together from several smaller bits at some date after 1428. Thus, in its account of events for the year 1384 an interpolated passage mentions the death of John Wycliffe, along with an accompanying reference to the later exhumation of his corpse, which we know occurred in 1428; therefore the text was compiled at some date after this event.[13]

C. L. Kingsford not only endorsed this interpretation, but also went further, delineating three separate texts – with terminal dates of 1401, 1405, and 1413 – from which the complete *Continuatio* was ultimately constructed. For its narrative from 1367 to 1401 Kingsford pointed to 'a brief Latin Chronicle possibly of Canterbury origin'.[14] Kingsford labeled this text the *Southern Chronicle*, extant in BL, Add. MS 11714, and which in his opinion was compiled between 1423 and 1426.[15] As for the portion of the *Continuatio* running from 1402 to 1413, Kingsford singled out a closely related English text known as 'Davies's Chronicle' (or the *English Chronicle*), whose narrative spans the years 1377 to 1461. But this text was itself taken from earlier bits, proven by the appearance of three textual divisions in its alignment with the *Continuatio* – one at 1401, another at 1405, and yet another at 1413.[16]

11 All of this has been worked out in G. B. Stow, 'The *Continuation* of the *Eulogium Historiarum*: Some Revisionist Perspectives', *EHR*, 119 (2004), 667–81.

12 A useful description of the continuation is provided in A. Gransden, *Historical Writing in England, II, c. 1307 to the Early Sixteenth Century* (London, 1982), 158 and note 5.

13 *Eulogium Historiarum*, i, l. Haydon also points out that BL, Galba E. VII is a later copy of the original text, since it 'is written in one hand apparently of the former half of the fifteenth century, and is remarkably free from erasures and interlineations. It is therefore in all probability not the autograph of the author of the Chronicle which it represents': ibid., xlix.

14 C. L. Kingsford, *English Historical Literature in the Fifteenth Century* (Oxford, 1913), 30.

15 Ibid., 275.

16 After observing that 'as far as 1401 the two works seem to have had a common Latin source which may have been of Canterbury origin', Kingsford noted that another source apparently terminated in 1405: 'since the resemblance of the English Chronicle to the *Continuation* after 1405 is not so close as before, it is possible that another of the common originals may have ended about this date': ibid., 29, 127. Furthermore, Kingsford noted that for its text from 1406 to 1413, the narrative of a version of the *Brut* found in Harley 53 'is very similar in its general character to *Davies's Chronicle*, though with some omissions and one or two slight additions': ibid., 123. From all of this Kingsford was led to the conclusion that 'the *Continuation*, *Davies's Chronicle*, and the version of the *Brut* in Harley 53 had a common English original between 1401 and 1413', and 'the fact that the *Continuation*

Of all these texts, by far the most important for our purposes is the *Southern Chronicle*, whose alignment with the *Continuatio* is worth analysis. Like the latter, the *Southern Chronicle* is also a composite, compiled from different texts at a date shortly after its *terminus ad quem* of 1422. For the period from 1367 to 1401 the *Southern Chronicle* was derived from a Latin text with a terminal date of 1401, while from 1402 to its conclusion in 1422 its narrative was taken from a completely different source.[17] But the most important point to note is that for their account of events from 1367 to 1401, the *Continuatio* and the *Southern Chronicle* convey similar accounts, and both texts were drawn from a common source for their narratives for this period. In Kingsford's words, 'as for the character of the *ultimate original* [my emphasis] the evidence of the *Southern Chronicle* would seem to show that down to 1401 it was a brief Latin Chronicle possibly of Canterbury origin: at all events the *Continuation* and the *Southern Chronicle* have a common Latin source … the verbal resemblances of the *Continuation* and the *Southern Chronicle* seem conclusive as to the existence of a Latin original ending in 1401'.[18]

Given that both the *Continuatio* and the *Southern Chronicle* were derived from a shared Latin original ending in 1401, we are presented with three possible explanations of why the crown-wearing reference should appear in the former narrative, while being absent from the latter:

1. The crown-wearing passage *was* present in the lost Latin original ending in 1401, but was subsequently deleted by the author of the 1367–1401 portion of the *Southern Chronicle*.

2. The crown-wearing passage was *not* present in the lost Latin original ending in 1401, which was then followed nearly verbatim by the author of the 1367–1401 portion of the *Southern Chronicle*.

3. The crown-wearing passage was *not* present in the lost Latin original ending in 1401, but was subsequently interpolated into the evolving text of the *Continuatio* by a later compiler.

Which of these options is the most convincing? Perhaps the most logical way of answering this query is to pose the question: Which of our texts more closely approximates to the lost Latin original ending in 1401? All things considered, it can be demonstrated that the *Southern Chronicle* comes closer to the mark. For one thing, like the Latin original, the first portion of the *Southern Chronicle* also concludes in 1401. For another, the *Southern Chronicle* presents an annalistic account of events across the reign of Richard that bears all the hallmarks of a tran-

ends with 1413 is rather to be taken as evidence for an English Chronicle which ended at that date than as affording any proof of the existence of a Latin original': ibid., 31. It seems worth observing that Kingsford's theory of multiple sources behind the complete *Continuatio* text has not met with universal approval. A dissenting opinion was presented by S. N. Clifford, who argued that 'it is very hard to accept that three separate chroniclers, working at roughly the same time in the fifteenth century, made use of some or all of these five chronicles, all now lost, as suggested by Kingsford. It is far more likely that one man was responsible for the composition of the whole …': 'An Edition of the *Continuatio* of the *Eulogium Historiarum*, 1361–1413' (unpublished M. Phil. thesis, University of Leeds, 1975), 28. For a reconsideration of Clifford's views, see Stow, 'The Continuation of the *Eulogium Historiarum*', 670–74. The *English Chronicle* has recently appeared in a new edition: W. Marx (ed.), *An English Chronicle 1377–1461* (Woodbridge, 2003).

17 Kingsford, *English Historical Literature*, 32.

18 Ibid., 30, 127 note 1.

scription from a similarly brief account of events from 1367 to 1401. In this regard it is important to point out that, in its presentation of events in the year 1398, the text of the *Southern Chronicle* flows more smoothly without the inclusion of the crown-wearing reference.[19]

Additional signs suggest that the composer of the *Southern Chronicle* produced a near duplicate of the short Latin original before him. For example, it appears that he copied from what might be called a sort of rough-draft narrative, dashed off hastily and containing several instances of sloppy, haphazard organization of principal events during the period 1367 to 1401. A clear indication of this is that the text of the *Southern Chronicle* is replete with numerous factual errors. Among the more notable of these are incorrect dates for John of Gaunt's Spanish expedition, Richard's demand for cash payments from the citizens of London, and the dates of Queen Anne's death and Richard's first Irish expedition (events which are presented in reverse chronological order).[20]

Since it appears that for the portion of its text extending from 1367 to 1401 the *Continuatio* was also derived from the short Latin original, it is worth considering their alignment. What quickly becomes apparent is that the *Continuatio* text presents numerous examples of alterations, emendations, and interpolations for its narrative from 1364 to 1401, all of which clearly indicate that the composer of the *Continuatio* deviated considerably from the original Latin text from which he copied his narrative. At critical and distinct junctures our text suddenly departs from its progenitor to add all sorts of afterthoughts and 'flashback' references, material that is oddly out of context with what precedes and follows these interjections.

Examples of this practice abound; here it will suffice to cite but a single example. In their accounts of 1386 both texts present a nearly verbatim account of the Wonderful Parliament, beginning with 'factum est parliamentum', and concluding with the appointment of Arundel as commander of the English naval fleet followed by Richard's restitution of lost liberties to the earl of Suffolk: 'eum libertati restituit'. At precisely this point, however, the texts diverge: the *Southern Chronicle* continues on with an account of Arundel's victories against the French fleet ('Comes Arundel omnes'), but the *Continuatio* interjects a backward-looking account of a parliament at Westminster in October 1385, concluding with a reference to the earl of March's designation as heir to the crown at 'Hibernia interemptus fuit'. At this point the *Continuatio* resumes its literal alignment with the *Southern Chronicle* at 'Comes Arundell'omnes'.[21]

Perhaps the most interesting example of how the *Continuatio*'s compiler borrowed from – and expanded upon – the shorter Latin text to 1401 concerns an interesting description of Richard II. There appears in the *Southern Chronicle* an important passage – brief, unadorned, and appearing as a sort of afterthought – that offers a description of Richard's character. This reference occurs at a most awkward place, sandwiched in between a brief account of Richard's expedition to Ireland in 1395 and an equally brief account of Queen Anne's death in 1394 (events which, as mentioned above, are herein presented in reverse chronological order):

19 BL, Add. MS 11714, fols. 11v–12r.

20 *Eulogium Historiarum*, iii, 359–61; BL, Add. MS 11714, fols. 11v–12r.

21 *Eulogium Historiarum*, iii, 359–61; BL, Add. MS 11714, fol. 11r.

> Rex Ricardus in divitiis et regalibus ornamentis praedecessores studuit excedere et ad Salomonis gloriam pervenere coepitque plus illis infra regnum formidari quamvis prole careret.[22]

> [King Richard endeavored to exceed all his predecessors in riches and royal regalia and to match the fame of Solomon, and he began to fear those within the kingdom, since he had no issue.]

In the *Continuatio* text, however, this description of Richard II, rather lengthy and homiletic in tone, appears as the last entry dealing with Richard's reign in 1399, and before going on to describe the coronation of Henry IV:

> Rex Ricardus in divitiis omnes praedecessores suos studuit excedere, et ad Salomonis gloriam pervenire; coepitque plus illis infra regnum post annum eius xi formidari quamvis prole careret] [*et animo bellicoso. In thesauris et jocalibus, in vestibus et ornamentis regalibus, in quibus vehementer excessit, in splendore mensae, in palatiis quae aedificavit, nullus in regibus eo gloriosior diebus suis. Et in maxima altitudinae suae gloriae subito appensus et inventus minus habens deponitur potens de sede, et statua percussa miserabiliter est contrita, arborque procera in medio terrae omnibus opulentiis privata, Vigili jubente Coelesti, succiditur, et in carcere perpetuo, videlicet, Castro Pontis Fracti, fit habitatio eius.*[23]

> [King Richard endeavored to exceed all his predecessors in riches, and to match the glory of Solomon; and after the eleventh year of his reign he began to fear those within the kingdom since he had no issue and lacked a warlike nature. In treasures and jewels, in dress and royal regalia, in which he far exceeded others, in the splendour of his table, in the palaces that he threw up, none of his contemporaries equaled him in royal splendour. But at the highest point of his power suddenly found wanting, he was deposed from the throne, and his image miserably struck down, and like a mighty oak in the middle of the land stripped of its power, by the command of a watchful heaven, he was struck down, and thrown into confinement, a prison, namely the castle of Pontrefact, was made his dwelling.]

What has happened here? It appears that the later compiler of the *Continuatio* has clearly derived Richard's character-description from the Latin original shared with the text of the *Southern Chronicle.* That this is the most logical conclusion is attested not only by the relocation placement of this passage to a more appropriate place in his narrative – at the conclusion of his account of Richard II's reign in 1399 – but also by the expanded version of the shorter and earlier passage found in the Latin original ending in 1401.

With all of this before us, we may draw the following conclusions. Firstly, both the *Continuatio* and the *Southern Chronicle* relied upon a common Latin original for their narratives from 1367 to 1401. Secondly, the *Southern Chronicle* – whose text clearly antedates that of the *Continuatio* – represents a close replica of this Latin original. Since, however, its text omits any reference to the crown-wearing passage, presenting instead a seamless account of events in 1398, the famous passage was

22 Ibid., fol. 12r.

23 *Eulogium Historiarum*, iii, 384.

never included in the Latin original with a terminal date of 1401. Thirdly, since the *Continuatio* was *also* compiled in part from this Latin original – and since its narrative clearly represents an expanded version of this shorter text, the crown-wearing passage can only be seen as yet another in a series of textual interpolations into one of the post-1401 component segments of the evolving *Continuatio* text, most likely that portion embracing the years 1367–1405.[24]

II

This revelation carries with it some important implications, not the least of which concerns some insights regarding the compiler's interests, access to sources, as well as his possible motives for insinuating a hostile depiction of Richard II into his narrative of events in the year 1398. Although never established with any certainty, some valuable clues regarding the author's identity are forthcoming from an analysis of the text. Several signs suggest that our author was a learned man, and quite possibly an ecclesiastic. From his careful reading of the text F. S. Haydon drew the conclusion that in the continuation of the original narrative we discover 'transpositions and amplifications of phraseology, and sometime additional particulars, the result, very likely, of new information and more extensive inquiry', and that 'the author was a person of greater cultivation than the compiler of the *Eulogium* itself'.[25] That the compiler may have been affiliated with the Grey Friars at Canterbury has been proposed by several scholars, and is generally the accepted view.[26]

24 That there *was* a component of the *Continuatio* with a terminal date of 1405 can be demonstrated by a comparison of its text with that of the English Chronicle. Until this date their narratives run roughly parallel; after this time, however, they follow different tracks: cf. Stow, 'Continuation of the *Eulogium Historiarum*', 677 note 50. It makes no sense to consider the segment which ends in 1401, since it has been demonstrated above that its text fails to include the crowning passage. Nor should we consider the portion of the *Continuatio* extending from 1405 to 1413, since it has also been shown above that this segment was most likely drawn from a later English text: cf. Kingsford, *English Historical Literature*, 31, 127 and note 1. At the other end of the spectrum, it is doubtful if the passage was inserted into the final version of the *Continuatio* compiled at some date considerably later than *c.* 1430. This interpretation takes on added significance when it is pointed out that under its account of events in 1385 the *Continuatio* contains a reference to Richard II's designation of Roger Mortimer, earl of March, as his successor. If the interpolated passage concerning Richard II's alleged designation of the earl was indeed inserted under Yorkist influence, it is highly unlikely that the copyist would at the same time inject anti-Ricardian sentiments. See further, M. V. Clarke and N. Denholm-Young, 'The Kirkstall Chronicle', in M. V. Clarke, *Fourteenth Century Studies*, ed. L. S. Sutherland and M. McKisack (Oxford, 1937), 107 note 5, where it is maintained that the reference was inserted 'under Yorkist influence'.

25 *Eulogium Historiarum*, lxx, lxxxi. Haydon's view is endorsed by E. J. Jones, 'The Authorship of the *Continuation of the Eulogium Historiarum*: A Suggestion', *Speculum*, 12 (1937), 196–202. See also Clifford, 'Continuation of the *Eulogium Historiarum*', 40: 'his knowledge of Latin was greatly inferior to that of the author of the Continuation itself'.

26 This, at any rate, is the conclusion reached by Gransden, who observes that it is 'fairly certain that the continuation was by a Franciscan friar who was possibly a member of the convent of Grey Friars in Canterbury': *Historical Writing in England, II*, 158; cf. J. I. Catto, 'An Alleged Great Council of 1374', *EHR*, 82 (1967), 764–71. See also J. Taylor, *English Historical Literature in the Fourteenth Century* (Oxford, 1987), 21, and Given-Wilson, 'The Manner of King Richard's Renunciation', 366–7 and note 1. Added support for a Canterbury affiliation is provided by the considerable attention paid to the role of the Friars Minor in Glendower's revolt, leading Derek Whitfield to remark that 'especially from 1401 to 1405, the *Eulogium* is a source of prime importance for the political history of

There are further indications that the author was very likely a contemporary observer of important events attending the Lancastrian revolution, and that he had access to important sources of information. For instance, it seems that he composed his text in successive drafts across the early 1400s, and that he frequently went back over previously written accounts in order to add bits and pieces of new information as well as second thoughts and new insights into his evolving text.[27] Moreover, he may very well have been an eye-witness to much that he records. It is often overlooked that the *Continuatio*'s account of events surrounding Richard's resignation in the Tower, along with its coverage of the parliament of 30 September 1399, seems to come from a particularly well informed source, perhaps an eyewitness. We are told, for example, that witnesses to this event took notes to be used in future proceedings, and that when Henry of Lancaster entered Westminster hall he carried before him the sword of state and then proceeded to the seat of his late father, which was next to that of the bishop of Carlisle.[28]

If the author were indeed an ecclesiastic, this helps to account for keen interest in the affairs of Thomas Arundel, archbishop of Canterbury.[29] Thus we are informed of the archbishop's criticism of the luxurious lifestyle enjoyed by many of Richard II's courtiers, and we are told of Richard's duplicitous behavior in his dealings with Thomas Arundel, the archbishop of Canterbury, in getting him to hand over his brother Richard for trial before the Revenge Parliament of 1397.[30] We further learn the particulars of Richard's sentence of exile imposed on Arundel, followed by the archbishop's opening address at the deposition parliament in 1399, as well as his sermon delivered at the accession of Henry IV.[31]

Perhaps owing to his fondness for Arundel, and especially his perceived mistreatment at the hands of the king, the author betrays throughout his narrative a personal and determined dislike for Richard II. Thus the *Continuatio* repeatedly calls attention to perceived wrong-doings at Richard's court in the late 1390s, whether on the part of the king or his corrupt courtiers. For example, the *Continuatio* portrays Richard as excessively vindictive in his cold and calculated treatment of Gloucester,

the English Province': 'Conflicts of Personality and Principle: the Political and Religious Crisis in the English Franciscan Province, 1400–1409', *Franciscan Studies*, 1, 17 (1957), 336.

[27] For example, and as demonstrated above, it is clear that the compiler followed the annalistic account of the lost Latin original for his material from 1364 to 1401. Since the final entry in this text relates the execution of the Lollard heretic William Sawtry, which took place in early March 1401 the author was at work shortly after this date. But since his text also incorporates material from the Lancastrian 'Record and Process', a version of which was in circulation in mid-1400, the author must have revised an already written draft in order to add this material. Yet another part of his text was composed before 27 April 1404, since the text refers to Philip the Bold, duke of Burgundy, as still alive when the text was composed, and the duke died on this date: R. Vaughan, *Philip the Bold* (London, 1962), 101. At the same time, the author is conspicuously well informed about and interested in Glyndwr's revolt, which he relates in considerable detail (*Eulogium*, iii, 388–401), and which suggests a possible eyewitness account, but which suddenly ends *in medias res* in 1405.

[28] *Eulogium Historiarum*, iii, 383.

[29] Gransden, for instance, notes that 'the loyalty of the Franciscan continuator of the *Eulogium Historiarum* was not to a secular magnate, nor exclusively to one ecclesiastic. However, probably because he had some connection with Canterbury, the continuator shows a marked regard for the archbishop [Thomas Arundel]. His attachment becomes particularly apparent towards the end of the fourteenth century, the period when he began writing': *Historical Writing in England, II*, 181.

[30] *Eulogium Historiarum*, iii, 376–7, 371–2.

[31] Ibid., 382–4.

Arundel, and Warwick during the 'Revenge Parliament' in 1397.[32] In addition, the narrative relates that Richard's purpose in convening the Shrewsbury parliament in January 1398 was to dispense with parliament altogether.[33] Our chronicle also states that Richard was never really interested in his subjects' welfare, and it refers to Richard's last will and testament as 'prejudicial to his kingdom'.[34]

Whatever his personal inclinations, our narrator recounts important events from a decidedly Lancastrian perspective, attested by his frequent adherence to the Lancastrian 'Record and Process'.[35] As an example, the *Continuatio* presents a unique version of the 'Revenge Parliament' of 1397 by drawing parallels between its actions and the 'Merciless Parliament' of 1388.[36] In its treatment of Richard's renunciation of the crown the *Continuatio* presents a similarly Lancastrian line. We are told that although Richard had promised to resign the crown at his meeting with Henry Bolingbroke at Conway, he took back this promise in the Tower, and was ultimately coerced to surrender of the crown 'absolute et sine conditione', and then proceeded to recite the document of surrender.[37] The account of Richard's death at Pontefract also adheres to the Lancastrian version in that it attributes his demise to 'voluntary starvation'.[38]

Although it appears that our author was driven by a variety of motives to insinuate the scandalous crown-wearing passage into his compilation, this in itself does not necessarily prove that the ceremonies alleged in the *Continuatio* never occurred. Indeed, it could be argued that the reference is consistent with Richard's determination to initiate what Nigel Saul refers to as 'the elaboration of courtly protocol', and a 'growing emphasis on ceremonial'.[39] Moreover, crown-wearings constituted by far the most dramatic of examples of Richard's efforts to highlight the formality and mystique of his royal office.

On numerous occasions Richard staged carefully orchestrated ceremonies where he attired himself in full royal regalia and sat enthroned wearing his crown. In May 1389 Richard had the royal crown transported to King's Langley, where, according to Michael Bennett, 'he presumably staged a crown-wearing to mark the declaration of his majority'.[40] The *Vita Ricardi Secundi* records that in 1390 both Richard and Queen Anne sat enthroned, wearing their crowns, at a banquet held at Kennington on the Feast of St Edward the Confessor as a way of displaying their royal dignity.[41] In the same year, according to the Westminster chronicler, Richard, along with his entire chapel royal, wore his crown during High Mass at Westminster Abbey on the

32 Ibid., 374–6.

33 Ibid., 377–8.

34 Ibid., 380–81.

35 On the wide distribution of the 'Record and Process' by Lancastrian sympathizers, see: Gransden, *Historical Writing in England, II*, 187, and Given-Wilson, *Chronicles of the Revolution*, 168–9. According to Given-Wilson, *Chronicles of the Revolution*, 64, Usk's 'account of a final conversation between the king and the archbishop before the latter went into exile is corroborated by the thirty-third and last of the charges brought against Richard in the "Record and Process"': ibid., 183–4.

36 *Eulogium Historiarum*, iii, 373–4.

37 Ibid., 382–3.

38 Ibid., 387.

39 Saul, *Richard II*, 342.

40 *Richard II and the Revolution of 1399*, 40.

41 G. B. Stow (ed.), *Historia Vitae et Regni Ricardi Secundi* (Philadelphia, 1977), 132.

Feast of the Translation of St Edward.[42] And two years later Richard celebrated Mass on the feast of St Edward, again wearing his crown.[43]

In other ways, too, Richard set out deliberately to establish 'a courtly style that suited his tastes and reflected his lofty conception of his office' in order to 'cultivate a loftier and more exalted image of himself as king', and to 'strengthen the power and authority of the Crown'.[44] Prominent among these additional initiatives was the demonstration of deference in Richard's presence, exemplified in the practice of kneeling before addressing the king.

Chroniclers' accounts attest several instances of this form of deference. The monk of Westminster reports that on 23 October 1385 the archbishop of Canterbury was reconciled with the king, and that Richard 'in his lust for glory and his eagerness to have from everybody the deference properly due to his kingship … allowed the archbishop to kneel before him to beg his pardon'.[45] One year later Sir John Holland approached the king and 'three times, before reaching him, he flung himself to the ground on his knees and arms; finally he rose to his knees and stretched his hands upwards and with tears and wails humbly begged the king for mercy'.[46] On another occasion Henry Knighton relates that when Gloucester, Arundel, and Warwick confronted Richard at Westminster on 17 November 1387, they found Richard seated on the royal throne in the Great Hall, and they genuflected three times before they were granted the opportunity to address the king.[47] Interestingly, Walsingham confirms this account, but says that Gloucester remained on his knees until he was bidden to rise by the king.[48] Again, in his *Concordia facta inter regem Riccardum II et civitatem Londonie*, Richard Maidstone describes in great detail the pomp and pageantry associated with Richard's entrance into London on 21–22 August 1392, including an account of the aldermen and keeper of the city approaching Richard on their knees before presenting him with the sword and keys of the city.[49]

Further recorded expressions of deference in Richard's presence indicate bowing and prostrating before addressing the king. The monk of Westminster reports that on the night of 24 February 1385 the duke of Lancaster visited the king at Sheen and, once in the king's presence, 'made to him the bow which propriety demanded'.[50] A

42 L. C. Hector and B. F. Harvey (eds.), *The Westminster Chronicle, 1381–1394* (Oxford, 1982), 450.

43 Cf. Saul, *Richard II*, 340 note 45.

44 Ibid., 339–40; and idem, 'Richard II and the Vocabulary of Kingship', 854. In support of this notion Saul cites Thomas Walsingham, who says that during the 'Revenge Parliament' of 1397 the Speaker of the Commons 'imputed to the king in his statements not human, but divine, honours, finding strange and flattering words hardly suitable for mere mortals; so that whenever he addressed the king, who was seated on his throne, he would extend his arms and supplicate with his hands, as if praying to him, entreating his high, excellent and most praiseworthy majesty that he might deign to concede these or those things. And the young king, courting honours and seeking praise, did not stop these words, as he should, but rather delighted in them': ibid.

45 *Westminster Chronicle*, 139.

46 Ibid., 159.

47 G. H. Martin (ed.), *Knighton's Chronicle* (Oxford, 1995), 414.

48 J. Taylor, W. R. Childs and L. Watkiss, *The St Albans Chronicle: The Chronica Maiora of Thomas Walsingham* (Oxford, 2003), 836.

49 T. Wright (ed.), *Political Poems and Songs Relating to English History* (2 vols., Rolls Series, 1859–61), i, 282–300. Lynn Staley, 'Gower, Richard II, Henry of Derby, and the Business of Making Culture', *Speculum*, 75 (2000), 80, says that Maidstone 'offered Richard a portrait of himself as triumphant over the powers both of time and of rebellion. Moreover, he did so in a way that is emphatically ceremonial, formal, hieratic, …'.

50 *Westminster Chronicle*, 112.

similar event took place on 30 December 1387, when a delegation of lords sought an audience with the king in the Tower. We are told that, 'on seeing the king, who was enthroned in the open near the chapel, [they] did him due reverence by three times prostrating themselves before, with the king's permission, they rose with diffidence to their feet …'.[51]

While it may appear at first appearance that the *Continuatio* account is consistent with these expressions of deference and respect, particularly with well-founded instances of crown-wearings, closer scrutiny suggests otherwise. It is important to point out that subtle – but profound – distinctions separate the *Continuatio* reference from all other known instances, and they call into question its credibility.

To begin with, the crown-wearing events reported by observers like the Westminster monk, Henry Knighton, and others were put on as *public* displays of royal magnificence. Known as 'festival crownings', they were associated with important events like celebrations of feast days, and were held either in Westminster hall or in some other accessible area in order to broadcast Richard's his regal authority. Furthermore, these events were traditional practices with earlier antecedents. As Nigel Saul puts it, 'the tradition of thrice-yearly crown-wearing sessions stretched back to early Norman times'.[52] The crown-wearing reference in the *Continuatio*, however, describes events in a different category. The passage states unequivocally that Richard staged elaborate crown-wearing ceremonies *within the king's chamber* ('in camera'). It is highly unlikely that these kinds of events were derived from any known precedents; according to Saul, 'no previous chronicler had commented on the extreme formality of such occasions, so there is the possibility that Richard's lofty demeanor was new'.[53]

All the same, it has been suggested that Richard may have modeled these highly formalized ceremonies on the behavior of his father, Edward the Black Prince. According to Saul, who cites a well-known reference in the so-called *Anonimalle Chronicle*, 'the first and most immediate source of the new formalism was almost certainly the Black Prince's court in Aquitaine … it was his habit to keep the Aquitanian nobility waiting for days on end for an audience, and then only to admit them to his presence on bended knee'.[54] Saul continues, 'this was behaviour of a kind that directly anticipates his son's at the festival crownings described by the *Eulogium* writer. Quite possibly, in assuming a more formal style, Richard was drawing on what he knew of the protocol of his father's court.'[55] Nevertheless, there are significant differences between these and the description provided by the *Continuatio* compiler. For instance, the *Anonimalle* reference states neither that the Black Prince staged these events *inside* the royal chamber, nor that the particular courtiers were made to stand silently therein for hours on end, and then forced to genuflect when recognized by his gaze.[56] It therefore appears that the highly unorthodox rituals

51 Ibid., 227.

52 Saul, *Richard II*, 342. For the view that the *Continuatio* refers to 'festival crownings', see E. H. Kantorowicz, *The King's Two Bodies. A Study in Mediaeval Political Theology* (Princeton, 1957), 29 and note 16.

53 Saul, *Richard II*, 342.

54 Saul, *Richard II*, 344–5.

54 Ibid., 345.

55 Ibid.

56 In addition, it is worth noting that the *Anonimalle* reference is itself not without difficulties. In the estimation of its editor the portion of the text that relating to the alleged ritual demanded by the

alleged in the *Continuatio* are *sui generis*, and without earlier Anglo-Norman or French exemplars.[57]

Further consideration of the *Continuatio* account throws up additional questions concerning its credibility. First of all, there is an apparent inconsistency concerning the timing of the alleged crown-wearings. The chronicle indicates that Richard staged these events either shortly after the consecration of Roger Walden as archbishop of Canterbury or just before the council at Nottingham. The date of Walden's consecration was 3 February 1398, and the council at Nottingham was convened on 30 June 1398, representing a gap of nearly five months.[58] Yet an analysis of Richard II's known itinerary for these months reveals that the king was rarely at Westminster during this period. During the spring and early summer of 1398 Richard was at Westminster on only the following dates: 1–4 April, 9 May, and then not again until 1 September, preferring instead to spend his time roaming around the midlands.[59] What this suggests in turn is that there is no real reason to take the *Continuatio* compiler's word for it that the events he describes necessarily occurred in the year 1398; they could just as easily have been staged at any date in Richard's reign – if they ever occurred at all.

This possibility, however, raises further complications. It is well known that crown-wearing ceremonies were put on by Richard II across several years, beginning in the mid-1380s and stretching into the early 1390s. If this were the case, there is every reason to expect that events of this magnitude and extravagance would have caught the eye of contemporary critics of Richard's policies, particularly those concerning matters within his court. As we have seen above, chroniclers were keen to record instances of deference and obeisance, particularly examples of crown-wearing events. What is more, at least one of these occurrences was of sufficient interest as to generate independent, corroborating notices in the narratives of Walsingham and the Westminster monk.[60] Surely, therefore, ceremonies on such an elaborate, extravagant, and unorthodox scale as described in the *Continuatio* would have been recorded by either the Monk of Westminster (to 1394), Henry Knighton (to

Black Prince in 1367 may not have been written by a contemporary, but perhaps 'by two other scribes writing between 1396 and 1399': V. H. Galbraith, *The Anonimalle Chronicle 1333 to 1381* (Manchester, 1927), xxiv. For a different view see A. F. Pollard, 'The Authorship and Value of the "Anonimalle" Chronicle', *EHR*, 53 (1938), 577–605.

57 Instead, the deference attributed to Richard II smacks of late Roman imperial hieratic practices, particularly those enforced at the court of Diocletian, where 'to such quasi-divinity the proper gesture was no longer salutation, but prostration, *adoratio*, *proskynesis* … To be one of the circle of *admissionales*, who regularly came into the sacred presence, was itself an honour and a symbol of high office in its own right. On their reception, such people would kneel and kiss the hem of the Emperor's robe': S. Williams, *Diocletian and the Roman Recovery* (New York, 1985), 111–12.

58 For the dates of Walden's elevation to the see of Canterbury, see F.M. Powicke and E. B. Fryde (eds.), *Handbook of British Chronology* (2nd edn, London, 1961), 211, 528.

59 Richard II's itinerary in 1398 is laid out in Saul, *Richard II*, 473. For Richard's wanderings in the midlands during this period see: Tout, *Chapters*, iv, 34; Saul, 'Richard II, York, and the Evidence of the King's Itinerary', in J. L. Gillespie (ed.), *The Age of Richard II* (Stroud, 1997), 81; M. Bennett, *Richard II and the Revolution of 1399* (Stroud, 1999), 130. Furthermore, the only dates which Richard might have seriously considered for 'solemn days' were the feast dates of Saints Edward the Confessor and John the Baptist (13 October and 24 June).

60 See notes 47 and 48 above.

1396), or Walsingham or other contemporary observers.[61] Yet nowhere in the entire corpus of late fourteenth-century chronicle literature do we encounter a description of events of the sort alleged by the *Continuatio* writer.[62]

In conclusion, it may very well be that towards the end of his reign Richard II 'began to tyrannize his people', in Walsingham's memorable phrase. But to cite the *Continuatio*'s crown-wearing reference among verifiable instances of *gravimina* that contributed to Richard II's downfall is to fly in the face of all that has been presented here. It has been demonstrated that the passage in question represents a later textual interpolation into a notoriously corrupt text; this in itself is enough to cast doubt on its credibility. More compelling is the revelation that this inflammatory passage was insinuated by an author motivated by either personal dislike of Richard or loyalty to the Lancastrian cause – or both – in order to limn a negative portrait of the king.[63] All things considered, then, the *Continuatio*'s fantastic story represents little more than yet another alleged historical incident in the reign of Richard II.

61 For a survey of chroniclers' assessments of Richard II see Saul, *Richard II*, 435ff. See also: G. H. Martin, 'Narrative Sources for the Reign of Richard II', in *The Age of Richard II*, 51–69; G. B. Stow, 'Chronicles Versus Records: The Character of Richard II', in J. S. Hamilton and P. J. Bradley (eds.), *Documenting the Past: Essays in Medieval History Presented to George Peddy Cuttino* (Wolfeboro, New Hampshire, 1989), 155–76.

62 Cf. the most complete description of Richard's character conveyed in the *Vita Ricardi Secundi*, 166, along with Walsingham's famous remark that Richard's courtiers resembled more 'knights of the bedchamber than of war'.

63 For the notion that the *Continuatio* compiler was anxious to impugn Richard's character see Terry Jones et al., *Who Murdered Chaucer?* (London, 2003), 47–8. His motives notwithstanding, it is interesting to speculate on the author's possible sources. It may be that ther compiler caught wind of some vicious rumor regarding the goings-on within Richard's court. For the role of rumour in the aftermath of the Lancastrian revolution in 1399, see P. Strohm, *England's Empty Throne: Usurpation and the Language of Legitimation, 1399–1422* (New Haven and London, 1998), 19–31, 106–14. Alternatively, the author could have drawn on the description of the protocol at the Black Prince's court, as presented in the *Anonimalle Chronicle*, which could have been in circulation in the early 1400s. For this idea I am indebted to a conversation with John Taylor.

WAS RICHARD II A TYRANT? RICHARD'S USE OF THE BOOKS OF RULES FOR PRINCES

Terry Jones

My question may seem a bit of a non-starter. For six hundred years, historians have been discussing the weaknesses of King Richard's character: his vanity, his superstitious nature, his capacity for self-delusion, his vindictiveness, his duplicity, his disregard for his subjects, his favouritism, his self-indulgence, his reliance on bad counsel, his lack of manliness, his fickleness, his introspection, his coldness and lack of social skills, his insecurity, his paranoia, his insanity and, of course, his megalomania. The whole thrust of Ricardian historiography has been: 'What went wrong?' How did this promising young ruler end up a tyrant, hated and despised by his people?

Recently, however, some scholars have begun questioning the basic premises of this tradition, and – before the momentum of this particular act of iconoclasm becomes unstoppable – I would like to jump on the band-wagon.[1]

It is worth noting that Henry IV avoids the outright accusation of tyranny in the official version of why Richard was deposed. He accuses Richard of 'evil government', of greed, of dissimulation, of acting arbitrarily, and (rather oddly) of rebuking certain lords too 'sharply and violently' in council, but the 'Record and Process' never actually goes so far as to accuse him of being an out and out tyrant.

Richard, for his part, certainly did not see himself as a tyrant. In fact he offered himself up as a champion *against* tyranny. In the Parliament of January 1397 – the first in which he was free of the baleful effect of his uncles and others who had tried to depose him in 1387/8 – he explained to the Commons why he wanted to support the king of France in his expedition against Gian Galeazzo, the lord of Milan. The king of France and the king of England, he said, were regarded as two of the most worthy and valiant Christian princes, 'and for this reason if they happen to know of any king, prince, or other person … who by tyranny would conquer and destroy the Christian people … they are bound by right … to destroy such a tyrant and destroyer, and restore and recover those oppressed and deprived of their estate'.[2]

Actually Richard's main reason for supporting the king of France, as he also explained to the Commons, was to re-affirm the peace between their two countries. The lords of Milan were by-words for tyranny – the 'tiraunts of Lumbardye', as Geoffrey Chaucer calls them in the *Legend of Good Women*.[3] They certainly made

1 G. B. Stow, 'Richard II in Thomas Walsingham's Chronicles', *Speculum*, 59 (1984), 68–102, and D. Biggs, *Three Armies in Britain* (Leiden and Boston, 2006).

2 *Rotuli Parliamentorum*, iii 340, translated in C. Given-Wilson, P. Brand and A. Curry (eds.), *The Parliament Rolls of Medieval England, 1275–1504* (digital edition, Leicester, 2005).

3 *Legend of Good Women*, F 372–80, in *The Riverside Chaucer*, ed. L. D. Benson (Boston, Mass., 1987). All references to Chaucer are to the *Riverside* edition.

no effort to explain their foreign policies to any representative assembly. Chaucer gives a good summary of what distinguished a rightful king from a tyrant in the eyes of Richard II's contemporaries: a rightful ruler's first duty is to care for his people; they are 'his treasure and his gold in coffer', he says, recalling the pseudo-Aristotelian *Secretum secretorum*.[4] By cementing the peace with France, Richard was acting as a rightful king by putting an end to a war that had impoverished both peoples. And one might add that, by freely and openly explaining to the commons the motives behind his foreign policy, he was certainly not behaving as you might expect a tyrant to behave.

Nowadays we tend to equate absolutism with despotism, but in the thirteenth and fourteenth centuries what distinguished a rightful king from a tyrant was not how much power he wielded but how he used that power. This view had its origins in Aristotle: '... among monarchical forms of government, the type which looks to the common interest is called Kingship ... Tyranny is a government by a single person directed to the interest of that person ...'.[5]

In the thirteenth century, Thomas Aquinas took up Aristotle's distinction between the rightful ruler and the tyrant: if '... a community of free men is ordered by a ruler in such a way as to secure the common good, such rule will be right and just ... If, however, the government is directed ... towards the private good of the ruler ... such a ruler is called a tyrant ... if just government belongs to one man alone, he is properly called a king.'[6]

The distinction was faithfully disseminated in one of the most influential of all medieval interpretations of Aristotle, the *De regimine principum* of Giles of Rome (1243–1316). Here is John Trevisa's English version of the original Latin: '... a kyng takeþ heede to þe comyne profit and a tyrand to his owne profit'.[7]

Giles' book was well-known in England. Edward III owned a copy in French, which was passed on to Henry of Grosmont, whose daughter, Blanche married John of Gaunt and was the subject of Chaucer's *Book of the Duchess*. Richard's uncle and arch-nemesis, Thomas of Woodstock, duke of Gloucester, owned a copy in Latin, and so too did Sir Simon Burley, Richard's tutor.

The *De regimine principum* was included in the arts curriculum at Paris and the English universities by the mid fourteenth century.[8] Ten years after Richard's usurpation, Thomas Hoccleve assumed that Henry, Prince of Wales, would be familiar with it.[9] It seems to me unthinkable that the young Richard II should not have been exposed to such a popular and influential disquisition on his duties as a prince and the distinction between rightful kingship and tyranny.

In any case, Aristotle's definition of tyranny was probably the only one widely

4 M. A. Manzalaoui (ed.), *Secretum Secretorum*, i (Early English Text Soc., 1977), 84.

5 Aristotle, *Politics*, trans. Ernest Barker, revised by R. F. Stalley (Oxford, 1995), 7, 100–101.

6 R. W. Dyson (ed.), *De Regimine Principum*, ch. iv, in *St Thomas Aquinas, Political Writings* (Cambridge, 2002), 9.

7 D. C. Fowler, C. F. Briggs, P. G. Remley (eds.), *The Governance of Kings and Princes*, John Trevisa's Middle English translation of the *De Regimine Principum* of Aegidius Romanus (New York and London, 1997), 333.

8 C. F. Briggs, *Giles of Rome's De Regimmine Principum – Reading and Writing Politics at Court and University, c.1275–c.1525* (Cambridge, 1999), 147.

9 Thomas Hoccleve, *Regement of Princes*, lines 2129–30, see also lines 2038–2135, in F. J. Furnivall (ed.), *Hoccleve's Works, The Regement of Princes and Fourteen Minor Poems* (Early English Text Soc., extra series, 72, 1897), 74–7.

understood in the fourteenth century.[10] It was used by John of Paris (1301–2): 'kingship properly understood can be defined as rule over a community perfectly ordered to the common good by one person … in a tyranny, the ruler intends only his own good'.[11] It was the basis of the Italian jurists' discussions of tyranny. Bartolus of Sassoferrato (1313–1357) wrote that where there is government by one man, he 'is called a lord if he inclines to a good and common end, a tyrant if he is inclined to pursue bad or [merely] personal ends'.[12] In 1324 the influential and controversial Marsilius of Padua put his own particular spin on it, stressing the consent of the people to be governed: 'A *kingly monarchy*, then, is a temperate government wherein the ruler is a single man who rules for the common benefit, and in accordance with the will or consent of the subjects. *Tyranny*, its opposite, is a diseased government wherein the ruler is a single man who rules for his own private benefit apart from the will of his subjects.'[13]

The political theorists of Richard II's day distinguished between tyranny and kingship not by how much power a ruler wielded, but by how he used it. So if we are to accuse Richard of being a tyrant we need to assess his rule within this context and the way in which he and his contemporaries defined tyranny.

In the summer of 1397, we are told, Richard II's rule suddenly changed in character and became tyrannical. He arrested the three lords who had challenged his kingship ten years before, reversed the legislation of the Merciless Parliament of 1388, required his subjects to swear new oaths to uphold measures approved in Parliament; he demanded that those who had supported the revolt of 1387–8 sue for his pardon in person, he demanded charters from the home counties that gave him 'carte blanche', and he attempted to censor foreign correspondence.[14] In other words he concentrated power into his own hands, demanding absolute obedience from his subjects. At the same time 'he began to cultivate a loftier and more exalted image of himself as king'.[15]

At the opening session of parliament, the chancellor Edmund Stafford, bishop of Exeter, spelt out the new deal. He '… took as his theme the words of the prophet Ezekiel – There shall be one king for all – showing upon many authorities of holy scripture that there would be one king and governor, and no kingdom could be governed in any other way: and that for the good governance of every king three things were required; first, that the king have the power to govern; second, that the laws by which he ought to govern should be kept and justly executed; third, that the subjects of the kingdom should be duly obedient to the king and his laws.'[16]

As far as we know, no one at the time objected to this as an obnoxious declara-

10 An exception is Walter Milemete's *On the Nobility, Wisdom, and Prudence of Kings*. This curious book is really a commentary of the *Secretum Secretorum*. It betrays no awareness of Aristotle himself, and even pre-dates Machiavelli in presenting the maintenance of kingly power as the ultimate goal, and the well-being of the people as simply a precautionary measure to assist in this. See C. J. Nederman (ed.), *Political Thought in Early Fourteenth-Century England* (Medieval & Renaissance Texts and Studies, 250, 2002), 15–62.

11 A. Monahan (ed.), *John of Paris On Royal and Papal Power* (New York and London, 1974), 7.

12 Bartolo of Sassoferrato, *Treatise on City Government*, ed. and trans. S. Lane, http://www.fordham.edu/halsall/source/bartolus.html

13 A. Gewirth (ed.), Marsilius of Padua, *Defensor Pacis* (Toronto, 1980), 27–8.

14 N. E. Saul, 'Richard II and the Vocabulary of Kingship', *EHR*, 110 (1995), 854; C. Given-Wilson, *The Royal Household and the King's Affinity* (New Haven and London, 1986), 186–7.

15 Saul, 'Richard II and the Vocabulary of Kingship', 854.

16 *Rotuli Parliamentorum*, iii, 348.

tion of despotic rule, and it is worth noting that Henry IV was happy to re-employ Stafford as chancellor in 1403. So his Parliamentary address of 1397 did his reputation no harm.

The equation of tyranny with absolutism is a modern one. In the Middle Ages, there was certainly much discussion about whether it was better to be ruled by one man, or by several or by many, but medieval political theorists believed that it was possible for one man to rule within the law, even if he wielded absolute power. And, almost to a man (Marsilius is an exception) they came down in favour of rule by one man – just as long as he was a king and not a tyrant – that is as long as he ruled in the interest of his people and not in his own interest.
If anyone was responsible for the hold which this idea had on Richard II's contemporaries, it was probably Thomas Aquinas.

Aristotle had outlined three types of government: Rule by One, Rule by the Few, and Rule by the Many. Each of these, he said, has a good manifestation and a bad manifestation. Rule by One Person, if it is good, we call Monarchy, if bad, Tyranny. Rule by the Few, if good, we call Aristocracy and, if bad, Oligarchy. Rule by the Many we call Constitutional Government or 'Polity', if it is good, and if it is bad Democracy. Of the 'perverted' forms of government, Aristotle says the worst is Tyranny, then Aristocracy, then Democracy. The good forms of government go in the opposite order: Constitutional Government or Polity is least good, followed by Oligarchy and the best (theoretically) Monarchy.
I say 'theoretically' because although Aristotle does indeed postulate an ideal form of kingship, in which one man should have absolute power, he does not offer it up as a universal panacea. Different forms of government suit different sorts of people, he says, and it is only amongst a certain type of people 'which tends to produce some particular stock (or family) pre-eminent in its capacity for political leadership' that such a king's rule will be best suited.[17]

Elsewhere, he rehearses the arguments in favour and against one-man rule and decides that on balance rule by more than one person is probably preferable: 'the judgement of a single man is bound to be corrupted when he is overpowered by anger, or by any other similar emotion; but it is no easy task to make everyone get angry and go wrong simultaneously … Is not the balance clearly in favour of the greater number?'[18]

Aristotle continues: 'It is clear from our argument, first, that the best form of political association is one where power is vested in the middle class, and, secondly, that good government is attainable in those cities where there is a large middle class.'[19]

But this was not a message that chimed with the political realities of the medieval world. Thomas Aquinas, for example, wrote his *De regimine principum* for Hugh III, the king of Cyprus (1267–84), and naturally he down-played Aristotle's preference for rule by the many and concentrated on his arguments for kingship.[20] Giles of Rome dutifully reproduced Aquinas's interpetation of Aristotle as if it were Aristotle's own: 'it is not to vnderstondynge þat þe philosofer wolde mene þat lordschepe

17 Aristotle, *Politics*, iii, 17, 131.
18 Ibid., iii, 15, 124–5.
19 Ibid., iv, 158–9.
20 *St Thomas Aquinas, Political Writings*, 17.

of manye is sympliche bettere þan lordschipe of oon ȝif eiþer is riȝtful, for he seith ofte in þe same Politikes þat a regne [kingship] is most worthi principate …'[21]

Aquinas's and Giles' reading of Aristotle acquired huge significance in the struggle between expanding papal power and emerging monarchical and imperial powers of Europe throughout this period. Dante, writing in anticipation of Henry VII of Luxembourg being crowned Holy Roman Emperor in 1309, waxes lyrical on the subject of monarchy: 'Mankind exists for its own sake and not for the sake of something else only when it is under the rule of a monarch, for only then are perverted forms of government (i.e. democracies, oligarchies and tyrannies), which force mankind into slavery, set right …'.[22]

William of Ockham and John Wyclif both come to the same conclusion.[23] Even the hard-headed Italian jurists like Bartolus of Sassoferrato, despite rehearsing the arguments *against* one-man rule, come down in its favour in the right circumstances. A city, Bartolus says, is best ruled by 'the multidude', larger populations by the aristocracy, but cities that rule over other cities are best ruled by a king.[24]

Even the rebels of 1381 had one-man rule in mind. At Smithfield, Wat Tyler demanded '… that no lord should have lordship in future, but it should be divided among all men, except for the king's own lordship'.[25] It was the very policy which was actively being pursued by the two most significant figures in Richard's council.

Sir Simon Burley, Richard's tutor, and Michael de la Pole – both some thirty years senior to their king – had been in service with Richard's father, the Black Prince, in Aquitaine, where they had, to use Nigel Saul's words: 'witnessed lordship at its most vigorous and assertive' and successful. 'They had seen the order that was brought by the rigorous exaction of the duty of obedience.'[26] And obedience to the king was required, according to the *De regimine principum*, even if the king lapses into a certain degree of tyranny: 'for a certain amount of tyranny may be better suffered than the harm that comes if men are disobedient to the prince and break his law'.[27] I feel sure that Sir Simon must have read that out to his pupil.

When Richard II took the rule of England into his own hands, he was simply putting into practice one of the generally accepted political theories on how to rule in the best interests of his subjects. So his seizure of power in 1397 is no guide to whether he suddenly became a tyrant or not. We need to look at what he did with that power.

What distinguished the rightful ruler from the tyrant was the promotion of the common good, but there was no doubt in the minds of any of the medieval political theorists about the chief objective of the rightful ruler: it was peace. Aquinas wrote that the 'multitude' should 'be established in the unity of peace'. Giles of Rome declared 'pees and vnytee of citeseyns schole be his final entent þat ȝeueþ [giveth] þe lawe …'. For Dante peace was: 'the goal to which all our human actions are

21 *The Governance of Kings and Princes*, 328.

22 P. Shaw (ed.), Dante, *Monarchia* (Scholarly Digital Editions, Birmingham, UK, 2006), Book I, ch. 12, 9.

23 William of Ockham, *A Short Discourse on the Tyrannical Government*, ed. A. S. McGrade (Cambridge, 1992), 128–9. Iohannis Wycliffe, *De civili dominio* (4 vols., London, 1885–1905), i, 201.

24 Bartolo of Sassoferrato, *Treatise on City Government*, as above, n. 12.

25 *Anonimalle Chronicle*, in R. B. Dobson (ed.), *The Peasants' Revolt of 1381* (London, 1970, 2nd edn, 1983), 164.

26 N.E. Saul, *Richard* II (New Haven and London, 1997), 119.

27 *Governance of Kings and Princes*, 388.

directed as to their final end', and Bartolus concurred: 'the peace and union of the citizens should be the final intention of the ruler'.[28]

Peace meant peace both inside the realm and outside. Both objectives presented overwhelming problems to the young Richard II and his counsellors, and both were inextricably linked. The pursuit of peace with France may have made good sense, in terms of the economy, the tax burden on ordinary people, and the devastation on the continent, but it was a dangerous policy to pursue, for it laid the monarchy open to easy charges of weakness and cowardice, from those magnates and men-at-arms who still saw the war with France as their greatest opportunity for gain and glory.

These men formed a pretty formidable opposition. The elderly French soldier, diplomat and author, and one-time chancellor of Cyprus, Philippe de Mézières, described the atmosphere in the English court and the great animosity between the doves and the hawks. He depicts the hawks as bristling Black Boars gathered around the young king – a miraculous White Boar: '… quite close to the crowned young White Boar stood several big Boars, black and bristling, who once were the sons of the powerful black Boar, who so many times by divine permission destroyed the rows of beautiful vines in the great field of golden lilies [France]'.[29]

Philippe picks out the earl of Arundel as the ringleader, and highlights the intimidating effect of the war party on those who wanted peace: 'It was true that there were some among the knights who no longer favoured the war, but through fear of the Black Boars and in particular a certain count of Arundel, they did not dare say a word nor support their king …'.[30]

Philippe de Mézières was writing in 1389 but, although many things had changed, there is no reason to think that the atmosphere between the warmongers and the peace party had been much different in 1383. Philippe implies that the animosity of the barons towards Richard was there from the very beginning of the reign. He even suggests that Richard was crowned *against their will*: 'The son of the great Black Boar is now reigning and he, by God's grace, has become white and shining, in contrast to his father. He has been crowned king of England against the will of some of the great princes. It is his firm intention to sheathe the sword and make a good peace with the king of France. But the great princes have so tied his hands that he can go no further in the matter.'[31]

The barons would certainly not have liked the policy of regal supremacy which Richard and his advisers pursued, no matter how many political theorists claimed it was the best form of government. The barons must also have been jealous of the influence men like Sir Simon Burley, Richard's tutor, had over the boy-king. Their historical spokesman, Walsingham, tut-tuts at the ostentatious familiarity with which, during the coronation, Sir Simon 'took the king up in his arms' – without waiting for him to be divested of his royal regalia – and carried him 'into the palace by the royal gate with crowds milling all round him and pressing upon him, so that on the way he lost one of the consecrated shoes through his thoughtlessness.'[32]

28 *Ibid*, III, ii, 327. St. Thomas Aquinas, *On Kingship*, ed. Gerald B. Phelan (Toronto, 1949, revised edn. by I. T. Eschmann, 2000), 65. Dante, *Monarchia*, I iv, 5. Bartolo, ca 8.

29 Philippe de Mézières, *Le Songe du Vieil Pelerin*, ed. G. W. Coopland (2 vols., Cambridge, 1969), i, 395. [trans. by Anna Soderstrom]

30 Ibid., 402–3.

31 Ibid., 186.

32 L. C. Hector and B. F. Harvey (eds.), *The Westminster Chronicle, 1381–1394* (Oxford, 1982), 416–17.

Did the magnates know from that moment that they were being side-lined? The first written record of their animosity does not appear in the chronicles until 1384, when the earl of Arundel could no longer hold back his hatred for the royal party. In full parliament at Shrewsbury he set aside any propriety and respect for his liege lord, to pour out his bile in public: 'You are aware, my lords, that any kingdom in which prudent government is lacking stands in peril of destruction; and the fact is now being illustrated before your eyes, since this country, which, as you know, began long ago through bad government to lose strength, is at present almost in a state of decay …'.[33] It is no wonder the sixteen-year-old king went white with rage and told Arundel 'to go to the Devil!'

The rebels of 1381 had offered an entirely different perspective: they blamed the misgovernment of England on the barons: 'the realm of England hath not been well governed a great space for the honour of the realm nor for the common profit by his uncles and the clergy …'.[34]

The benefits of peace with France were of no interest to the hawks; the mass of the population may have been impoverished by the war abroad and the taxation to run it may have provoked massive revolts in both countries, but the magnates took their cut of booty and ransoms, expanded their affinities and gained fame and glory. The French chronicler, Jean le Beau remarked: 'the war-loving nobles had long conspired against Richard on several occasions while he was seeking peace with France, because they had found war a source of considerable profit'.[35] And naturally the desire for profit meant that the common soldiery were all in favour of war. As Froissart put it: 'the poorer knights and archers were of course for war, as their sole liveliehood depended on it'.[36]

For a man like Gloucester, the war with France must have appeared to be the only way of supporting himself in the manner in which he hoped to become accustomed. His father, Edward III, had left him no territorial endowment, and even though he had been raised to an earldom and granted £1,000 a year to maintain it, he had to collect the money in rents from alien priories which were already in financial difficulties, and he probably never received his full due. It must have been galling: he was twelve years older than the king, a son of Edward III, and yet he had to stand by and watch courtiers like de Vere (who came from one of the poorest families amongst the titled nobility) being lavished with rewards which should have been going to him.[37]

Gloucester was not going to let peace break out if he could help it. He joined his brother, Lancaster, in the peace embassy of 1383, but Froissart reports his treachery in the negotiations. Gloucester secretly told his friends 'that he would never agree to any peace with France, whatever negotiations might be taken in hand on the subject, if it were not an honourable one' by which he meant all the surrendered towns had to be returned and the 1,400,400 francs still unpaid must be paid in full – both of which were impossible demands. But he 'declared, that as long as he lived he should

33 Ibid., 67–9.

34 J. Froissart, trans. Lord Berners in Dobson (ed.), *The Peasants' Revolt of 1381*, 141–2.

35 R. Mott, 'Richard II and the Crisis of 1397', in I. Wood and G. A. Loud (eds.), *Church and Chronicle in the Middle Ages, Essays presented to John Taylor* (London, 1991), 169; Jean le Beau, *Chronique de Richard II, 1377–1399*, ed. J. A. C. Buchon, Collection des Chroniques Nationales Françaises, XXV, supplement ii (Paris, 1828), 2–3.

36 J. Froissart, *Chronicles*, ed. T. Johnes (2 vols., London, 1852), ii, 495.

37 Saul, *Richard II*, 178–9, 121.

never change these sentiments; in which he was joined by many of the barons of England, particularly the earl of Arundel … though they dissembled their opinions in public from seeing how much the king of England was bent on peace'.[38]

Let us be quite clear: this was treachery of the first order. Gloucester was supposed to be negotiating on behalf of the king, and yet he was secretly undermining Richard's policy. It was a treachery about which Philippe de Mézières warned the two young kings (in 1383 Richard was fifteen and Charles VI was only fourteen). 'When peace comes to be discussed … the generals I mentioned above and their followers will profess themselves very anxious for peace, but will always be ready … to strangle the proposed plan at its birth, and there lies the great danger, for neither you nor your brother of England is old enough to penetrate the disguise of these enemies of peace.'[39]

At twenty-seven, Gloucester must have been a formidable opponent for anyone, let alone his fifteen-year-old nephew. Once again Froissart paints a vivid and convincing portrait of the animosity which the duke bore Richard and the utter contempt with which he treated him. Gloucester 'had conceived a great hatred to his nephew, the king of England, and could in no way speak well of him … When the king sent for him, if it was his pleasure he would come, but more frequently he stayed at home; and when he obeyed, he was always the last to come and the first to depart. On giving his opinion, it must be implicitly followed, for he would not suffer to be contradicted. He then took leave, mounted his horse, and set off for a handsome castle he had in Essex … from his rough manner, [he] was more dreaded by the king than any of his uncles, for, in his speech, he never spared him. The king was always submissive to him, and whatever he asked was instantly granted.'[40]

The earl of Arundel showed equal hatred of Richard, even though he was rich, secure and not particularly challenged by the ambitions of the court party. However, he had grown up in a world in which English chivalry had triumphed over the French. He would have been fifteen when Edward III signed the Treaty of Brétigny, and perhaps he had always longed to repeat the glory of those heady days. Perhaps he just did not like the new court ways, in which the manly militarists of Edward's court had been replaced by an artsy group of culture-vultures. Maybe he simply hated having to bow and scrape to a boy twenty-one years his junior, and watch the established aristocracy side-lined at court by jumped-up newcomers.

The 28-year truce with France of 1396 was one of Richard's outstanding achievements. It had taken a lot of courage to pursue it in the teeth of the most bitter opposition from his magnates and the military establishment. The policy had, amongst other things, provoked a major baronial revolt in 1387 and had nearly resulted in Richard's deposition. And yet, with great skill and determination, the young king continued to seek peace with the country's old enemy abroad. It had taken thirteen years to achieve it.

The next year Richard was to achieve peace at home, which meant, according to the books of rules for princes, the establishment of kingly rule in the teeth of baronial opposition. Almost from the moment of Richard's accession, Arundel, Gloucester and their associates had treated him with disgraceful contempt, but in 1386 they went further and stripped him of all privacy and dignity in his household

38 Froissart, *Chronicles*, ii, 495.
39 *Le Songe du Vieil Pelerin*, ii, 72.
40 Ibid., ii, 637.

affairs. As Richard wrote to Albert of Bavaria: several noblemen '… have for long and since we were of tender years traitorously conspired to disinherit our crown and usurp our royal power, raising themselves with many abettors of their iniquity to rebel against our royal will, publicly condemning our faithful servants to death and doing whatsoever they pleased at their own will. Thus have they striven damnably to spend their malice even upon our person, having wrongly usurped the royal power by going about among our privy affairs, so that they have left us hardly anything beyond the royal name.'[41]

By crushing the rebel magnates, and bringing the country under his sole rule, Richard could claim to have brought internal peace to the kingdom, as he did to the Byzantine emperor, Manuel Palaeologus: '… we have by our own valour trodden on the necks of the proud and haughty … and have restored to our subjects peace, which they had troubled, and which by God's blessing shall endure for ever'.[42] Unfortunately for Richard, God's blessing lasted barely a couple of years. But at that moment, Richard could rightly claim that he had struggled long and hard to put into practice the ideals of one-man kingly rule as recommended by all the political theorists of the day.

In the light of this, it might be interesting to look at some of the associated charges that are even now levelled against him: for example, the charge that he was driven by his own personal vanity and that he seemed to want to present himself as some sort of god.

Now it might well be that Richard II was a very vain person. Indeed, considering his birth and upbringing, it would be a miracle if that were not the case. Indeed, that may have been exactly what his uncles disliked about him – maybe he was a conceited little brat. Actually we do not know. However, we should beware of assuming that, as king, his acts of policy stemmed from his personal failings. We can demonstrate, for example, that displays of magnificence did not necessarily originate in Richard's personal vanity, but in the books of rules for princes.

Aristotle did not go into much detail about the need for kingly splendour, but he noted that the one who rules will always want to distinguish himself from the ruled: 'so long as one is ruling and the other is being ruled, the ruler seeks to mark distinctions in outward dignity, in style of address, and in honours paid'.[43]

In the twelfth century, John of Salisbury explained that it was right and proper for a prince to appear magnificent: '… the prince stands on a pinnacle which is exalted and made splendid with all the great and high privileges which he deems necessary for himself. And rightly so …'. Giles of Rome seemed to be fascinated by the topic and spent many pages discussing how a king should be magnificent.[44] Another tract on kingship, *De quadripartite regis specie*, presented Richard with: 'a spectacular picture of the king as a figure of Solomonic wisdom and magnificence'.[45] This was a tract a copy of which Richard actually owned, and to make its point it has a glamorous picture of Richard on the first page.

Oddly enough, even the radical religious reformers thought it incumbent on a king to display his splendour. The *Tractatus de regibus* (a free adaptation of Wyclif's

41 Mott, 'Richard II and the Crisis of 1397', 175.

42 A. R. Myers (ed.), *English Historical Documents, 1327–1485* (London, 1969), 174–5.

43 Aristotle, *Politics*, 92.

44 *Policraticus* Book IV ch. 1; *The Governance of Kings and Princes*, I, ii, 81.

45 L. Staley, *Languages of Power in the Age of Richard II* (Pennsylvania, 2005), 121.

De Officio Regis) states that since legitimate kings rule by the right of God '… þai nedid to mayntene þo regale [their royal appurtenances and treasure], for by defoulynge her off [damaging them], her state goþ away [their royal authority is diminished]. And for þis cause kynges schulden be riche in men and godes, for ellis myght thai not holde þis state þat God haþ ȝiven to hem.'[46]

And this was really the key. As John of Salisbury put it, the importance of kingly display demonstrated the prince's relationship with the Almighty: 'the prince is … a kind of likeness on earth of the divine majesty … The power which the prince has is therefore from God … who, therefore, resists the ruling power, resists the ordinance of God' [Romans 13:2].[47]

This association of a rightful king with divine power went back, as usual, to Aristotle.[48] Thomas Aquinas saw the king as God's Justice of the Peace: the king '… is to be in the kingdom what the soul is in the body, and what God is in the world'.[49] Even Marsilius of Padua, who actually championed the election of rulers rather than hereditary succession, saw the hereditary monarch as the equivalent of the lord of the universe: 'the rule of the hereditary monarch is more similar to the governance or rule of the universe; for in the universe there is always, immutably, a single ruler, as it is said in the twelfth book of the Philosophy, last chapter: "One ruler let there be, because things do not wish to be ordered badly."'[50]

The *Secretum secretorum* took the same line: a king '… is likened to God … and therfor it sitte to hym þat he be stedfast and high and all his werkes proper and comvne [correct and available to all]'.[51]

Against this background of well-known and much-debated political theorizing, Thomas Walsingham's comments on Richard II's appearance at the Parliament of 1397 seem distinctly disingenuous. Walsingham claims that the Speaker of the Commons, Sir John Bushy: 'imputed to the king in his statements not human, but divine, honours, finding strange and flattering words hardly suitable for mere mortals … And the young king, courting honours and seeking praise, did not stop these words, as he should, but rather delighted in them.'[52]

Walsingham, clearly writing after the deposition, is pulling out all the stops for a piece of propaganda. For example, he calls Richard 'the young king', but in 1397 Richard was thirty. Did Walsingham (or any other chronicler for that matter) ever call anyone else of that age 'young'? Did Walsingham call the thirty-year-old Gloucester the 'young' duke when he was clamouring to restart the war with France in 1385? Of course not. A man of thirty was a fully-grown man in 1397 just as he is today.

Walsingham was merely parroting Thomas Arundel's smear campaign against Richard which he initiated in his address to parliament on 6 October 1399: '… no

46 *Tractatus de regibus* in J.-P. Genet (ed.), *Four English Political Tracts of the Later Middle Ages* (Camden Society, 4th series, 18, London, 1977), 7–8.

47 John of Salisbury, *Policraticus*, Book IV.

48 Aristotle, *Politics*, III, 13, 117.

49 Aquinas, *On Kingship*, 54.

50 Marsilius, *Defensor Pacis*, 71. Marsilius is actually quoting not from the *Politics* but from the *Metaphysics* xii, 10: 'Too many kings are bad – let there be one!' Aristotle, *Metaphysics*, ed. H. Lawson-Tancred (London, 1998, revised edn 2004), 388.

51 *Secretum secretorum*, 69–70.

52 'Annales Ricardi Secundi et Henrici Quarti', in H. T. Riley (ed.), *Chronica et Annales* (Rolls Series, 1866), 210; see also Saul, 'Richard II and the Vocabulary of Kingship', 854.

longer, as was the case before, will boys rule in the realm, but the lord says to you that "a man will rule the people". For that saying of the apostle's in Corinthinans 13: "When I was a child I spake as a child, I understood as a child, I thought as a child", could not inappropriately be used of the past rulers of this realm of yours … he who ruled understood as a child … just as a boy loves vanity, in the same way a man understands truth and wisdom … When therefore a boy reigns, will alone reigns, and reason is exiled … From this danger we have been freed, because a man rules: … And thus in the place of a boy willfully running riot, a man will now rule over the people …'.[53]

Walsingham picks up Arundel's spin, and deliberately attributes to Richard's 'vanity' the whole question of 'divine honours', the relationship of king and God and the use of elevated forms of address. And yet both Arundel and Walsingham must have been perfectly familiar with the theoretical background. Perhaps even more dishonestly, they also chose to ignore the political realities of the day; which were that, if the king of England wished to play a part in international affairs, he had to adopt the manners and ways of European court culture.[54]

Nigel Saul, commenting on the Field of the Cloth of Gold meeting between the English and French monarchs, notes that 'Richard had to spend lavishly on the ceremonies because of the considerations of power play involved. To be effective on the international stage a king had to appear kingly. If he arrived at a conference poorly arrayed, as an English observer says that Charles VI did at Ardres, he would have been written off as a ruler of no consequence.'[55]

Since the days of Charlemagne, the French court had practised a formal behaviour more elaborate than probably any other court in Europe.[56] By the latter part of the fourteenth century, the French court was very much the trend-setter for Europe. If Richard II was to marry the daughter of the king of France, and become part of that family, he had no choice but to adopt their ways and their grander forms of address. As Nigel Saul puts it: 'Richard's encouragement of the form "your majesty" was probably intended … to raise him to a position of equal standing with the French king.'[57] Walsingham's and Arundel's entirely successful attempt to smear Richard by pretending that the elevated style was simply the result of Richard's vanity, was all part and parcel of the thorough-going propaganda exercise mounted by Richard's usurper and his circle of advisers.

So far, I have tried to show that Richard II's policies were driven by the political theories of the day. There is one book of rules for princes, however, which I have not yet mentioned.[58] It is perhaps the most interesting of them all, since it was

[53] *Rotuli Parliamentorum*, iii, 424.

[54] For a very interesting commentary on Arundel's use of Richard's 'youth' and 'lack of manliness' see C. Fletcher, 'Manhood and Politics in the Reign of Richard II', *Past and Present*, 189 (2005), 3–39.

[55] Saul, *Richard II*, 231.

[56] Saul, 'Richard II and the Vocabulary of Kingship', 871.

[57] Ibid., 872.

[58] I also have not mentioned another book of advice written for Edward III: William of Pagula's *Admonition to Edward III*. Pagula demonstrates little knowledge of Aristotle's *Politics* but he does assert the duty of the king to care for his people. His book, however, confines itself to an attack on *purveyance*: 'the right of the king and his immediate family to provide for themselves when touring the realm by confiscating local goods or purchasing them at a fixed, non-negotiable price'. See Nederman (ed.), *Political Thought in Early Fourteenth-Century England*, 63–139.

most probably written, or rather translated, specifically for Richard. In his *Tale of Melibee*, Chaucer tactfully omits a reference to the dangers of having a boy-king on the throne,[59] and chooses to translate a book which deals with precisely the issues that preoccupied Richard and his advisers throughout the reign. Most surprisingly, Richard's performance of his office adheres to the guidelines prescribed in the *Melibee* almost as if he were following them deliberately. But then, perhaps he was.

The *Melibee* is ultimately based on the *Liber de consolationis et consilii* by the thirteenth-century notary, Albertano of Brescia. The *Liber* was translated by Renaud de Louens in 1336 as the *Livre de Melibee et de Dame Prudence*, and, significantly, a recent commentator tells us that Renaud 'presented his translation as a call to rebellious barons for moderation, peace, and reconciliation'.[60] Considering that Richard was surrounded by rebellious barons, it may be that something of the same motive lay behind Chaucer's translation of the *Melibee* into English.

Strictly speaking *The Tale of Melibee* is not a 'Mirror for Princes'; that is, it is not a book of general instruction for princes. It is, rather, a book of advice to princes *on a specific topic*: on how to take counsel, and, as we have seen, whose counsel the king should take was one of the over-riding political issues of the day.

As an instruction manual, the *Melibee* uses an almost modern technique. First it offers a specimen council meeting, taken by a young man, Melibee, and narrates in some detail what happens at that meeting. Then Melibee asks his wife Prudence what she thought of his council, and she analyses the meeting point by point, and, without sparing her consort's blushes, tells him exactly everything he did wrong. She then offers him her advice, and encounters from him all the usual objections about listening to the advice of women. However, she finally persuades him, by her reason, and he submits to her 'maistrie'. The final part of the book is an object lesson in 'conflict resolution', with Dame Prudence acting as a discrete go-between, and gradually weaning her husband away from revenging himself upon his enemies to clemency.

One of the key components in council-taking, according to the *Melibee*, is of course choosing your counsellors: make sure you know your friends from your enemies and choose the oldest and wisest from amongst your friends: 'thou shalt considere which of hem been moost feithful and moost wise and eldest and most approved in conseillyng; and of hem shalt thou aske thy conseil …'.[61]

This would not have suited the opposition barons. They did not want the king listening to his friends – however wise or elderly they were. The barons wanted him to listen to *them* – and *only* them, and they were prepared to go to almost any lengths to make sure that happened. Yet instead of seeking the counsel of his uncle Gloucester or the earl of Arundel, Richard chose to confer with 'a mixture of well-established royal servants and followers of the Black Prince'.[62]

John Gower, in his mendacious and disgraceful *Tripartite Chronicle*, accuses Richard of not listening to the advice of older men: 'He took the base, immature

59 At line 1199 Chaucer omits 'And Solomon says, "Woe to the land that has a child as a lord …"'.

60 A. Graham, 'The Anonymity of Albertanus: A Case Study from the French', *Journal of the Early Book Society*, 3 (2000), 198–201.

61 *Tale of Melibee*, lines 1154–7.

62 Given-Wilson, *Royal Household and King's Affinity*, 184.

counsel of fools to himself, and caused the principles of older men to be rejected.'[63] This is a lie. After 1390 Richard consistently employed tried and trusted (and sometimes elderly) councillors such as Sir Richard Stury, who had been one of Edward III's councillors 'intimate with the king', and Sir Edward Dalingridge, a former retainer of Arundel, and Sir Lewis Clifford, another experienced knight of the king's household.

Earlier, when Richard had first become king, the chief amongst his counsellors was his old tutor, Sir Simon Burley. Burley was then in his forties, with a vast amount of experience behind him, both in military and diplomatic affairs. From 1377 Burley became a powerful figure in the realm. 'As vice-chamberlain from 1377 he had immediate and automatic access to the king; and, more importantly, he had control of others' access to the king. The likelihood is that he was a key figure in the development of court policies in the 1380s.'[64] Burley perfectly fitted the sort of councillor recommended by the *Melibee*: '… clepen to youre conseil of youre freendes that been of age, swiche as han seyn and been expert in manye thynges and been approved in conseillynges'.[65] Burley's power and the rewards he reaped naturally made him a hated figure in the barons' eyes. A great lord, such as Gloucester, must have resented having to kow-tow to a man of such relatively low birth – even though Burley was nearly twenty years his senior. It must have been galling to a son of Edward III to sometimes have to go through a commoner to gain access to the king.

And this was yet another major complaint of the magnates: they resented the fact that Richard seemed to pay more regard to ability than to rank. Indeed the idea that 'nobility' resides in the man himself rather than in an accident of birth forms a sort of Greek chorus to Richard's reign. It was a running theme throughout Chaucer's works,[66] and Richard himself chose to listen to the counsel of such low-born creatures as Michael de la Pole, John Beauchamp of Holt, Sir William Bagot, and Sir Nicholas Brembre. And, naturally, he promoted these men to high positions and gave them generous rewards, as the books of rules for princes recommended.

J. F. Baldwin remarked: '… the work of the council came to depend mainly upon men of minor estate. In the matter of salaries and wages, the ordinance of 1390, requiring the equitable payment of all members, was quite ignored, while the king's policy again was to give rewards only in special cases, and with greater generosity to the men of lower rank.'[67] After 1397, Baldwin continues, Richard laid even more emphasis on these trained experts: 'taken altogether the council had never before been so clearly outlined as a staff of expert men'.[68]

Once again, Richard was following the advice contained in the *Melibee*: 'Senec seith "… swiche thynges as he noght ne kan, he shal nat been ashamed to lerne hem, and enquere of lasse folk than himself".'[69]

This was, of course, intolerable to the magnates, and Adam of Usk voiced their complaints with candid clarity: 'It was in this King Richard's nature to debase the

63 John Gower, *The Major Latin Works of John Gower: The Voice of One Crying and the Tripartite Chronicle*, ed. E. W. Stockton (Seattle, 1962), 290.

64 Saul, *Richard II*, 113.

65 *Tale of Melibee*, lines 1163–4.

66 For example: *The Wife of Bath's Tale*, III, lines 1109–16 and *Gentillesse.*

67 J. F. Baldwin, *The King's Council in England during the Middle Ages* (Oxford, 1913), 132.

68 Ibid., 142.

69 *The Wife of Bath's Tale*, line 1071.

noble and to exalt the ignoble – as he did with this Sir William [Bagot], for example, and other such low-born men whom he elevated to great positions …'.[70]

The Westminster chronicler gives us a good account of the battle over counsel-taking early in the reign. In the Parliament of November 1383, the Lords temporal tried to take over control of the government, maintaining that Richard's illustrious royal predecessors 'had been ruled by the advice of their lords, and for as long as the control of those lords had been accepted the realm of England was a land of plenty and brilliant prosperity. The king, however, was of the opposite way of thinking: he said that he was unwilling to be ruled or led exclusively by their advice, but he was content to accept with all deference and docility the guidance of his council, composed as it was of the kingdom's picked and tested men.'[71] There is a nice clash here between the simplistic vision of the days when the barons ruled and all was milk and honey in the realm, and Richard's hard-headed insistence on picking the best men in the kingdom for the job, regardless of rank.

Richard's overall policy of pursuing peace is also a major theme of the *Melibee*. It is neatly combined, in the book, with the importance of following expert opinion rather than the prejudices of those with vested interests. The young Melibee's council starts with the hot-heads clamouring for war, but then it is the turn of the 'wise men', and they turn out to be the professionals: the surgeon, the physician and the lawyer. They put the arguments against war each from their own professional point of view. And Dame Prudence, when she summarizes the meeting, tells her husband that these were the people he should have listened to.

Peace, as we have seen, was the prime objective of rightful kingship according to every book of rules for princes since Aristotle. In order to adhere to that policy *vis à vis* France, Richard had to ignore those in his council who clamoured for war: the Black Boars described by Philippe de Mézières, who 'with loud voys … criden werre! Werre!'

The *Melibee* continues: 'up roos tho oon of thise olde wise, and with his hand made contenaunce that men sholde holden hem stille and yeven hym audience. "Lordynges, quod he, ther is ful many a man that crieth werre! werre! that woot ful litel what werre amounteth. Werre at his bigynnyng hath so greet an entryng and so large, that every wight may entre whan hym liketh, and lightly fynde werre; but certes what ende that shal therof bifalle, it is nat light to knowe. For soothly, whan that werre is ones bigonne, ther is ful many a child unborn of his mooder that shal sterve yong by cause of thilke werre, or elles lyve in sorwe and dye in wrecchednesse. And therfore, er that any werre bigynne, men moste have greet conseil and greet deliberacion." '[72]

This passage is echoed in the diplomatic language of John of Gaunt's commission to negotiate peace with France in 1383: '… the living disasters of war, such as Christian bloodshed, the widespread destruction and sacrilegious devastation of Churches, Monasteries and other holy sites, the ravishing of virgins, the rape of married women and the most wicked defilement of other women, the most unholy

70 C. Given-Wilson (ed.), *The Chronicle of Adam of Usk, 1377–1421* (Oxford, 1997), 61–3.
71 *Westminster Chronicle*, 55.
72 *Tale of Melibee*, lines 1036–1043.

oppression of innocent people, and other evil and despicable acts …'.[73] Could Chaucer have had a hand in drafting this text?

There is one occasion, however, when Richard did *not* follow the precepts of the *Melibee* with regard to council-taking. The young French squire, Jean Creton, who witnessed the events of the deposition at first hand, describes how, when Richard was in Ireland and first heard of Henry Bolingbroke's invasion, he was misled by the wicked counsel of the duke of Aumerle. What is interesting is that in order to show how Richard's counsel-taking was, on this occasion, defective, Creton takes us – almost blow-by-blow – through principles enunciated in the *Melibee*.

First of all, Richard calls his council when he is still in the first flush of rage at hearing the news: 'It seemed to me that the king's face at this turned pale with anger, while he said, '"Come hither, friends; good Lord, this man designs to deprive me of my country."'[74] The *Melibee* specifically warns against counsel-taking whilst in the grip of ire: 'he that is irous and wroth, he ne may nat wel deme; and he that may nat wel deme, may nat wel conseille'.[75]

Like Melibee, himself, Richard next forgets to select his council from his old and experienced friends; instead, according to Creton, 'he caused the young and old of his council to assemble …'.

The council advises him to set out immediately to stop Henry. But Richard then contravenes another rule of the *Melibee* by secretly receiving council from the duke of Aumerle, who treacherously persuades him to wait: 'werke nat alwey in every nede by oon counseillour allone; for somtyme bihooveth it to been conseilled by manye'.[76] Creton laments: 'the king put more trust in him [Aumerle] than in all his friends: by his counsel was the whole of the other defeated and set aside'.[77] Creton's account suggests that the *Melibee* was familiar enough to his readers for them to have been aware of the mistakes that Richard was making at that stressful and crucial moment in his reign.

In terms of Richard's governance, however, the most remarkable exemplar in the *Melibee* is that given by Dame Prudence as counsellor and intercessor.

Woman as guide and mediatrix, suing for mercy in the face of the implacable wrath of her consort, is a theme that runs through not just the *Melibee* but through a lot of Chaucer's work. In the Prologue to *The Legend of Good Women*, Queen Alceste (identified with Queen Anne) successfully pleads with the irascible God of Love (identified with Richard) to spare the poet's life. Chaucer also incorporated the concept into his short poem, *An ABC*: God, the King, is unswerving in his justice, and therefore mankind needs Mary, as Queen, to intercede and plead for mercy. Chaucer is actually presenting a political theory of the day as a religious image. He addresses the Virgin:

73 T. Rymer, *Foedera, Conventiones, Litterae etc.*, ed. G. Holmes (20 vols., London, 1704–35), vii, 407.

74 Jean Creton, *A Translation of a French Metrical History of the Deposition of King Richard II*, ed. J. Webb, in *Archaeologia*, 20 (1819), 55.

75 *Tale of Melibee*, line 1124.

76 Ibid., lines 1169–1171.

77 Creton, *Metrical History*, 58.

> Soth is that God ne granteth no pitee
> Withoute thee; for God of his goodnesse
> Foryiveth noon, but it like unto thee.[78]

The idea of the queen acting as intercessor was not new in Richard's day. In Edward III's reign, the most famous instance of the queen's intercession was when Queen Philippa pleaded for the lives of the burghers of Calais in 1347. Anne of Bohemia's role was marked out for her even before she arrived in England. The parliament roll of November/December 1381 records how Richard intends to pardon the rebels: 'out of reverence for God and His sweet mother St Mary, and at the special request of the noble lady, the Lady Anne, daughter of the noble prince Charles, late emperor of Rome, soon, if it please God, to be queen of England …'.[79] The same entry in the parliamentary roll emphasizes, as Prudence does in the *Melibee,* the importance of clemency in bringing about reconciliation and peace: '… also to the end that the same subjects should be the more strongly inclined to remain faithful and loyal in future, as they were before the said uprising; of his special grace he has pardoned the said commons …'.

When Anne arrived, she lived up to their expectations. Whether she herself actually motivated many or, indeed, any of the pardons with which her name is associated, is not really the point. If the king were to fulfil his role as the stern and implacable judge, like the God of Chaucer's *ABC* who 'of his goodnesse foryiveth noon', then he needed a route to clemency. As Richard Maidstone put it: 'The queen will be able to speak in behalf of her grateful people: What a man does not dare, the woman alone can.'[80]

Such a role was expected of Anne by all ranks of society, as the citizens of London made clear when they handed her a bill at the beginning of 1382: 'Since it pertains to your most benign piety to assume … the role of mediatrix between your most illustrious prince and most powerful lord and our lord the king, just as did our other lady Queens who preceded your most excellent highness in your realm of England, may it be pleasing to your most clement and preeminent nobility to mediate with our lord the King in a such wise with gracious words and deeds.'[81]

Whatever was expected of her, Anne took on the role of Melibee's Prudence in a lot of high-profile cases, and at least one chronicler gives the impression that she, herself, was perfectly capable of initiating it. In 1384 the former mayor of London, John of Northampton, according to the Westminster chronicler, would have been put to death 'but for the chance presence of the queen, who in a plea for his life threw herself at the king's feet and humbly begged that Northampton should not die'.[82] Anne also led the pleas for clemency for the six judges who had been condemned to death by drawing and hanging for the dreadful crime of 'denouncing the 1387 council to the king only months after advising the lords on the terms of its appointment'.[83]

[78] Chaucer, *An ABC*, lines 137–9.

[79] *Rotuli Parliamentorum*, iii, 103.

[80] P. Strohm, 'Queens as Intercessors', in his *Hochon's Arrow: The Social Imagination of Fourteenth-Century Texts* (Princeton, 1992), 110.

[81] Ibid., 105.

[82] *Westminster Chronicle*, 93.

[83] Saul, *Richard II*, 194. See also G. H. Martin (ed.), *Knighton's Chronicle 1337–1396* (Oxford, 1995), 503.

There is only one recorded instance of Anne interceding unsuccessfully, and that was in 1388 when she begged for the life of Sir Simon Burley. But of course, in that instant, she was not pleading with her consort, the king; she was pleading with the duke of Gloucester, and he did not seem particularly interested in playing by the books of rules for princes.

Alongside these high-profile cases, Anne was constantly begging forgiveness for less glamorous miscreants – even for those who had transgressed against her royal consort and herself, exactly as Dame Prudence does in the *Melibee.* In February 1382 Anne sought pardon for a certain Thomas Faringdon 'for the offences in the late insurrection of London'.[84] Faringdon's offences touched directly on Richard, for he was accused of confronting the king at Mile End, where he 'criminally, treasonably and irreverently grabbed the reins of the king's horse and as he detained the king, spoke the following or similar words: "Revenge me on that false traitor the prior, for he has falsely and fraudulently seized my tenements; do right justice in my case and deign to restore my tenements to me; otherwise, know that I am strong enough to do justice on my own account and to secure my possession and entry to those tenements."'[85] No little matter for a king to overlook, especially a king who was having problems getting respect from his barons, and yet at his queen's behest, just like Melibee, Richard relented.

> For lo, the gentil kynd of the leoun!
> For whan a flye offendeth him or byteth,
> He with his tayl awey the fly smyteth
> Al esily; for, of his genterye,
> Him deyneth nat to wreke him on a flye,
> As doth a curre or elles another beste.[86]

Three months later Anne begs mercy for 'Godschalk van Han Kon for having abraded and broken the arms of the king and queen, depicted on the Conduit in London'.[87] During the remainder of that year, the *Calendar of Patent Rolls* records her seeking mercy no fewer than four more times – twice more for men implicated in the Revolt of 1381. In the next year she sought pardons six times, on one occasion for a certain 'Agnes Martyn, condemned to death for larceny, and committed to prison because she was pregnant'. In 1384 Anne was credited with seeking the king's pardon seven times. There are no supplications in 1385, one in 1386, seven again in 1387; and from then to 1394, when she died, there are another thirty-four instances of her seeking clemency for miscreants at the hands of the king.

One occasion is particularly curious. On 30 November 1391 Queen Anne secured a pardon for 'Juliana, wife of John Gylle of Hamelden … condemned when pregnant … for having with other thieves unknown gone into the house of Percival le Walssh at Hoo … and there stolen his goods, viz. an ouche [*a brooch or a cluster of gems*] value two marks, silver spoons and mazers, value 4l., a silk gown furred with miniver, value 4l., a pair of rosaries of "beryle", value 26s. 8d., woollen cloth and sheets, value 4l., and 10 marks in money, and for having with other felons on

84 *CPR 1381–5*, 103.
85 Dobson (ed.), *Peasants' Revolt of 1381*, 210.
86 *Legend of Good Women*, F 391–6.
87 *CPR 1381–5*, 114.

the same day at Hoo beaten Agnes, wife of the said Percival, gouged out her eyes and cut out her tongue …'.[88]

It is possible to imagine the *Daily Mail* readers of the day being outraged at the pardoning of a villain who had participated in such a brutal crime, and yet the more thoughtful might have recalled how Dame Prudence, in the *Melibee*, reacted to an eerily similar case. The *Melibee* starts with three of Melibee's old enemies breaking into his house with ladders, beating his wife, Dame Prudence, and wounding his daughter so badly that she is left for dead. Yet even given this dreadful assault on herself and her daughter, Dame Prudence begs her husband to forgive the wrong-doers, and even personally negotiates their pardon. Queen Anne could claim she was simply putting Dame Prudence's principles into practice.

Incidentally, could it be to the pardons of Agnes Martyn and Juliana that Anne's epitaph on her tomb refers? 'Devoted to Christ, she was well-known for her deeds: always ready to give gifts to the poor, she settled quarrels *and relieved pregnant women* …'.

It was not only Queen Anne who followed Dame Prudence's example, however; Richard himself consistently employed one of the techniques she demonstrates in the book. Melibee accuses his wife of not caring about his honour. At this Prudence makes 'a show of anger': 'Thanne bigan dame Prudence to maken semblant of wrathe …'. Melibee is shocked into submitting himself wholly to her guidance, at which point, Prudence describes the theory behind 'making semblant of wrath'. She says: 'I make no semblant of wratthe ne anger, but for youre grete profit. For Salomon seith, "He is moore worth that repreveth or chideth a fool for his folye, shewynge hym semblant of wratthe, than he that supporteth hym and preyseth hym in his mysdoynge …"'.[89]

Richard would have learned from Giles of Rome that, while a king should be both feared and loved, it was better to be loved: 'eyþer is needful – to be drad and iloued – for not alle ben so good and parfit þat þey wollen leue euel doynge for loue of honest and of þe comyn profit … Naþalees bettere it is to be loued þan idrad …'.[90] And this is exactly what Dame Prudence's 'semblant of wrathe' is designed to achieve: the king shows initial anger but then, once the offender has submitted to his royal authority, the monarch is free to show mercy.

Richard's use of this technique helps to explain several otherwise mysterious episodes; take the curious case of 'Haxey's Bill'. In 1397 Richard was apparently furious with the commons for presenting him with a bill to regulate his household expenditure – a meddling in his private affairs which he considered beyond the competence of the commons and an affront to 'his regality and his royal majesty'. He demanded a scapegoat, and the commons duly offered up the unfortunate Thomas Haxey, as the 'originator' of the Bill. This allowed Richard 'graciously' to forgive the commons and promise them 'good lordship' in future, and – having threatened them with the stick – he now handed them a sizeable carrot: 'and further, the king himself said to the commons that they were bound to him in many ways, and now especially, inasmuch as he, for their ease and tranquility, would abstain from making or demanding a charge from them in tenths or fifteenths, nor did he think to charge

88 *CPR 1391–6*, 8.
89 *Tale of Melibee*, lines 1687–1713.
90 *The Governance of Kings and Princes*, 392.

them in future for any such charge concerning his own body or person'.[91] Richard was following the kingly tradition of a display of anger followed by a show of mercy.

Richard also applied the same principle to his treatment of Thomas Haxey himself. Haxey was condemned to death as a traitor, but, four days later, the archbishop of Canterbury and all the prelates 'humbly prayed of the king that it might please him of his grace to have pity and mercy for the said Thomas',[92] and Richard handed him over to the Church. Within three months Haxey, who was a clerk, had recovered all his benefices, and on 27 May 1397 he was granted an unconditional pardon. Chris Given-Wilson comments: 'This curious dichotomy between Richard's initial fury and his subsequent clemency has prompted speculation that there was more to the affair of Haxey's Bill than meets the eye.'[93] Was it all set up by Richard himself in order to show the commons the limits beyond which they could not go? I suggest it might be simply a case of Richard following the prescription in the *Melibee*: a display of just kingly anger followed, upon the suit of some intercessor, by a demonstration of mercy.

The Shrewsbury Parliament of 1398 saw the same thing, when the eighty-year-old Lord Cobham was tried for his part in the 1386 Commission of Government and for helping to condemn Sir Simon Burley and James Berners in 1388. He was found guilty and condemned to be drawn, hanged, beheaded and quartered. Once again, however, having vented the royal fury and demonstrated his justice, Richard 'moved by pity, to the reverence and honour of God, of his special grace pardoned the said John Cobham … and granted him his life …'.[94] Cobham lived to take his revenge in Henry's first parliament, and – since he was not attempting to follow any books of rules for princes – assisted in the prosecution of the former king's friends.

There is even a written account of the young Richard following the prescribed 'anger/mercy' routine in an earlier parliament. The Westminster Chronicler records how in the Parliament of October–November 1383 the lords complained that the king was listening to 'unsound advice' and needed to listen to them exclusively. Richard replied that he 'was unwilling to be ruled or led exclusively by their advice'. This, according to the chronicler created 'a considerable stir of indignation among the lords'. However, 'the king acted in this situation with great shrewdness and discernment … he began by rebuking the effrontery of the lords with a certain sternness so that by the use of winning language he might the more readily recall to his dominion the hearts of the less exalted classes which were in some degree estranged from him'.[95]

It is worth bearing in mind that Richard was only sixteen at this time. It is unlikely that the proud thirty-year-old duke of Gloucester or the belligerent 37-year-old earl of Arundel liked being bossed around by a 'stern' sixteen-year-old. Perhaps therein lay the source of their bitter hostility to Richard. It may even be that Chaucer is poking gentle fun at Richard's intimidating demeanour, when he describes in *The Legend of Good Women*, the curiously fearsome God of Love (who is identified with Richard):

[91] *Rotuli Parliamentorum*, iii, 340.
[92] Ibid., 342.
[93] C. Given-Wilson, Introduction to *Parliament Rolls of Medieval England*.
[94] *Rotuli Parliamentorum*, iii, 383.
[95] *Westminster Chronicle*, 55.

For sternly on me he gan byholde,
So that his loking dooth myn herte colde.[96]

The God of Love is only dissuaded from punishing Chaucer severely when Queen Alceste pleads for mercy.

We even have a picture of Richard wearing his 'stern' expression, as Queen Anne intercedes on behalf for the citizens of Shrewsbury (plate 1).[97]

Plate 1. Richard II showing the stern face of justice in the Shrewsbury Charter, 1389

96 *Legend of Good Women*, F 239–240.
97 The Shrewsbury Charter of 1389, reproduced in Saul, *Richard II*, plate 15.

Plate 2. Richard's frown as remembered in the Corpus Christi College, Cambridge, copy of the Book of Benefactors of St Albans Abbey, early fifteenth century

His frowning brows are also evident in his portrait in the *Book of Benefactors of St. Albans Abbey* (plate 2).[98]

It may have been this severe demeanour that the magnates were complaining about in the Record and Process: that they were 'often so sharply and violently rebuked and reproved by the king'.[99]

It may also be that Richard's reputation for having a quick temper grew out of this self-same mannerism. There can be little doubt that Richard lost his patience with the likes of Archbishop Courtenay and the earl of Arundel (for example when the earl displayed his contempt for the dead Queen Anne at her funeral), but there are as many instances in the chronicles of Richard exerting a calming influence. The Westminster chronicler tells us that in 1388 when the duke of Gloucester quarrelled in full parliament with his brother, the duke of York, Richard calmed them both down: 'they would have hurled themselves upon each other had not the king *with characteristic mildness and goodwill*, been quick to calm them down'.[100]

To take another example: in 1385, when John of Gaunt visited Richard at Sheen, wearing full armour, because he was afraid that those around the king wished to take his life: 'The king answered him amiably, giving him, in mild and soothing language a positive assurance that he would see to it that in future there should be

[98] Corpus Christi College, Cambridge, MS 7, fol. 206.

[99] C. Given-Wilson (ed.), *Chronicles of the Revolution, 1397–1400* (Manchester, 1993), 179.

[100] *Westminster Chronicle*, 329.

improvement and reform in those respects in which there had been injustices in the past.'[101] And still in 1398, Richard is acting as the peace-broker between his nobles. When Henry of Hereford quarrels (fatefully for Richard as it turns out) with the duke of Norfolk, Richard, in council, tries to reconcile them: 'And when they were come before the king and his council, the king said to them himself, "My lords, make matters up; it will be much better." '[102]

Whoever the *Melibee* was written for, Richard, his queen and his council followed the precepts and techniques set out in that book with remarkable fidelity. The fact that they have never been given credit for their concern to play by the books of rules for princes, is scarcely surprising, given the scale of the propaganda pumped out after 1399 by Richard's usurper.

The central ingredients in Henry's propaganda campaign were the charges brought against Richard. So how did he measure up to them? For a start, is it true that he failed to take proper counsel? In 1383, the lords complained that Richard 'did not listen to the advice of the nobility as he should and as his predecessors had done'.[103] In other words, the magnates were demanding for themselves more say in the running of the country. Their criticism is a measure of their discontent with the way royal policy was excluding them from power, but is no indication in itself of how the country was being governed.

In 1386 the main complaints related to peculation by the king's ministers, but it is hard to justify the venom with which the barons launched their attacks. It is quite likely that Michael de la Pole enriched himself through his office, but, as he protested, his accusers were applying double standards. Everyone was at the same game. When Thomas Arundel, then bishop of Ely, took over the chancellorship from de la Pole, he helped himself to 'certain liberties and profits granted by ancient charter to his predecessors in the see', but he went through the fiction of resigning the great seal for the day, so that nominally there was no conflict of interest. And in 1409 he pulled the same trick again, when he was generously granted – free of all charges and for life – the castle and lordship of Queensborough in Kent.[104]

There is no reason to see Richard's ministers as extraordinarily acquisitive despite the clamour of the magnates. I say 'magnates' advisedly, for even though the attack in the Parliament of 1386 was nominally mounted by the commons, it is pretty clear that there was constant liaison between the commons and the lords, and it is easy to guess who was running the show.[105] As Chris Given-Wilson puts it, this attack on the king's ministers was not 'a crusade for impartial justice; it was simply another stick with which to beat the hated courtiers'.[106]

In 1399 the Record and Process distributed the blame for the 'evil government' equally between the king's advisers and Richard himself. It is the king who is charged 'for his evil government', which, it turns out, consists of giving 'the goods and possessions of the crown to unworthy persons …'. The phrase begs a lot of questions. 'Unworthy persons'? In whose opinion 'unworthy'? In the opinion of

[101] Ibid., 115.
[102] *Chronicles of the Revolution*, 103–4.
[103] Saul, *Richard II*, 112.
[104] J. S. Roskell, *The Impeachment of Michael de la Pole in 1386* (Manchester, 1984), 196.
[105] See Saul, *Richard II*, 159–160.
[106] C. Given-Wilson, 'Richard II and his Grandfather's Will', *EHR*, 93 (1978), 335.

those who did not benefit sufficiently from those rewards and preferment? In short, the lords of 1399, like their counterparts in 1383, were complaining that Richard gave rewards and preferment to the *wrong* people – that is, not to them.

In Henry's first parliament, Lord Cobham attacked Richard's 'worthless counsellors' and their 'wicked counsel'.[107] Yet what precisely was so evil and worthless about them? J. F. Baldwin's comment from 1913 seems to sum it up: 'The chronicles of the time generally speak of Richard's councillors as enemies of the law, and it is customary still to regard them as indulging in a public policy of a most fatuous kind. It is fair to observe, however, that the king's supporters were not a body of adventurers, much less were they *novi homines* or mere personal favourites. As a rule they were men of experience and ability, some of them the younger sons of good families, who had taken positions in the royal household, and had gained advancement from one office to another.'[108]

Thomas Arundel, freshly re-invented as archbishop of Canterbury, expounded in the same parliament at some length on the evils of Richard's government: 'And furthermore he said, that people ought especially to consider in what state this same honourable realm, which had so long endured with such bad government, waste and ruin, would have been, if it had been placed under good and just government and ruled by wise and suitable counsel, as it should by right have been; which realm, with its goods, wealth, riches, abundance, commodities and various other advantages, he wished to see take its place among all the other realms of the world.'

To take the last point first. When it came to England 'taking its place in the world', England was doing just that – thanks to the peace with France. Richard had brought England onto the world stage as a co-equal with the Valois royal house. He, himself, had even been sounded out about the possibility of becoming Holy Roman Emperor. England, under Richard did not need the help of the likes of Arundel to take its place in the world. It was doing very nicely, thank you.

What about Archbishop Arundel's other accusation? Had there been 'waste and ruin'? Had Richard's rule been driven by greed and extravagance, as the Record and Process claimed, and imposed 'needlessly grievous and intolerable burdens up the people'?[109]

In 1386 the rebellious barons chose to concentrate on the fiscal mismanagement of the royal household. The main outcome of that year's parliament was the establishment of a Commission of Government (composed almost entirely of the king's enemies) to pry into the recesses of the king's expenditure – without restraint or limit. As the Westminster chronicler recorded it, the intrusion into the king's privacy was absolute. The Commission was empowered to enter the royal household '… and all the offices thereof and all our other courts, offices, and places *as often as they please* [my italics]; and to cause to be brought before them *where and when they please*, such rolls, records, and other muniments and evidences as they see fit …'.[110]

And yet, according to Chris Given-Wilson, the expenditure of the royal household, between 1377 and 1384, had been kept at 'an admirably low level' of between £13,500 and £16,000 – below Edward III's spending. There was a slight rise between

107 *Chronicles of the Revolution*, 204.
108 Baldwin, *King's Council.*
109 *Chronicles of the Revolution*, 173.
110 *Westminster Chronicle*, 173.

1384 and 1386 although only marginally higher than Edward's last years, and 1386 to 1389, presumably thanks to the Commission, saw the expenditure drop to an average of £12,800 per year – 'the cheapest three-year period for the wardrobe throughout the years 1360–1413'.[111] The Commission of 1388 was clearly designed not to rectify a financial problem but to humiliate the young king, and to bring him to heel.

When Richard took more control of the government he seems to have acted with the best interests of his subjects at heart. In 1389, he was not only rigorous in eliminating corruption, he also mitigated taxes that had been granted at the Cambridge Parliament. With an agreement with France in his pocket (if indeed he had pockets) Richard was able to postpone a levy on moveables until 1391, and did not in fact call for it until 1393.[112] So he did not impose 'intolerable burdens' in the early 1390s. In 1393/4, however, Richard established the principle that taxes could be raised in peacetime as well as war,[113] and of course, Henry was able to make good political capital out of this in the Record and Process – even though Henry, himself, had not the slightest intention of doing otherwise.

In the Parliament of January 1397, Richard asked the commons for a grant of a fifteenth and a tenth but had to be content with 'twelve pence in the pound on every kind of merchandise, and three shillings per tun of wine ... And also the subsidy on wool, hides and woolfells ... for five years.'[114] A year later Richard did indeed levy unprecedented taxes obtaining the wool subsidy for life plus one and a half fifteenths and tenths with no conditions, but he made a point of linking these grants to a general pardon for past rebellions – excluding those who had joined the rebellious barons of 1387, who were told that they must sue for individual pardons. In other words, the grants he obtained from the commons were to be regarded as punishment for past misdemeanors, and this, as we shall see in a moment, made a lot of difference.

The subsidies were large but did they involve 'waste and ruin' and, if so, for whom? They would certainly have affected the merchant classes and the well-off, who purchased their wares, but the vast majority of Richard's subjects, the peasantry, would have been hardly affected at all. It is not easy to see how such subsidies could have made Richard a tyrant. The people who complained were wealthy and powerful, and perhaps Richard was looking to the welfare of a wider and humbler segment of his subjects in whom the wealthy and powerful had little interest.

Historians can speculate that Richard's taxation of 1398 was just the thin end of the wedge, and that Richard would have gone on to more and more outrageous acts, but it is equally possible that, when he came back from Ireland, he would have mitigated the subsidies as he had in 1389, in line with the anger/mercy theory, as expounded in the *Melibee*.

It can also be argued that the same theory lay behind the 'blank charters' and the pardons that Richard started exacting. It may well be that Richard, acting in accordance with the anger/mercy policy, saw the *cartes blanches* as establishing a sort of 'year zero', from which date all his subjects were committed to complete

111 Given-Wilson, *Royal Household and the King's Affinity*, 79.
112 Saul, *Richard II*, 235.
113 Ibid., 260–61.
114 *Rotuli Parliamentorum*, iii, 341, translation by C. Given-Wilson in *Parliament Rolls of Medieval England*.

obedience, leaving the king free to exercise his clemency and to dispense fair and impartial justice to all. But past transgressions had to be admitted before they could be properly forgiven. What is more, there were some transgressions that simply could not be forgiven, without doing violence to the concept of fair and impartial justice.

The political theories of the day demanded that the conscientious ruler punish and correct his rebellious subjects without favour or partiality; to fail to punish those who rebelled was a dereliction of duty. As Giles of Rome put it: 'For by cause of riȝtwisnesse þe riȝtful man scholde no man spare. Þerfore it is iseid, vii Politicorum, þat he þat doþ wel spareth no man; for not for fader noþer for sone noþer for frend noþer for oþer scholde men spare to do wel.'[115]

The just king had to show no favour to father, son nor any other, and he was expected to make a show of this. Perhaps this is the reason why, when the duke of Gloucester was arrested in 1397, Richard himself went to Pleshy to carry out the arrest. Considering Gloucester's irascible and high-handed character, it was a pretty brave thing for Richard to do and not something he needed to do, unless he was demonstrating his determination to act out the correct role of kingship – showing no favour even to those of his own blood.

Rather than being perfidious and faithless in revoking his pardons to Arundel, Gloucester and Warwick and the rest, Richard was fulfilling his duty to punish those that rebelled. The pardons, in themselves, had been forced out of him and were contrary to the concept of good government as expounded in the books of rules for princes. What king in his right mind would have freely pardoned those who had risen up in armed rebellion against him, who had been on the point of deposing him, who had publicly displayed contempt for him, who had secretly and treacherously tried to undermine his policy of peace with France, and who had tortured, executed or exiled something like forty of his closest friends and followers? It would have been a travesty of justice, as Richard and his advisers would have understood it, if the king did not finally bring these rebellious and treacherous barons to account.

Richard was not exacting 'revenge' in 1397, he was meting out long-overdue punishment, and yet his actions have gone down in history as vindictive and treacherous. Why?

That there was a concerted attempt to alter the record and to establish a sanitized account of the usurpation of 1399 is beyond question. We know that Henry sent letters to all the abbeys and major religious churches in the kingdom demanding that they send their chronicles to him for examination, along with 'certain persons who were knowledgeable about chronicles'.[116] The ostensible reason for this was to search for evidence of Henry's claim to the throne, but it is quite obvious that Henry had another purpose.

The very fact that not a single English chronicle is in the slightest degree critical of Henry's usurpation is in itself a pretty good indication that some homogenizing hand was stirring the pot. The usurpation was an act of ultimate treachery. It was also illegal, since it was the seven-year-old Edmund Mortimer, not Henry, who was the primogenitary heir to the throne, and yet not one voice, amongst the English chroniclers, is raised in protest. Each chronicler obediently praises Henry's actions,

115 *The Governance of Kings and Princes*, 391.
116 *Chronicles of the Revolution*, 124.

and damns Richard. Is that not strange? Were there really no dissenting voices? Did not one chronicler feel that an injustice might have been done, or worry that the law might not have been followed to the letter?

It seems that Henry's real business, in calling in the chronicles, was to ensure that a single, politically correct version of the usurpation prevailed. On the continent, beyond the reach of Henry's heavy hand, an eye-witness to the events of 1399, Jean Creton, was free to record his disgust at the treachery of Henry and the men who flocked to his banner.[117]

Did nobody in England think along the same lines? Or did nobody dare write it down? Or, if someone *did* write it down, did it not survive? Clearly those involved were aware that the truth might be repressed; Creton explains that he wrote his account because, when the earl of Salisbury was seized alongside his sovereign, he begged Creton to make sure the true story got out: 'For which cause, I have taken the trouble to fulfil the promise that I made him, in the great sorrow and peril in which I left him.'[118]

The English chronicles, on the other hand, bear nervous witness to the sort of intimidation that Henry and his censors must have brought to bear. After the usurpation some manuscripts became full of erasures and corrections. For example, a new scribe took over the *Dieulacres Chronicle* and tut-tutted at things the previous writer had written sympathetic to Richard. The *Kirkstall* writer simply did a Vicar of Bray, and joined Henry's party. *Letter-Book H of the City of London* had cut out of it two and a half folios, covering the days of the usurpation.

Then there were the disparaging references to John of Gaunt in the St Albans *Historia Anglicana*, which were altered after Gaunt's son seized power – presumably because of 'the dread which the monks of St. Albans had of falling under the displeasure of the new Lancastrian king'.[119] In another manuscript, Thomas Walsingham busily altered even slightly compromising references to Henry's father, and marked in the margins: 'cave quia offendiculum'. According to V. H. Galbraith, the Walsingham manuscript known as Royal 13.E.ix 'was barely finished when the revolution of 1399 made it necessary to remove the most dangerous quires, containing the *Scandalous Chronicle*, and to erase a whole series of small *offendicula*, sometimes a mere word, but often whole sentences'.[120]

A new nervousness of offending the usurper had polluted the cloisters and scriptoria of England. As part of this propaganda offensive, the official version of the deposition, the Record and Process, gave future writers and historians a template of what was acceptable to the new regime. As Chris Given-Wilson remarks, it is 'a version of events which placed the need to justify the usurpation above the demands of truth'.[121] That it was perceived as a piece of propaganda is borne out by the fact that it was circulated around some monasteries for inclusion in their chronicles.

But Henry did more than simply impose an official version of events upon the

117 Creton, *Metrical History*, 237–9.

118 Ibid., 239.

119 E. M. Thompson (ed.), *Chronicon Angliae auctore monacho quodam Sancti Albani* (Rolls Series, 1874), xxiii.

120 V. H. Galbraith, 'Thomas Walsingham and the *St. Albans Chronicle*, 1272–1422', *EHR*, 47 (1932), 24; see also Stow, 'Richard II in Walsingham's Chronicle', 81. Recently an earlier date for the removal of the *Scandalous Chronicle* has been proposed. See J. Taylor, W. Childs and L. Watkiss (eds.), *The St Albans Chronicle*, i: *1376–94* (Oxford, 2003), lii–lv.

121 *Chronicles of the Revolution*, 168.

entire country; he also undertook the daunting task of changing the nation's collective memory about Richard to produce a black hole of propaganda in which Richard's reputation could be sunk without trace. G. B. Stow has convincingly argued that the most famous description of Richard's megalomania – in which he sits on the throne from dinner till vespers, speaking to no one and getting all who catch his eye to bow – is a later textual interpolation specifically designed to blacken Richard's character.[122]

If Henry was putting pressure on the chroniclers to whitewash his regime, there is no reason to suppose he did not also put pressure on his poets. Chaucer does not seem to have responded, but the aging Gower produced the *Tripartite Chronicle* – a ludicrous presentation of what the aging poet thought the usurper wanted him to say. He paints Richard as 'wicked', 'greedy', 'poisonous', 'infatuated', 'false', 'cunning', 'two-faced', 'juvenile', 'violent', 'evil' and 'offensive to one and all'. The king is served by 'fawning' counsellors, by 'a haughty, treacherous, greedy, wicked Earl, who was Chancellor by means of a thousand trickeries', and his 'hungry, pernicious dogs' are always ready to hand. Henry, on the other hand, is 'noble', 'worthy', 'a friend to piety'. Here is a typical passage: 'Then the noble Henry, a friend to all honour, came into full bloom and was mightier than all. Just as the rose is the crown of flowers, he was the best of good men, the protector of the English … the model of virtues, the most excellent of the excellent …'.[123]

What is equally remarkable is the lengths to which both chroniclers and poets went back through their own material trying to bring the past into line with the new political realities. The *Tripartite Chronicle* was specially penned for the Lancastrian propaganda machine, but Gower also went back into his past writings and tried, as best he could, to alter the record so it would appear that his admiration for Henry and misgivings about Richard pre-dated the usurpation. The first version of his *Vox clamantis* reads as if it were written while Richard was still a boy, and, while highly critical of the advisers who surround the king, expresses high hopes for the young king himself: 'May the day be near on which you, most handsome of kings, will go forth in aureate splendour behind four snow-white horses. And may the shoutings of praise such as Augustus once had at Rome be yours anew. … O good king, may you stand sublime in a vanquished world …'.[124]

The work is often cited as an example of Gower turning against the king, relatively early in the reign, for it has been supposed that sometime between 1381 and 1386 Gower rewrote his criticisms of the counsellors to lay the blame on Richard himself: 'The king, an undisciplined boy, neglects the moral behaviour by which a man might grow up from a boy … Vainglory makes these youthful comrades vain … Sin springs up on every side of the boy, and he, who is quite easily led, takes to every evil.'[125] If Gower had, indeed, written these words in Richard's reign, one could only marvel at both the courage of the writer and the indulgence of the monarch. J. H. Fisher has, however, suggested that Gower did not insert the eulogy to Richard until 1386 and the 'undisciplined boy' passage until at least 1391.[126]

122 G. B. Stow, 'Richard II in the *Continuatio Eulogii*: Yet Another Alleged Historical Incident?', above.

123 Gower, *Tripartite Chronicle*, trans. Stockton, 314.

124 Gower, *Vox clamantis*, Book VI, lines 1180–90, trans. Stockton, 248–49.

125 Ibid., 232.

126 J. H. Fisher, *John Gower* (London, 1965), 108.

Even these revised dates, however, are probably untenable. A few lines further on, Gower writes: 'his destiny does arise out of this wrongdoing'. How could the poet have known Richard's fate in 1391? Gower has let the cat out of the bag. The whole concoction of lies fits perfectly into the template of 'spin' that Archbishop Arundel laid down in his address to Henry's first parliament: Richard the undisciplined boy full of vainglory. The second version of the *Vox clamantis* must have been written after the usurpation, but modified to make it look as if it had been written earlier.

Gower did exactly this sort of retrospective correction with another work, the *Confessio amantis*, in an attempt to bring it into line with the new political correctness; this time we catch him at it red-handed. The poem, which Gower tells us he wrote in 1393, had originally been dedicated to Richard. Later manuscripts, however, contain a new dedication to Henry of Lancaster:

> This bok, upon amendment
> To stonde at his commandement,
> With whom myn herte is of accord,
> I sende unto myn oghne lord,
> Which of Lancastre is Henri named:
>
> *Confessio amantis*, Prol. 83–7

In 1393, however, Henry was not Henry of Lancaster. 'Duke of Lancaster' was his father's title, and Henry presumably would not have wanted to upset the old man by grabbing his inheritance too early. Gower, however, must have been aware of the anachronism, for he tries (rather comically) to cover it up in a rubric: 'First it is declared how in the sixteenth year of King Richard the Second, John Gower composed this book and finally completed it, and how he then dedicated it with special reverence to his noblest lord, his lord Henry of Lancaster …'. He then realizes his mistake and adds: '*then Earl of Derby*'.[127]

There is another possible clue to the sort of pressure which the owners of manuscripts must have felt at this time. Gower's dedication to Richard – along with an allusion to Chaucer and a final dedication to the king – survives in only eleven manuscripts. According to Fisher, however, there are another twenty manuscripts 'now lacking the leaves on which one or both of the passages would be found'.[128] It is possible that the lack of these leaves is due to ordinary wear and tear, since they represent the beginning and end of the poem, but it would interesting to examine these manuscripts to see how many, if any, had the pages deliberately removed.

Under Henry, poets and chroniclers alike had to glorify the usurper and vilify the deposed king.[129] Henry's reign also heralded an unprecedented wave of intimidation and censorship. The statute *De haeretico comburendo* not only established the use of terror to force critics of the commercialized Church to toe the line, it also included provision for confiscating (and presumably burning) books 'contrary to the catholic faith'. Eight years later Archbishop Thomas Arundel introduced even more draconian measures, this time aimed specifically at books in English. Steven Justice writes: 'No other European country knew such a restriction, and in theory it

127 P. Nicholson, 'The Dedications of Gower's *Confessio amantis*', *Mediaevalia*, 10 (1984), 174.

128 Fisher, John Gower, 116.

129 P. Strohm, 'Hoccleve, Lydgate and the Lancastrian Court', in D. Wallace (ed.), *The Cambridge History of Medieval English Literature* (Cambridge, 1999), 659.

would have condemned the large, rich corpus of English religious writing – Rolle, the *Cloud*, sermon literature, even confessional manuals – as well as virtually all English vernacular poetry.'[130]

At the same time, Arundel also introduced an early version of Orwell's 'Thought Police' by ordering the heads of universities to investigate any students who held views 'sounding ill for the Catholic faith or good customs'. That is an extremely wide net to cast: 'sounding ill' and anything against 'good customs'. No wonder Thomas Hoccleve could write without irony: 'Be war of thought, for it is perillous.'[131] The only way for a poet to survive in 1409 was to become a good donkey and patiently wear the bridle that Arundel provided.

> But se how that the worthi prelacie,
> And vnder hem the suffissant clergy,
> Endowyd of profound intelligence,
> Of al this land werreyen thi sentence; [make war on your opinion]
> That selue same to me were a bridel,
> By which wolde I gouerned ben and gyed. ...[132] [ruled and guided]

By comparison, the censorship of letters from abroad which Richard had imposed, to keep track of the activities of Arundel and Henry in exile, was nothing.
As Douglas Biggs has argued, the support which Henry enjoyed during his rebellion was not due to outrage at his treatment at the hands of the king, but to the ambitions and opportunism of the 'coalition of the disaffected': 'the great men of the realm who joined Henry did so for their own reasons rather than, as layers of pro-dynastic propaganda would have us believe, to aid the cause of the disenfranchised heir of John of Gaunt'.[133]

Even after Richard's capture, it is clear that the usurper's followers were fearful of popular support for the rightful king.[134] Richard obviously inspired affection in many who knew him. His Cheshire archers, for example, were in the habit of calling him 'Dicken' and are credited with saying: 'Dycun, sleep quietly while we guard you.' And those who worked for the king showed remarkable loyalty: the clerks, who in the final years of the reign were 'among the king's closest companions and advisors ... were in no wise fair-weather friends. Their devotion to their royal master well outlasted his ability to reward and promote them.'[135]

A contemporary French writer tells the story of the squire Jenico Dartasso, who refused to throw off the king's cognizance of the white hart, even when it was clear that Henry had triumphed, and who was thrown into jail for his loyalty.[136] And this sort of act of loyal bravado was by no means an isolated instance. *The Brut* tells how the usurper's own son was so grieved to leave Richard's side that Richard had to urge him to obey his father.[137]

130 S. Justice, 'Lollardy', in *The Cambridge History of Medieval English Literature*, 676.
131 Hoccleve, *The Regement of Princes*, line 267.
132 Ibid., lines 361–6.
133 Biggs, *Three Armies in Britain*, 264.
134 J. H. Wylie, *History of England under Henry the Fourth* (4 vols., London, 1884–98), i, 67.
135 Saul, *Richard II*, 336.
136 B. Williams (ed.), *Chronicque de la Traison et Mort de Richard Deux Roy Dengleterre* (London: English Historical Society, 1846; reprinted 1964), 210–11.
137 F. W. D. Brie (ed.), *The Brut* (Early English Text Soc., original series, 131, 136 (1908, repr. 2000)), 545.

The Record and Process accuses Richard of being indifferent to the fate of his subjects, but to which 'subjects' was it referring? Richard's policy of peace with France certainly meant he was not protecting the interests of those barons, commanders and men-at-arms who saw war as their best chance for affluence and influence, but it was certainly in the interests of the ordinary people: the peasantry of England, who had suffered at the hands of the tax-gatherers to finance the war, and those of France who had, in addition, suffered the dreadful depredations of military violence. Richard demonstrated a great deal of courage in sticking to his goal despite the 'bristling Black Boars' breathing down his neck; he would have had a much easier time if he'd gone along with the hawkish ambitions of his senior magnates, but he stuck to the policy which, as he had learnt from all the books of rules for princes, would best benefit his most ordinary and humble subjects.

And there is evidence for Richard's concern for ordinary folk. At the age of eighteen, for example, he defied his uncle, John of Gaunt, during the Scottish expedition of 1385. Having reached Edinburgh, Gaunt was urging that they should cross the Firth of Forth and press further into Scottish territory, but Richard resisted because, he said, so many of the 'humbler and lowlier members of our army' would die of starvation.[138] This is the same king who, as a youth, had sought pardon for the rebels of 1381. Perhaps it was Richard's concern for the welfare of his humbler subjects which gave offence to some of his magnates.

In 1395 Philippe de Mézières presented Richard with a 'Letter' in which he sketched out the ideal kingly realm, using the image of a 'delectable garden': 'All tyranny and harsh rule was banished from the garden, though there was a king, who stood for authority and the common good, and he was so loved and looked up to that he might have been the father of each and all. And no wonder, for he had such concern for the welfare of his subjects, dwellers in the garden …'.[139] Perhaps this was the kind of king Richard was aspiring to be? He and his nobles certainly seemed to adopt Philippe's phraseology. In Henry's first parliament one of the complaints lodged by that vindictive old man, Lord Cobham, was that Richard's companions and counsel 'used to describe themselves as the king's foster-children, and, with insufferable disdain, even took to announcing this in public, as they did for example when they presented their appeal with the words, "We, the foster-children of King Richard, etc.".'[140] If Richard was trying to establish a paternalistic kingly regime, in line with Philippe's vision and the books of rules for princes, his concept of his people went beyond the narrow interests of the magnates and encompassed everyone, great and small.

If we tear ourselves away from the rhetoric of the Record and Process and the hysterical prejudice of the chronicles, written and re-written as they were in the wake of the successful usurpation and under the hawk-eye of the guilt-ridden usurper, we will find precious little evidence that Richard was unpopular in the country at large.

Douglas Biggs writes: 'It was not the easy, popular rebellion, that Lancastrianized chronicles and forged government documents would like us to believe, and Richard of Bordeaux was not a mentally incompetent tyrant who gave up his crown with an

138 *Westminster Chronicle*, 129–31.

139 Philippe de Mézières, *Letter to King Richard II*, ed. G. W. Coopland (Liverpool, 1975), 54.

140 *Chronicles of the Revolution*, 204.

ease bordering on alacrity … The Revolution of 1399 was a close-run affair, and one that rested on a series of unlikely alliances and on no small amount of luck for Henry of Lancaster and his coalition of the disaffected.'[141]

Richard, I would argue, was not a 'tyrant' in the sense that word was understood at the time. On the contrary, he was a monarch who tried to live by the books of rules for princes, who sought to protect his humbler subjects from policies which, while bringing wealth and success to the magnates, brought only ruin and destruction to ordinary folk. Richard never forgot the lesson of the rule books that his subjects were 'his treasure and his gold in coffer'. The argument could be put that Richard II's reign was a bold experiment in ideal kingship and that Henry IV had to invent Richard's unpopularity – just as he invented his tyranny.

141 Biggs, *Three Armies in Britain*, 276–7.

COURT VENUES AND THE POLITICS OF JUSTICE

Anthony Musson

The fourteenth century encompasses a significant chapter in the evolution of the judicial system in England. During this period various (often overlapping) influences were in evidence and there was considerable experimentation in the agencies and personnel employed to administer justice.[1] Historians have traditionally set such changes against a background of conflict between the crown and the parliamentary commons with apparent tensions emerging from the centralising tendencies of royal government and a preference on the part of the localities for devolved judicial powers.[2] A more nuanced interpretation, however, favours constructive dialogue between the crown and the parliamentary classes over issues of judicial administration that in turn brought about 'a remarkably integrated system that linked the centre to the provinces and for the first time established a permanent judicial presence by the crown in the localities' in the form of the assize circuits and the justices of the peace.[3]

Yet in balancing this equation little consideration has so far been afforded the practical realities of holding judicial sessions (whether at Westminster or in the provinces) and in particular what part national, regional or local politics played in influencing the choice of or determining the venues in which court sessions were actually held. The comparatively fixed nature of the higher royal courts at Westminster from the late fourteenth century onwards and assumptions about where sessions were held have skewed views on the administration of justice and overlooked the political (let alone economic, architectural and geographical) considerations involved in the location of court venues. The complexity of the relationship between royal government and the political elite (whose residences and power bases were in the provinces) has also been underestimated. Many of the latter themselves had a stake in the judicial processes, not just as justices of the peace or through sitting on oyer and terminer commissions, but through the exercise of jurisdictional powers in their own private spheres. Historians of the fourteenth century can be guilty, myself included, of privileging the administration of royal justice over the (continued) exercise of private justice. Definable in both geographical and jurisprudential terms, private jurisdiction comprised a range of adjudicatory powers that could legitimately be exercised over certain types of persons in specially convened

1 A. Musson and W. M. Ormrod, *The Evolution of English Justice: Law, Politics and Society in the Fourteenth Century* (Basingstoke, 1999).

2 B. H. Putnam, 'The Transformation of the Keepers of the Peace into the Justices of the Peace, 1327–1380', *TRHS*, 4th series, 12 (1929), 19–48.

3 Musson and Ormrod, *Evolution*, 191. (See also N. Saul, 'Conflict and Consensus in Local Society', in *Politics and Crisis in Fourteenth Century England*, ed. J. Taylor and W. Childs (Gloucester, 1990), 38–54.)

courts as a consequence of (one or all of) three circumstances: holding a franchise;[4] the fealty owed by military or quasi-military service; possession of a manor.[5]

The present paper is naturally limited in scope and cannot hope to address all these issues in the detail they deserve,[6] but it nevertheless attempts to shift the focus in the debate on the politics underlying the administration of justice from the purely structural, the 'grand design' which has already been satisfactorily charted, to the experiential, the physical and practical reality of holding judicial sessions. Tensions between centre and locality can to some extent be perceived in this area, though again it is not a straightforward polarisation between the two and there are points where notionally centre and locality meet. They surface, first, in an obvious sense in terms of geography, as characterised by court location and the distance litigants physically had to travel in order to sue in the royal courts at Westminster, though (as outlined below) this was not a phenomenon that posed problems purely for 'central' justice. Tensions can also be hypothesised with regard to contrasts in the psychological impact of royal justice, the visual experience of going to court, especially the way that the architecture of a particular building could promote, reflect and convey ideals and notions of law, authority and the exercise of justice.[7] In examining court venues and associated visual experiences, I shall also be considering how the balance of public and private power in late medieval England was maintained and the extent to which the lofty ideals of royal justice were compromised or thwarted by the practical realities of holding judicial sessions.[8]

In the later Middle Ages the king, at the apex of the judicial system, was the focal point for claims for justice and offered litigants redress in his courts if they sought it. Geography probably played an important part in determining whether to bring an action and where to initiate it.[9] Judicial power, although theoretically centred on the person of the king, was normally exercised in his name by specially appointed royal judges. Over the course of the thirteenth and fourteenth centuries justice came to be given both a fictional royal presence and a more fixed physical location in Westminster Hall, the great hall of the royal palace of Westminster, where parliament was often convened and where the higher courts of king's bench, common pleas

4 Public jurisdictional responsibility of differing levels bestowed on an individual by the king or exercised by ancient custom, the authority for which (*quo warranto*) had been vouched for in court. See D. W. Sutherland, *Quo Warranto Proceedings in the Reign of Edward I* (Cambridge, 1963).

5 W. O. Ault, *Private Jurisdiction in England* (New Haven and London, 1923), 1–8.

6 I am grateful to the British Academy for funding this research which is part of a larger project entitled 'Law and Image: An Historical Iconography of Law, 1200–1500'.

7 G. Fairclough, 'Meaningful Constructions – Spatial and Functional Analysis of Medieval Buildings', *Antiquity*, 66 (1992), 348–66; J. M. Steane, *The Archaeology of Power: England and Northern Europe AD 800–1600* (Stroud, 2001); J. M. Steane, *The Archaeology of the Medieval English Monarchy* (rev. edn, London, 1999).

8 For a discussion on the visual impact of the state see J. Watts, 'Looking for the State in Later Medieval England', in *Heraldry, Pageantry and Social Display in Medieval England*, ed. P. Coss and M. Keen (Woodbridge, 2002), 243–67.

9 Correspondence from the fifteenth century indicates that geography played an important part in litigation strategy: an opponent could be facing suits brought by the same party both at Westminster and in his home region: see the Paston v. Aslake dispute (*The Paston Letters and Papers of the Fifteenth Century*, ed. N. Davis (2 vols., Oxford, 1971–6), i, 7–12; ii, 505–7. See also Louis A. Knafla's analysis in 'The Geographical, Jurisdictional and Jurisprudential Boundaries of English Litigation in the Early Seventeenth Century', in *Boundaries of the Law: Geography, Gender and Jurisdiction in Medieval and Early Modern Europe*, ed. A. Musson (Aldershot, 2005), 131–48.

and exchequer, which heard the suits of litigants and supervised the operation of lower courts, were normally based. Although the requirement in Magna Carta that common pleas should be 'in some fixed place' did not originally imply that the court should be restricted to a single location (nor that this should be identified with Westminster), merely established centres of royal government – so that litigants should not be inhibited from seeking redress on account of the king's peripatetic lifestyle, the clause came to be glossed as implying common pleas should normally be held at Westminster.[10] Unless a person were living within relatively close proximity to the capital, the courts located within their own county would normally be more accessible than the central courts, assuming of course that the locally based courts could fulfil a litigant's needs. Having a tribunal such as the court of common pleas in a fixed location, however, presumably engendered would-be litigants' confidence in the system, knowing that the justices would at least be at Westminster hearing cases. That the journey did not necessarily deter people can be demonstrated by the instances of peasants from as far afield as the west country seeking redress in the court of common pleas and in king's bench.[11]

On arrival at Westminster, litigants would enter the palace through the great gateway built in 1287–8 and encounter the eleventh-century great hall of William Rufus, the largest in existence in Europe at that time. Measuring around 240 feet long, 69 feet wide, and 92 feet high, Westminster Hall still stands today, more or less in the form it assumed as a result of the late fourteenth-century rebuilding (re-roofing and other refurbishments) undertaken by Richard II (who did not live to see its completion in 1404).[12] The hall in the early years of the fourteenth century had similar dimensions to its enhanced counterpart (though it was probably not quite so high as the roof space was raised in the 1390s to incorporate the hammer-beam roof), but the building was almost windowless apart from a clerestory and may well have been aisled (though this is not known for sure). When the courts were in session the court of common pleas was stationed on the west wall near the entrance to the exchequer (which was housed in a separate building), while the court of king's bench (and later the court of chancery) were positioned at the south end of the hall on a raised dais. The courts were enclosed by wooden partitions and so formed self-contained units within the spacious hall. It is not clear exactly what visitors would have experienced in terms of the overall state of the buildings. The palace itself had suffered damage from several fires (including one in 1315), from the elements (especially flooding from the Thames) and from problems associated with rot and

10 M. T. Clanchy, 'Magna Carta and the Common Pleas', in H. Mayr-Harting and R. I. Moore (eds.), *Studies in Medieval History Presented to R. H. C. Davis* (London, 1985), 219–32.

11 P. R. Schofield, 'Peasants and the Manor Court: Gossip and Litigation in a Suffolk Village at the Close of the Thirteenth Century', *Past and Present*, 159 (1998), 1–42; R. Faith, 'The "Great Rumour" of 1377 and Peasant Ideology', in R. H. Hilton and T. H. Aston (eds.), *The English Rising of 1381* (Cambridge, 1984), 43–52. Note, too, the unfortunate experience of the fictional litigant in the *London Lickpenny*, who braved the journey to Westminster, but was apparently unable to obtain redress owing to his lack of wherewithal to expedite matters (R. H. Robbins (ed.), *Historical Poems of the Fourteenth and Fifteenth Centuries* (New York, 1959),130–4).

12 R. A. Brown, H. M. Colvin and A. J. Taylor (eds.), *The History of the King's Works: the Middle Ages* (2 vols., London, 1963–5), i, 45–7, 491–2, 527–33, 543–5; C. Wilson, 'Rulers, Artificers and Shoppers: Richard II's Remodelling of Westminster Hall, 1393–99', in D. Gordon, L. Monnas and C. Elam (eds.), *The Regal Image of Richard II and Wilton Diptych* (London, 1997), 33–59; J. Goodall, 'The Medieval Palace of Westminster', in C. and J. Riding, *The Houses of Parliament: History, Art, Architecture* (London, 2000), 49–61.

mould. Consequently in the early fourteenth century it was noted that only the great hall, painted chamber and exchequer buildings were 'in a tolerable state of repair'. By the 1380s there were even structural questions raised over the stability of the walls of the great hall.[13]

The central courts, however, were not based solely at Westminster during the fourteenth century and for long periods were in fact resident in York, owing to the military operations against Scotland.[14] As Mark Ormrod has cogently argued, the presence in York of the central organs of royal administration for nearly twenty years of the period 1298–1338 not only established it as a home from home for the English government and a competing capital to London/Westminster, but offered an incentive to northerners to use the central courts by setting up the notion of a very real alternative (on their doorstep) to travelling to Westminster, a perception that was perpetuated well into the 1360s.[15]

For litigants attending the central courts in York, however, the architectural experience was entirely different: Westminster Hall's dimensions and grandeur clearly brooked no architectural rival. York Castle was the county's judicial headquarters, but the great hall there could not accommodate all the various judicial departments and so they were spatially distributed around the castle area and elsewhere in the city (at times in St Mary's Abbey, the Minster chapter house and the Guildhall). The exchequer of receipt took over the stone keep known as Clifford's Tower, the most visually prominent part of the castle, while other buildings were repaired or especially constructed to accommodate sessions. On the occasion of the first removal from Westminster, records show that a temporary wooden building was erected for the court of common pleas and all its customary court furniture duplicated. This was later dismantled and a new 'great hall' built in 1319–20. The court of king's bench sat in the old hall along with the exchequer.[16] Unfortunately we do not have the dimensions or architectural designs of these castle buildings,[17] but as Ormrod notes, 'the contrast between the permanent and spacious accommodation of Westminster palace and the ad hoc arrangements for the housing of the court and administration in York should not be overdone, for until the fourteenth century both the royal household and the majority of government offices were quite used to the regular disruption and lack of comfort that were the inevitable accompaniments to itinerant kingship'.[18] If anything the visual element may have been enhanced by the cumulative effect of the having the different venues dotted around the medieval city. Equally with the courts operating in largely separate spheres (unlike the close

13 Colvin, *King's Works*, i, pp. 504–5, 528. The positioning of buttresses to support the walls in 1385–7 may have been an admission of this.

14 They were also removed briefly during the 1390s by Richard II in a fit of pique against the city of London: see C. M. Barron, 'The Quarrel of Richard II with London, 1392–7', in F. R. H. du Boulay and C. M. Barron (eds.), *The Reign of Richard II: Essays in Honour of May McKisack* (London, 1971), 173–201.

15 W. M. Ormrod, 'Competing Capitals? York and London in the Fourteenth Century', in S. Rees Jones, R. Marks and A. J. Minnis (eds.), *Courts and Regions in Medieval Europe* (York, 2000), 79–98.

16 Colvin, *King's Works*, ii, 891–2; T. P. Cooper, *The History of the Castle of York* (London, 1911), 105–7.

17 Most drawings by sixteenth and seventeenth century artists depict Clifford's Tower. There are a few views of the buildings of the castle bailey, though the medieval buildings have either been altered or replaced (B. Wilson and F. Mee, *The City Walls and Castles of York: The Pictorial Evidence* (York, 2005), 70–6).

18 Ormrod, 'Competing Capitals?', pp. 91–2.

proximity they were used to in Westminster Hall) the atmosphere within them may have altered. While the courts were undoubtedly busy, the noise and bustle would not have been magnified to the same extent and it is unlikely that concessionary stands were sold in York Castle to match the plethora of shops that apparently operated in Westminster Hall.[19] The royal government's presence must have dominated the city of York, however, and made an impact on its inhabitants in a way that was not possible (or so readily apparent) at Westminster.

As the York experience highlights, one of the requirements for the staging of major sessions would have been sufficient space to accommodate not just the judges, their clerks and the parties, but all manner of local officials, jurors and other attendees. In addition to its sojourn in York, there were frequent occasions during the fourteenth century when the court of king's bench left Westminster and held its sessions in the provinces, usually sitting as a court of first instance and delivering gaols in the county in which it visited. Indeed, during the period 1290–1339 the court of king's bench spent fifty per cent of its time in the provinces.[20] The venues for its visits varied from royal castles and established centres to smaller sites, where probably the full paraphernalia of the court was not erected,[21] or, indeed, where sessions may have been held in the open air.[22] It is not entirely clear whether the responsibility for choosing the particular place for sessions lay with the chief justice or the chancellor.[23] Although the king's bench was the highest court in the land (bar parliament) and represented a physical manifestation of the king's duty to exercise justice, interestingly, it does not seem to have been deemed essential for the court to have sat in notable or prestigious buildings: in 1336 when at Northampton two private houses were rented by the judges, one in which their proceedings took place, the other in which bills were entertained.[24]

If the venue were not a royal castle or specially rented accommodation, it is to be presumed other arrangements had to be made to house the court. Obtaining the permission of someone with the requisite authority over the building ought therefore to have been a necessary first step, but there are signs that common courtesy was sometimes ignored. For example, in 1340 royal justices tried to hold pleas in the London Guildhall (then a thirteenth-century construction 90 feet long by 50 feet wide),[25] but were challenged by the city corporation, who maintained that the justices only had the right to sit in London at the Tower (for general eyres) or Newgate (for gaol deliveries).[26] In 1358, when the court of king's bench attempted

19 J. H. Baker, 'Westminster Hall', in idem, *The Common Law Tradition: Lawyers, Books and the Law* (London, 2000), 252.

20 Musson and Ormrod, *Evolution*, 194–205 (Appendix). Correspondingly from 1340 to 1399 the court spent 74% of its time at Westminster.

21 G. O. Sayles (ed.), *Select Cases in the Court of King's Bench, VI*, (Selden Society, 82, London, 1965), xi–xii.

22 The king's bench (or at least chief justice Shareshull) visited Stratford Langthorn (Essex), where the county court (at least in the thirteenth century) may well have been held in the open air: R. C. Palmer, *The County Courts of Medieval England, 1150–1350* (Princeton, NJ, 1982), 19.

23 Putnam assumes that it was 'Shareshull's choice of place for holding courts under his various commissions': B. H. Putnam, *The Place in Legal History of Sir William Shareshull* (Cambridge, 1950), 87.

24 TNA:PRO, KB 27/305 *rex* m. 17; Putnam, *Shareshull*, 261 note 76. Unfortunately, we do not know the dimensions or the architectural features of these houses.

25 C. M. Barron, *The Medieval Guildhall of London* (London, 1974), 21–2.

26 R. R. Sharpe (ed.), *Calendars of the Letter Books of the City of London: Letter Book F* (London, 1904) pp. 59–60; D. Crook, *The Records of the General Eyre* (London, 1982), 187.

Plate 1. St Mary's Abbey, York, the 'hospitium'

to hold its sessions 'in a certain hall' in the episcopal palace at Wells (possibly the now ruined six-bay hall added by Bishop Burnell in the late thirteenth century),[27] the justices were prevented from sitting and were informed by the bishop's attorney that they were infringing the franchise of the bishop.[28] In 1334, apparently as a result of intimidation, the justices of king's bench were compelled shift venue (from the guildhall?) and hear pleas somewhere outside the city of Lincoln.[29]

During the thirteenth century itinerant royal justices held sessions of the general eyre (an omnicompetent judicial agency) in a variety of locations, including hearing pleas of the liberties of St Peter's, York and St Mary's, York in the nave of the Minster and the *hospitium* of St Mary's Abbey (plate 1) respectively, which would have required prior liaison with the institutions concerned.[30] With the eyre's suspension in 1294, however, the holding of eyres took on a political (as well as a financial) dimension.[31] In several cases the crown used the vacancy in an episcopal see to institute eyre proceedings. In Kent (1313–14) the crown took advantage of its control of the archbishop's temporalities to house the eyre proceedings in the archbishop's impressive great hall at Canterbury (which was at that date second only to Westminster Hall in size, measuring 168 feet long, 64 feet wide and 40 feet high). Sessions were arranged concurrently with crown pleas sitting at one end of the hall and civil pleas at the other.[32]

27 M. Thompson, *Medieval Bishop's Houses in England and Wales* (Aldershot, 1998), 50–51.

28 *King's Bench, VI*, 121–2.

29 Ibid., xxvi. They may possibly have held their sessions in the castle, which although geographically within the city technically lay outside its jurisdiction.

30 Crook, *Records of the General Eyre*, 148.

31 D. Crook, 'The Later Eyres', *EHR*, 97 (1982), 245, 248–9.

32 F. W. Maitland, L. W. V. Harcourt and W. C. Bolland (eds.), *The Eyre of Kent, 6 & 7 Edward II* (Selden Society, 24 and 27, London, 1910–12), i, lii–liii; ii, xii; Steane, *Archaeology of Power*, 64, 66. The palace was destroyed by the Puritans in the seventeenth century.

The imposition of an eyre on the city of London in 1321 (at the behest of the Despensers) constituted an overtly political use of the judicial mechanisms. In accordance with the articles of the eyre, representatives of the city were required to show their charters and requisite authority for exercising their liberties. Sessions were initially held in the Greater and Lesser halls on the third floor of the White Tower, the keep of the Tower of London, a suitably imposing building architecturally, built by William the Conqueror and regularly symbolically whitewashed.[33] This apparent vision of royal majesty and superiority was nevertheless undermined and compromised in reality since the judges were obliged to move location (after their Whitsun adjournment) in order for proceedings to resume. Edward II was having the Tower fortified against potential insurrection and, fearing for the safety of his queen, Isabella, who was expecting her fourth child, had her 'childbed' located on the floor formerly occupied by the justices. Justices hearing civil pleas were forced to find makeshift accommodation in a smithy located in the second ward of the Tower, while crown pleas were located in a small house adjoining it.[34]

The extent to which the architectural setting mattered to contemporaries or was deliberately chosen to impress can only be conjectured, though most buildings where judicial sessions would normally have been held would through their very nature be imposing in some respects or have leant themselves to enhancing the gravity of the proceedings. Contemporaries would nevertheless have been aware that justice was not their sole function and that halls, for instance, had several purposes including being a place for feasting and other public events (just as Westminster Hall itself was used for coronation feasts and the distribution of food to the poor). The Gothic architectural style we are familiar with today in churches and cathedrals influenced the building of ordinary houses and even infused the architecture of the great tithe barns. We should perhaps not be too surprised then that judicial sessions were not only held in churches on occasion, even ordinary houses (not unknown since manorial courts would normally be held in the hall of the manor house), but also granges or barns.[35]

In the shires, as is well known, a royal presence was further impressed upon public consciousness through a hierarchy of courts and a mixture of regular and ad hoc sessions operating under the crown's jurisdiction. Under special oyer and terminer commissions they attended a designated location in the shire to hear and determine a specific complaint. The particular venue was chosen by the plaintiff with the advantage that the case was then tried on home turf rather than on neutral ground in a particular court elsewhere.[36] This meant that the sessions could be convened in well-established fora (such as Exeter or Oxford),[37] or alternatively small or fairly remote places (such as Stow on the Wold, Gloucestershire or Sedgley and Pensnett,

33 Colvin, *King's Works*, ii, 714.

34 H. M. Cam (ed.), *Year Books of Edward II: The Eyre of London 14 Edward II* (Selden Society, 85, 86, London, 1968–9), i, xxxvi, 105.

35 In 1253 the crown pleas (including criminal trials) of the Rutland eyre were apparently held in a 'grange' at Oakham Castle, an outbuilding in the castle grounds equivalent to a roomy barn: see C. A. F. Meekings, 'The Rutland Eyre of 1253: a Correction', in idem, *Studies in Thirteenth-Century Justice and Administration* (London, 1981), 617.

36 R. W. Kaeuper, 'Law and Order in the Fourteenth Century: the Evidence of Special Oyer and Terminer Commissions', *Speculum*, 54 (1979), 734–84.

37 TNA:PRO, JUST 1/192 mm. 1, 2, 12 (Exeter); /1421 mm. 16, 21, 18d, 20d (Oxford).

Staffordshire).[38] The ability to nominate the venue did not always work out in the plaintiff's favour, especially where the other party was able to obtain the authority to alter it. John Botetourt for example, petitioned the crown that the hearing of a dispute against Peter Bucskyn and others should be held at Thetford where the damage was caused (as per the oyer and terminer commission for which he had sued). Bucksyn had obtained a writ transferring the case to Norwich, but had then allegedly prevented both Botetourt and the justices assigned to the case (presumably at Botetourt's request as permitted) from approaching the city of Norwich.[39]

The crown's scheduled judicial visits during any legal year were comparatively few, but were undoubtedly memorable events in the calendar. The twice or thrice-yearly visitations of the assize justices (assigned by royal commission to a geographical circuit of counties) were intended to bring routine and certainty to the hearing of land litigation,[40] in spite of complaints in the early fourteenth century from one quarter that assizes had not been heard in the west Midlands for twelve years.[41] Perceptual problems as to the exact location of the venue arose on account of the stipulation in Magna Carta (c. 18) that assizes ought to be held in the county town, a place normally identified with the name of the county itself and regarded as the administrative centre of the shire. Thus York was the administrative hub for Yorkshire, Lancaster for Lancashire, Gloucester for Gloucestershire, Nottingham for Nottinghamshire, Lincoln for Lincolnshire and so on.[42] As well as being the place where the assizes were ordained to be held it was supposed to be coterminous with the venue at which the county court met.[43]

This was all very well in theory, offering certainty of location and accessibility to litigants within the county, but 'the principal and chief towns of every of the counties' was far too vague in its implication and the association with 'the shire courts of the same counties' did not really help. First, the sheriff, the king's representative in the shires, theoretically had an administrative centre in the bailey of a royal castle situated in, or in close proximity to, the major county town, where he presided over the monthly meetings of the county court in the 'shire house' or 'hall of pleas'.[44] Identification of judicial sessions with the crown may have been attenuated, however, by the fact that the castle where county sessions were held was not necessarily in royal custody or ownership.[45] In the 150-year period 1272–1472, for example, only York, Canterbury and Newcastle witnessed no discontinuity between castle and county. During the same period eight of the twenty-five county castles were only ever temporarily linked to the crown, while of the remaining seventeen (with the exception of the three already mentioned) all experienced a break in royal custody at some point, the split becoming permanent in the cases of Sherborne

38 TNA: PRO, JUST 1/299/5 (Gloucs.); *CPR 1354–8*, 618 (Staffs.).

39 TNA:PRO, SC 8/35/1731; *CPR 1321–4*, 312–13.

40 Except where the geographical location suffered from being a frontier and possible war-zone as in the case of Northumberland (and other northern counties) during the early fourteenth century: see C. M. Fraser (ed.), *Ancient Petitions Relating to Northumberland* (Surtees Society, 176, 1966), 115–16.

41 TNA:PRO, SC 8/327/E832. This was an exaggerated claim that can be well and truly refuted by the legal records: see C 66/161–86; JUST 1/1394, /1403, /970, /292, /310, /1406, /1413.

42 For a full list of county venues see Palmer, *County Courts*, 312 (Appendix II).

43 6 Richard II c. 5 (*Statutes of the Realm*, ii, 27); M. H. Mills, 'The Medieval Shire House (Domus Vicecomitis)', in J.C. Davies (ed.), *Studies Presented to Hilary Jenkinson* (London, 1957), 254–7.

44 Mills, 'Shire House', 251–74.

45 J. Rickard, *The Castle Community: English and Welsh Castle Personnel, 1272–1422* (Woodbridge, 2002), 7–8.

(Dorset), Carlisle (Cumberland) and Old Sarum (Wiltshire). Secondly, not every shire had an obvious, predominant or sole county town. A number of counties (such as Norfolk and Suffolk, Bedfordshire and Buckinghamshire, Nottinghamshire and Derbyshire, Surrey and Sussex) were united under a single sheriff with one of the counties usually being the dominant partner providing the main focus for county sessions.[46] Some counties, such as Middlesex and Cornwall had multiple venues for the county court.[47] Thirdly, in geographical terms, distances within a county could be considerable, while in political terms, fourth and finally, the location of the assizes (and even the county courts) could be (and were) moved at will, sometimes in rotation, at other times on a more permanent basis. These problems signify the complexity of the experience in individual counties and highlight the practical implications there were for the administration of justice.

Looking at the counties of the south-west of England, for example, Hampshire and Devon were straightforward in terms of their venues, having administrative centres at Winchester and Exeter respectively. Cornwall, Wiltshire, Somerset and Dorset were more complicated cases. From the early thirteenth century Launceston and Bodmin shared monthly sessions of the county court in the ratio 2:1. Richard, earl of Cornwall, however, reversed the situation and accorded Bodmin all but three of the sessions.[48] His successor in title, Edmund, moved the Bodmin sessions to Lostwithiel in 1286–7 and had a special hall constructed to hold the county court and other judicial sessions.[49] In 1398 the county courts were still being held at Launceston and Lostwithiel.[50]

Wilton was traditionally the venue for the county court in Wiltshire, but in 1280 there were suggestions that it should be moved to Marlborough or Devizes.[51] The sheriff's offices, however, were not located in Wilton itself, but in the nearby Salisbury castle (Old Sarum), where the main county gaol was located (either within it or nearby). With the removal of the see and the town to a new position, the gaol at New Salisbury also became the focus for assizes and gaol delivery from the late thirteenth century,[52] although Old Sarum continued to be used as a base by the sheriff and as a site for the trial of prisoners, in spite of its increasingly archaic position.[53] It was not until about 1485 that the sheriff finally moved his headquarters to Fisherton Anger, a suburb of Salisbury.[54] In spite of the apparent association from their nomenclature, Somerton was not initially the county town for Somerset, nor was Dorchester the administrative centre for Dorset. In the latter county, most activity centred around Sherborne, where eyres, assizes and gaol deliveries where

46 R. B. Pugh, *Imprisonment in Medieval England* (Cambridge, 1968), 59–60.

47 The Middlesex venues were Brentford, Ossulstone (near Tyburn) and Stonecross (near St Mary le Strand).

48 P. L. Hull (ed.), *The Caption of Seisin of the Duchy of Cornwall (1337)* (Devon and Cornwall Record Society, new series, 17, 1971), 4.

49 *Rotuli Parliamentorum*, i, 296. For further discussion see below.

50 G. O. Sayles (ed.), *Select Cases in the Court of King's Bench VII* (Selden Society, 88, London, 1971), 100.

51 *VCH Wiltshire*, v, 13.

52 Old Sarum gaol deliveries were increasingly held at New Salisbury in the fourteenth century (e.g. TNA:PRO, JUST 3/144 m. 4; /161 m. 15).

53 For example: TNA:PRO, JUST 3/147 mm. 2, 18.

54 *VCH Wiltshire*, v, 21; Pugh, *Imprisonment*, 83.

regularly convened during the thirteenth and fourteenth centuries[55] until Edward III's reign when use of Dorchester as a venue picked up.[56] From the twelfth century until the 1280s, Ilchester seems to have been the preferred location for the county gaol in Somerset and the venue for the county court. The administrative centre was then switched to Somerton for about eighty years (though not without ensuing complaints),[57] until interest in Ilchester was deliberately revived somewhere between 1366 and 1371.[58]

Given the situations faced in particular counties it is not surprising that complaints to the crown emanated from several county communities concerning the distances travelled to attend courts and where they were held. The community of Sussex, for example, resented having to go to all the way to Guildford for sessions (as a result of the combined bailiwick and the lack of a venue) and in 1320 for the sake of accessibility sought to have the county court and gaol located in the same place within their own county. They were informed the sheriff should inquire where the court might best be placed and inform the king,[59] but sixteen years later, the location of both shire court and gaol was still something of an issue in the county.[60] Although a location was initially unspecified, Chichester was favoured as a venue[61] and the county court was held there at least in the 1340s.[62] Lewes, however, became the venue for the county court in the fifteenth century though a county gaol was not established there until 1487.[63]

A request from the community of Berkshire in about 1315 for the common gaol of the county (situated in Windsor castle) to be relocated in the town of Wallingford, cited several compelling reasons. They claimed the distance to be travelled and the route taken (through the perilous paths of the Chilterns and through the greatly flooded Thames) not only meant that there was a risk of felons escaping or being rescued, but also that ordinary people were being impeded and put off from coming to sue and indeed many had perished in the attempt.[64] Such reasons, however, were clearly not as compelling to the king, who resolutely declined to have the gaol situated anywhere other than Windsor. Following a further petition emphasising the real hardship faced by those attending (not only in terms of accessibility, but also the lack of food to nourish them during sessions) the promise of an inquiry into the matter was at least gained.[65]

55 For example: Crook, *Records of the General Eyre*, 63, 73, 105, 160; TNA:PRO, JUST 1/1422 mm. 58–59d, /1448 mm. 21, 26, 28, 34–37, 45.

56 For example, TNA:PRO, JUST 1/1422 mm. 56–57, 60–67; /1434 mm. 60d, 62–64; /1445 mm. 27–28d; JUST 3/144 m. 3; /161 mm. 17, 21.

57 TNA:PRO, SC 8/118/5895.

58 *VCH Somerset*, iii, 283; Palmer, *County Courts*, 312–13; Pugh, *Imprisonment*, 66–7.

59 TNA:PRO, SC 8/4/158.

60 TNA:PRO, SC 8/4/157. See also SC 8/73/3615.

61 TNA:PRO, SC 8/259/12913; Colvin, *King's Works*, ii, 613. In the early thirteenth century the then sheriff had been instructed to build a gaol on the site of the former castle, but the land was subsequently given to the Grey Friars and the gaol never built.

62 Palmer, *County Courts*, 13.

63 Pugh, *Imprisonment*, 76–7.

64 TNA:PRO, SC 8/2/67.

65 *Rotuli Parliamentorum*, i, 300a (no. 44). The king's reluctance may have stemmed in part from the fact that surveys revealed that much work on Wallingford castle (which pertained to the earldom of Cornwall, but following the death of successive earls had reverted to the crown) was required. It is interesting to note, however, that with the Black Prince's elevation as duke of Cornwall, a new 'hall

Similarly, the people of Staffordshire living around Newcastle under Lyme requested in the early fourteenth century that the assizes be held in the town of Stafford because it was a royal town and in the middle of the county, rather than at Lichfield, as the distance to travel was intimidating and put them to considerable expense. The royal response was that the justices should hold their sessions in a location that would be 'for the ease of the county'.[66] It was not until the statute of 1387–8 that there was formal recognition that the stipulation in previous legislation for sessions to be held in the major county towns was 'in part prejudicial and grievous to the people of divers counties of England'. As a compromise it was enacted that the chancellor (in consultation with the justices) would be able to provide remedy for anyone who was so disadvantaged.[67] It is not clear whether this implies an equitable remedy would be forthcoming if required or merely that when contemplating assize venues the chancellor would consult with the assize justices as to the most convenient location for local people.[68]

Other practical problems presented themselves, though, when decisions were pending on where a court was to be placed. The friars minor of Bury St Edmunds display in their petition of 1302 a 'NIMBY' attitude towards the proposed removal and rebuilding of the courthouse of Cattishall with good reason it seems. The friars' church (they said) was used as a refuge by people attending the court and for their horses when the weather was rainy or stormy and inevitably at other times when people were assembled for court sessions their religious devotions were disturbed by the noise and throng of people. They argued that the courthouse should be rebuilt close to the town of Bury St Edmunds so that people could have more convenient recourse to it.[69]

The location of the assize visits was therefore something of an issue in local politics despite the fact that they were comparatively closer to home than the courts at Westminster. From 1285 there were also options for cases that had been initiated by writ in the court of common pleas at Westminster to be part heard in the shires by the circuit justices under *nisi prius* provisions.[70] This was of particular interest to people in northern counties,[71] but also those in the south-west of England. Thomas de la Bere, for example, was granted a hearing before the justices of assize in Somerset on financial grounds because his plea had been adjourned at Westminster on numerous occasions leaving him greatly impoverished from all the travel.[72] It was not just Westminster that could prove a long way away. Alice de Folville asked for a *nisi prius* hearing next time the justices came to Rutland claiming she was in danger of death and could not travel all the way to York (where the central courts were stationed) without considerable harm and expense.[73] The popularity of this

of pleas' and prison were built at Wallingford in 1359 with further expenditure on the great hall taking place in 1375 (Colvin, *King's Works*, ii, 851–2).

66 TNA:PRO, SC 8/64/3181.

67 11 Richard II c. 11 (*Statutes of the Realm*, ii, 55).

68 Pugh, *Imprisonment*, 287.

69 TNA:PRO, SC 8/1/21; printed in G. O. Sayles (ed.), *Select Cases in the Court of King's Bench II* (Selden Society, 57, London, 1938), cxxxvi–cxxxvii. See also *CPR 1301–7*, 367.

70 M. M. Taylor, 'Justices of Assize', in J. F. Willard, W. A. Morris and W. H. Dunham (eds.), *The English Government at Work, 1327–1336* (3 vols., Cambridge, MA, 1940–50), iii, 240–1.

71 For example: TNA:PRO, SC 8/41/2035 (Cumberland).

72 TNA:PRO, SC 8/32/1600.

73 TNA:PRO, SC 8/46/2293.

Plate 2. Helmsley Castle (Yorkshire)

opportunity is suggested not only by the steady growth in business during the course of the fourteenth century, but also by requests in the 1350s that the powers of the justices be extended.[74]

The *nisi prius* option could be challenged and countered, however, so as to deliberately inhibit the ability of an opponent to attend court. Thomas Beauchamp, earl of Warwick, for instance, requested that the hearing of a case in which he was a party be held at Westminster rather than in the form of a *nisi prius* hearing in Cornwall as previously granted to his villein, David Tregoys. Since the latter came from Cornwall, Beauchamp's successful application appeared to be restricting Tregoys' (clearly a person of lower status) opportunity to attend a convenient legal forum.[75] From this and other cases it appears that what ostensibly was intended to be a

74 A. J. Verduyn, 'The Attitude of the Parliamentary Commons to Law and Order under Edward III' (unpublished D.Phil. thesis, University of Oxford, 1991), 129–30.

75 TNA:PRO, SC 8/22/1055.

concession to the accessibility of justice could in fact become another weapon in the litigant's armoury.[76]

When judicial sessions were actually held in the provinces they were usually convened in castles.[77] This was partly for historical political reasons, but also practical reasons of space and the need for proximity to the gaol, which was usually at or near the castle. Accordingly, the king's pivotal role as law-giver and earthly judge was emphasised in the provinces in some areas through the deliberate fostering of notions of authority and jurisdiction inherent in archaic architectural forms, notably the heavy-looking keeps of castles dating from the eleventh and twelfth centuries, such as those at Newcastle (Northumberland), Peveril (High Peak, Derbyshire), Helmsley and Richmond (Yorkshire) (plate 2).[78] Alterations may have been made elsewhere within the castle area, but the visually striking, solid keeps were retained. Arguably many of these castles once possessed (and in some cases continued to hold) strategic importance or were located in frontier zones, which may account for their imposing structure. Their military significance aside, they were invariably used for judicial purposes (both routine and special sessions) and so contributed to the experience of the prisoners brought to the castle gaol (and later tried), the various types of jurors and the litigants attending for civil pleas held there.[79] Notions of power and authority were especially instilled at the entrances to castles where the inner buildings would be approached through fortified gateways or heavy-looking barbicans as at Scarborough and Sherborne castles, for example.[80]

The holding of judicial sessions in castles was perhaps initially incidental to their purpose as buildings, yet increasingly became identified with it and provided another strand of visual experience, one that associated the exercise of justice with authority and power, but in doing so leant heavily on a past architectural tradition to reinforce that image. Even when some castles had ceased to have a military function and had been abandoned or pulled down, as at Worcester and Bedford, judicial sessions were at least notionally rather than physically held in or at the castle.[81] Warwick gaol was not located inside the castle, though documentary evidence (including an investigation of the physical state of the gaol) implies that it was and (as with Worcester and Bedford) commissions were issued in the fourteenth and fifteenth centuries for the delivery of the castle gaol.[82] Contemporary acknowledgement of this psychological connection can also be found in Lydford Castle, a courtroom and prison purpose-built to a design deliberately intended to equate it in people's minds with the jurisdictional power and authority that had come to be associated with castle buildings (plate 3). Lydford formed the administrative nerve centre for the royal forest of Dartmoor and from the early thirteenth century was the jurisdictional headquarters for the stannaries of Devon. Prisoners were housed

[76] For example: TNA:PRO, SC 8/107/5323.

[77] Not all towns holding sessions or possessing gaols had castles: Aylesbury, for example, was location for the county gaol, but had no castle in which to locate it (Pugh, *Imprisonment*, 77).

[78] D. J. Cathcart King, *The Castle in England and Wales: An Interpretative History* (London and New York, 1988), 67–73; A. Pettifer, *English Castles* (Woodbridge, 1995), 51, 191–3, 295–8.

[79] For example: TNA:PRO, JUST 3/53/2, /74/3, /75, /76, /141A; Crook, *Records of the General Eyre*, 64, 137–8, 147–9, 172–3.

[80] The imposing John of Gaunt gateway at Lancaster Castle dates from *c.* 1405.

[81] Colvin, *King's Works*, ii, 559, 888.

[82] For example: TNA:PRO, C 66/132 m. 13d (Worcester), /133 m. 24d (Bedford), /159 m. 16d (Warwick); Pugh, *Imprisonment*, 72.

Plate 3. Lydford Castle (Devon)

and tried in the distinctive building constructed around the turn of the thirteenth century (probably at the crown's instigation, though it belonged to the earldom of Cornwall by the 1230s). Visually Lydford differs from orthodox castles in that there are no elaborate gateways or obvious fortifications. The main surviving building, which seems to be perched on a hill, in outward appearance is a keep of two stories. In fact archaeological investigation has shown that the hill is man-made and hides an earlier building that was 52 feet square and possessed walls 10 feet thick. These walls formed the ground floor of the original structure, the upper level of which was demolished shortly after it was built. Two new levels were added to the earlier one (at some point in the thirteenth century) with thinner walls containing narrow slit windows. Earth was then piled in a mound around the outside of the old walls of the former ground floor (and mostly inside so as to relieve pressure on the walls), giving the impression of an earlier style of castle building.[83]

Judging from the surveys carried out on royal possessions in the shires, buildings housing royal courts were at times in a considerable state of disrepair. In order to hold sessions of the revived general eyre in 1329 considerable repair work had to be done to Northampton Castle, the great hall, great chamber, lower chapel and other buildings having burned down in 1318.[84] The great hall at Sherborne, for instance, the venue for eyres, assizes and gaol deliveries required considerable work doing to it during the thirteenth century, but by 1315 the hall was once again in a dilapidated state and in need of attention.[85] In 1320 the sheriff of Warwickshire complained that the gaol and hall where the county court sat were collapsed and in a ruinous state

83 A. D. Saunders, 'Administrative Buildings and Prisons in the Earldom of Cornwall', in T. Reuter (ed.), *Warriors and Churchmen in the High Middle Ages: Essays Presented to Karl Leyser* (London, 1992), 204–8.

84 Colvin, *King's Works*, ii, 753. The estimated cost of repair to the castle was over £1,000. In the event, only the great hall was rebuilt especially for the eyre sessions.

85 Colvin, *King's Works*, ii, 833.

allegedly to the extent that prisoners could no longer be kept there nor the court sessions be held.[86] The castle at Shrewsbury, similarly described as 'very much out of repair' in 1336, was 'ruinous' by the turn of the century and its buildings considerably neglected. Little seems to have been done to ameliorate the situation even by the mid fifteenth century.[87] How accurate and reliable the surveys were may depend upon who was undertaking them and the underlying agenda. Ironically, repairs for court buildings were often allocated from royal judicial revenues. For example, amercements from the Yorkshire eyre were deployed to defray the cost of building works at York Castle in 1257.[88] Chronic underfunding, combined with intermittent royal interest, war, natural phenomena and perhaps poor quality materials and bad workmanship, all may have served in various instances to undermine the visual spectacle of royal justice in the provinces.

As a result of the inadequacy of numerous royal castles, or for other exigencies,[89] sessions were frequently transferred to city guildhalls or other 'halls of pleas'. Gloucester county court customarily met in the guildhall,[90] while a 'hall of pleas' in the town of Nottingham regularly hosted gaol delivery sessions.[91] Guildhalls were the venues for deliveries of the city gaols (and of Newgate) by royal justices,[92] but also for the pleas held by the civic authorities. Not only would the building be identified with the city, rather than the crown, in terms of the psyche of people attending, but the insignia of the city was also on prominent display. Similarly, the gateways to ecclesiastical institutions (as well as towns) in the upper chambers of which judicial sessions were sometimes held were decorated with the statuary associated with the church and the heraldic shields of patrons and benefactors. Other buildings 'borrowed' for royal sessions were equally self-referential statements of their owner's prestige. The great hall (built *c.* 1289) that formed part of the complex at Lostwithiel (later known as the Duchy palace), dealing not only with stannary business, but sessions of the county court and gaol deliveries, was conceived on a grand scale with Westminster Hall as the model. We do not know the exact dimensions, but the eighteenth-century engraving by Nathaniel Buck coupled with the available archaeological evidence point towards a sizeable building.[93]

To what extent then did the holding of royal judicial sessions in privately owned venues compromise the image of royal justice? It is not possible to pursue this line in depth here,[94] but it is possible that familiarity with the architectural design and detail caused people to identify with the owner of the building rather than the crown. In certain judicial arenas images associated with local dignitaries and their jurisdictional networks (badges, coats of arms and other insignia) were probably more prevalent visually (operating repeatedly on the conscious and subconscious

86 TNA:PRO, SC 8/3/136.
87 Colvin, *Kings Works*, ii, 837.
88 Colvin, *King's Works*, ii, 890.
89 For convenience sometimes prisoners had to travel from gaol to the venue where the assizes where being held .
90 TNA:PRO, SC 8/114/5683.
91 Pugh, *Imprisonment*, 64–5. Ironically the 'hall of pleas' in the town of Nottingham normally used for judicial sessions was in disrepair and so a building in the outer bailey of the castle was prepared for the eyre sessions in 1330: see Colvin, *King's Works*, ii, 761.
92 Crook, *Records of the General Eyres*, 148 (York), 150 (Lincoln); Pugh, *Imprisonment*, 309–10.
93 Saunders, 'Administrative Buildings', 208–10.
94 This issue is discussed more fully in my forthcoming book *Seeing Justice: Law and Image in Late Medieval England.*

mind of participants) and more durable than royal symbols.[95] The realities of local (private) power may have been visually reinforced to the detriment of royal (public) judicial authority. This may especially have been the case in locations used for peace sessions that were not normally crown venues and which would be readily identified with the owner. In counties such as Hampshire and Worcestershire, the sessions were generally held in Winchester and Worcester respectively.[96] In the mid to later fourteenth century, Yorkshire peace sessions were not concentrated on York, but held in a number of venues around the county, including castles such as Scarborough, Pickering, Knaresborough and Helmsley.[97]

At Helmsley, for example, home to the lords Roos, the approach ways to and through the castle were deliberately engineered so as to create a particular impression of awe and jurisdictional authority. Visitors to Helmsley coming from York would find that the route taken to gain entry to the castle then was not a direct one. The south gate offered an impressive formal approach involving almost a circuit of the boundary curtain walls which was intended to impress the onlooker with the magnificence of the setting and its buildings. After crossing the two bridges spanning a double circuit of ditches, visitors would arrive in the main public area of the castle. The great hall, probably aisled, was located to the west, but estate business and court hearings (including peace sessions) were probably carried out in the main receiving chamber of the East Tower (built around 1190–1227) (plate 2). A prominent architectural feature of the castle, the East Tower's 'location, scale and orientation suggest that it was intended to be seen from the town as a potent symbol of the lord's wealth and power'.[98] This visual experience would be especially potent when the owner of the venue was himself a member of the peace commission, although there is no evidence that the lords Roos (William and John), were among the working justices and attended sessions personally.[99]

This paper has examined some of the venues used for royal judicial sessions and identified some of the problems faced by the crown in trying to ensure justice was administered both 'centrally' and in the provinces. While architectural setting did play a significant part, the crown was on occasion thwarted in its desire to hold sessions in a particular venue and was frequently forced to compromise owing to the practical realities of space and as a result of its own financial constraints, particularly in its inability or disinclination to keep its premises in a good state of repair. The choice of venue had considerable political implications and was often the subject of petitions to parliament which even led to legislation on the matter. It was the crown's resort to using buildings which it did not control, however, that raises interesting political questions. The resulting situation did not necessarily work to the crown's detriment but certainly appears more complex than a straightforward competition between 'centre and locality', between royal control and private jurisdiction. Coinciding with a greater decentralisation of royal justice, holding judicial

95 This is also the conclusion of Watts, 'Looking for the State', 264–7.

96 For example: B. H. Putnam (ed.), *Proceedings before the Justices of the Peace in the Fourteenth and Fifteenth Centuries: Edward III to Richard III* (London, 1938), 208, 231, 417.

97 A. Musson, 'Attitudes to Royal Justice in Fourteenth-Century Yorkshire', *Northern History*, 39 (2002), 176.

98 J. Clark, *Helmsley Castle* (English Heritage Guide, London, 2004), 12.

99 Putnam, *Proceedings*, 463, 467; S. Walker, 'Yorkshire Justices of the Peace, 1389–1413', in idem, *Political Culture in Later Medieval England*, ed. M. J. Braddick (Manchester, 2006), 86–7.

sessions in buildings with civic, baronial or ecclesiastical owners enabled the crown to satisfy an increasing desire for local autonomy while also maintaining its provision of judicial sessions without incurring the same level of financial expense. It could also be argued that where the king was unable to utilise his own buildings and royal judicial sessions were held in premises in baronial, civic or ecclesiastical hands, the consequent royal association in fact heightened the prestige and worship of the owners and so was to the mutual advantage of all parties. The exercise of justice was thus characterised by an intermeshing of public and private interests, which was symbolically highlighted through identification with external and internal architectural features.

MORALITY AND OFFICE
IN LATE MEDIEVAL ENGLAND AND FRANCE

Christopher Fletcher

Modern historians and literary critics share a common tendency which sometimes distorts their interpretations of past societies and the texts produced by them. Both groups of scholars reflect their own societies in preferring what is new or original over what is well-established, derivative or commonplace. The very word 'commonplace' carries its own negative connotations in modern English, denoting a feeling or idea which is ordinary, lacking originality or individuality, and hence uninteresting.[1] In making our own judgements about the intellectual and literary achievements of our contemporaries, such an attitude may be fair enough. But in examining cultures which by no means shared these values – fourteenth-century England, for example – they have often produced a certain kind of blind spot, a mis-assessment of priorities, in particular when it comes to understanding the role of ancient and well-established prejudices in the practice of everyday life. This article is focused on one particular area in which distaste for the hackneyed and the unoriginal has probably led astray a number of commentators on late medieval English society. It is concerned with the operation of morality, and in particular moralising literature, in the regulation of local office holders, a group and a set of functions which assumed ever greater importance with the expansion of the fiscal and judicial functions of the royal government in the late thirteenth and early fourteenth centuries.

'Morality' is almost as unappealing a word to an early 21st-century sensibility as 'commonplace'. With nineteenth-century social movements lurking dimly in the collective subconscious, it summons up a strong association with the sanctimonious drawing of a moral, especially after the fact. Yet the sense intended here dates from rather before 'morality' went so seriously out of fashion, to something rather more like, for example, Hegel's use of *Moralität* to refer to what is universal or general in human values, by contrast to the customary ethics denoted by *Sittlichkeit*.[2] Such a distinction has a particular resonance when it is the later Middle Ages which are at issue, dominated as this period was by the vision of law codified expertly by St Thomas Aquinas: that all law is derivative of eternal law, the law of God; that the expression of that law in the world is natural law; and that human beings approximate to these regulations by the particular determinations of positive law.[3] In this

1 *Oxford English Dictionary*, s.v. 'commonplace'; *Collins Cobuild English Dictionary*, ed. John Sinclair et al. (London, 1995), s.v. 'commonplace'.

2 G. W. F. Hegel, *Elements of the Philosophy of Right*, ed. A. W. Wood, trans. H. B. Nisbet (Cambridge, 1991), 133–98; A. W. Wood, 'Hegel's Ethics' in F. C. Beiser (ed.), *The Cambridge Companion to Hegel* (Cambridge, 1993), 211–33 esp. 217–18.

3 St Thomas Aquinas, *Summa Theologica*, Ia IIae, qu. 94–7, IIa IIae, qu. 57. The relevant extracts are printed in *Selected Political Writings*, ed. A. P. d'Entrèves, trans. J. G. Dawson (Oxford, 1965), 113–47, 163–4. For a brief summary, see J. A. Alford, 'Literature and Law in Medieval England', *PMLA*, 92 (1977), 941–51.

sense, morality denotes norms of behaviour which contain a reference to a universal level in a way which overlaps with forms of social life which we would describe as religious.

For some years now, literary critics and historians have been interested in a group of texts composed in late thirteenth- and fourteenth-century England which are sometimes described as complaint, sometimes as satire, sometimes as the literature of social protest or social unrest, all of which share a moralising perspective on contemporary society.[4] These texts were initially assumed to be the expression of the grievances of the common people, which is to say the peasantry, who were presumed to have responded to the oppressions of royal and seigneurial officials with bitter complaints or satirical lampoons which subsequently found their way from oral tradition into written poetry.[5] Poems such as the *Song of the Husbandman*, written in English around 1340, complained of the exactions of royal officials who obliged the poor farmer to pay the same debt over and over, took his oxen and obliged him to sell his seed corn, just as bad weather further reduced his circumstances.[6] The *Song against the King's Taxes*, meanwhile, a macaronic poem in Anglo-Norman and Latin, tells of the abuses which accompanied the raising of a royal tax of a fifteenth and a concurrent levy on wool.[7] The poor people pay but the rich escape. The people are so oppressed that they may rise in rebellion. The guilty will get what they deserve at Judgement Day. Perhaps the most widely commented upon of these texts, however, has been *The Simonie*, sometimes denoted by modern commentators as 'On the Evil Times of Edward II'.[8] Seemingly composed soon after the deposition of Edward II, this poem is found together with Middle English romances and devotional works in the famous Auchinleck MS, which was perhaps put together in a London bookshop round about 1330.[9] This poem, which, unusually for this kind of literature, survives in three manuscripts, condemns the corruption and venality of those in power, and in particular how 'their actions fail to correspond with the pretensions of their offices'.[10]

Since the 1980s, historians and literary critics have considerably refined the way in which they consider the social origins and audiences of these texts. It is generally accepted that these works were not the work of those impoverished smallholders whose sufferings they portray, as was at first assumed. The earlier examples of this

4 R. H. Robbins, 'Middle English Poems of Protest', *Anglia*, 78 (1960), 193–203; J. Coleman, 'The Literature of Social Unrest', in Coleman, *English Literature in History, 1350–1400: Medieval Readers and Writers* (London, 1981), 57–156; J. R. Maddicott, 'Poems of Social Protest in Early Fourteenth Century England', in W. M. Ormrod (ed.), *England in the Fourteenth Century: Proceedings of the 1985 Harlaxton Symposium* (Woodbridge, Suffolk, 1986), 130–44; T. Turville-Petre, *England the Nation: Language, Literature and National Identity, 1290–1340* (Oxford, 1996), 181–217.

5 Robbins, 'Middle English Poems of Protest'; R. W. Kaeuper, *War, Justice and Public Order: England and France in the Later Middle Ages* (Oxford, 1988), 326–7; J. R. Maddicott, *The English Peasantry and the Demands of the Crown, 1294–1341* (Past and Present Supplement 1, Oxford, 1975), 13, 67 – although even in this early study Maddicott is concerned to assert only the 'comparatively' humble social standing of those who could have composed such a work in English.

6 *Political Songs of England: From the Reign of John to that of Edward II*, ed. Thomas Wright, repr. with an introduction by P. Coss (Cambridge, 1996), 149–53.

7 *Political Songs*, ed. Wright, 182–7.

8 *The Simonie: A Parallel Text Edition*, ed. D. Embree and E. Urquhart (Heidelberg, 1991).

9 L. H. Loomis, 'The Auchinleck MS and a Possible London Bookshop of 1330–1340', *PMLA*, 57 (1942), 595–627.

10 Maddicott, 'Poems of Social Protest', 133.

kind of writing are in Anglo-Norman or Latin, or are even macaronic compositions in a mixture of both languages. This would seem to exclude the peasantry, since they would not have been sufficiently conversant in either of these languages to understand these works, let alone write them. Moreover, these same texts clearly draw much of their material not from oral tradition but from a sophisticated written tradition of Latin satire stretching back to the twelfth century and beyond.[11] Even those of these texts which are in Middle English are now generally thought unlikely to have been composed amongst the lower ranks of society, on the grounds of the sophistication of the metrical forms being deployed, and the academic and literary pedigree of the themes invoked.[12] This has left commentators in some difficulty as to how to present the audiences and authors of these texts. Some, notably John Maddicott, have re-interpreted them as being written, if not by peasants themselves, then by educated men, perhaps clerics, perhaps literate laymen of a moral bent, who were very much in sympathy with the sufferings of the poor, and were therefore able to act as their spokesmen, championing their cause in the pursuit of a better world.[13] Others, such as Janet Coleman, have taken a different approach, seeing these works as part of a literature 'by and for' a broadly defined 'middle class', which was nonetheless motivated by a moral world view.[14] Although the term 'middle class', as Coleman is aware, might be considered somewhat misleading when applied to fourteenth-century England, it does duty in denoting a group of literate laymen otherwise mainly defined by what they were not. Not clergymen, not peasants, and not dukes or earls nor even lesser tenants-in-chief, the county gentry find themselves grouped together with local urban elites in a 'middle class' whose common tastes and common literacy were not always accompanied by equivalent social status.

Whether seen as clerkly figures decrying the faults of the times in anticipation of William Langland, or else as gentry or urban precursors to John Gower, quite capable of simultaneously condemning the sufferings of the poor and their troublesome faults, this re-assignment of the social reference of the literature of 'social protest' has created some difficulty in understanding its social function. The problem is rather similar to that posed by the constant protests by the parliamentary commons of the late fourteenth century against livery and maintenance. Those who complained against the distribution of badges and robes and the payment of annuities by lordly patrons were in precisely the same social group as those who received these condemnable gifts.[15] In the same way, the county and urban elites who furnished the vast majority of local officials were apparently responsible for composing poetic complaints about the misdeeds of the selfsame officers, which

[11] On which see J. Peter, *Complaint and Satire in Early English Literature* (Oxford, 1956); J. A. Yunck, *The Lineage of Lady Meed: The Development of Mediaeval Venality Satire* (Notre Dame, Indiana, 1963).

[12] Maddicott, 'Poems of Social Protest', 133; Coleman, *English Literature in History*, 62–5; A. Musson and W. M. Ormrod, *The Evolution of English Justice: Law, Politics and Society in the Fourteenth Century* (Basingstoke, 1999), 166–70; G. Kane, 'Some Fourteenth-Century "Political" Poems', in G. Kratzmann and J. Simpson (eds.), *Medieval English Religious and Ethical Literature: Essays in Honour of G.H. Russell* (Woodbridge, Suffolk, 1986), 82–91.

[13] Maddicott, 'Poems of Social Protest'.

[14] Coleman, *English Literature in History*, 64.

[15] N.E. Saul, 'The Commons and the Abolition of Badges', *Parliamentary History*, 9 (1990), 302–15, esp. 310.

others from the same social milieux then read, listened to and copied for later consultation. How can this apparent paradox be resolved?

One solution to this troublesome state of affairs has been to redefine the literature of social protest as 'satire'. This approach has the virtue of re-inscribing works like the *Song of the Husbandman* and, especially, *The Simonie* in a tradition of estates literature and venality satire which stretches back to early medieval and even ancient models.[16] That said, this long perspective on the development of literary forms also has the less desirable effect of minimising the relevance of these texts to the societies in which they were written.[17] The literature of 'complaint' is made a mere literature of 'entertainment', positioned at the more serious end of a spectrum which runs from savage condemnation to lampoon.[18] In this view, because they are traditional and literary in content, and because they were read by members of an established order which was 'perfectly capable of laughing at itself', the texts ought to be distinguished from later works such as *Piers Plowman* and its imitators – such as *Richard the Redeless* and *Mum and the Sothsegger* – which do suggest particular ways in which the system might be changed.[19]

Such a view is by no means universally held. Richard Firth Green, for example, has observed that the appearance of traditional themes drawn from satire and even sermons in verses which circulated during the rising of 1381 does not mean that these 'letters of John Ball' are of no importance.[20] On the contrary, they demonstrate that the rebels, although conservative in their world view, were able to make use of these well-established tropes in motivating their collective action.[21] As Green notes, the rebels were reactionaries, not revolutionaries; Luddites, as it were, not Bolsheviks.[22] Such an interpretation could easily be applied to the fourteenth-century literature of complaint. This literature, although traditional in content, need not therefore be seen as unconnected with its world. Its programme, although well-established, was not non-existent: the system need not be transformed, but its particular abuses could certainly be brought to an end if everybody behaved in accordance with the requirements of their estate.

Writers such as Maddicott and Coleman are fully aware of such possibilities. Yet, in a different way, they too remain subject to the understandable desire to stress what is new in these works, and so discard those parts of these poems which had

16 On which see R. Mohl, *The Three Estates in Medieval and Renaissance Literature* (New York, 1933); Peter, *Complaint and Satire*; Yunck, *The Lineage of Lady Meed*; S. Wenzel, *Preachers, Poets and the Early English Lyric* (Princeton, NJ, 1986), 174–208.

17 A similar comment is made of an allied set of texts in R. F. Green, 'John Ball's Letters: Literary History and Historical Literature', in Barbara A. Hanawalt (ed.), *Chaucer's England: Literature in Historical Context* (Minneapolis, 1992), 176–200, esp. 188.

18 Kane, 'Some "Political" Poems', 88; Peter, *Complaint and Satire*, 36; Musson and Ormrod, *Evolution of English Justice*, 166.

19 Ibid.

20 Green, 'John Ball's Letters'.

21 A rather more extreme elaboration of a similar approach, in which the 'letters' are seen as *the* significant textual creation of the Peasants' Revolt, is S. Justice, *Writing and Rebellion* (Berkeley, Calif., 1994). See the comments of A. Prescott, 'Writing about Rebellion: Using the Records of the Peasants' Revolt of 1381', *History Workshop Journal*, 45 (1998), 1–28, esp. 9, 13–18.

22 Green, 'John Ball's Letters', 189. Green presents this as a counterargument to those who consider that, because the verses of John Ball's letters were conventional, they could not have any reference to contemporary events. As he notes: 'even if we could show that every single line in these letters could be paralleled somewhere in the complaint tradition, we would still not be justified in arguing that they had no specific relevance for the Peasants' Revolt'.

already been recited a thousand times before. Maddicott focuses on the introduction of complaints against royal taxation and royal justice, arguing that there was quite simply more to complain about in the early fourteenth century.[23] Coleman sees the novelty less in the content of these works, and more in the milieu from which they emerged and to which they were addressed, the newly literate 'middle class'.[24] Such perspectives certainly seem preferable to dismissing these works as mere entertainment. But at the same time, they risk losing something too, something related to the traditional, commonplace origins of these texts. For none of the interpretations of these texts fully explains why anybody should want to read them, listen to them recited or have them copied. Literature regarded solely from the perspective of the conditions of its creation, even if these conditions are historicised, tends to be expelled from its social world, in the sense that it is regarded as evidence of that society rather than as a functioning part of it. Like a museum exhibit, it is something to be understood with reference to its historical context and literary antecedents, carefully marked on a card by the glass case; but it is no longer seen in use, doing something in the society which kept using it after its initial production.

In the remainder of this article, I would like to suggest a different perspective from which to regard texts like *The Simonie*, one which places them back as an organic part of the society which saw fit to produce them and to make use of them. It is proposed that these texts served what might be called a 'confessional' function, forming part of a process by which the gentry and urban social groups from which officers were drawn inculcated into themselves values which had previously come from outside. In adapting themes which had first reached the laity in the form of sermons, and which before that had been circulated to clerical audiences in the similar aim of internal moral regulation, these texts suggest how what has been labelled satire and complaint could serve a disciplining function for a social group which furnished at first new audiences, and at length new authors too.

Before exploring this interpretation of the fourteenth-century English texts, however, it might help to consider a comparative example which has often been taken to be a contrasting one: that of late medieval France. Peeking over the fence at this parallel history and historiography yields a number of clues about how it might be possible to look at the exercise of morality in the political society of late medieval England. For writers on the growing penetration of royal government into French society in the later Middle Ages have long drawn out the importance of moral ideas in this process. In a highly influential article of 1962 Raymond Cazelles examined how, from the reign of St Louis, successive legislative initiatives took 'reformation' as their goal and as a source of legitimacy.[25] The focus of ordinances of 'reform' beginning with the king's return from Crusade in 1254 was on the specific misdeeds and moral comportment of royal officials in the localities, described as the 'reformatio regni'. Under Louis IX this was an overtly moral or religious exercise, the extension of his own personal conversion to the entire kingdom.[26] It built on an

23 Maddicott, 'Poems of Social Protest', 141–2.

24 Coleman, *English Literature in History*, passim.

25 R. Cazelles, 'Une exigence de l'opinion depuis Saint Louis: La réformation du royaume', *Annuaire Bullétin de la Société Historique Française* (1962–3), 91–9.

26 P. Contamine, 'Réformation: un mot, une idée' repr. in Contamine, *Des pouvoirs en France, 1300–1500* (Paris, 1992), 37–47, at 39–40. This article was originally published in J.-Ph. Genêt and B. Vincent (eds.), *Etat et église dans la genèse de l'Etat moderne* (Madrid, 1984).

earlier inquiry, carried out by mendicants before the king's departure, which was primarily confessional rather than judicial in character: a cataloguing of deeds done in his name so that he might set sail with his conscience in order.[27] Perhaps unsurprisingly, this movement took on a very different character after Louis' death. Under the last Capetians, 'reformatio' came to be as much a means of legitimising royal intervention as of taming the excesses of the king's representatives in the localities. Reforming ordinances and the activities of the king's *enquêteurs-réformateurs* now served as much to secure the king's revenues and protect royal rights as to protect his people from the depredations of his officials.[28]

Earlier comparisons between late medieval England and France have tended to take 'reformatio' to be a belated and unusually religious echo of English movements of 'secular reform', which stretched back at least to Henry I's coronation oath, and which were to establish a healthy tradition running through the reform movements of 1215, 1258 and 1297, the Ordinances of 1311, the crisis of 1340–1, and beyond.[29] By comparison, the movement of reformation begun by St Louis seems an anaemic and short-lived development if, following Cazelles, it is seen to have passed its heyday after the crises which followed Crécy and Poitiers. Following this chronology, R. W. Kaeuper concludes that, after the upheavals of the 1340s and 1350s, 'reformatio' waned in France, just as Estates assemblies failed to produce the 'second phase' of reform which was embodied in the English parliament.[30] Kaeuper combines this with a second absence, that of the literature of satire and complaint with which we began, to conclude that fourteenth-century Frenchmen were less concerned about 'the sheer weight of the emerging royal apparatus of government' than their contemporaries in England.[31]

Even at the time Kaeuper drew these comparisons, however, historians of medieval France had already begun to revise Cazelles's account of the chronology of 'reformatio' and of the continuing political, social and cultural resonance of this theme. To begin with, Philippe Contamine suggested that the peak of the demand for reform came not in the aftermath of Poitiers, but in the first twenty years of the fifteenth century, fading out thereafter only to emerge once again in the final decades of the Middle Ages.[32] The work of Bertrand Schnerb and Jacques Krynen has further improved understanding of the importance of 'reformatio' in the late fourteenth and fifteenth centuries.[33] This movement was promoted first by the appropriation of the language of moral and administrative reformation by John the Fearless, duke of Burgundy, in his struggle with Louis, duke of Orléans for control of government during the madness of Charles VI. It was encouraged by members of the university

[27] R. Telliez, 'Le contrôle des officiers en France à la fin du Moyen Age: une priorité pour le pouvoir?' in L. Fellier (ed.), *Contrôler les agents du pouvoir* (Limoges, 2002), 191–209 at 204.

[28] Cazelles, 'Réformation'; J. B. Henneman, 'Enquêteurs-réformateurs and fiscal officers in fourteenth-century France', *Traditio*, 24 (1968), 309–49.

[29] Kaeuper, *War, Justice and Public Order*, 270–315.

[30] Ibid., 298.

[31] Ibid., 340–1, quote at 341.

[32] Contamine, 'Réformation'.

[33] For what follows see B. Schnerb, 'Caboche et Capeluche: Les insurrections parisiennes au début du XVe siècle', in F. Bluche and S. Rials (eds.), *Les Révolutions Françaises: Les phénomènes révolutionnaires en France du Moyen Age à nos jours* (Paris, 1989), 113–30; J. Krynen, *L'Empire du Roi: Idées et croyances politiques en France, XIIIe–XVe siècle* (Paris, 1993), esp. 432–8. Convenient narratives of these events in English can be found in R. Vaughan, *John the Fearless* (London, 1966); R. C. Famiglietti, *Royal Intrigue: Crisis at the Court of Charles VI, 1392–1420* (New York, 1986).

of Paris, who saw in the confused circumstances of the first decades of the fifteenth century an opportunity to promote their own ideas of good government.[34] This ill-fated alliance of the Burgundian noble faction, university intellectuals and the Paris mob was to reach its chaotic apogee in the general insurrection led by the butchers of Paris in 1413. After depositing the long and rambling set of demands known as the 'ordonnance cabochienne' – itself a confection of earlier ordinances of 'reformatio' – this reform movement finally degenerated into a series of mob entries into royal residences, armed with a predictable list of officers to be expelled. These actions had their own moralistic slant, for with each occasion that the rioters made their appearance in the house of Charles VI or his eldest son, Louis of Guyenne, they took the opportunity to lecture those present on the extravagant lifestyles of those at court, and on how their misdeeds led the king to overtax his people.[35]

In the last thirty years or so, morality has emerged as a central theme in the development of the ideology of the late medieval 'royal state' in France. Claude Gauvard, Jacques Krynen and others have brought out the centrality of morality in the understanding of politics for a number of late fourteenth- and early fifteenth-century writers. Gauvard points to the emergence of a new type of literary work which addressed matters of doctrine, but was nonetheless inspired by events, all whilst keeping the value of a general, universal principle.[36] For these writers, it was impossible to disassociate political reform from moral reform. Christine de Pizan's *Livre de Prudence et de Prod'ommie de l'homme*, for example, although it is moral and theoretical in its overall aspect and structure, nonetheless features numerous passages which address contemporary problems.[37] The corruption of officers, the flattery of courtiers, the power of clientage, all these general themes are related to the particular circumstances of the hegemony of Louis of Orléans over the court of mad King Charles VI.[38] In taking this line, Christine did no more than follow the same method as a number of her contemporaries. Eustache Deschamps' poems, to take a second outstanding example, have a word to say about almost every significant political event of the last quarter of the fourteenth century, from the revolts at Montpellier and the French victory at Roosebeke, to the debâcle at Nicopolis and the fate of Richard II.[39] For Deschamps, in a traditional moral fashion familiar from Latin or Middle English satire and complaint, each of the particular evils of the age were caused by the failure of each to fulfil his alloted role: 'each and every one fails in his estate' (*chascun se defait en son estat*) and 'each and every one behaves contrary to his rank and trade' (*chascun fait contre son metier*).[40] In text after text from late fourteenth- and early fifteenth-century France the evils of the times – be

34 See esp. B. P. McGuire, *Jean Gerson and the Last Medieval Reformation* (University Park, Pennsylvania, 2005).

35 Famiglietti, *Royal Intrigue*, 117, 119, 124–5; Schnerb, 'Caboche et Capeluche', 126.

36 C. Gauvard, 'Christine de Pizan et ses contemporains: l'engagement politique des écrivains dans le royaume de France aux XIVe et XVe siècles', in L. Dulac and B. Ribémont, *Une femme de lettres au Moyen Age: Etudes autour de Christine de Pizan* (Orléans, 1995), 105–128, esp. 108.

37 Ibid., 107.

38 Compare Christine de Pizan, *Le Livre des Fais et Bonnes Meurs du Sage Roy Charles V*, ed. S. Solente (2 vols., Paris, 1936–40) which arrives at a similar result from the opposite direction, presenting a generalising 'mirror for princes' through the medium of Charles V's alleged correspondence to the ideals of kingship found in the *De Regimine Principum* of Giles of Rome, in the pseudo-Aristotelian *Secreta Secretorum* and similar works.

39 Gauvard, 'Christine de Pizan', 110–11.

40 Krynen, *Empire du Roi*, 250.

they military defeats, civil disorder, the king's madness or whatever – are blamed on the egoism, ambition and pride which corrupt individual souls. Contemporary sins are all the worse in that, contaminating each estate, they infect all of society.[41] From Philippe de Mézières to Jean Gerson, commentators on contemporary politics were in their nature moralists also, drawing lessons on the particular issues of the day from the universal values of morality.[42] All this was brought to realisation in the demands for moral reform, first brought in by the allies of John the Fearless, and then fatally appropriated by the Paris mob.

The theme of morality has been central to recent analyses of the expansion of royal authority in France: the expectations it raised and contemporary conceptions of how the reform of the body politic might be pursued. Ideas of the correct ordering of society which were so well established as to constitute moral commonplaces were used by political writers, noble politicians and restless mobs to approach problems which had only reached the importance they did as a result of the expanding fiscal, judicial and administrative functions of the royal state. Royal officials were to be assigned a morally constraining social function just like all the other estates of the realm, the difference being that the other estates were less often the principal targets of royal ordinances and popular protest.

What do historians of medieval England have to learn, if anything, from all this? Is it just that the French monarchy was inherently a more moralistic or religious institution, organised around its 'roy très chrétien'? Certainly, the focus on morality found in recent surveys of French political writing and political events would seem to fit in rather well with the moralistic reformist impulse which a number of writers have found in the writings of William Langland and John Gower and, behind these, to the earlier literature of complaint.[43] Kaeuper's contrast between English grumbling about the misdeeds of royal officials and French acceptance of the mechanisms of the royal state now seems overdrawn, to say the least. His demarcation of a purely 'secular' movement of reform in England also seems to overstep the mark. As J. T. Rosenthal long ago pointed out, there was often a moralistic slant to the condemnation of evil counsellors in English political crises from the twelfth to the fifteenth centuries.[44] This fact gives much of the colour to narrative accounts of political crises, but it also goes some way to explaining their explosions of violence, the intensity of the hatred which royal counsellors and officials could inspire. The moral sins of the courtiers of Edward III's last years as targeted in the Good Parliament of 1376 are a case in point.[45] In a rather different way, it is clear that distaste for the dishonourable activities of Edward II were not restricted to monastic chroniclers; and, after his fall, accusations about his sexuality provided useful ammunition for those who supported his removal.[46] In the early reign of Richard II, the importance

41 Ibid.

42 Ibid., 242–96. See, in general, J. Krynen, *Idéal du prince et pouvoir royal en France à la fin du Moyen Age (1380–1440): Etude de la littérature politique du temps* (Paris, 1981).

43 See A. Middleton, 'The Idea of Public Poetry in the Reign of Richard II', *Speculum*, 53 (1978), 94–114; and the works of John Maddicott and Janet Coleman discussed above.

44 J. T. Rosenthal, 'The King's "Wicked Advisers" and Medieval Baronial Revolts', *Political Science Quarterly*, 82 (1967), 595–618.

45 C. Fletcher, 'Virtue and the Common Good: Sermons and Political Practice in the Good Parliament, 1376', in K. Jensen and M. Rubin (eds.), *Charisma and Religious Authority* (forthcoming).

46 H. Johnstone, 'The Eccentricities of Edward II', *EHR*, 48 (1933), 264–7; P. Chaplais, *Piers Gaveston: Edward II's Adoptive Brother*, 1–3, 108–14; W. M. Ormrod, 'Monarchy, Martyrdom and Masculinity:

assigned to the moral comportment of courtiers could serve to explain political crisis in and of itself, with no need to stray into any more controversial matters, such as the legitimacy of armed resistance to the monarch, or the imposition of a new 'Continual Council'.[47] For the St Alban's chronicler (admittedly, a Benedictine monk) the repudiation of the king's friend, Robert de Vere, of his wife, a niece of the duke of Gloucester and a cousin of the king, was not only *a* cause but *the* sole and sufficient cause of the crisis which culminated in the battle of Radcot Bridge and the 'Merciless Parliament' of 1388.[48] For other writers on the same events, it was clear that the blame for the kingdom's troubles lay wholly with 'the governors and closest counsellors of the king, living viciously, deluding the said king, and not attending to the business of the king and kingdom'.[49] It is their vices that leave the king destitute and oblige him to tax his people. No need to resolve genuine disagreements about tax, the conduct of war or the authority of the king. It is vice that is to blame.

Certainly, when it is the moral faults of those in power which are at issue, then this kind of commentary assumes the same role of a 'shared grumble' which John Maddicott ascribed to the literature of 'social protest'.[50] As Bishop Thomas Brinton of Rochester observed in the opening of a sermon which he preached during the political crisis of 1376, each person loves to hear the faults of others condemned, but when their own vices are recited, they are less receptive.[51] It seems clear that the literature of complaint could fulfil such a role, and even provide rebels with verses to spur them to action against their oppressors.[52] But it also seems unlikely that this was the intention of the majority of those who compiled or read these works, whether they were preachers urging the conversion of county or urban elites, or if they were drawn from these very groups themselves. Of course, we might wish simply to discard this intention, and to observe, reasonably enough, that it is at least as important to observe how these works were received, understood and re-used by men like the rebels of 1381. But we can also observe that, given the manuscript context of these works, and the reaction of, say, William Langland to the use of his reforming vision for seditious purposes, such radical usages were probably not the most common or ordinary use of these texts.[53] For the most part, their social role was a rather different one, either as the tool of preachers seeking to persuade the

England in the Later Middle Ages', in P. H. Cullum and K. J. Lewis (eds.), *Holiness and Masculinity in the Middle Ages* (Cardiff, 2004), 174–91. And see above, J. Burgtorf, '"With my life, his joyes began and ended": Piers Gaveston and King Edward II of England Revisited'.

47 C. Fletcher, *Richard II: Manhood, Youth and Politics* (forthcoming), ch. 8.

48 Thomas Walsingham, *The St Albans Chronicle, 1376–1394*, ed. J. Taylor and W. R. Childs, trans. L. Watkiss (Oxford, 2003), 822.

49 *Favent*, 1–2: '… gubernatores et proximi conciliarii regis, viciose viuentes, dictum regem deludentes, negocia regis nec regni prospicientes, sed sibi ipsis mamona iniquitatis pluries per nephas amplectentes. Sub quorum umbra peccati rex egenus mittitur, en ut regnum, decimis leuatis et subsidiis, plaga magna percutitur.'

50 Maddicott, 'Poems of Social Protest', 139.

51 *The Sermons of Thomas Brinton, Bishop of Rochester (1373–1389)*, ed. M. A. Devlin (Camden Society, 3rd series, 85, London, 1934), 315.

52 See esp. Green, 'John Ball's Letters'.

53 After the rebels quoted his verse, Langland seems to have introduced a number of revisions to the C-version of his text to evade the possibility that the 'commons' from whom the king derived his power in the ideal kingdom might be interpreted as the common people, and not as their legitimate representatives, those of the knightly class. See S. Crane, 'The Writing Lesson of 1381', in Hanawalt (ed.), *Chaucer's England*, 201–21 at 211–12.

office-holding class of the need to reform, or as part of the efforts of that same class to discipline itself.

In France, when writers like Christine de Pizan, Philippe de Mézières or Eustache Deschamps criticised the moral failings of their contemporaries, they addressed themselves to these same people, or those of the same class, not to those whom they hoped would overthrow them. They did so by connecting the events of their time to moral absolutes, and so consciously gave meaning to the present day by relating it to values which were hackneyed, commonplace or, to put it another way, universal. The same could be said of those preachers who condemned the faults of the court to Charles VI and his queen to their faces; whose lessons were, so says the monk of St Denis, at first piously accepted by the king, but sadly abandoned once his madness returned.[54] Of course, this could be a dangerous game, and when the same criticisms were taken up by the duke of Burgundy or the Paris crowd, the impact of such strictures could be profoundly seditious. But, at the base, this kind of moral discourse was intended, at least initially, to bring about repentance in the sinner, not to inspire violent action amongst those who suffered from his misdeeds.

Much the same can be said of the literature of social protest which circulated in England. Its manuscript context tends to suggest either that it was intended for use by preachers, or for private reading by the literate laity – that is to say, precisely the classes who made up the office-holding elites of county and urban communities.[55] The division between the two types of manuscript can, indeed, be exaggerated, and a sermon, particularly a Middle English sermon, could equally well do service as confessional reading for a pious laymen concerned to improve himself and his fellows. It too was conservative and commonplace in themes and content, innovating only insofar as it attached new groups and new abuses to well-established schema of the faults of each estate.

Far from condemning the commonplace aspects of the literature of 'complaint' as timeless material without purchase on contemporary reality, and going on to concentrate solely on those parts of these works which seem to refer to new social realities, it would seem better to stress how the traditional origins of these texts facilitated their social function and practical impact. These works lose out if we try to see them as an external comment on society or events; or as an external intervention, a polemical attempt to change the way things are. They make rather more sense if we see them as the surviving remnants of social practices which sought to discipline the behaviour of all societies' members, and in particular those with authority deriving from office. Moralistic commentaries on medieval society – like sermons and confessional works – set out a moral structure which appealed to a higher system of values than that to be found in this world. They did this in the expectation of disciplining the class who owned and presumably read them. The close proximity between sermon writing and complaint literature has often been remarked upon in the past, but the tendency is still to see this in terms of a development from one to the other – literature drawing on material to which it gained access through the

[54] *Chronique du religieux de Saint-Denys*, ed. L. Bellaguet (6 vols., Paris, 1839–52), iii, 266–75.

[55] Maddicott, 'Poems of Social Protest', 136–9; Coleman, *English Literature and History*, ch. 3; P. Coss, 'Introduction', in *Political Songs of England: From the Reign of John to that of Edward II*, ed. Thomas Wright (Cambridge, 1996), lx–lxv.

medium of sermons.[56] Yet it is possible to view things differently, considering the two as different parts of the same project, re-adapting well established moral themes to fit the circumstances of the day, but still drawing their power from the traditional vision of society which underlay them both. To work out how this might be so, I would like to return in the final section of this article to one suggestion with which we began: that the literature of 'complaint' could better be seen as a 'confessional' literature, which shared many of its functions, as well as themes, with contemporary preaching. In particular, I would like to explore how a work like *The Simonie* might profitably be compared with a sermon preached some sixty years after the poem's composition, but which shares many of its concerns, and which continues to draw its power from them.

The sermon *Redde racionem villicationis tue* of Thomas Wimbledon was first delivered at St Paul's Cross, London during the political crisis of 1386–8.[57] Its theme, taken from Luke 6:10, might be roughly translated as 'give an account of your charge'. According to the preacher, Our Lord Jesus Christ is like the steward who sends out his men through the ages of the world to work on his vineyard, that is: the Church. Just as in looking after the material vine there are diverse tasks to be accomplished, so in the Church (which here means Christian society) there are three 'offices': priesthood, knighthood and labourers. To priests it falls to cut away the branches of sin. To knights it falls to prevent wrongs and thefts, to maintain God's law, and to keep the land from foreign enemies. To labourers it falls to work bodily so as to obtain the livelihood of all. Each estate needs the other. Wimbledon then goes on to consider how God will call each 'office' to account for its 'bailly' – its charge – on the Day of Judgement.[58]

This extremely traditional account of the functions of the three estates reads like the photographic negative of the picture of the 'times' given by the literature of complaint, in which each and every one has his function and yet, as a consequence of sin, fails to fulfil it.[59] In *The Simonie*, the cause of recent war, hunger, crop failure and animal murrain is clear to see. This is the 'coueytise and symonie' that causes everyone, from priests to knights to doctors to lawyers to the king's ministers, to corrupt their allotted function in the pursuit of gain.[60] It is these sins which brought on the famines of Edward II's reign, although it also seems that it was pride in particular that promoted strife amongst the lords.[61] The impression of seeing two sides of the same moralistic coin is intensified when Thomas Wimbledon turns first to the responsibilities and likely sins of the clergy, and then to 'the secunde baylif'. This, it becomes clear, is not to be restricted to 'temperal lordis that hauen gouernayle of peplis' but is also to include all those 'that kepyng hath of eny comunyte,

56 G. R. Owst, *Literature and Pulpit in Medieval England* (2nd edn, Oxford, 1961), 548–93; Yunck, *Lineage of Lady Meed*, 239–58.

57 *Wimbledon's Sermon: Redde Rationem Villicationis Tue*, ed. I. K. Knight (Pittsburgh, 1967).

58 It is notable that 'balliva' was the standard term to denote the charge of an office. Sheriffs, for example, could be referred to as 'ballivus domini Regis'. They in turn were answered to by their own bailiffs in each hundred. See G. H. Fowler (ed.), *Rolls from the Office of Sheriff of Bedfordshire and Berkshire, 1332–1334* (Bedfordshire Historical Record Society, Quarto Memoirs, 3, 1929), 4, note 34b.

59 For this traditional division, see Mohl, *The Three Estates*, 316–23.

60 *The Simonie*, ed. Embree and Urquhart, A version, lines 289–354.

61 Ibid., lines 379–468.

as kynges, princys, maires and schyreuys [i.e. sheriffs] and justices'.[62] These men are to be asked: why have you come into your office? Was it to help the people, destroy falsehood and further truth, or to win goods and worldly worship?[63] If your office was taken more for 'thyn owne worldly profyt than for help of the comunyte', then you are a tyrant, as Aristotle says.[64] For many people desire such 'states' to oppress those they hate and to take gifts. Of such men God said, 'They have reigned, but not of me; they have been princes, but I know them not.'[65] Wimbledon then invoked the example of Rehoboam, son of Solomon, who, having taken the counsel of the young, decided to oppress those in his charge.[66] Finally, the preacher drew the moral. It was good for every ruler of communities that he be not led by fools, nor by any other who had no love for the community.[67] 'For wyte he wel, be he neuere so hygh, that he shal come byfore his heighere to yelde rekenyng of his bayle.'[68]

On one level, Wimbledon's sermon can be taken as a reaction to the events of the years in which it was written and delivered. His sermon is a lively and powerful theorisation of the nature of office and its moral charge in a period when office-holders were being rushed to summary execution for their alleged misdeeds.[69] But his general theme had a far greater moral resonance which explains its continuing success as a written tract in the fifteenth century. Wimbledon's sermon survives in no fewer than fifteen manuscripts, two of these in Latin, the rest in English. It sometimes rubs shoulders with material meant for the use of preachers, sometimes with confessional treatises such as the *Two Ways* of John Clanvowe, composed around the same time by that seasoned administrator and diplomat to Richard II before his departure on Crusade.[70] It thus deserves to be classed together with the literature of complaint not only in the themes it addressed but also in the nature of its later textual life. Despite the contemporary relevance of Wimbledon's sermon, it was those aspects which were already commonplace which account for its later success as a written tract. Speaking of similar matters in the 1320s, the *Simonie* had already complained of 'justices, shirreues, meires' and 'baillifs' who should maintain right, but instead make night of the fair day. No justice can be obtained from them without money.[71] When the king sends out for taxes, the poor are burdened excessively.[72] He should look for treasure close at hand amongst the justices, sheriffs, escheators and the chancellor.[73] Those who have office soon become rich. They should do the king's will but instead fill their purses.[74] The sheriff's subordinates, the bailiffs and

62 *Wimbledon's Sermon*, 70.

63 Ibid., 80.

64 Ibid., 80–1.

65 Ibid., 81.

66 Ibid., 81–2.

67 *Wimbledon*, ed. Knight, 82. 'be he lord or king' is a contemporary marginal addition in one manuscript only, the fifteenth-century MS Harley 2398. Other manuscripts refer simply to 'leders', the 'lorde' or 'reuler' of communities.

68 Ibid., 83.

69 See further Fletcher, *Richard II*, ch. 8.

70 Ibid., 3–22. The editor of this sermon misidentifies Clanvowe's treatise in Oxford, University College MS 97 as concerning an 'account of a voyage made by Sir John Clanvowe'. The correct identification as the *Two Ways* is in John Clanvowe, *Works*, ed. V. J. Scattergood (Cambridge, 1975).

71 *The Simonie*, ed. Embree and Urquhart, A version, lines 289–94.

72 Ibid., lines 301–6.

73 Ibid., lines 319–24.

74 Ibid., lines 325–36.

beadles, are no better, dedicated as they are to grieving poor men at the assizes.[75] There was nothing original in what Wimbledon said about royal officers, but that did not make what he had to say any less powerful.

The search for originality or its absence in Wimbledon's sermon or *The Simonie* is something of a distraction when we are not assessing their literary merit, but their late medieval social function. From this latter point of view, what matters is how, like their French contemporaries, the authors and audiences of these texts considered the theme of moral reformation to be the most powerful, most important response to both specific political upheavals and to longer term injustices. They fitted traditional moral concerns into a structure of responsibility which could apply to any office. To Thomas Wimbledon, the penalty of failure to pursue the profit of the 'community' was clear: the pains of Hell which dominate the second half of his sermon. These pains also found a more immediate resonance in the vengeance visited upon royal officers in recent history. Neither the insurgents of 1381 nor the commons of 1388 were afraid of helping their opponents into the fires of eternity with the aid of a little worldly rough justice.

If the office-holding audience read these barbed, threatening commentaries and felt themselves agreeably entertained, it would be more than a little surprising. Although the writers of these works tended to balk at the social implications of their criticisms the moment they were taken up by movements of popular unrest, they were not above invoking the terrors of popular sedition to give extra urgency to their strictures. This, I think, has to be seen as the function of these works, a function entwined with the need to control the ever more important activities of those in local elites from whose ranks royal officers were drawn. In the absence of an established doctrine of popular sovereignty in either England or France, moralistic discourse provided both a means of self-control for officers, and a legitimising structure of values for rebellion. In the end, the latter strengthened the power of the former, even if this was not the initial intention of those who first beseeched royal officers to reform themselves. The terrors of Hell would have been all the more vivid when they were reinforced by the memory of the coming of their bestial, nightmarish agents on earth, and by the expectation that they might soon come again.

[75] Ibid., lines 337–42.